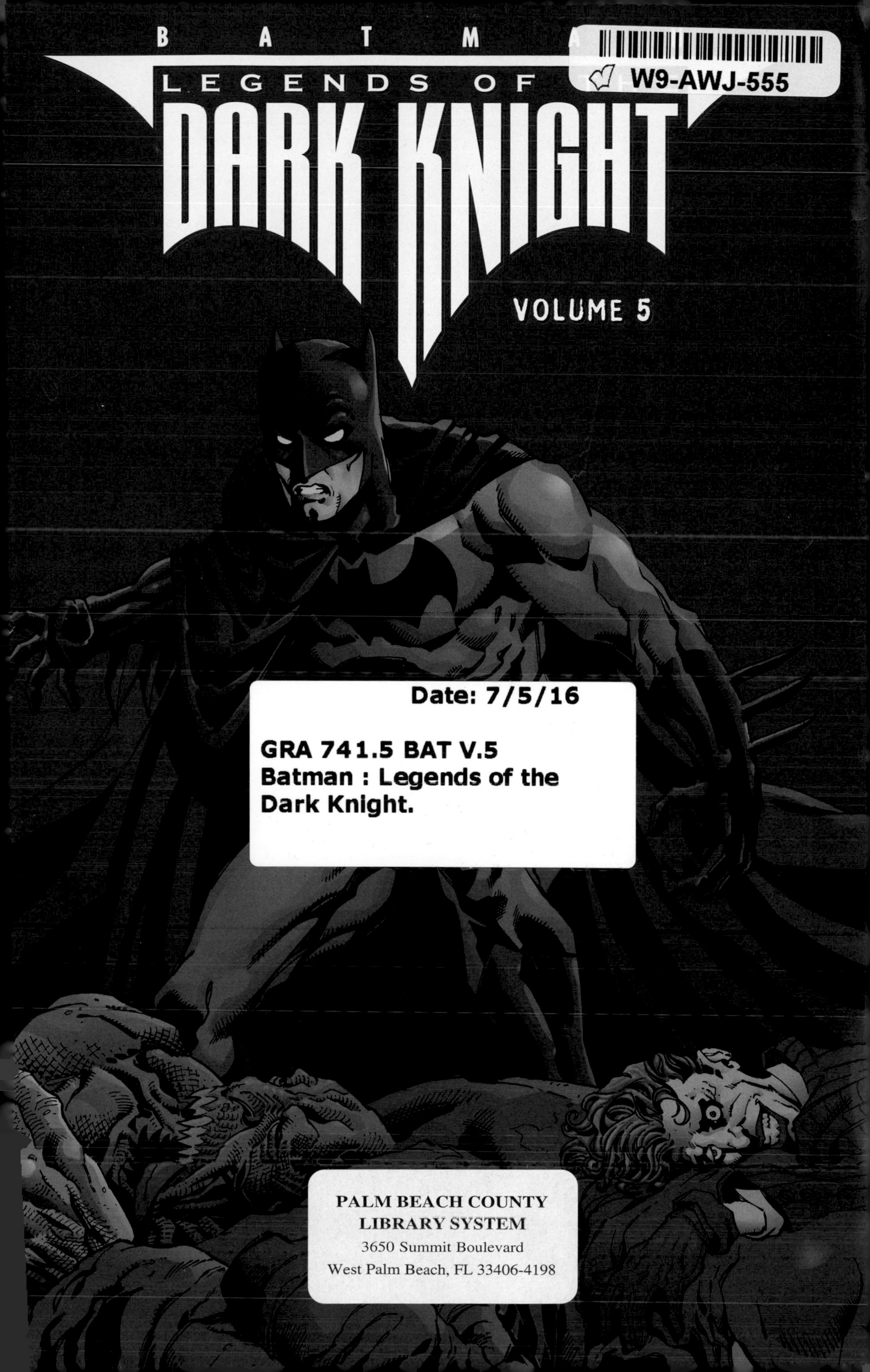
BATMA
LEGENDS OF
DARK KNIGHT
VOLUME 5

HANK KANALZ KRISTY QUINN ALEX ANTONE EDITORS – ORIGINAL SERIES
JESSICA CHEN ASSISTANT EDITOR – ORIGINAL SERIES
JEB WOODARD GROUP EDITOR – COLLECTED EDITIONS
LIZ ERICKSON EDITOR – COLLECTED EDITION
DAMIAN RYLAND PUBLICATION DESIGN

BOB HARRAS SENIOR VP – EDITOR-IN-CHIEF, DC COMICS

DIANE NELSON PRESIDENT
DAN DIDIO AND JIM LEE CO-PUBLISHERS
GEOFF JOHNS CHIEF CREATIVE OFFICER
AMIT DESAI SENIOR VP – MARKETING & GLOBAL FRANCHISE MANAGEMENT
NAIRI GARDINER SENIOR VP – FINANCE
SAM ADES VP – DIGITAL MARKETING
BOBBIE CHASE VP – TALENT DEVELOPMENT
MARK CHIARELLO SENIOR VP – ART, DESIGN & COLLECTED EDITIONS
JOHN CUNNINGHAM VP – CONTENT STRATEGY
ANNE DEPIES VP – STRATEGY PLANNING & REPORTING
DON FALLETTI VP – MANUFACTURING OPERATIONS
LAWRENCE GANEM VP – EDITORIAL ADMINISTRATION & TALENT RELATIONS
ALISON GILL SENIOR VP – MANUFACTURING & OPERATIONS
HANK KANALZ SENIOR VP – EDITORIAL STRATEGY & ADMINISTRATION
JAY KOGAN VP – LEGAL AFFAIRS
DEREK MADDALENA SENIOR VP – SALES & BUSINESS DEVELOPMENT
JACK MAHAN VP – BUSINESS AFFAIRS
DAN MIRON VP – SALES PLANNING & TRADE DEVELOPMENT
NICK NAPOLITANO VP – MANUFACTURING ADMINISTRATION
CAROL ROEDER VP – MARKETING
EDDIE SCANNELL VP – MASS ACCOUNT & DIGITAL SALES
COURTNEY SIMMONS SENIOR VP – PUBLICITY & COMMUNICATIONS
JIM (SKI) SOKOLOWSKI VP – COMIC BOOK SPECIALTY & NEWSSTAND SALES
SANDY YI SENIOR VP – GLOBAL FRANCHISE MANAGEMENT

BATMAN: LEGENDS OF THE DARK KNIGHT VOLUME 5

PUBLISHED BY DC COMICS. COMPILATION COPYRIGHT © 2015 DC COMICS. ALL RIGHTS RESERVED.

ORIGINALLY PUBLISHED ONLINE AS LEGENDS OF THE DARK KNIGHT DIGITAL CHAPTERS 66-68, 70-84
COPYRIGHT © 2013, 2014, 2015 DC COMICS. ALL RIGHTS RESERVED. ALL CHARACTERS, THEIR DISTINCTIVE
LIKENESSES AND RELATED ELEMENTS FEATURED IN THIS PUBLICATION ARE TRADEMARKS OF DC COMICS.
THE STORIES, CHARACTERS AND INCIDENTS FEATURED IN THIS PUBLICATION ARE ENTIRELY FICTIONAL.
DC COMICS DOES NOT READ OR ACCEPT UNSOLICITED IDEAS, STORIES OR ARTWORK.

DC COMICS, 4000 WARNER BLVD., BURBANK, CA 91522
A WARNER BROS. ENTERTAINMENT COMPANY.
PRINTED BY RR DONNELLEY, SALEM, VA, USA. 10/2/2015.
FIRST PRINTING. ISBN: 978-1-4012-5814-6

LIBRARY OF CONGRESS CATALOGING-IN-PUBLICATION DATA

MARZ, RON.
BATMAN : LEGENDS OF THE DARK KNIGHT. VOLUME 5 / RON MARZ ; ILLUSTRATED BY PETE WOODS.
PAGES CM
ISBN 978-1-4012-5814-6 (PAPERBACK)
1. GRAPHIC NOVELS. I. WOODS, PETE, ILLUSTRATOR. II. TITLE.
PN6728.B36M267 2015
741.5'973—DC23
2015028555

PEFC Certified

Printed on paper from
sustainably managed
forests and controlled
sources

PEFC
PEFC/29-31-75   www.pefc.org

BATMAN
LEGENDS OF THE
DARK KNIGHT

VOLUME 5

AARON LOPRESTI · DOUG WAGNER · MARC GUGGENHEIM
RON MARZ · SCOTT KOLINS · J. TORRES
WRITERS

AARON LOPRESTI · MATTHEW DOW SMITH · FEDERICO DALLOCCHIO
CULLY HAMNER · DEREC DONOVAN · SCOTT KOLINS
MATTHEW CLARK · WADE VON GRAWBADGER
ARTISTS

WENDY BROOME · ALEJANDRO SANCHEZ · RICO RENZI · DAVE MCCAIG
ULISES ARREOLA · CARRIE STRACHAN
COLORISTS

SAIDA TEMOFONTE · DERON BENNETT
LETTERERS

CULLY HAMNER
COLLECTION COVER ARTIST

BATMAN created by BOB KANE

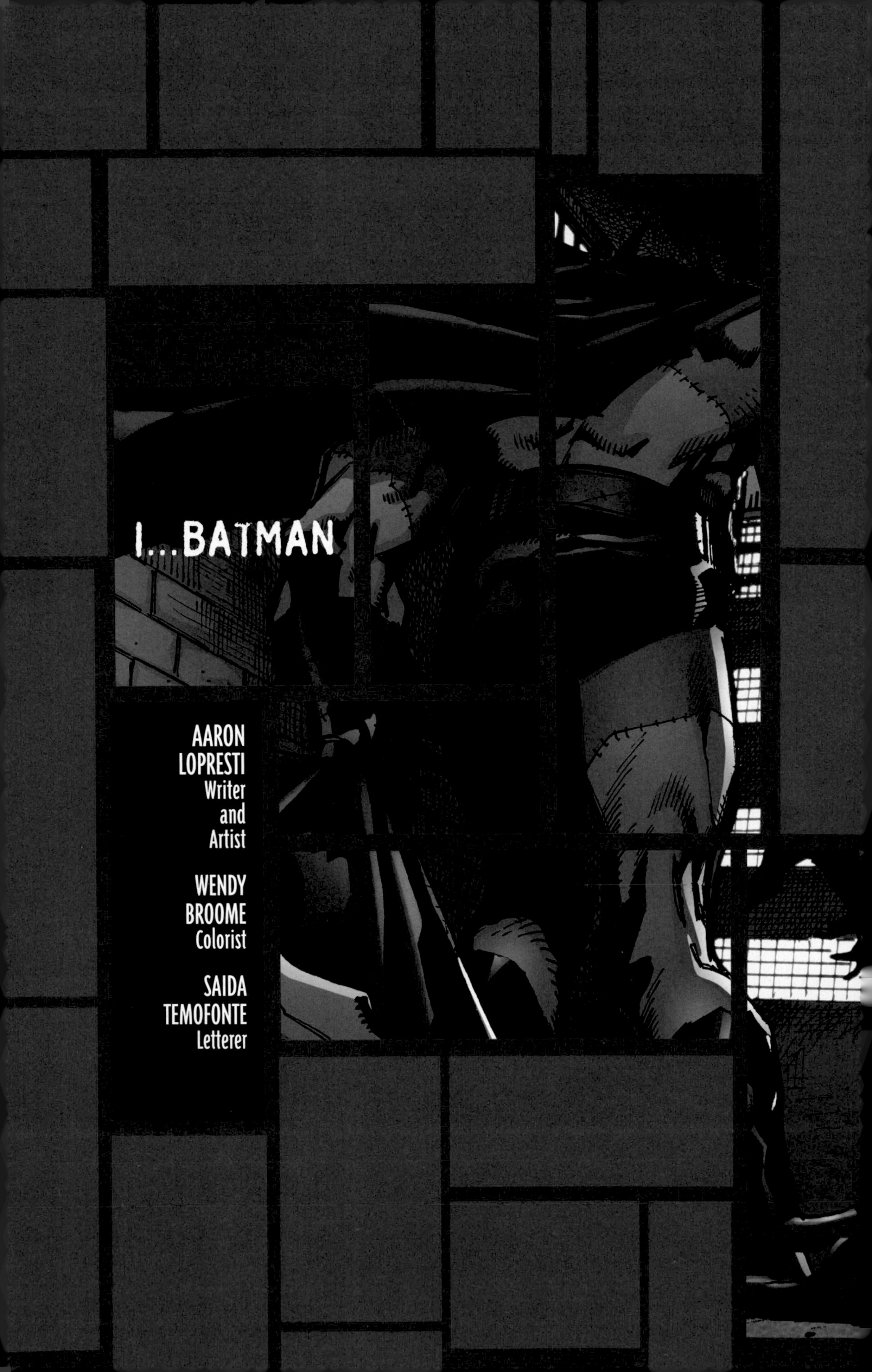
I...BATMAN
AARON LOPRESTI Writer and Artist
WENDY BROOME Colorist
SAIDA TEMOFONTE Letterer

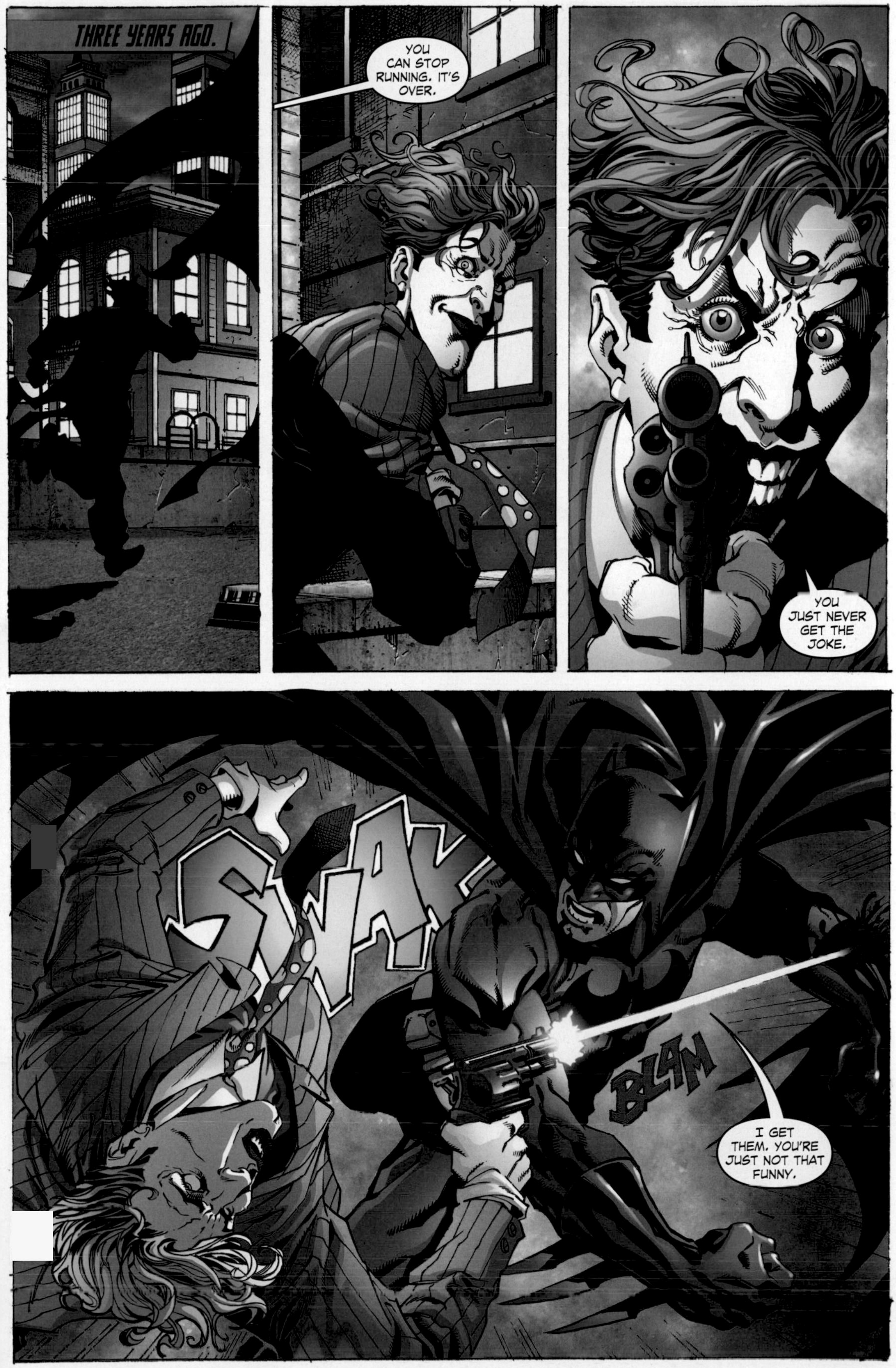
THREE YEARS AGO.
YOU CAN STOP RUNNING. IT'S OVER.
YOU JUST NEVER GET THE JOKE.
SKAK
BLAM
I GET THEM. YOU'RE JUST NOT THAT FUNNY.

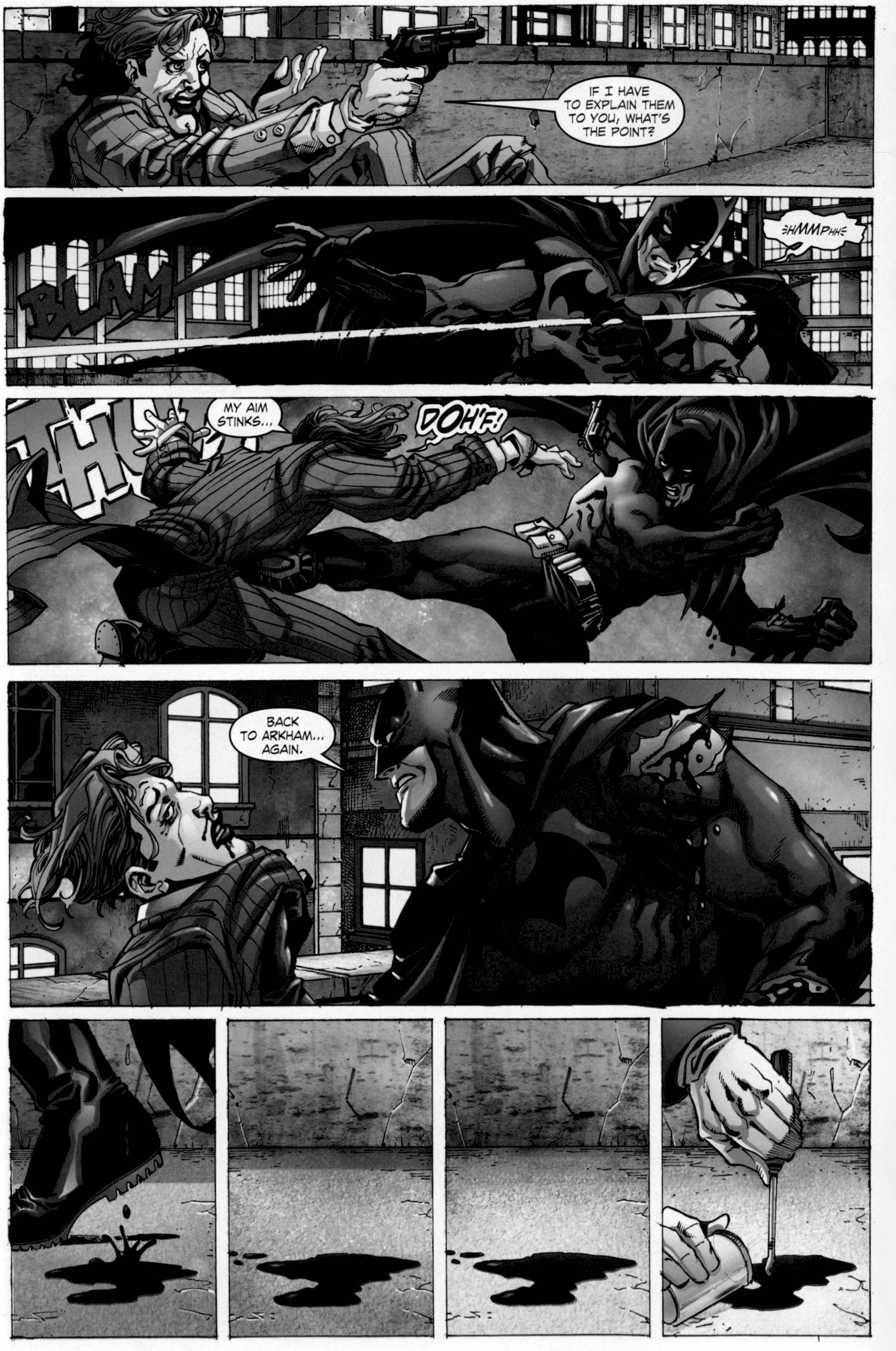
IF I HAVE TO EXPLAIN THEM TO YOU, WHAT'S THE POINT?
BLAM
HMMPHH
MY AIM STINKS...
DOH'F!
BACK TO ARKHAM... AGAIN.

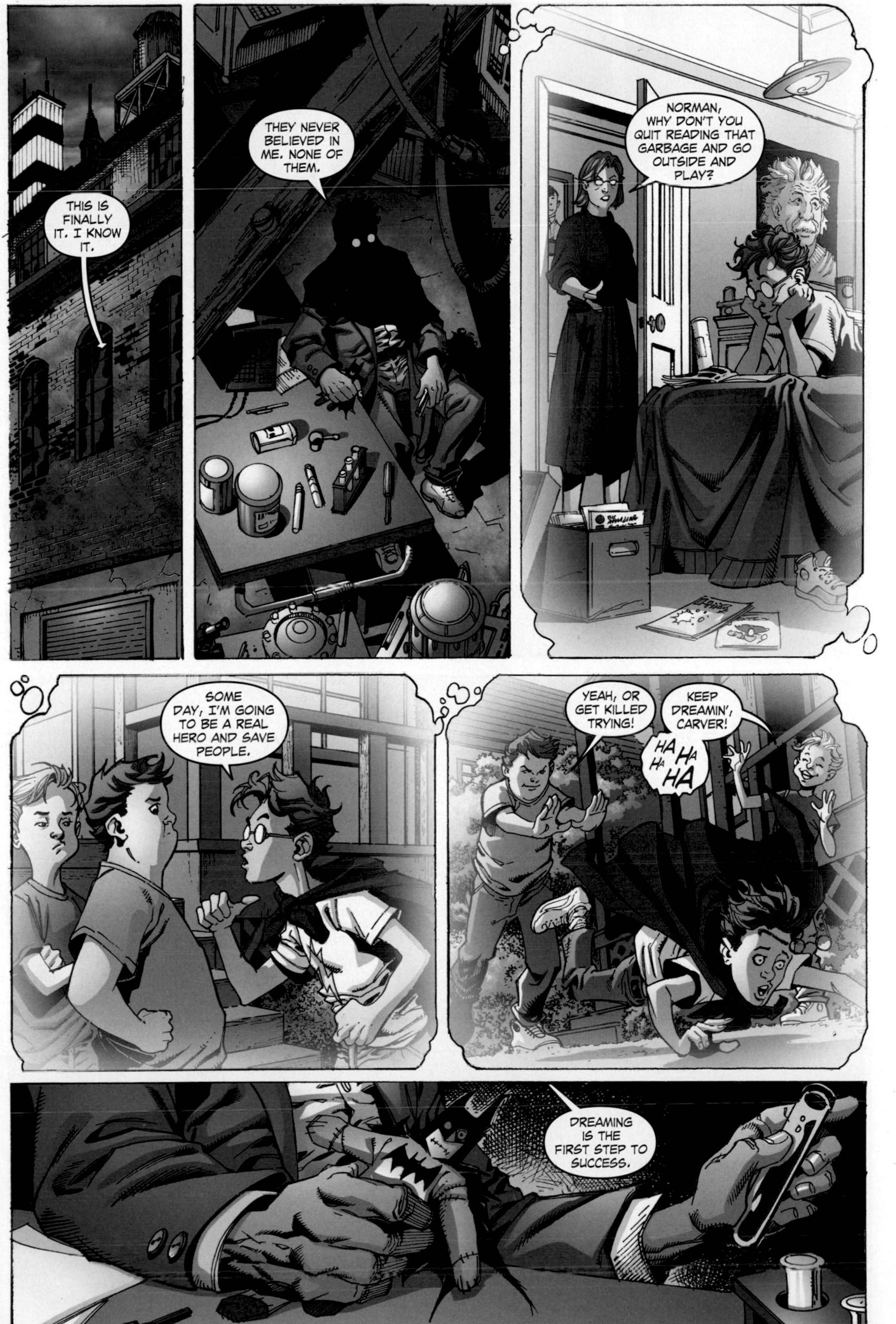
THIS IS FINALLY IT. I KNOW IT.
THEY NEVER BELIEVED IN ME. NONE OF THEM.
NORMAN, WHY DON'T YOU QUIT READING THAT GARBAGE AND GO OUTSIDE AND PLAY?
SOME DAY, I'M GOING TO BE A REAL HERO AND SAVE PEOPLE.
YEAH, OR GET KILLED TRYING!
KEEP DREAMIN', CARVER!
HA HA HA HA
DREAMING IS THE FIRST STEP TO SUCCESS.

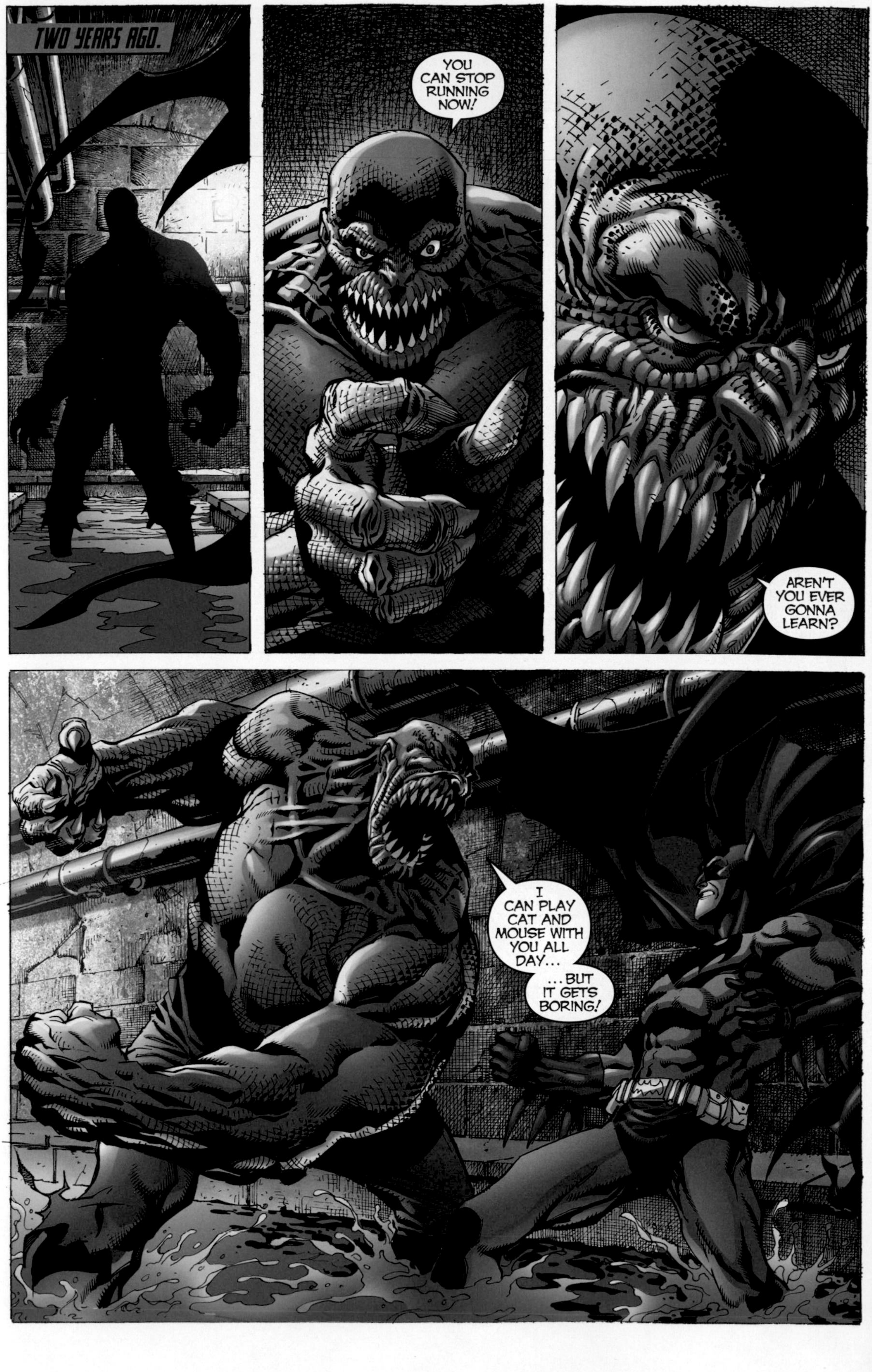
TWO YEARS AGO.
YOU CAN STOP RUNNING NOW!
AREN'T YOU EVER GONNA LEARN?
I CAN PLAY CAT AND MOUSE WITH YOU ALL DAY...
...BUT IT GETS BORING!

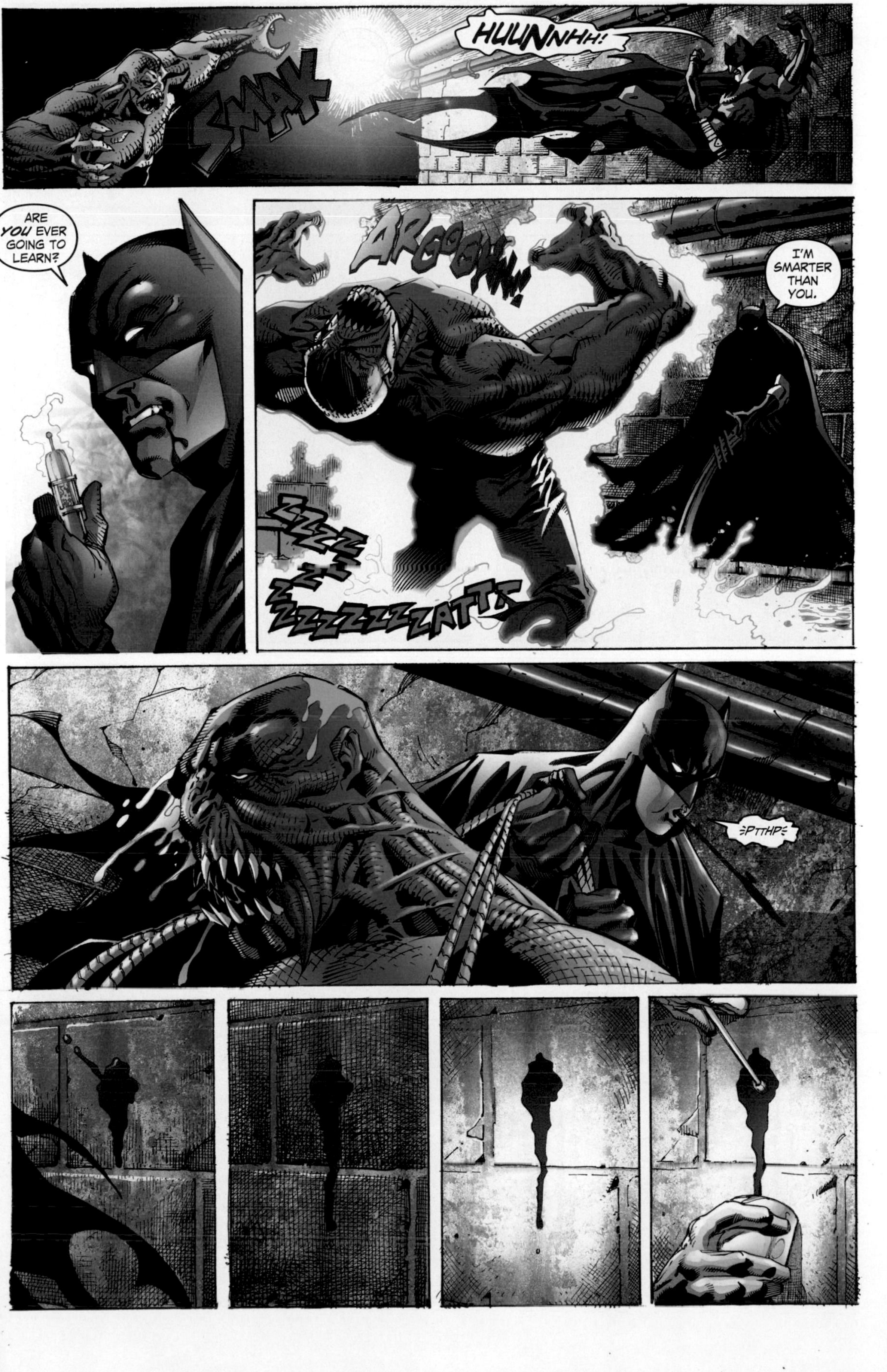
SMAK
HUUNNHH!
ARE YOU EVER GOING TO LEARN?
ARGGGHH!!
I'M SMARTER THAN YOU.
ZZZZZ
ZZ
ZZZZZZZZATTT
PTTHP

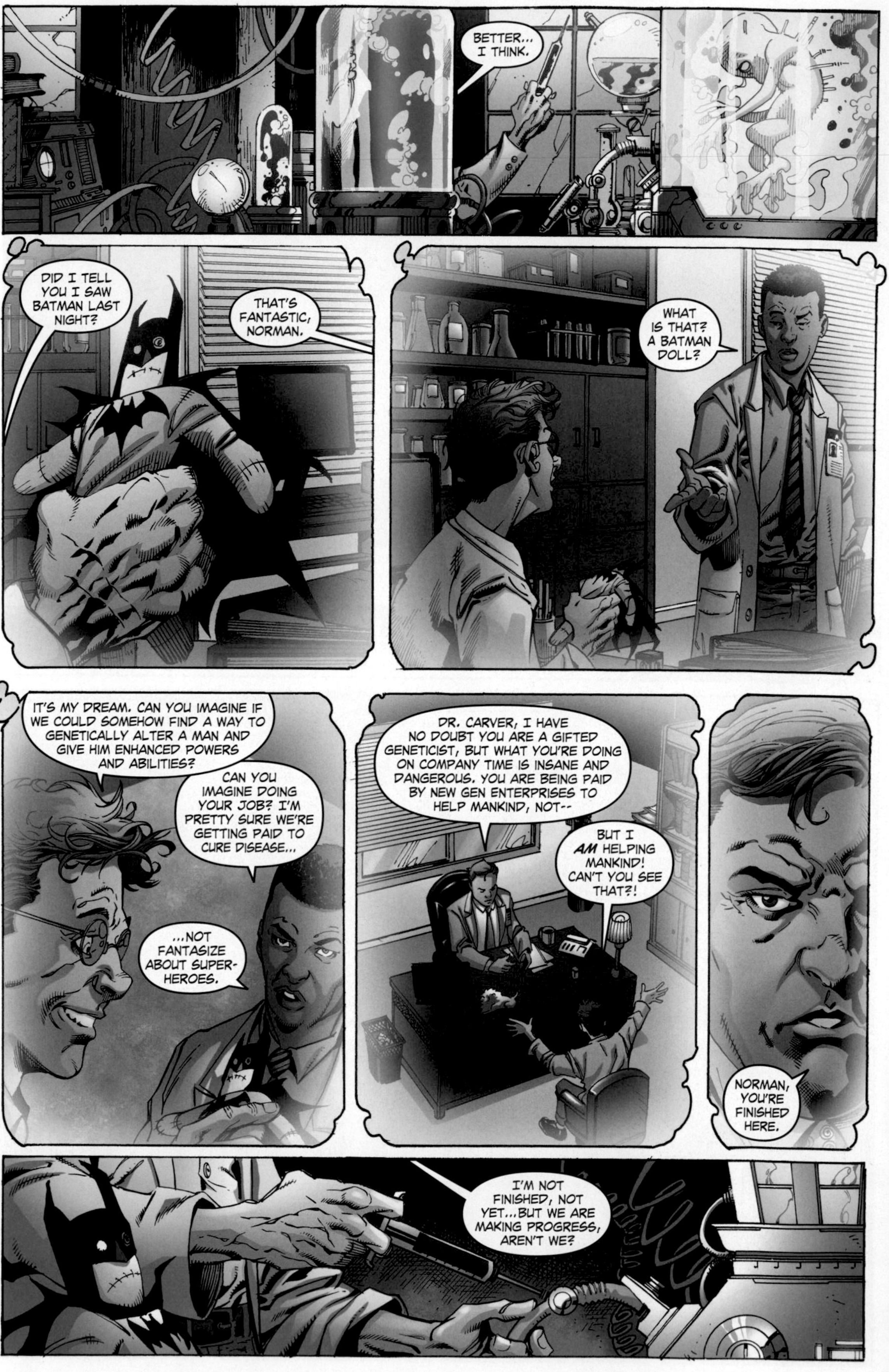
BETTER... I THINK.
DID I TELL YOU I SAW BATMAN LAST NIGHT?
THAT'S FANTASTIC, NORMAN.
WHAT IS THAT? A BATMAN DOLL?
IT'S MY DREAM. CAN YOU IMAGINE IF WE COULD SOMEHOW FIND A WAY TO GENETICALLY ALTER A MAN AND GIVE HIM ENHANCED POWERS AND ABILITIES?
CAN YOU IMAGINE DOING YOUR JOB? I'M PRETTY SURE WE'RE GETTING PAID TO CURE DISEASE...
...NOT FANTASIZE ABOUT SUPER-HEROES.
DR. CARVER, I HAVE NO DOUBT YOU ARE A GIFTED GENETICIST, BUT WHAT YOU'RE DOING ON COMPANY TIME IS INSANE AND DANGEROUS. YOU ARE BEING PAID BY NEW GEN ENTERPRISES TO HELP MANKIND, NOT--
BUT I AM HELPING MANKIND! CAN'T YOU SEE THAT?!
NORMAN, YOU'RE FINISHED HERE.
I'M NOT FINISHED, NOT YET...BUT WE ARE MAKING PROGRESS, AREN'T WE?

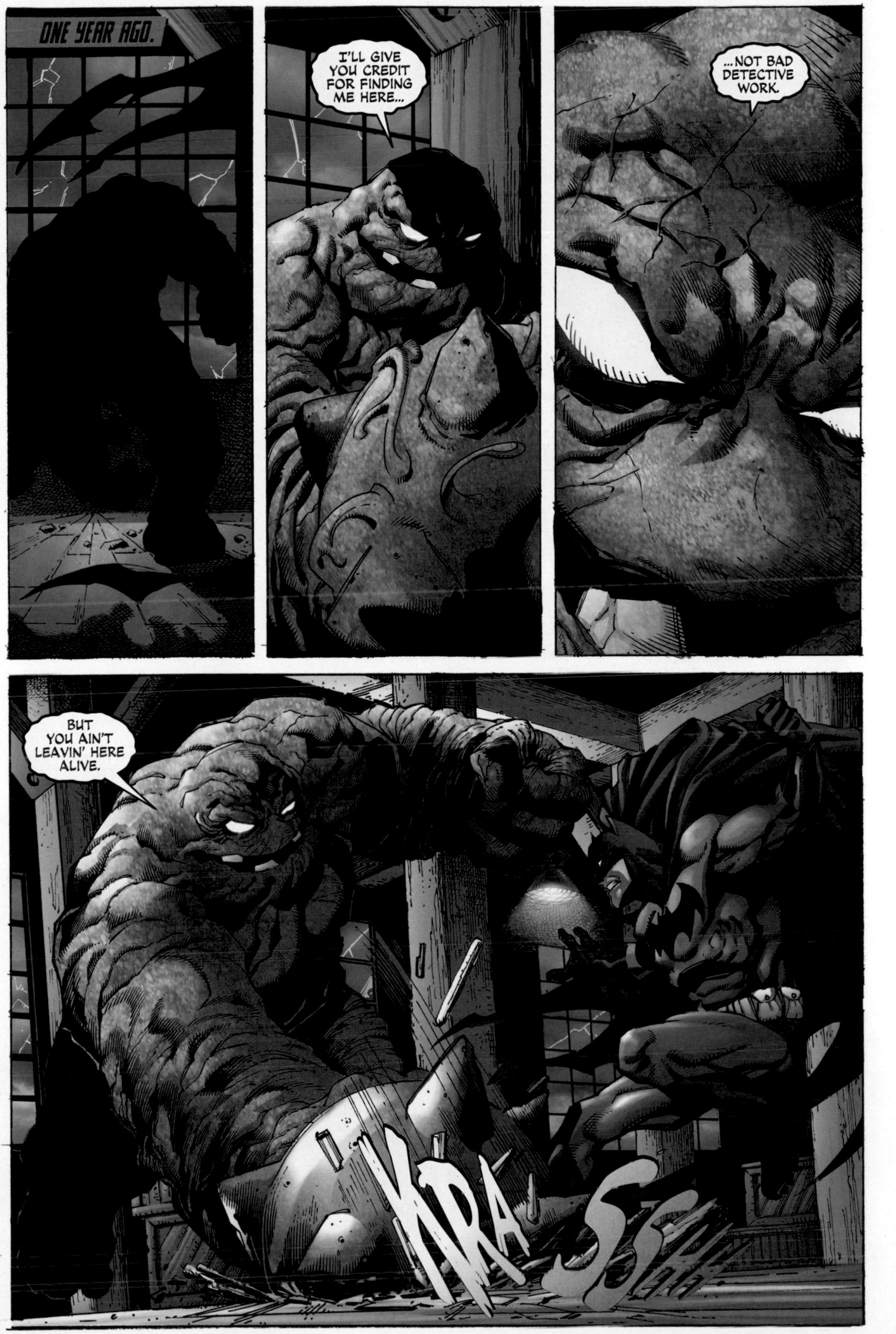
ONE YEAR AGO.
I'LL GIVE YOU CREDIT FOR FINDING ME HERE...
...NOT BAD DETECTIVE WORK.
BUT YOU AIN'T LEAVIN' HERE ALIVE.
KRASSSH

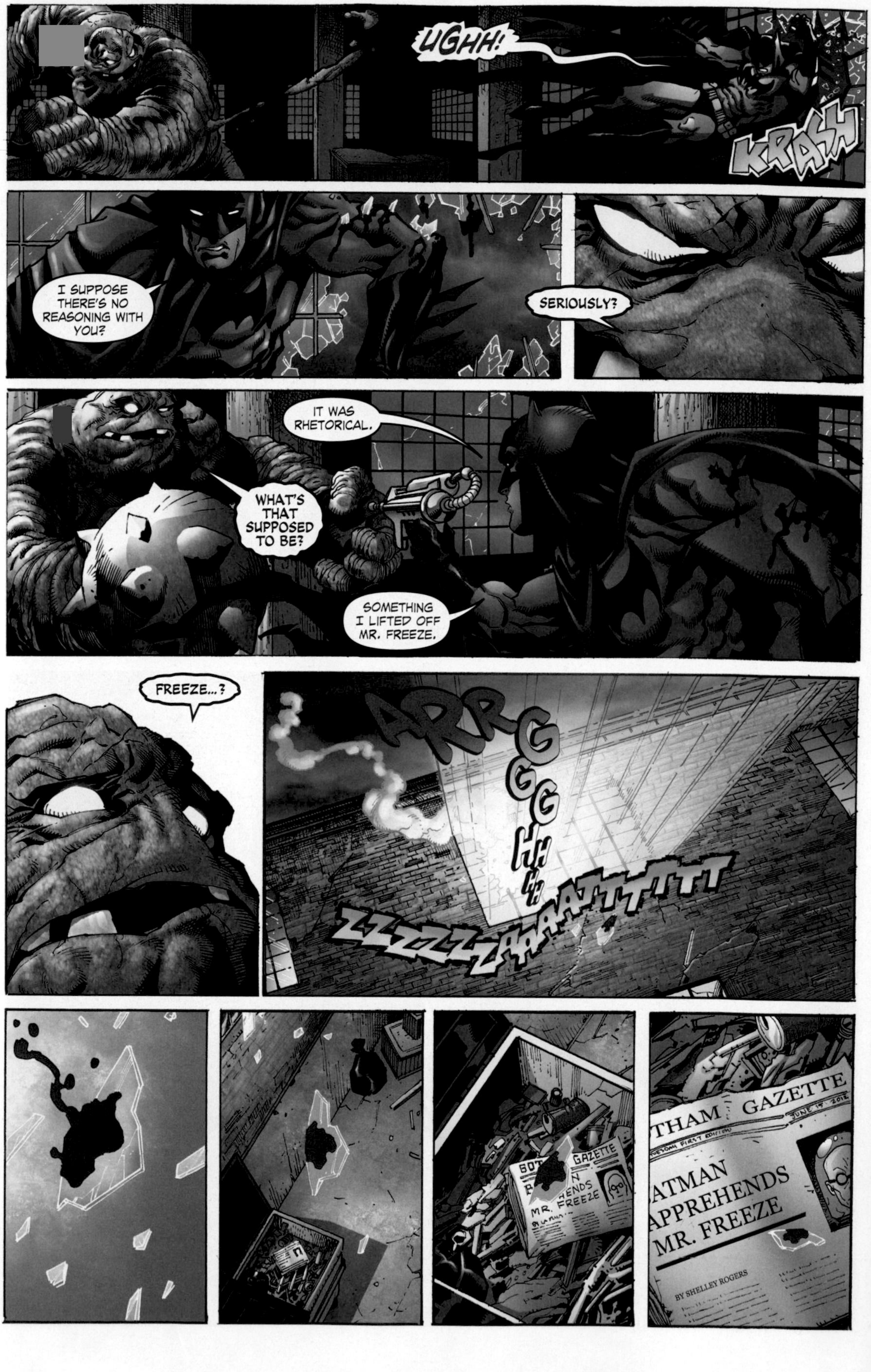

UGHH!
KRASH
I SUPPOSE THERE'S NO REASONING WITH YOU?
SERIOUSLY?
IT WAS RHETORICAL.
WHAT'S THAT SUPPOSED TO BE?
SOMETHING I LIFTED OFF MR. FREEZE.
FREEZE...?
ARRGGGHH
ZZZZZZAAAATTTTTTT
THAM GAZETTE
ATMAN APPREHENDS MR. FREEZE
BY SHELLEY ROGERS

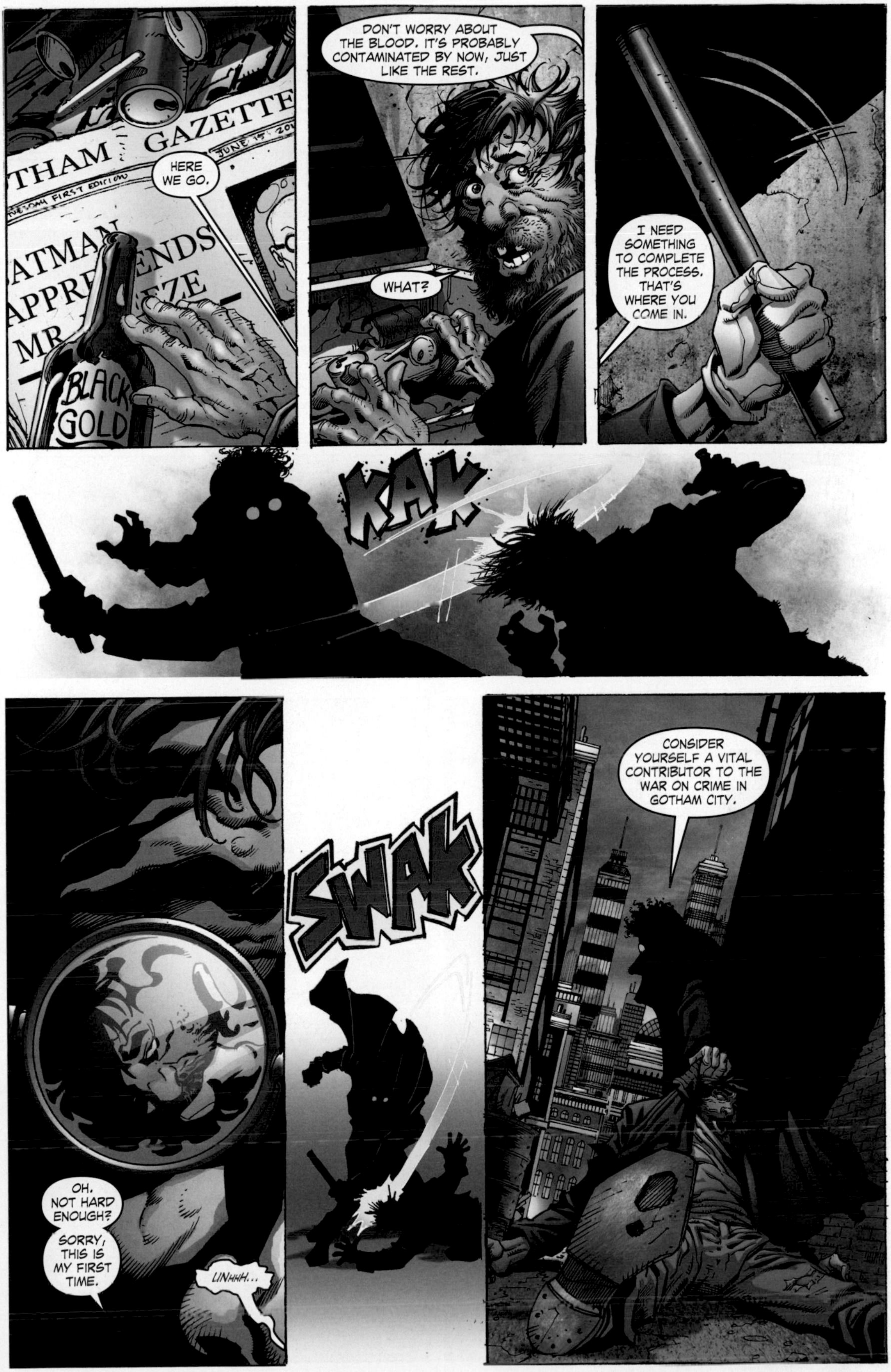

GOTHAM GAZETTE
BATMAN APPREHENDS MR. FREEZE
HERE WE GO.
BLACK GOLD
DON'T WORRY ABOUT THE BLOOD. IT'S PROBABLY CONTAMINATED BY NOW, JUST LIKE THE REST.
WHAT?
I NEED SOMETHING TO COMPLETE THE PROCESS. THAT'S WHERE YOU COME IN.
KAK
OH. NOT HARD ENOUGH?
SORRY, THIS IS MY FIRST TIME.
SWAK
UNHHH...
CONSIDER YOURSELF A VITAL CONTRIBUTOR TO THE WAR ON CRIME IN GOTHAM CITY.

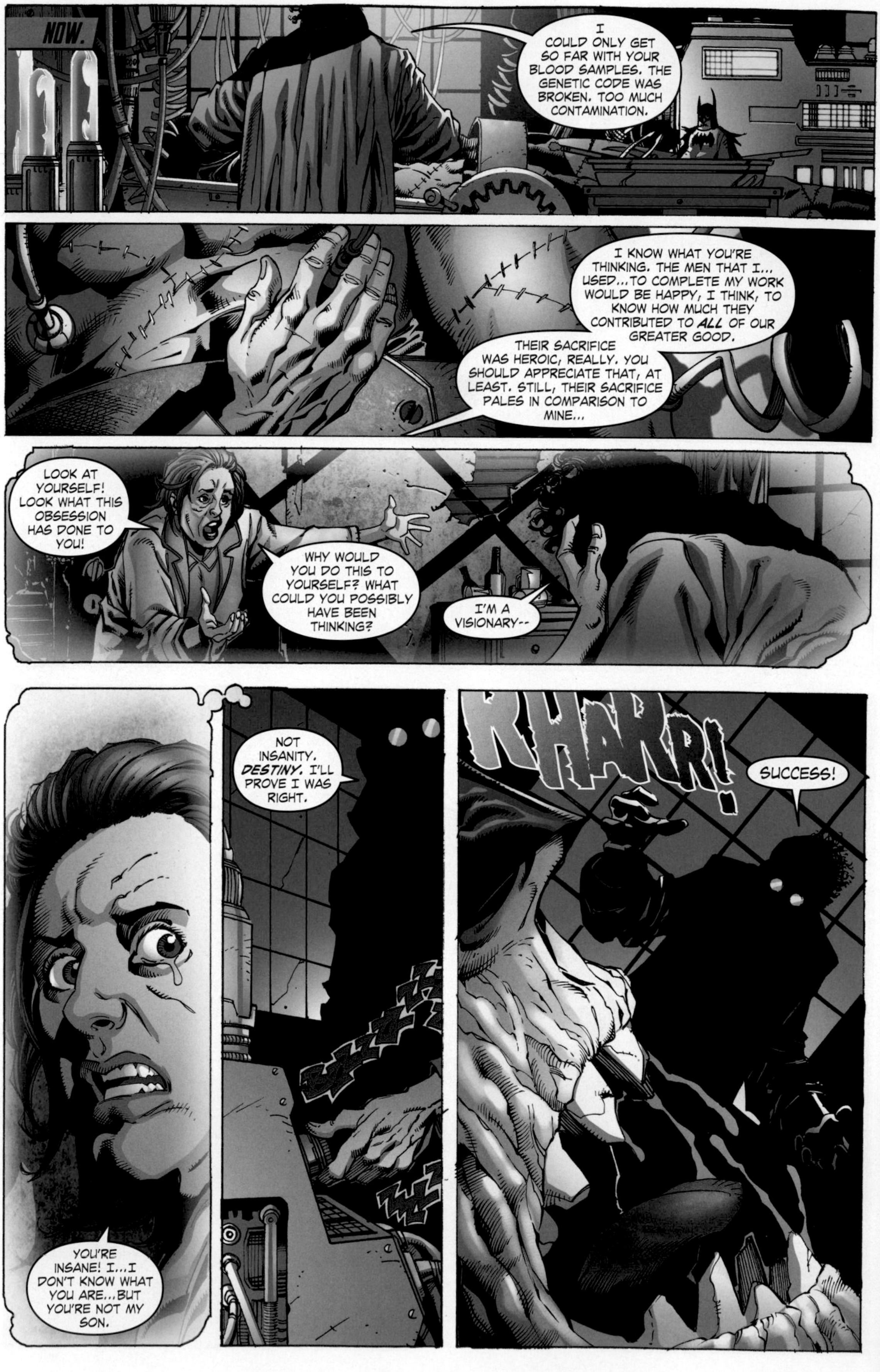
NOW.
I COULD ONLY GET SO FAR WITH YOUR BLOOD SAMPLES. THE GENETIC CODE WAS BROKEN. TOO MUCH CONTAMINATION.
I KNOW WHAT YOU'RE THINKING. THE MEN THAT I... USED...TO COMPLETE MY WORK WOULD BE HAPPY, I THINK, TO KNOW HOW MUCH THEY CONTRIBUTED TO ALL OF OUR GREATER GOOD.
THEIR SACRIFICE WAS HEROIC, REALLY. YOU SHOULD APPRECIATE THAT, AT LEAST. STILL, THEIR SACRIFICE PALES IN COMPARISON TO MINE...
LOOK AT YOURSELF! LOOK WHAT THIS OBSESSION HAS DONE TO YOU!
WHY WOULD YOU DO THIS TO YOURSELF? WHAT COULD YOU POSSIBLY HAVE BEEN THINKING?
I'M A VISIONARY--
YOU'RE INSANE! I...I DON'T KNOW WHAT YOU ARE...BUT YOU'RE NOT MY SON.
NOT INSANITY. DESTINY. I'LL PROVE I WAS RIGHT.
RHARR!
SUCCESS!

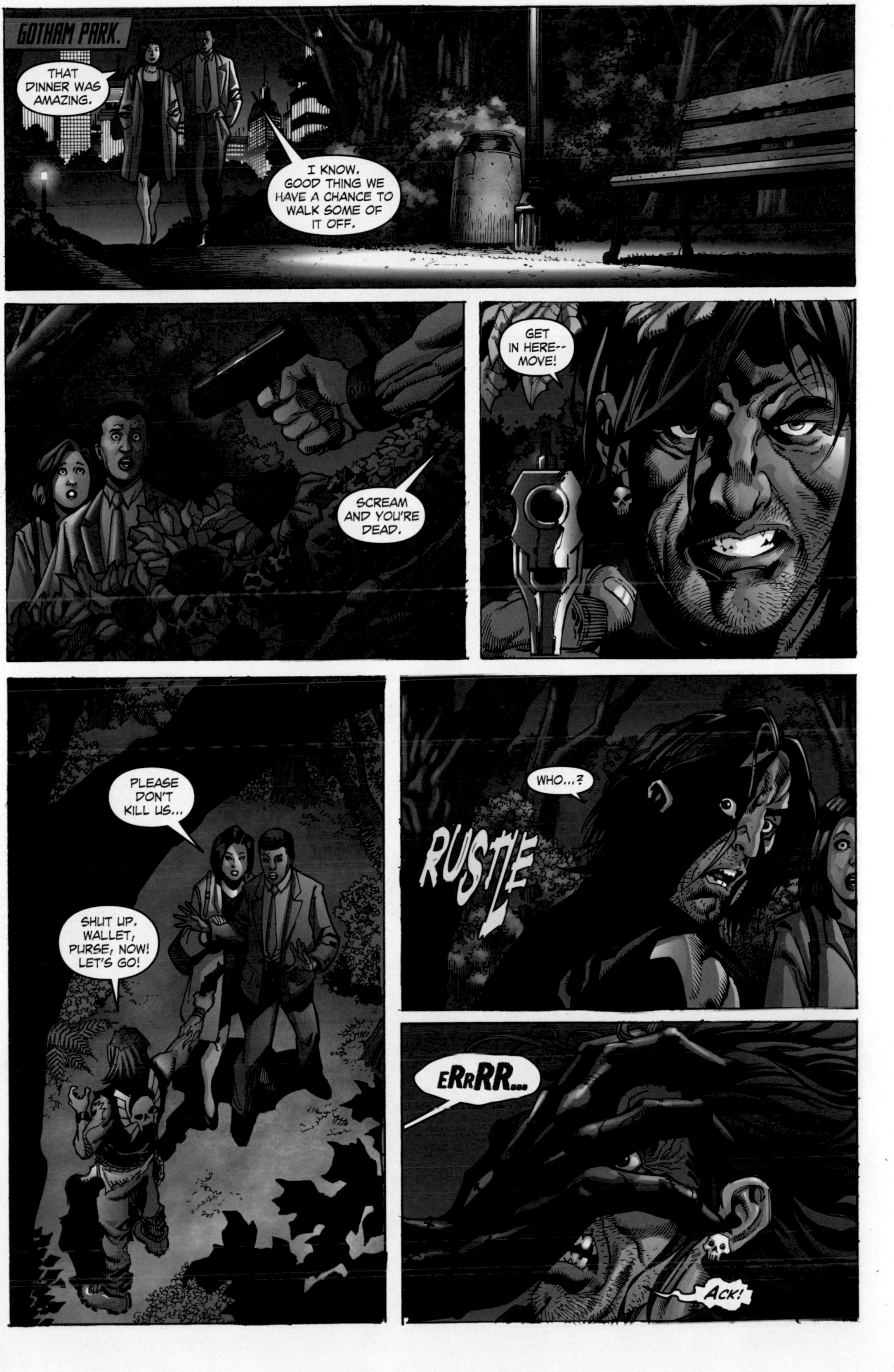
GOTHAM PARK.
THAT DINNER WAS AMAZING.
I KNOW. GOOD THING WE HAVE A CHANCE TO WALK SOME OF IT OFF.
SCREAM AND YOU'RE DEAD.
GET IN HERE-- MOVE!
PLEASE DON'T KILL US...
SHUT UP. WALLET, PURSE, NOW! LET'S GO!
WHO...?
RUSTLE
ERRRR...
ACK!

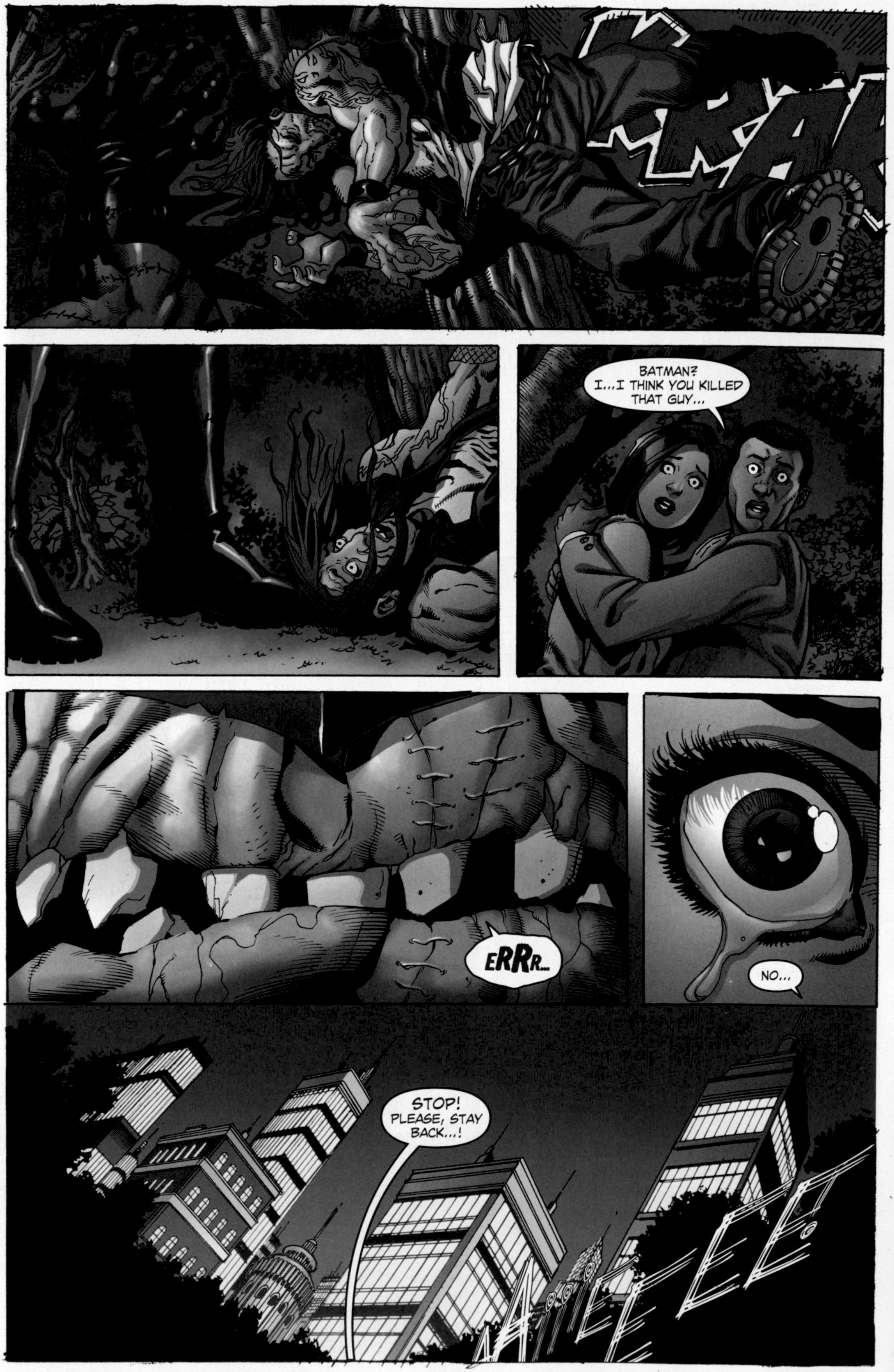
KRAK
BATMAN? I...I THINK YOU KILLED THAT GUY...
ERRR...
NO...
STOP! PLEASE, STAY BACK...!
AAIIEEEEE

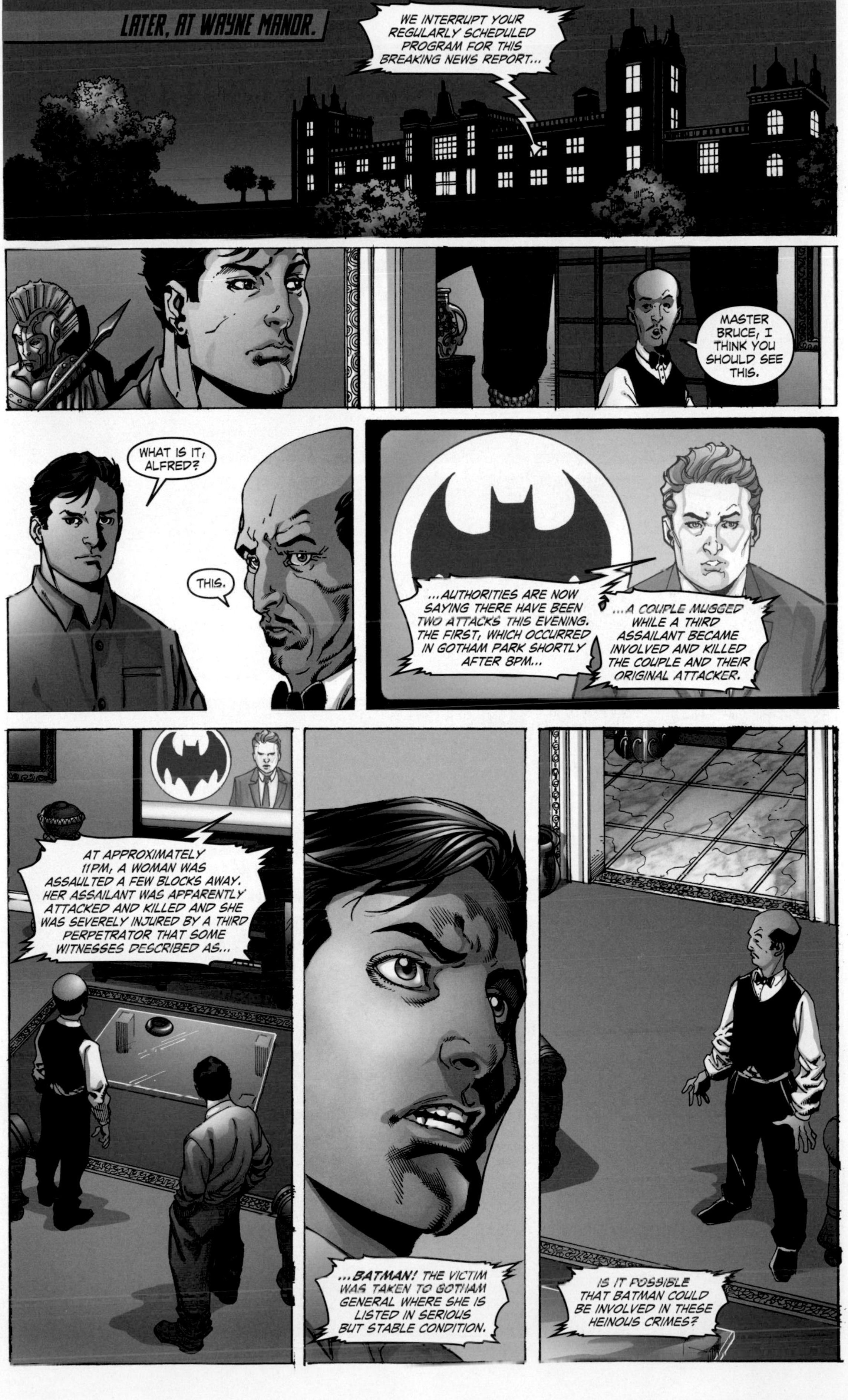
LATER, AT WAYNE MANOR.
WE INTERRUPT YOUR REGULARLY SCHEDULED PROGRAM FOR THIS BREAKING NEWS REPORT...
MASTER BRUCE, I THINK YOU SHOULD SEE THIS.
WHAT IS IT, ALFRED?
THIS.
...AUTHORITIES ARE NOW SAYING THERE HAVE BEEN TWO ATTACKS THIS EVENING. THE FIRST, WHICH OCCURRED IN GOTHAM PARK SHORTLY AFTER 8PM...
...A COUPLE MUGGED WHILE A THIRD ASSAILANT BECAME INVOLVED AND KILLED THE COUPLE AND THEIR ORIGINAL ATTACKER.
AT APPROXIMATELY 11PM, A WOMAN WAS ASSAULTED A FEW BLOCKS AWAY. HER ASSAILANT WAS APPARENTLY ATTACKED AND KILLED AND SHE WAS SEVERELY INJURED BY A THIRD PERPETRATOR THAT SOME WITNESSES DESCRIBED AS...
...BATMAN! THE VICTIM WAS TAKEN TO GOTHAM GENERAL WHERE SHE IS LISTED IN SERIOUS BUT STABLE CONDITION.
IS IT POSSIBLE THAT BATMAN COULD BE INVOLVED IN THESE HEINOUS CRIMES?

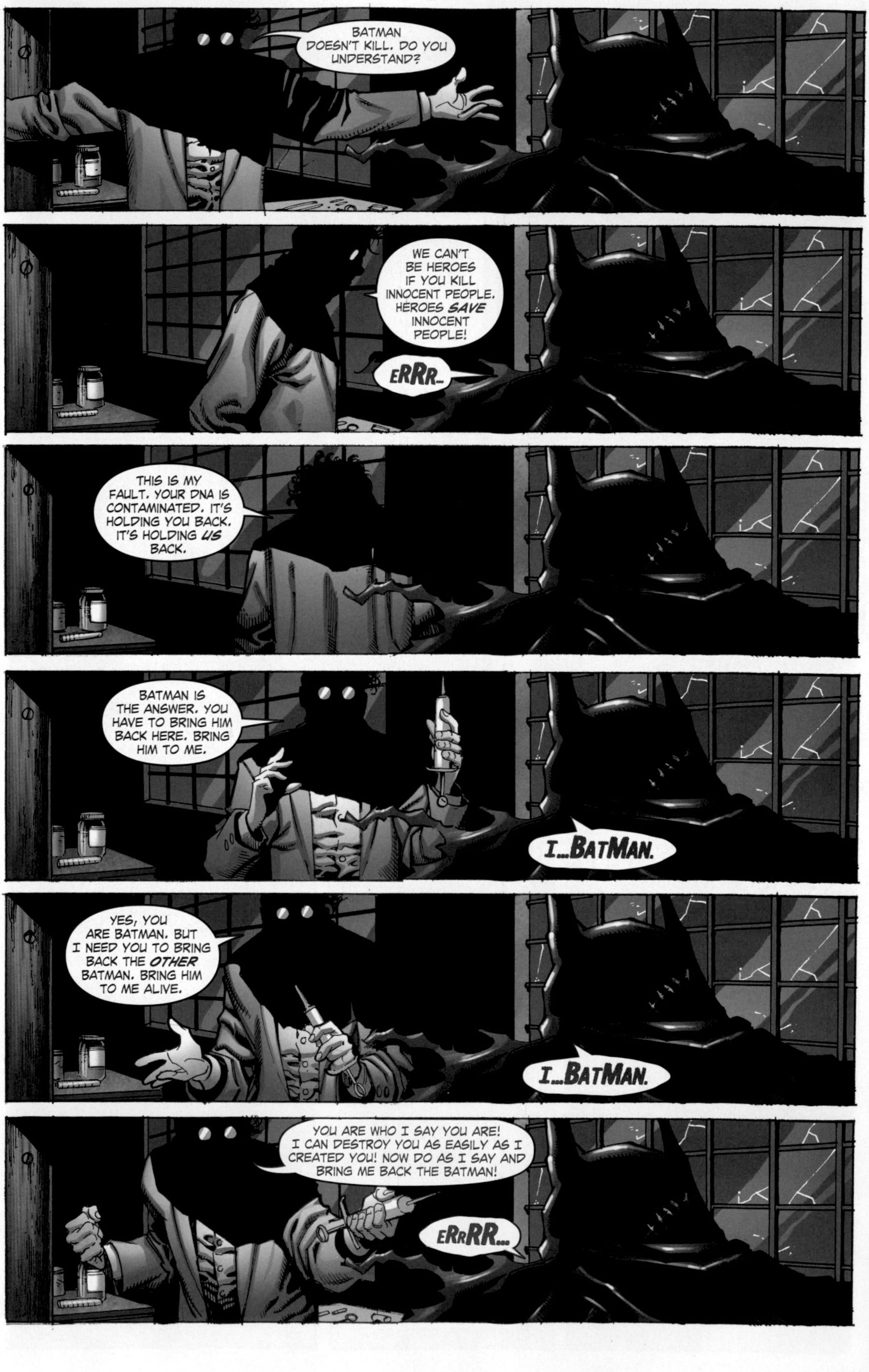
BATMAN DOESN'T KILL. DO YOU UNDERSTAND?
WE CAN'T BE HEROES IF YOU KILL INNOCENT PEOPLE. HEROES SAVE INNOCENT PEOPLE!
ERRR...
THIS IS MY FAULT. YOUR DNA IS CONTAMINATED. IT'S HOLDING YOU BACK. IT'S HOLDING US BACK.
BATMAN IS THE ANSWER. YOU HAVE TO BRING HIM BACK HERE. BRING HIM TO ME.
I...BATMAN.
YES, YOU ARE BATMAN. BUT I NEED YOU TO BRING BACK THE OTHER BATMAN. BRING HIM TO ME ALIVE.
I...BATMAN.
YOU ARE WHO I SAY YOU ARE! I CAN DESTROY YOU AS EASILY AS I CREATED YOU! NOW DO AS I SAY AND BRING ME BACK THE BATMAN!
ERRRR...

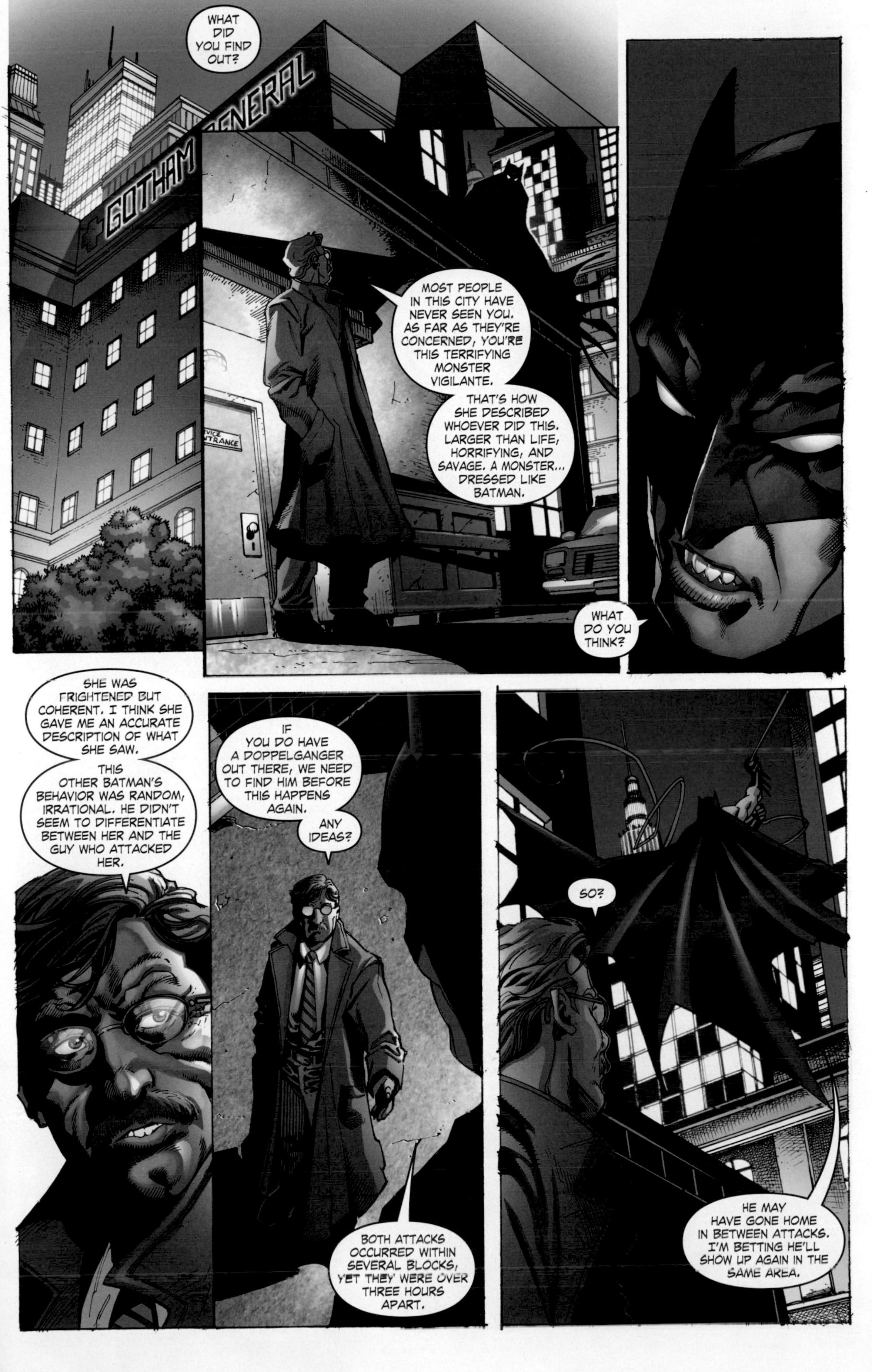
WHAT DID YOU FIND OUT?
GOTHAM GENERAL
MOST PEOPLE IN THIS CITY HAVE NEVER SEEN YOU. AS FAR AS THEY'RE CONCERNED, YOU'RE THIS TERRIFYING MONSTER VIGILANTE.
THAT'S HOW SHE DESCRIBED WHOEVER DID THIS. LARGER THAN LIFE, HORRIFYING, AND SAVAGE. A MONSTER... DRESSED LIKE BATMAN.
WHAT DO YOU THINK?
SHE WAS FRIGHTENED BUT COHERENT. I THINK SHE GAVE ME AN ACCURATE DESCRIPTION OF WHAT SHE SAW.
THIS OTHER BATMAN'S BEHAVIOR WAS RANDOM, IRRATIONAL. HE DIDN'T SEEM TO DIFFERENTIATE BETWEEN HER AND THE GUY WHO ATTACKED HER.
IF YOU DO HAVE A DOPPELGANGER OUT THERE, WE NEED TO FIND HIM BEFORE THIS HAPPENS AGAIN.
ANY IDEAS?
BOTH ATTACKS OCCURRED WITHIN SEVERAL BLOCKS, YET THEY WERE OVER THREE HOURS APART.
SO?
HE MAY HAVE GONE HOME IN BETWEEN ATTACKS. I'M BETTING HE'LL SHOW UP AGAIN IN THE SAME AREA.

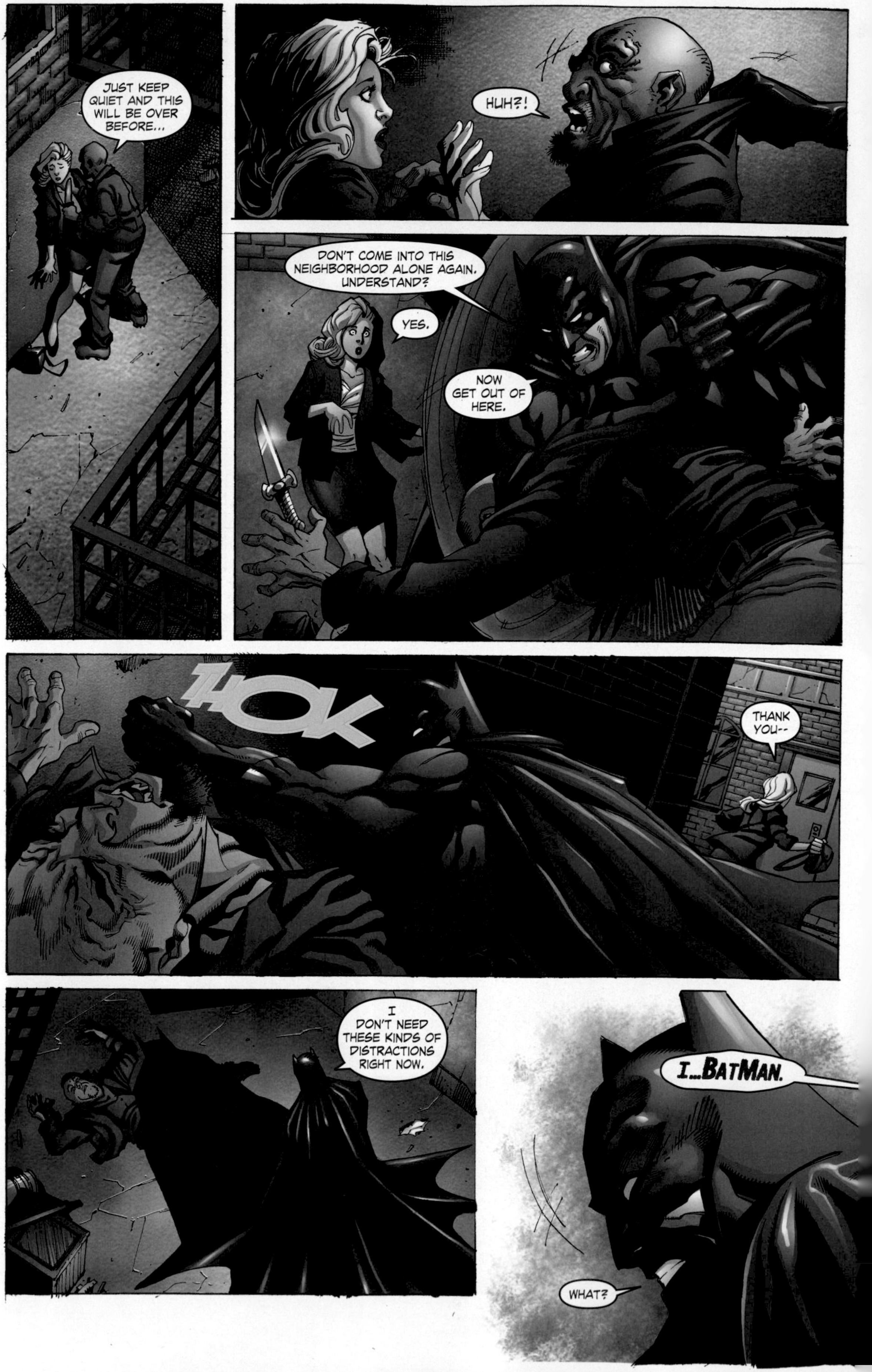

JUST KEEP QUIET AND THIS WILL BE OVER BEFORE...
HUH?!
DON'T COME INTO THIS NEIGHBORHOOD ALONE AGAIN. UNDERSTAND?
YES.
NOW GET OUT OF HERE.
THOK
THANK YOU--
I DON'T NEED THESE KINDS OF DISTRACTIONS RIGHT NOW.
I...BATMAN.
WHAT?

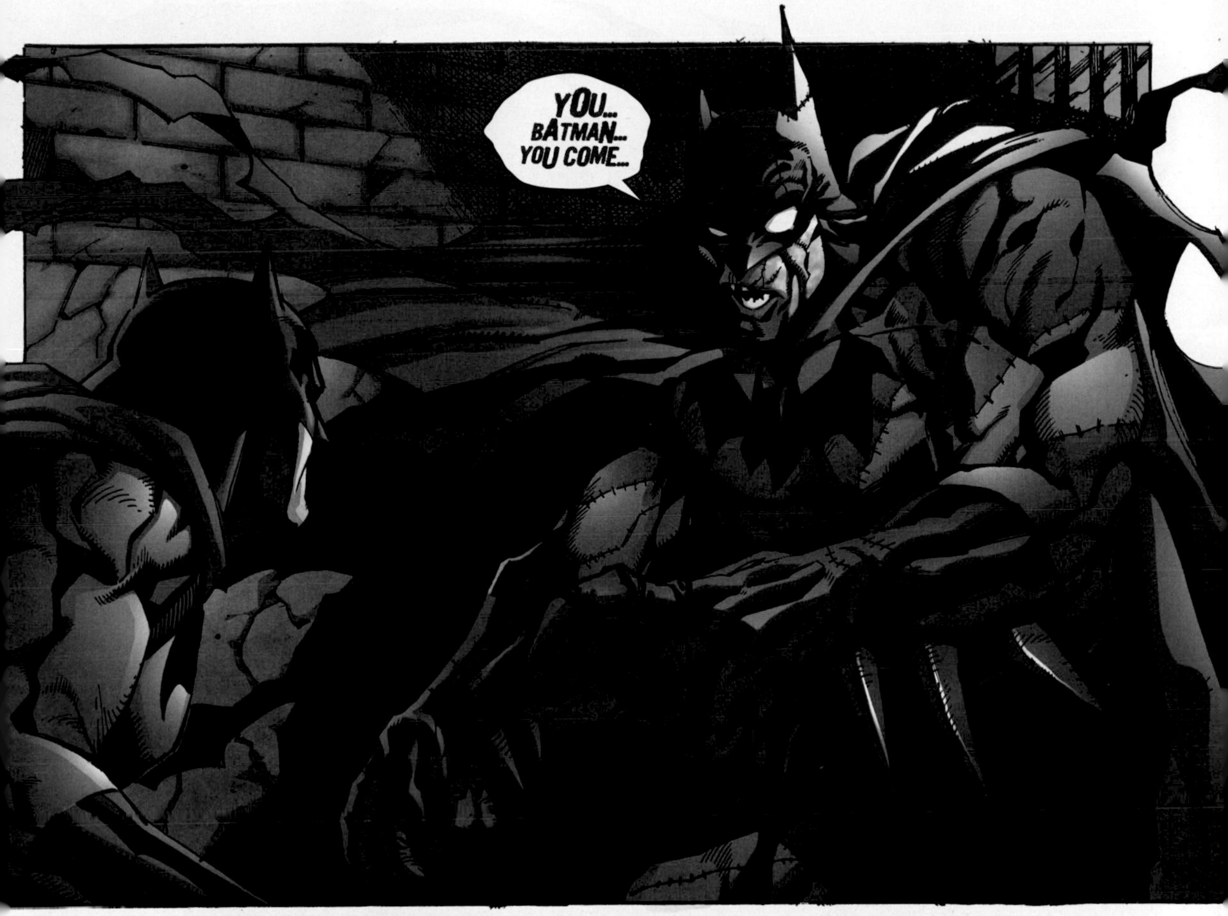
YOU... BATMAN... YOU COME...

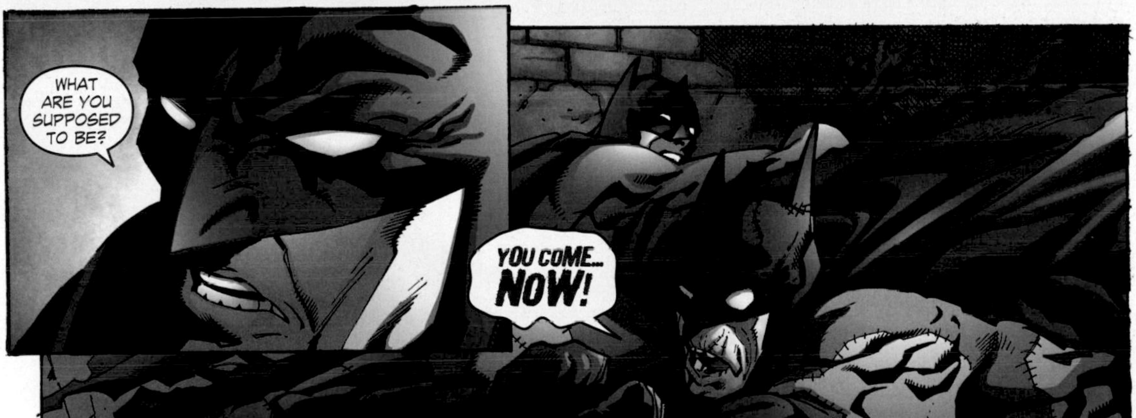
WHAT ARE YOU SUPPOSED TO BE?
YOU COME... NOW!

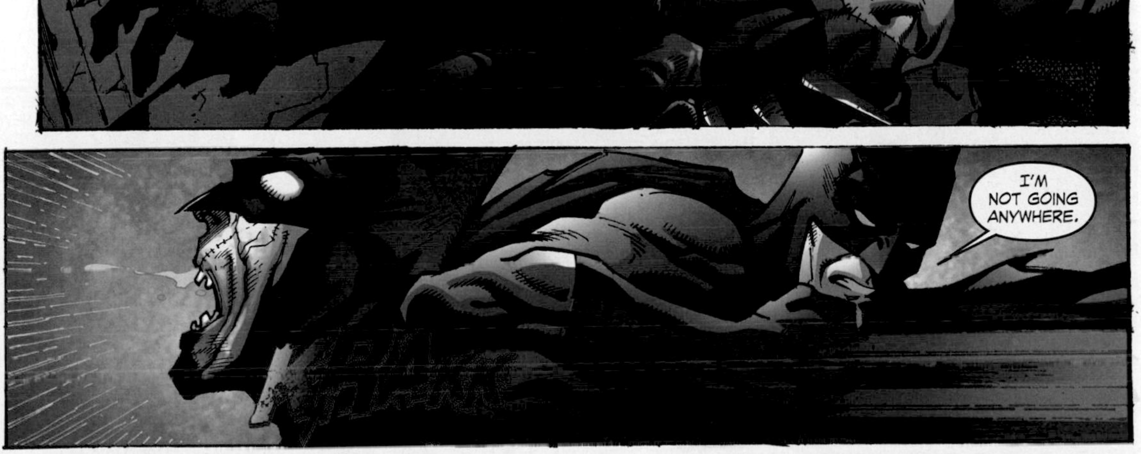
I'M NOT GOING ANYWHERE.

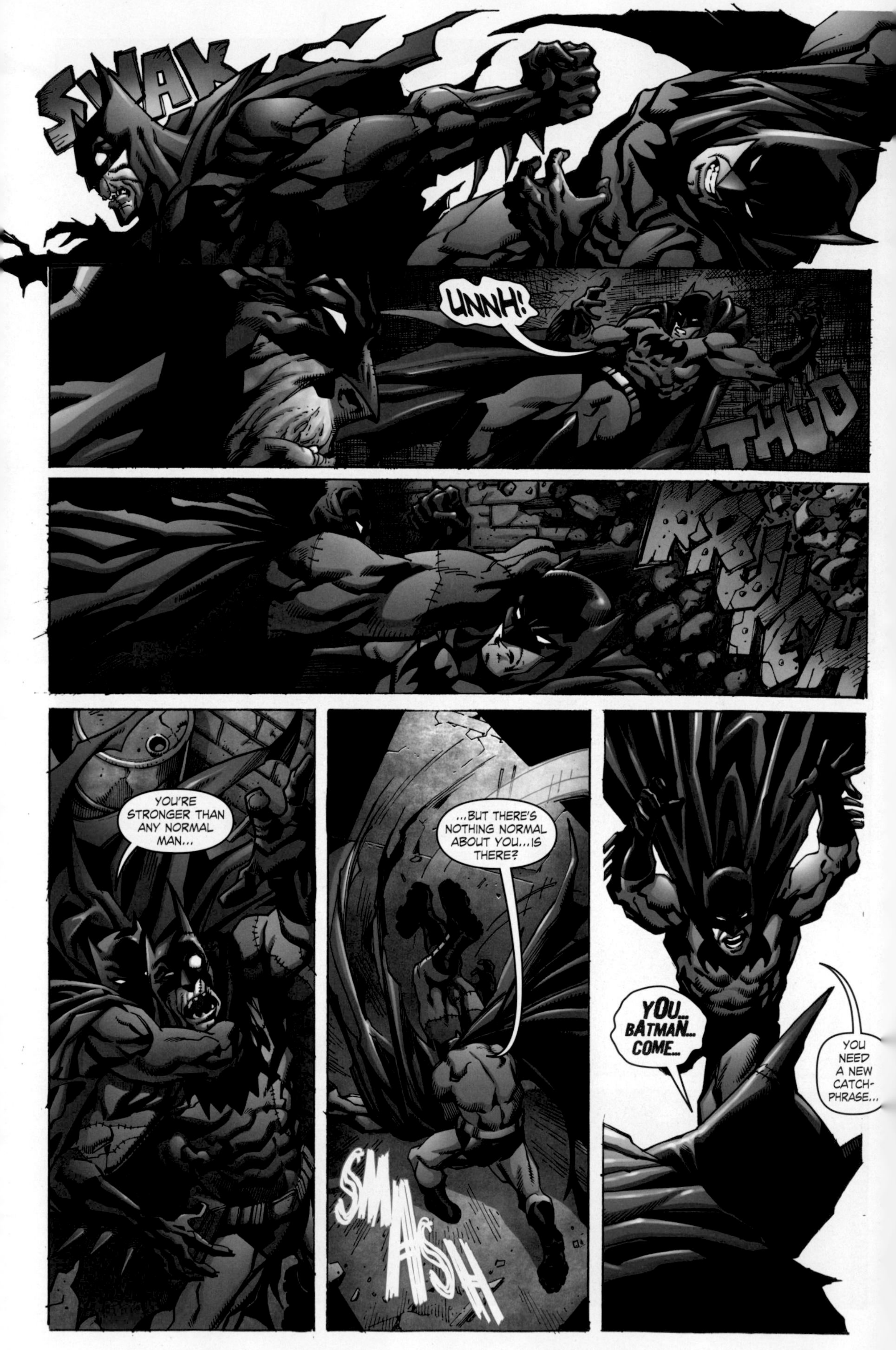
SWAK
UNNH!
THUD
YOU'RE STRONGER THAN ANY NORMAL MAN...
...BUT THERE'S NOTHING NORMAL ABOUT YOU...IS THERE?
SMASH
YOU... BATMAN... COME...
YOU NEED A NEW CATCH-PHRASE...

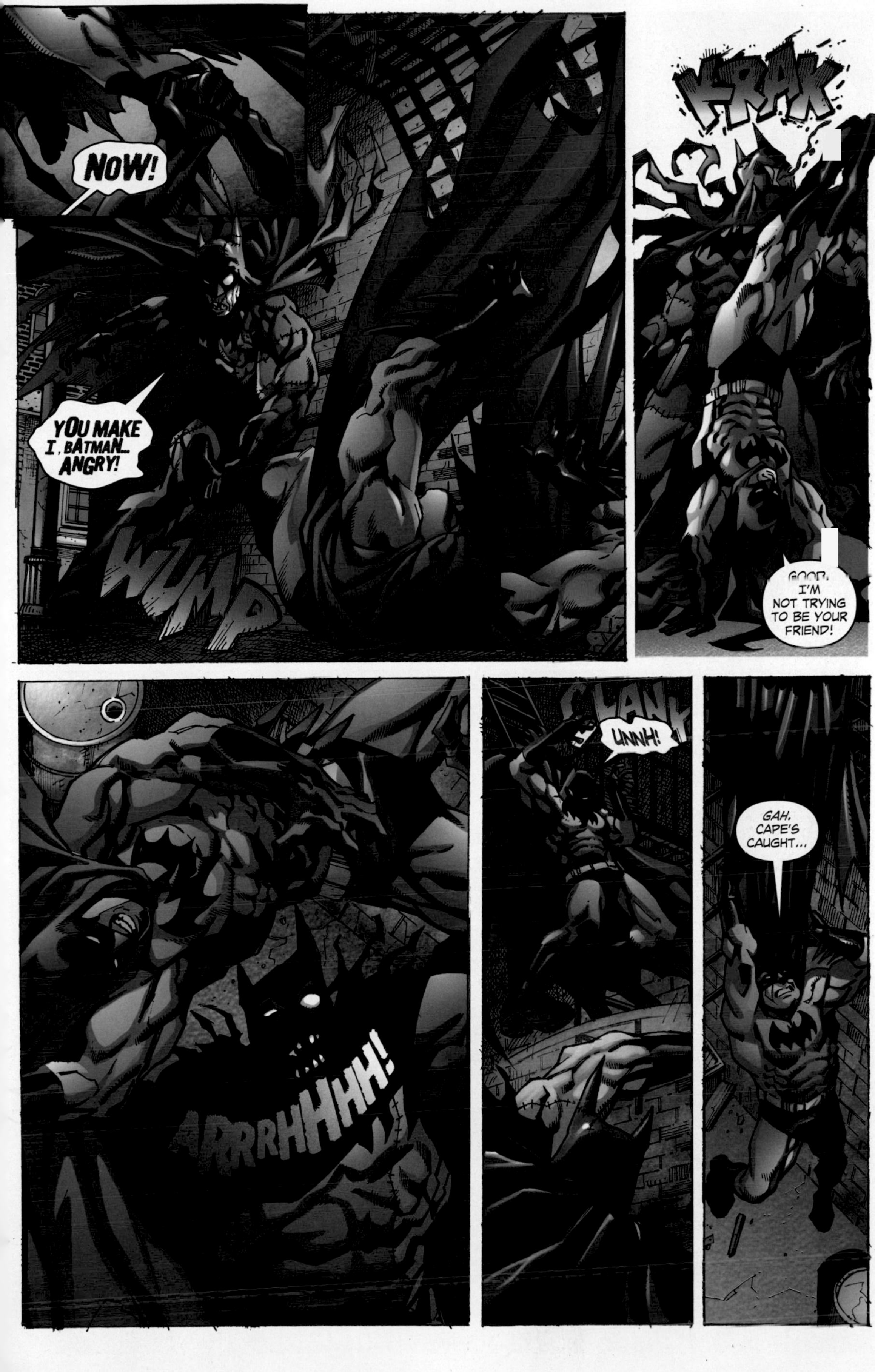
NOW!
YOU MAKE I, BATMAN... ANGRY!
WUMP
KRAK
GOOD. I'M NOT TRYING TO BE YOUR FRIEND!
ARRRHHHH!
UNNH!
GAH. CAPE'S CAUGHT...

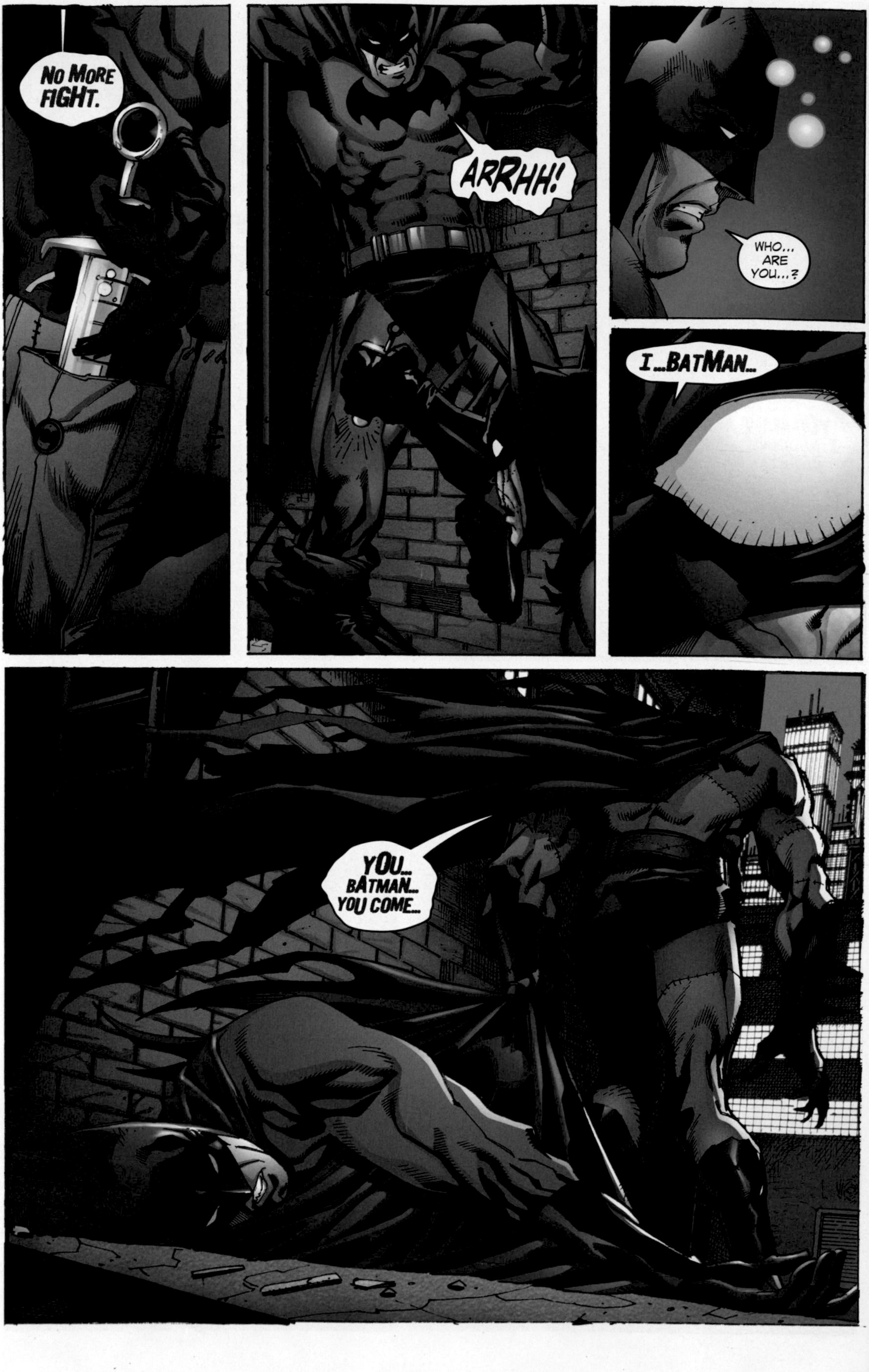
NO MORE FIGHT.
ARRHH!
WHO... ARE YOU...?
I...BATMAN...
YOU... BATMAN... YOU COME...

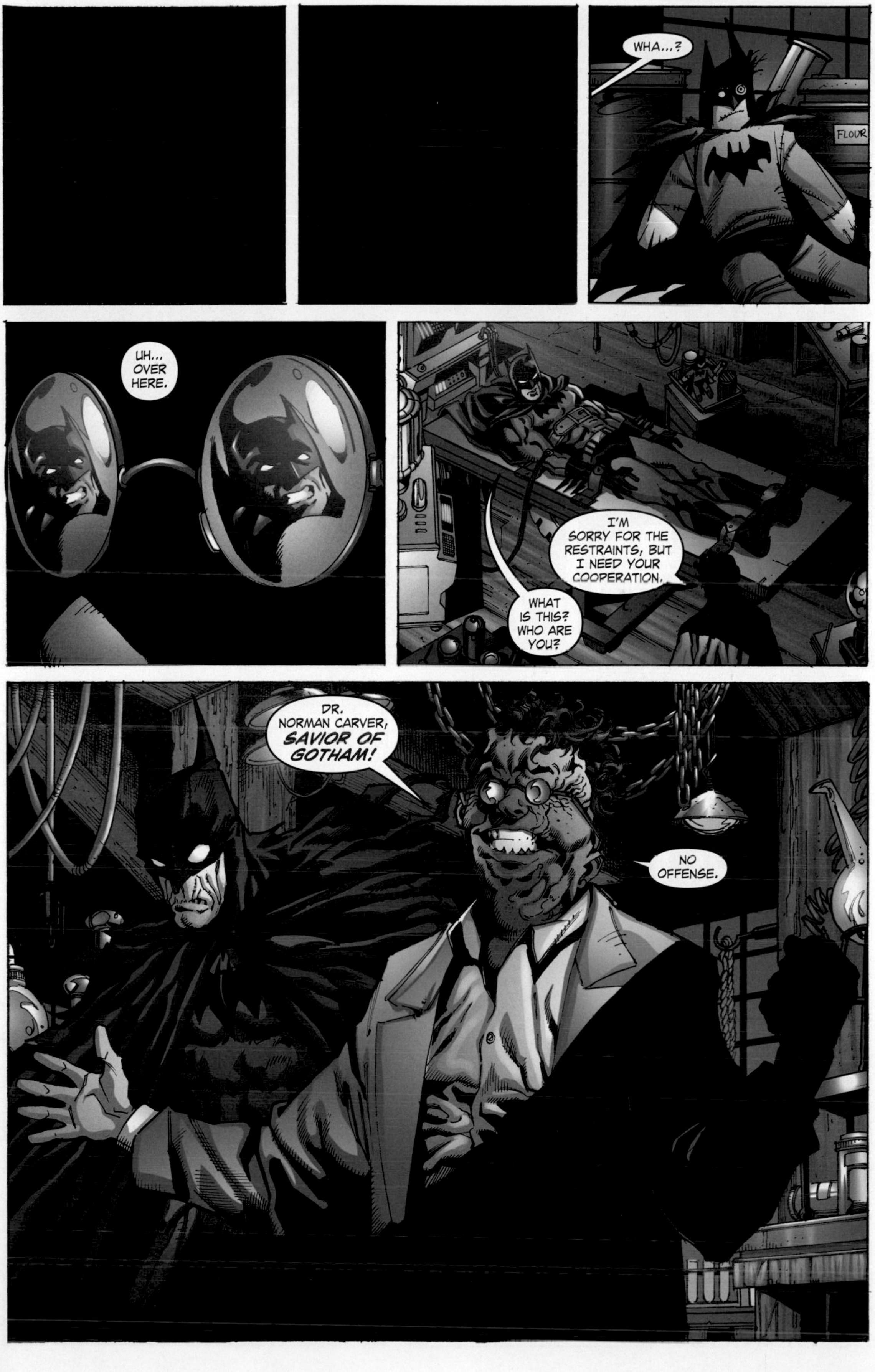

WHA...?
FLOUR
UH... OVER HERE.
WHAT IS THIS? WHO ARE YOU?
I'M SORRY FOR THE RESTRAINTS, BUT I NEED YOUR COOPERATION.
DR. NORMAN CARVER, SAVIOR OF GOTHAM!
NO OFFENSE.

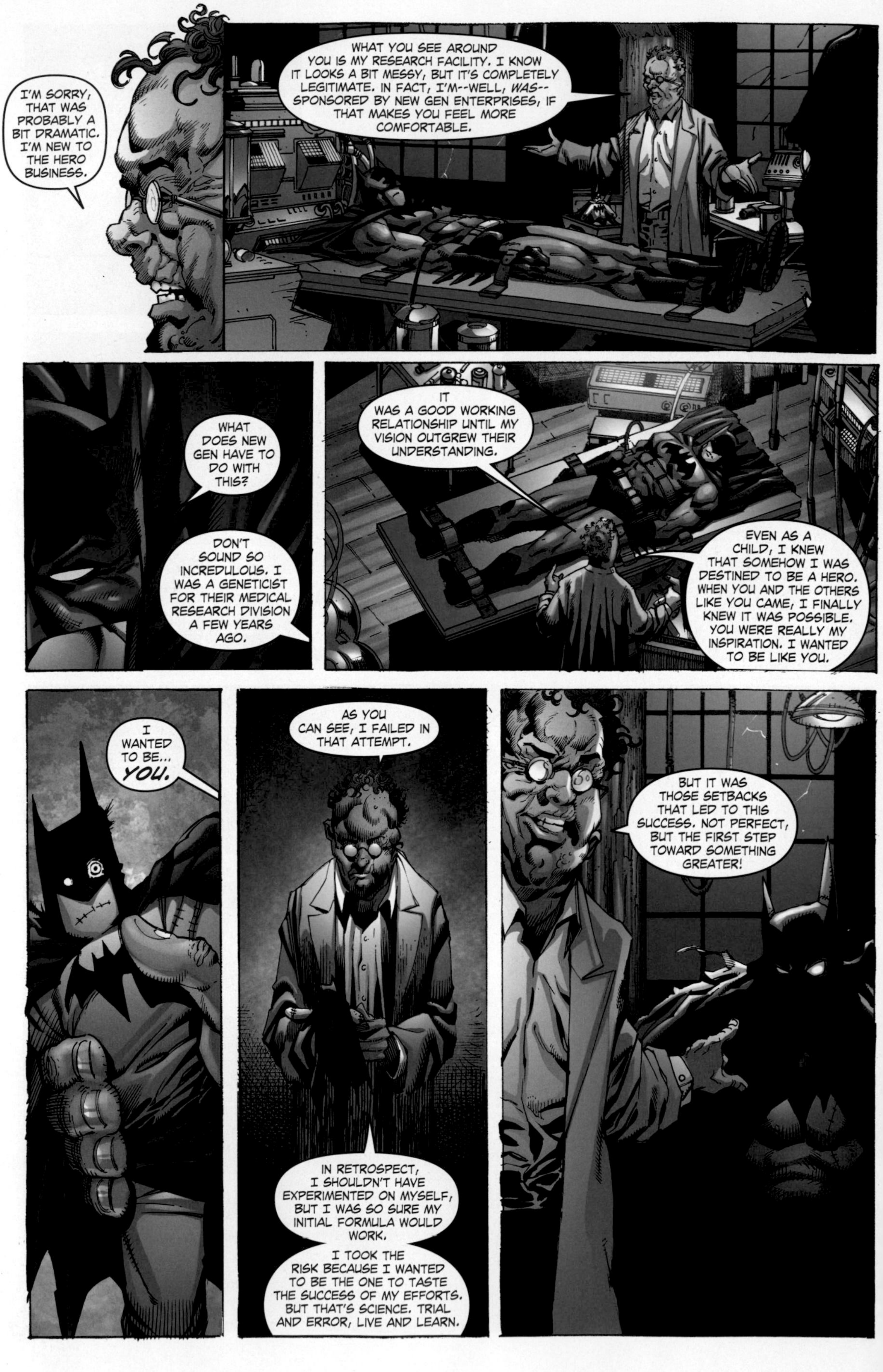
I'M SORRY, THAT WAS PROBABLY A BIT DRAMATIC. I'M NEW TO THE HERO BUSINESS.
WHAT YOU SEE AROUND YOU IS MY RESEARCH FACILITY. I KNOW IT LOOKS A BIT MESSY, BUT IT'S COMPLETELY LEGITIMATE. IN FACT, I'M--WELL, WAS--SPONSORED BY NEW GEN ENTERPRISES, IF THAT MAKES YOU FEEL MORE COMFORTABLE.
WHAT DOES NEW GEN HAVE TO DO WITH THIS?
DON'T SOUND SO INCREDULOUS. I WAS A GENETICIST FOR THEIR MEDICAL RESEARCH DIVISION A FEW YEARS AGO.
IT WAS A GOOD WORKING RELATIONSHIP UNTIL MY VISION OUTGREW THEIR UNDERSTANDING.
EVEN AS A CHILD, I KNEW THAT SOMEHOW I WAS DESTINED TO BE A HERO. WHEN YOU AND THE OTHERS LIKE YOU CAME, I FINALLY KNEW IT WAS POSSIBLE. YOU WERE REALLY MY INSPIRATION. I WANTED TO BE LIKE YOU.
I WANTED TO BE... YOU.
AS YOU CAN SEE, I FAILED IN THAT ATTEMPT.
IN RETROSPECT, I SHOULDN'T HAVE EXPERIMENTED ON MYSELF, BUT I WAS SO SURE MY INITIAL FORMULA WOULD WORK.
I TOOK THE RISK BECAUSE I WANTED TO BE THE ONE TO TASTE THE SUCCESS OF MY EFFORTS. BUT THAT'S SCIENCE. TRIAL AND ERROR, LIVE AND LEARN.
BUT IT WAS THOSE SETBACKS THAT LED TO THIS SUCCESS. NOT PERFECT, BUT THE FIRST STEP TOWARD SOMETHING GREATER!

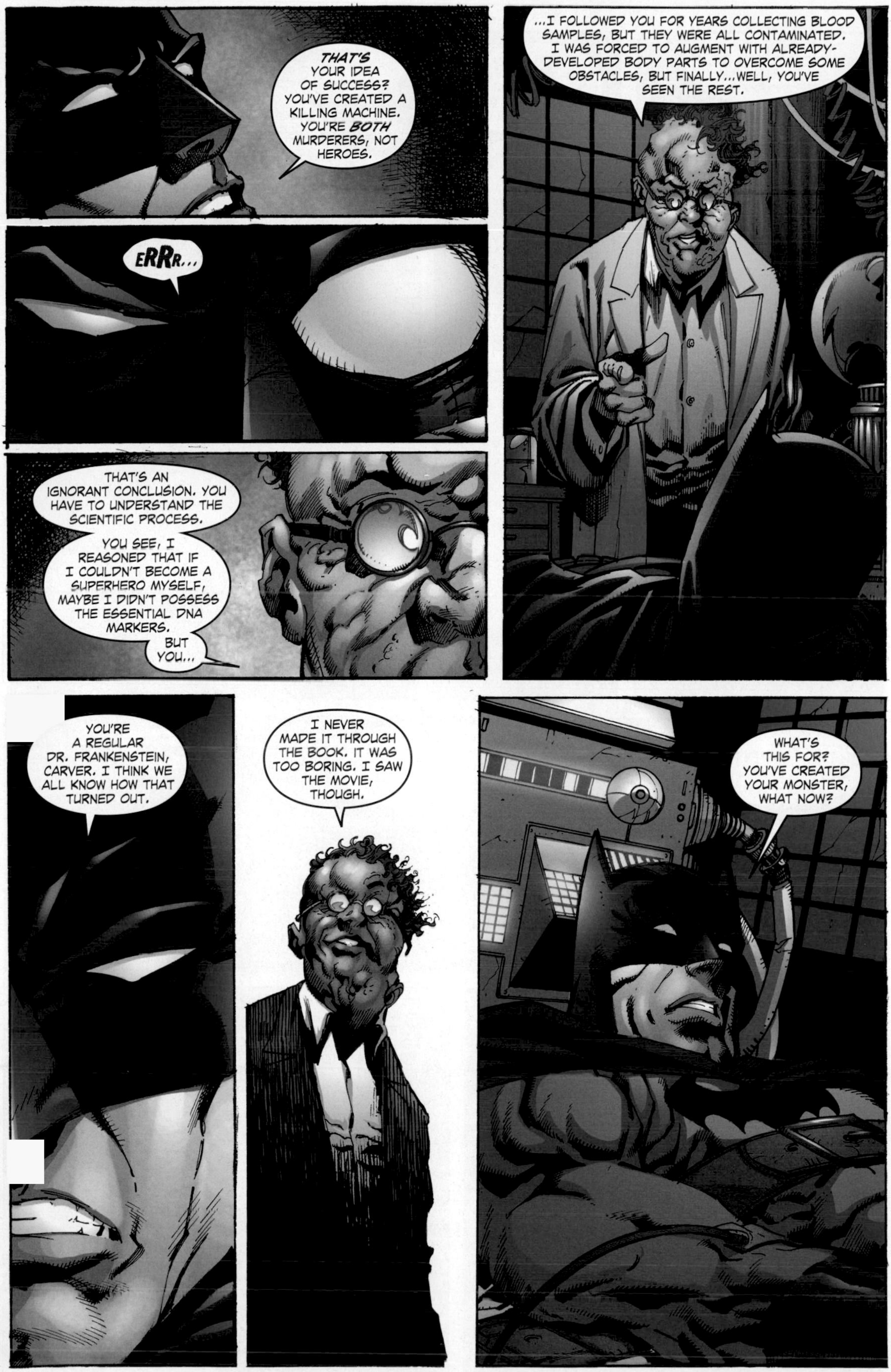
THAT'S YOUR IDEA OF SUCCESS? YOU'VE CREATED A KILLING MACHINE. YOU'RE BOTH MURDERERS, NOT HEROES.
ERRR...
THAT'S AN IGNORANT CONCLUSION. YOU HAVE TO UNDERSTAND THE SCIENTIFIC PROCESS.
YOU SEE, I REASONED THAT IF I COULDN'T BECOME A SUPERHERO MYSELF, MAYBE I DIDN'T POSSESS THE ESSENTIAL DNA MARKERS.
BUT YOU...
...I FOLLOWED YOU FOR YEARS COLLECTING BLOOD SAMPLES, BUT THEY WERE ALL CONTAMINATED. I WAS FORCED TO AUGMENT WITH ALREADY-DEVELOPED BODY PARTS TO OVERCOME SOME OBSTACLES, BUT FINALLY...WELL, YOU'VE SEEN THE REST.
YOU'RE A REGULAR DR. FRANKENSTEIN, CARVER. I THINK WE ALL KNOW HOW THAT TURNED OUT.
I NEVER MADE IT THROUGH THE BOOK. IT WAS TOO BORING. I SAW THE MOVIE, THOUGH.
WHAT'S THIS FOR? YOU'VE CREATED YOUR MONSTER, WHAT NOW?

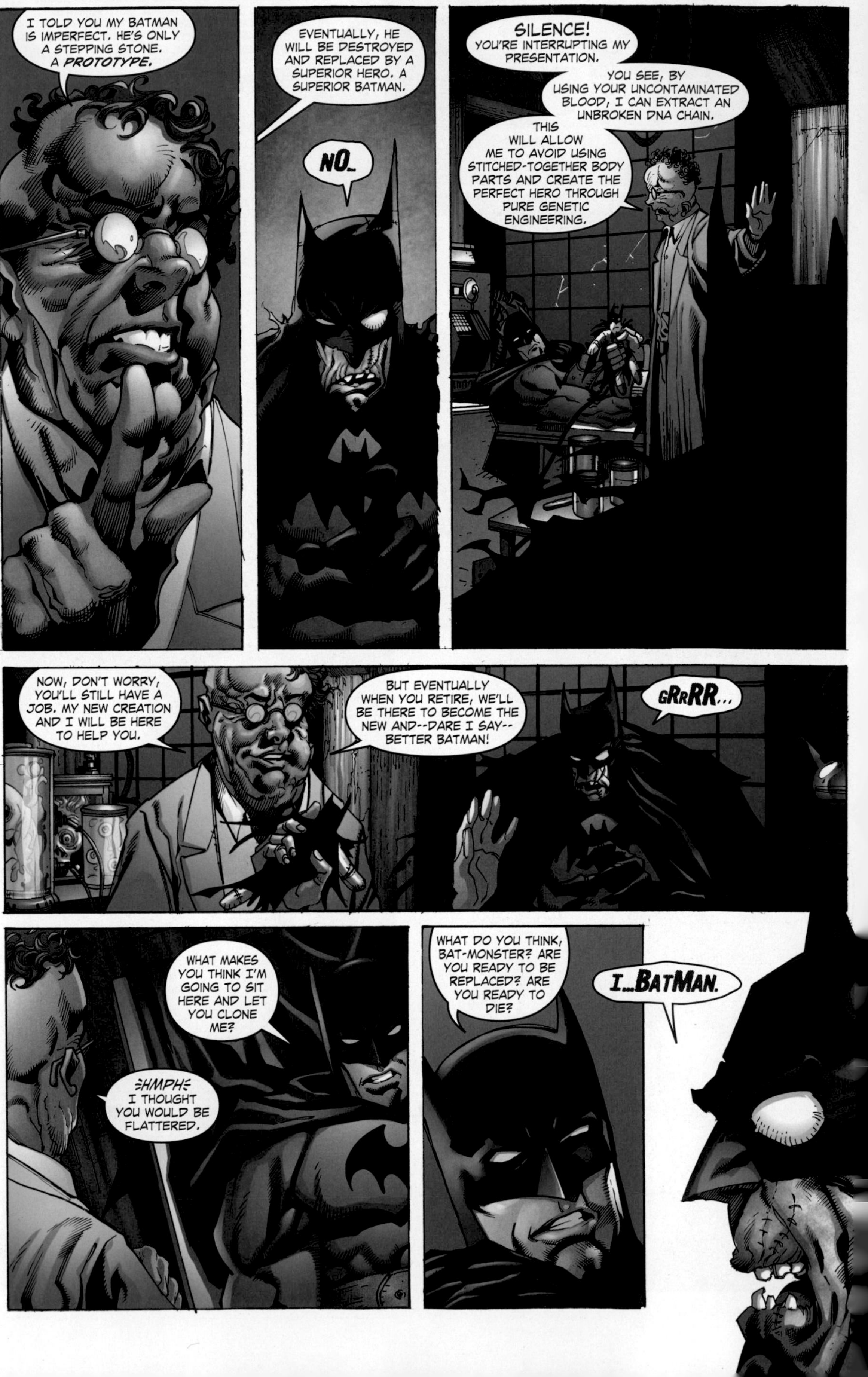
I TOLD YOU MY BATMAN IS IMPERFECT. HE'S ONLY A STEPPING STONE. A *PROTOTYPE.*
EVENTUALLY, HE WILL BE DESTROYED AND REPLACED BY A SUPERIOR HERO. A SUPERIOR BATMAN.
NO...
SILENCE! YOU'RE INTERRUPTING MY PRESENTATION.
YOU SEE, BY USING YOUR UNCONTAMINATED BLOOD, I CAN EXTRACT AN UNBROKEN DNA CHAIN.
THIS WILL ALLOW ME TO AVOID USING STITCHED-TOGETHER BODY PARTS AND CREATE THE PERFECT HERO THROUGH PURE GENETIC ENGINEERING.
NOW, DON'T WORRY, YOU'LL STILL HAVE A JOB. MY NEW CREATION AND I WILL BE HERE TO HELP YOU.
BUT EVENTUALLY WHEN YOU RETIRE, WE'LL BE THERE TO BECOME THE NEW AND--DARE I SAY--BETTER BATMAN!
GRRRR...
WHAT MAKES YOU THINK I'M GOING TO SIT HERE AND LET YOU CLONE ME?
HMPH I THOUGHT YOU WOULD BE FLATTERED.
WHAT DO YOU THINK, BAT-MONSTER? ARE YOU READY TO BE REPLACED? ARE YOU READY TO DIE?
I...BATMAN.

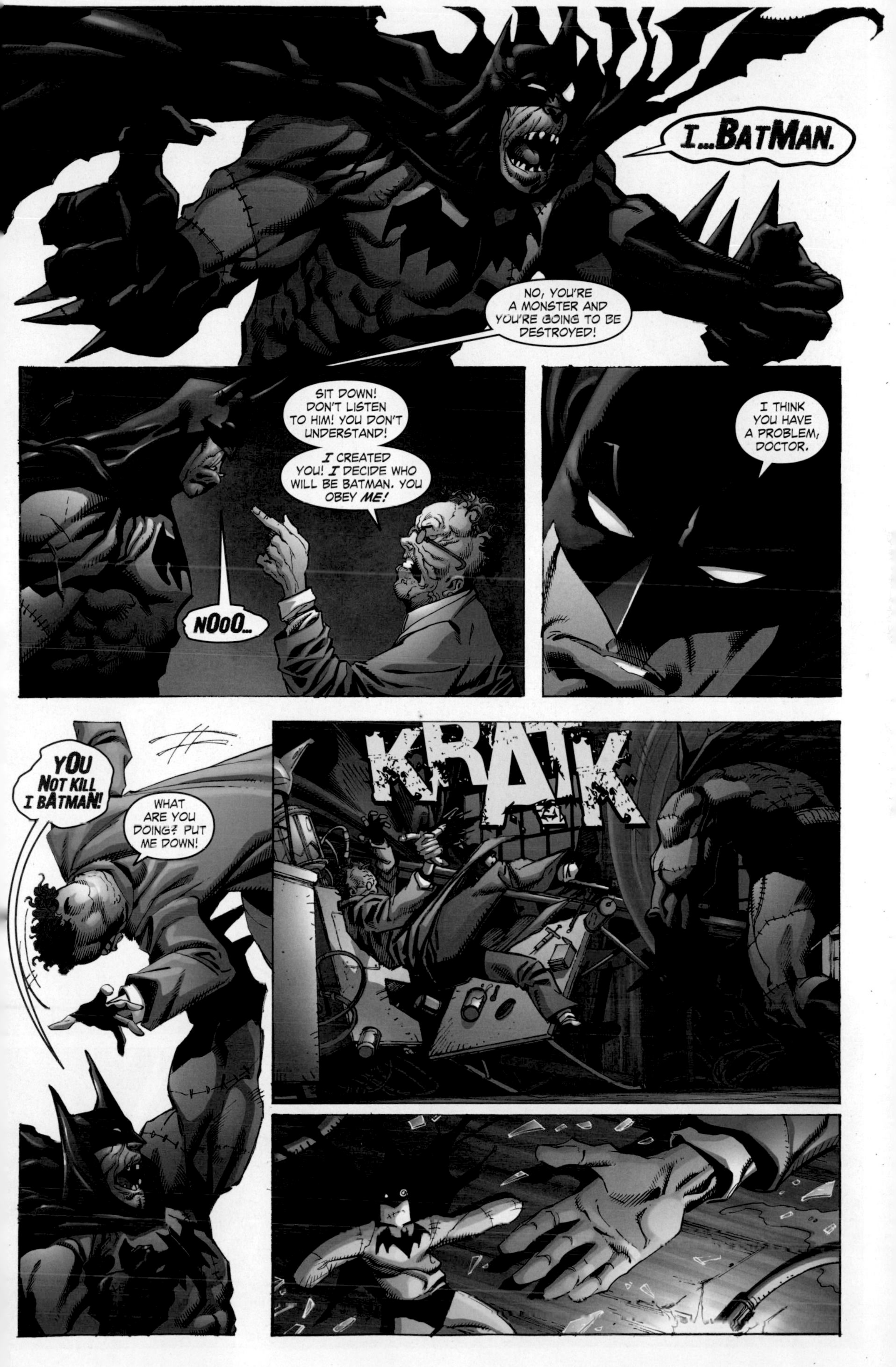
I...BATMAN.
NO, YOU'RE A MONSTER AND YOU'RE GOING TO BE DESTROYED!
SIT DOWN! DON'T LISTEN TO HIM! YOU DON'T UNDERSTAND!
I CREATED YOU! I DECIDE WHO WILL BE BATMAN. YOU OBEY ME!
NOOO...
I THINK YOU HAVE A PROBLEM, DOCTOR.
YOU NOT KILL I BATMAN!
WHAT ARE YOU DOING? PUT ME DOWN!
KRAK

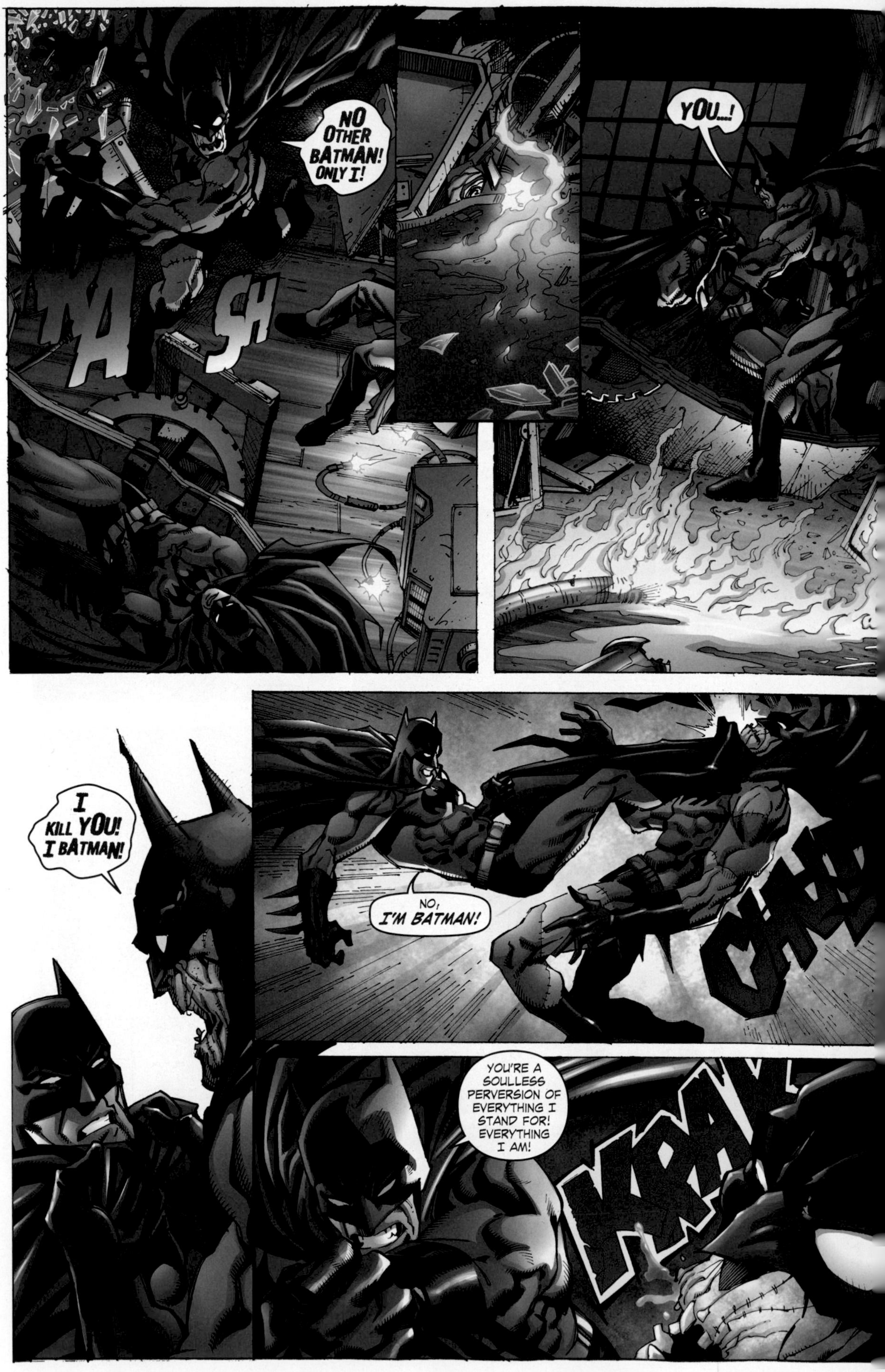
NO OTHER BATMAN! ONLY I!
YOU...!
I KILL YOU! I BATMAN!
NO, I'M BATMAN!
YOU'RE A SOULLESS PERVERSION OF EVERYTHING I STAND FOR! EVERYTHING I AM!

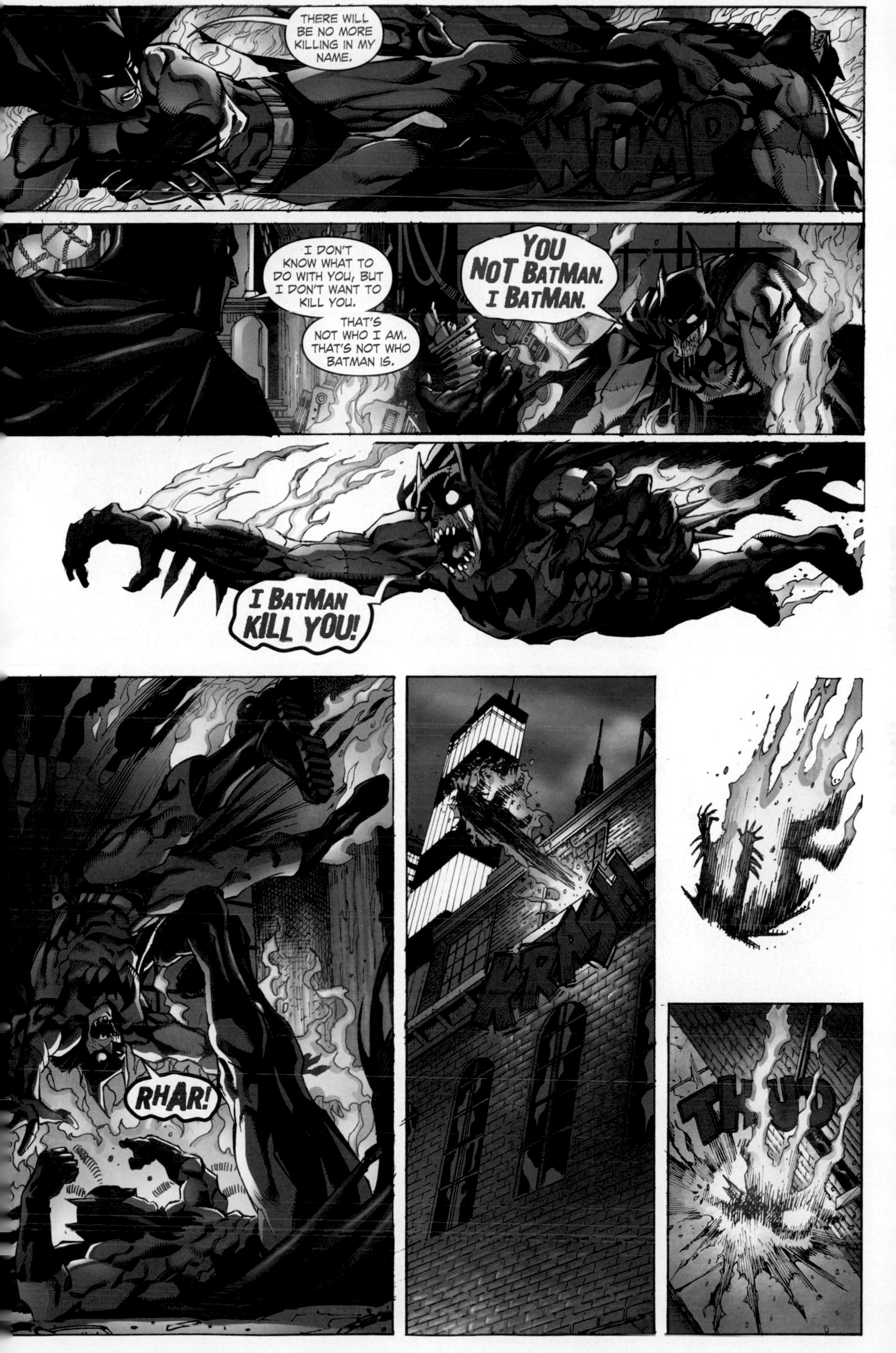
THERE WILL BE NO MORE KILLING IN MY NAME.
WUMP
I DON'T KNOW WHAT TO DO WITH YOU, BUT I DON'T WANT TO KILL YOU.
THAT'S NOT WHO I AM. THAT'S NOT WHO BATMAN IS.
YOU NOT BATMAN. I BATMAN.
I BATMAN KILL YOU!
RHAR!
KRAASH
THUD

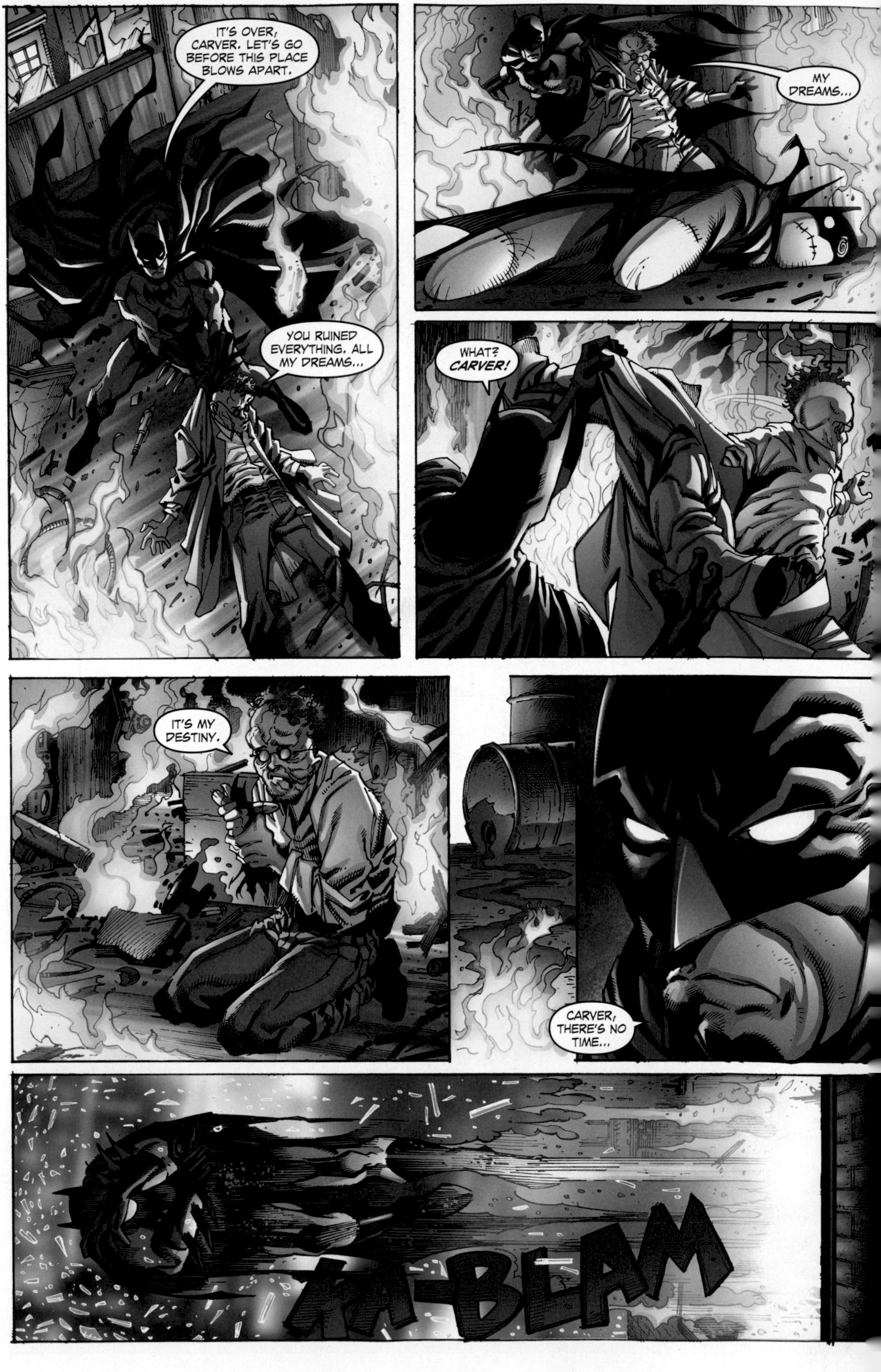
IT'S OVER, CARVER. LET'S GO BEFORE THIS PLACE BLOWS APART.
YOU RUINED EVERYTHING. ALL MY DREAMS...
MY DREAMS...
WHAT? CARVER!
IT'S MY DESTINY.
CARVER, THERE'S NO TIME...
KA-BLAM

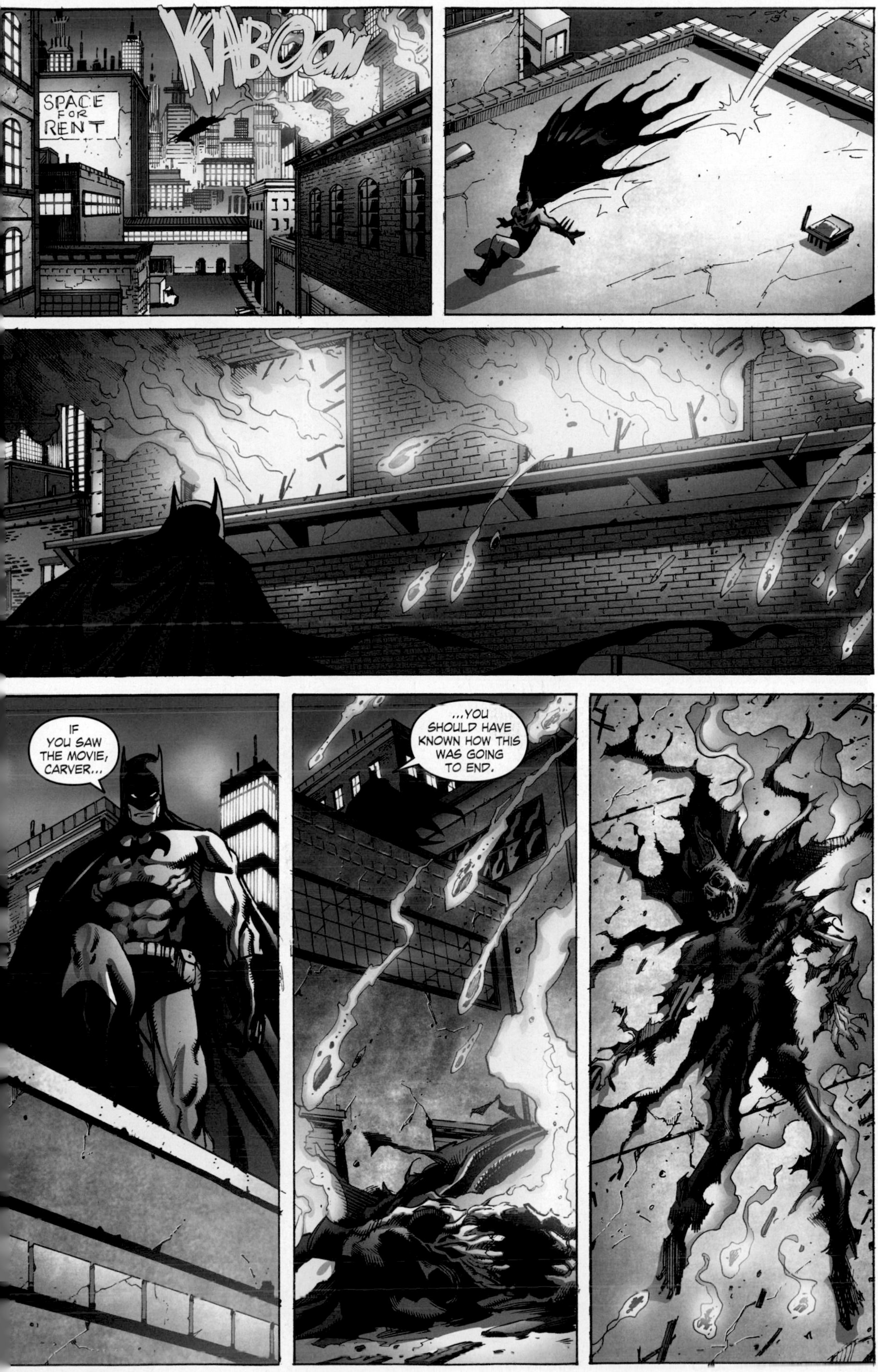
KABOOM
SPACE FOR RENT
IF YOU SAW THE MOVIE, CARVER...
...YOU SHOULD HAVE KNOWN HOW THIS WAS GOING TO END.

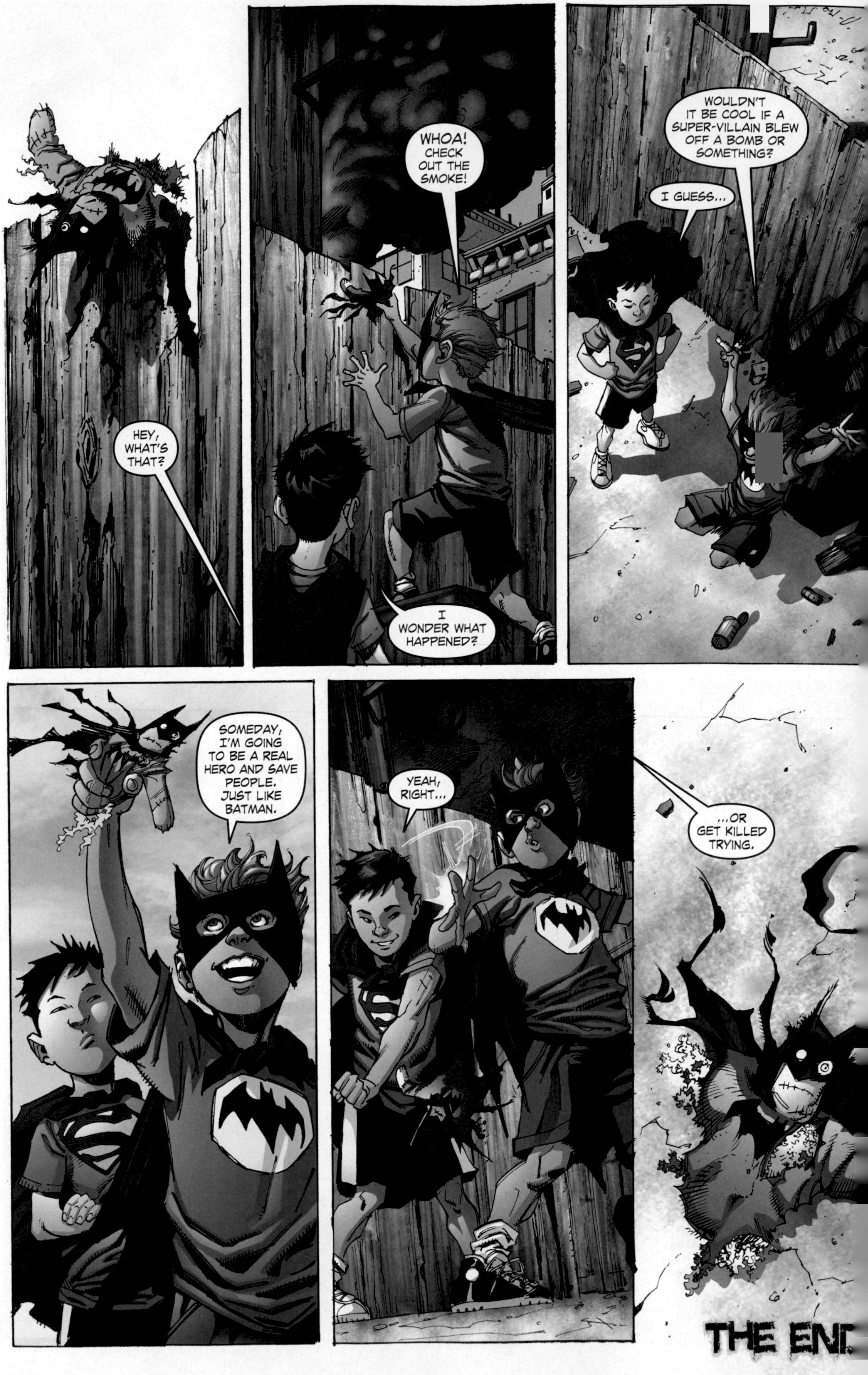
HEY, WHAT'S THAT?
WHOA! CHECK OUT THE SMOKE!
I WONDER WHAT HAPPENED?
WOULDN'T IT BE COOL IF A SUPER-VILLAIN BLEW OFF A BOMB OR SOMETHING?
I GUESS...
SOMEDAY, I'M GOING TO BE A REAL HERO AND SAVE PEOPLE. JUST LIKE BATMAN.
YEAH, RIGHT...
...OR GET KILLED TRYING.
THE EN

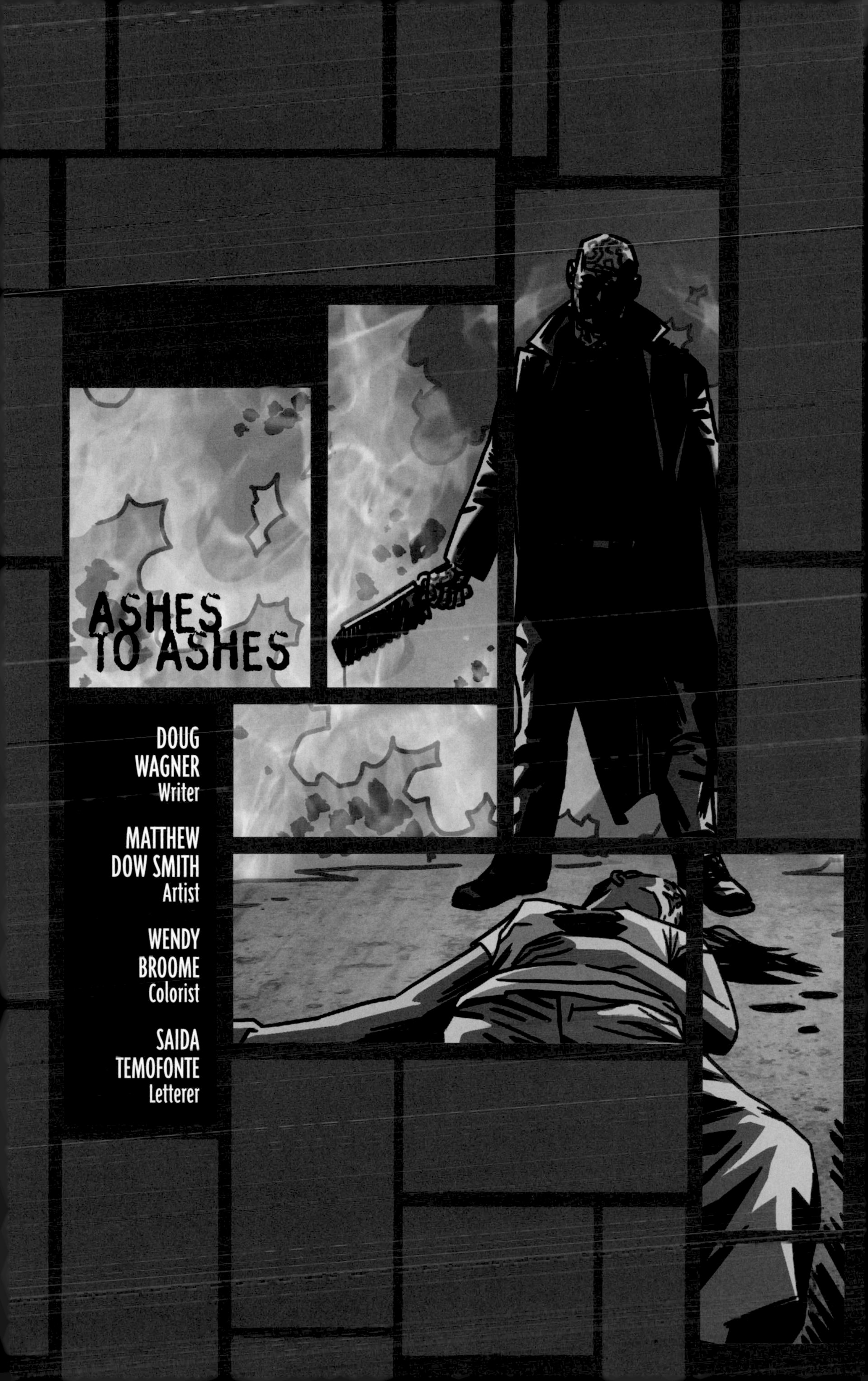
ASHES TO ASHES
DOUG WAGNER Writer
MATTHEW DOW SMITH Artist
WENDY BROOME Colorist
SAIDA TEMOFONTE Letterer

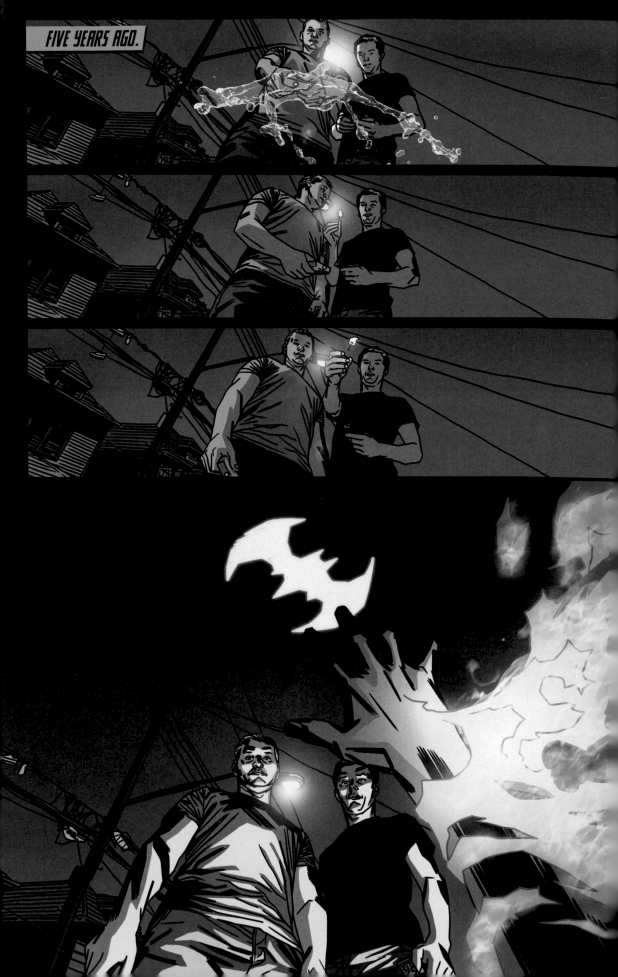

FIVE YEARS AGO.

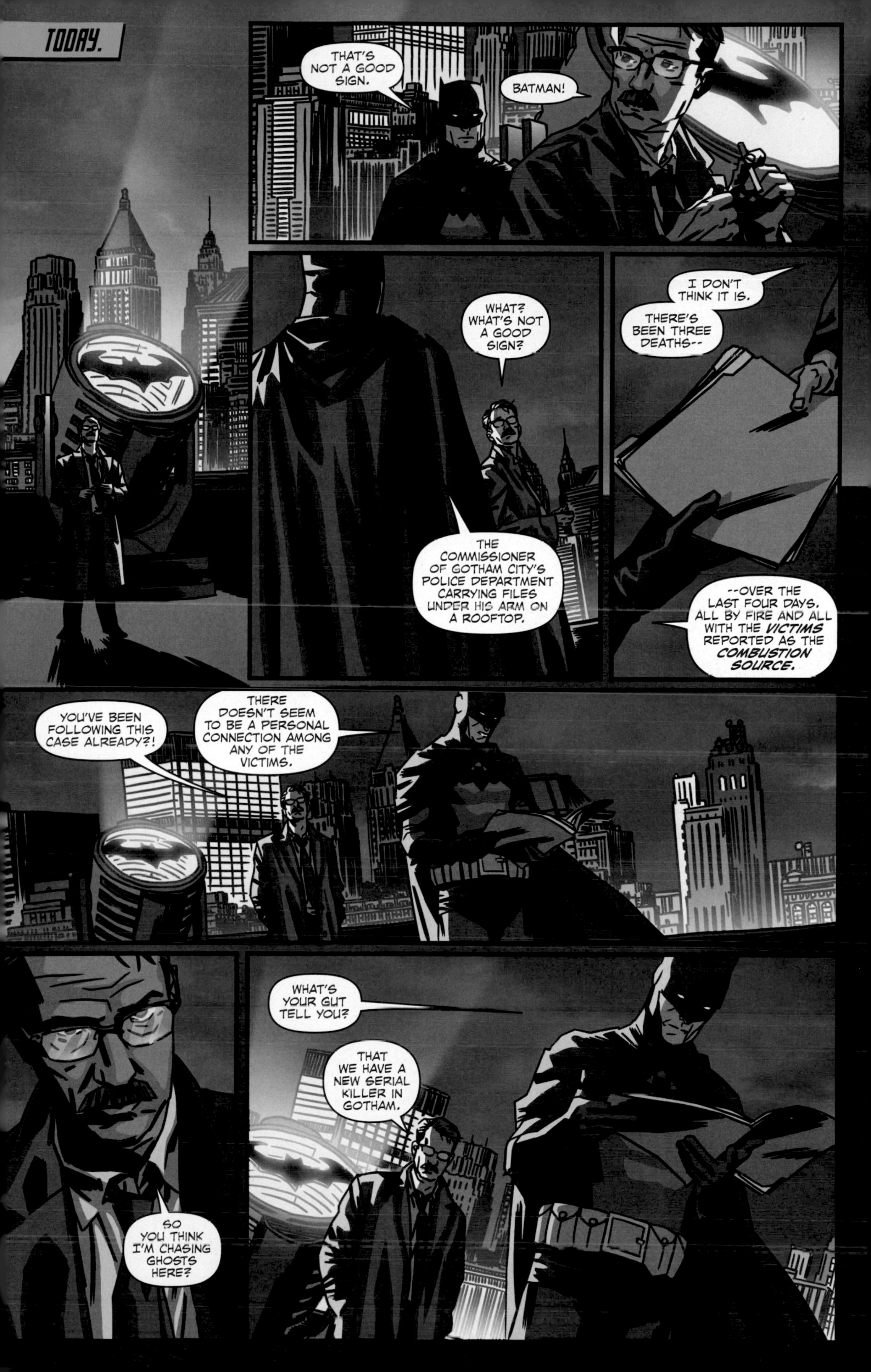
TODAY.
THAT'S NOT A GOOD SIGN.
BATMAN!
WHAT? WHAT'S NOT A GOOD SIGN?
THE COMMISSIONER OF GOTHAM CITY'S POLICE DEPARTMENT CARRYING FILES UNDER HIS ARM ON A ROOFTOP.
I DON'T THINK IT IS.
THERE'S BEEN THREE DEATHS--
--OVER THE LAST FOUR DAYS. ALL BY FIRE AND ALL WITH THE VICTIMS REPORTED AS THE COMBUSTION SOURCE.
YOU'VE BEEN FOLLOWING THIS CASE ALREADY?!
THERE DOESN'T SEEM TO BE A PERSONAL CONNECTION AMONG ANY OF THE VICTIMS.
SO YOU THINK I'M CHASING GHOSTS HERE?
WHAT'S YOUR GUT TELL YOU?
THAT WE HAVE A NEW SERIAL KILLER IN GOTHAM.

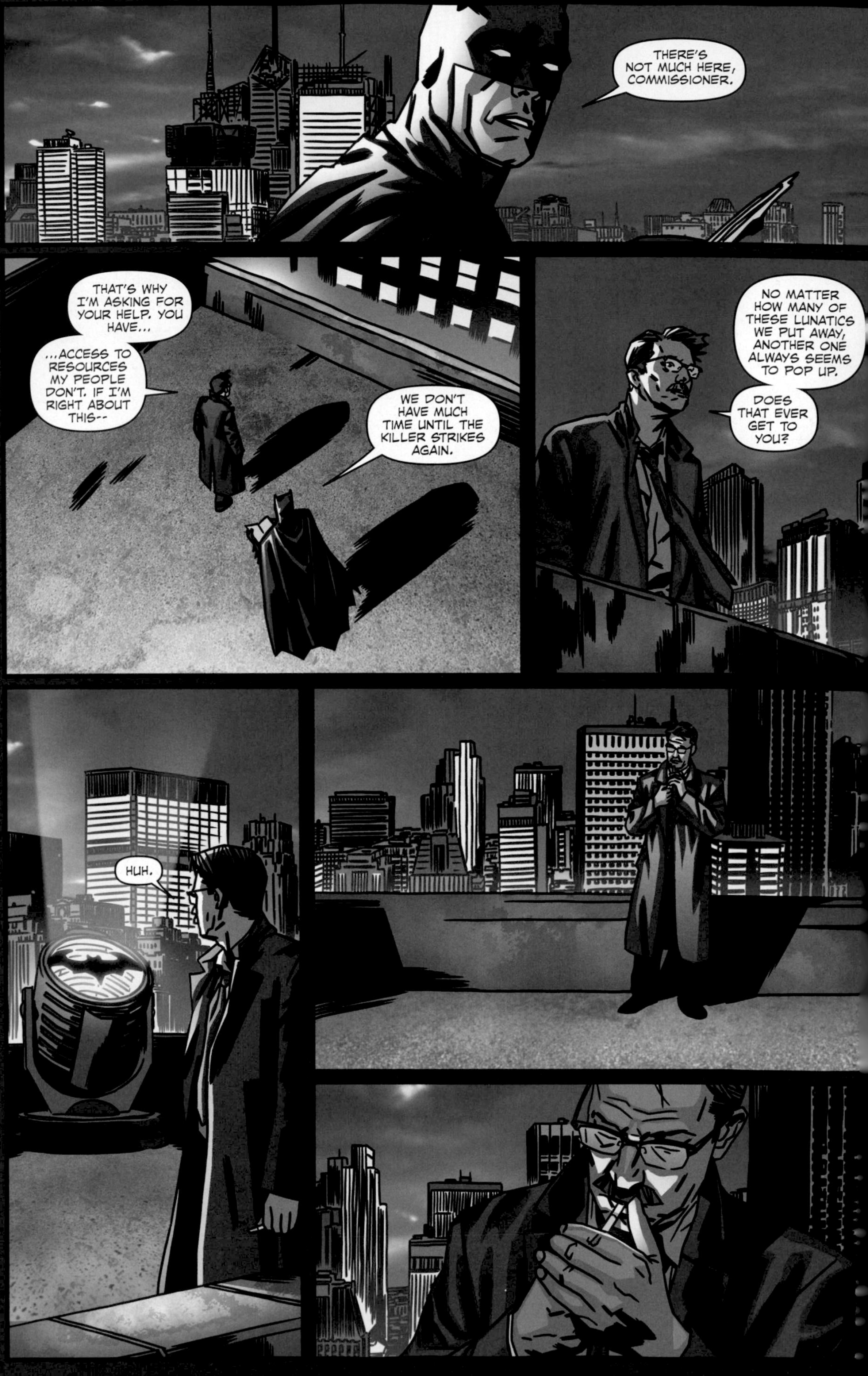
THERE'S NOT MUCH HERE, COMMISSIONER.
THAT'S WHY I'M ASKING FOR YOUR HELP. YOU HAVE...
...ACCESS TO RESOURCES MY PEOPLE DON'T. IF I'M RIGHT ABOUT THIS--
WE DON'T HAVE MUCH TIME UNTIL THE KILLER STRIKES AGAIN.
NO MATTER HOW MANY OF THESE LUNATICS WE PUT AWAY, ANOTHER ONE ALWAYS SEEMS TO POP UP.
DOES THAT EVER GET TO YOU?
HUH.

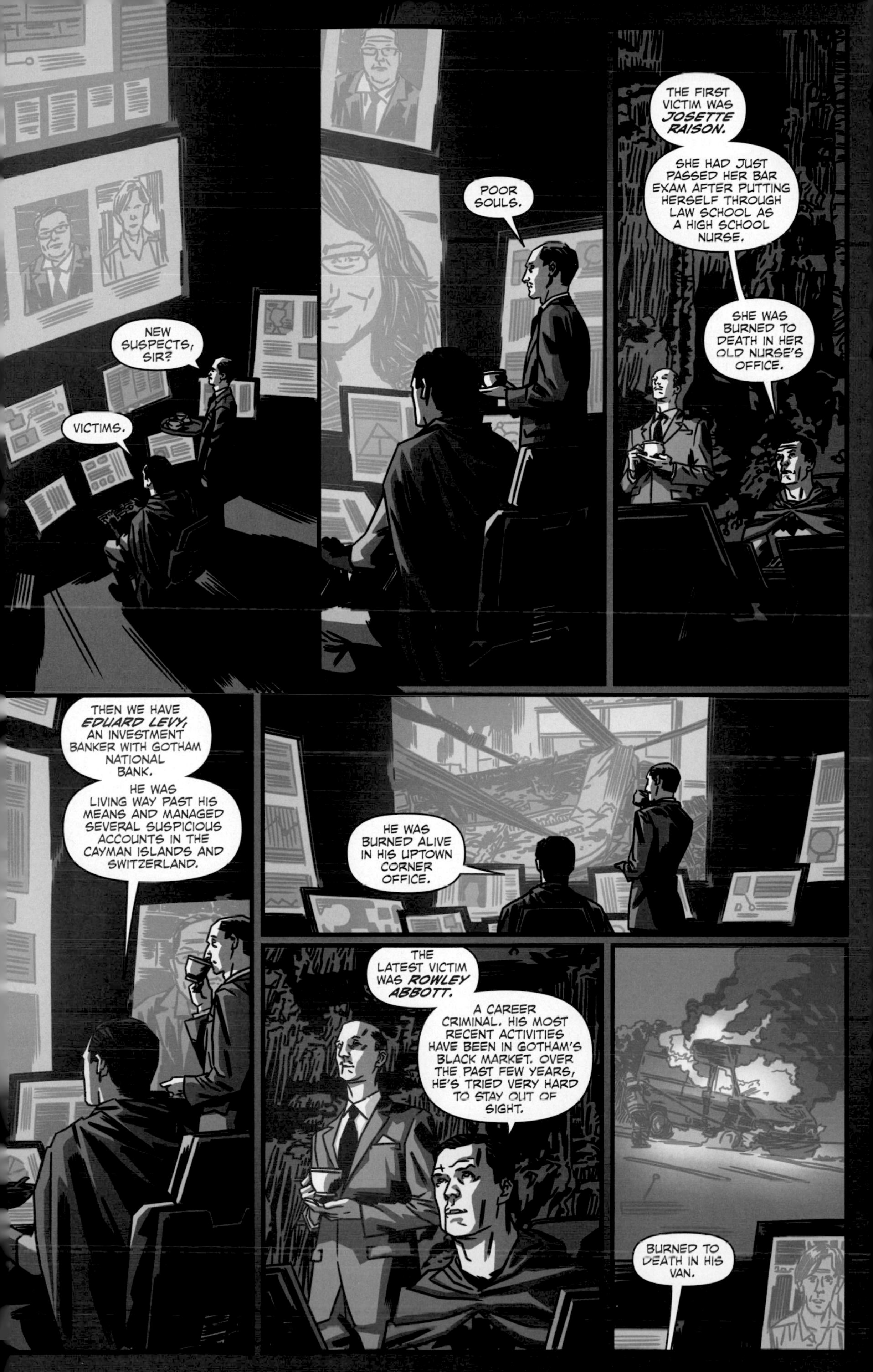
NEW SUSPECTS, SIR?
VICTIMS.
POOR SOULS.
THE FIRST VICTIM WAS ***JOSETTE RAISON.***
SHE HAD JUST PASSED HER BAR EXAM AFTER PUTTING HERSELF THROUGH LAW SCHOOL AS A HIGH SCHOOL NURSE.
SHE WAS BURNED TO DEATH IN HER OLD NURSE'S OFFICE.
THEN WE HAVE ***EDUARD LEVY,*** AN INVESTMENT BANKER WITH GOTHAM NATIONAL BANK.
HE WAS LIVING WAY PAST HIS MEANS AND MANAGED SEVERAL SUSPICIOUS ACCOUNTS IN THE CAYMAN ISLANDS AND SWITZERLAND.
HE WAS BURNED ALIVE IN HIS UPTOWN CORNER OFFICE.
THE LATEST VICTIM WAS ***ROWLEY ABBOTT.***
A CAREER CRIMINAL. HIS MOST RECENT ACTIVITIES HAVE BEEN IN GOTHAM'S BLACK MARKET. OVER THE PAST FEW YEARS, HE'S TRIED VERY HARD TO STAY OUT OF SIGHT.
BURNED TO DEATH IN HIS VAN.

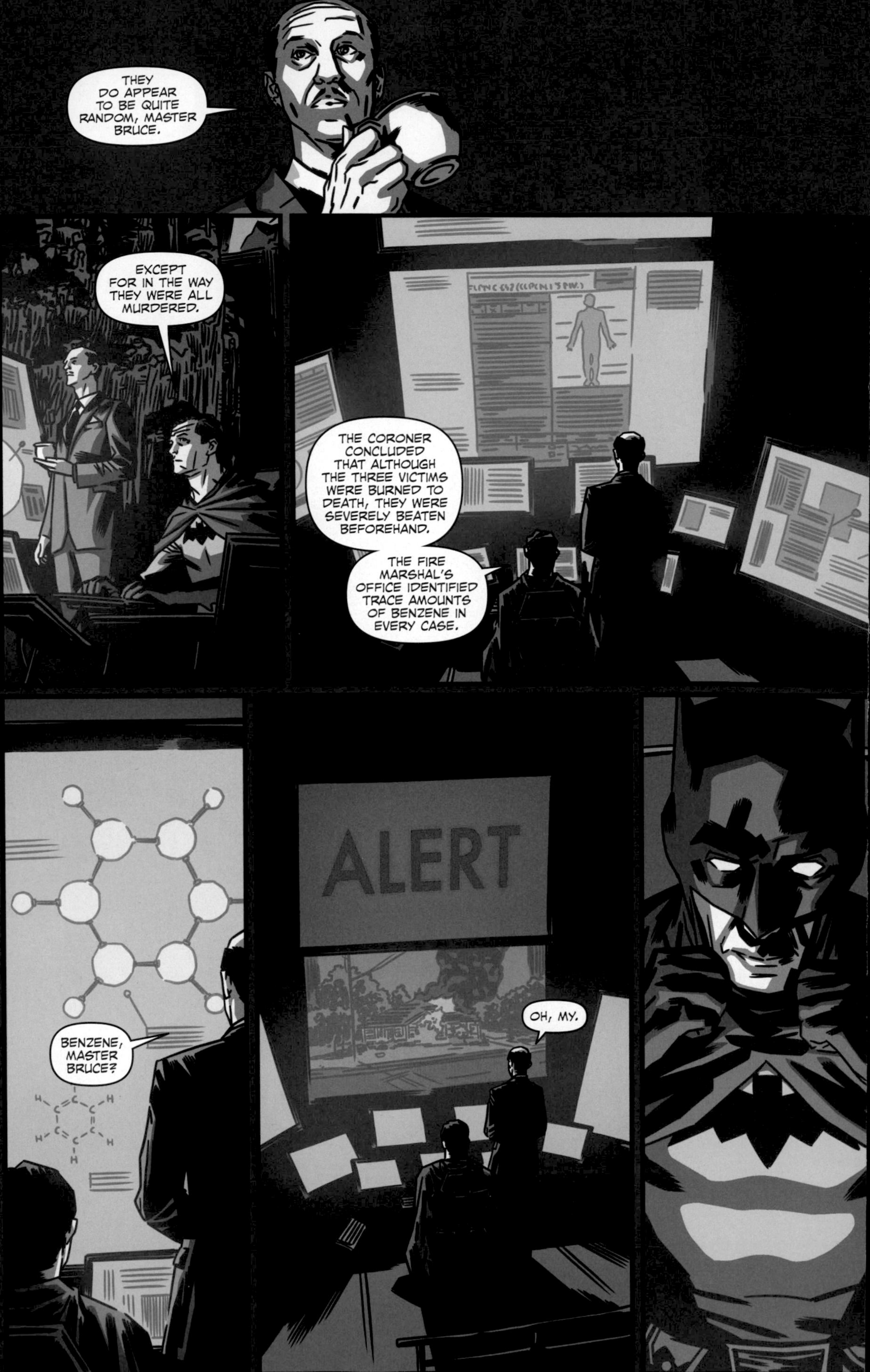
THEY DO APPEAR TO BE QUITE RANDOM, MASTER BRUCE.
EXCEPT FOR IN THE WAY THEY WERE ALL MURDERED.
THE CORONER CONCLUDED THAT ALTHOUGH THE THREE VICTIMS WERE BURNED TO DEATH, THEY WERE SEVERELY BEATEN BEFOREHAND.
THE FIRE MARSHAL'S OFFICE IDENTIFIED TRACE AMOUNTS OF BENZENE IN EVERY CASE.
BENZENE, MASTER BRUCE?
ALERT
OH, MY.

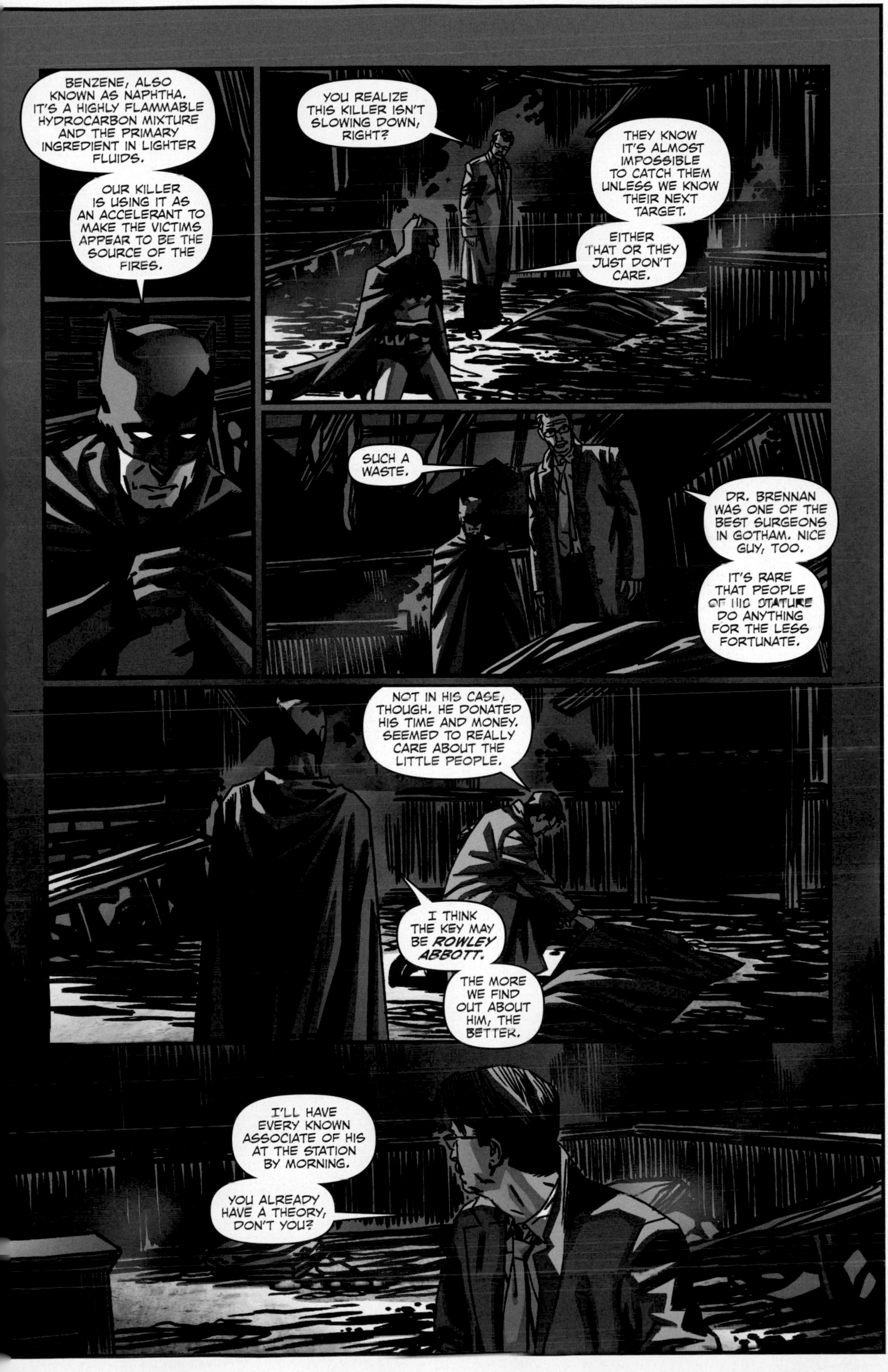

BENZENE, ALSO KNOWN AS NAPHTHA. IT'S A HIGHLY FLAMMABLE HYDROCARBON MIXTURE AND THE PRIMARY INGREDIENT IN LIGHTER FLUIDS.
OUR KILLER IS USING IT AS AN ACCELERANT TO MAKE THE VICTIMS APPEAR TO BE THE SOURCE OF THE FIRES.
YOU REALIZE THIS KILLER ISN'T SLOWING DOWN, RIGHT?
THEY KNOW IT'S ALMOST IMPOSSIBLE TO CATCH THEM UNLESS WE KNOW THEIR NEXT TARGET.
EITHER THAT OR THEY JUST DON'T CARE.
SUCH A WASTE.
DR. BRENNAN WAS ONE OF THE BEST SURGEONS IN GOTHAM. NICE GUY, TOO.
IT'S RARE THAT PEOPLE OF HIS STATURE DO ANYTHING FOR THE LESS FORTUNATE.
NOT IN HIS CASE, THOUGH. HE DONATED HIS TIME AND MONEY. SEEMED TO REALLY CARE ABOUT THE LITTLE PEOPLE.
I THINK THE KEY MAY BE *ROWLEY ABBOTT.*
THE MORE WE FIND OUT ABOUT HIM, THE BETTER.
I'LL HAVE EVERY KNOWN ASSOCIATE OF HIS AT THE STATION BY MORNING.
YOU ALREADY HAVE A THEORY, DON'T YOU?

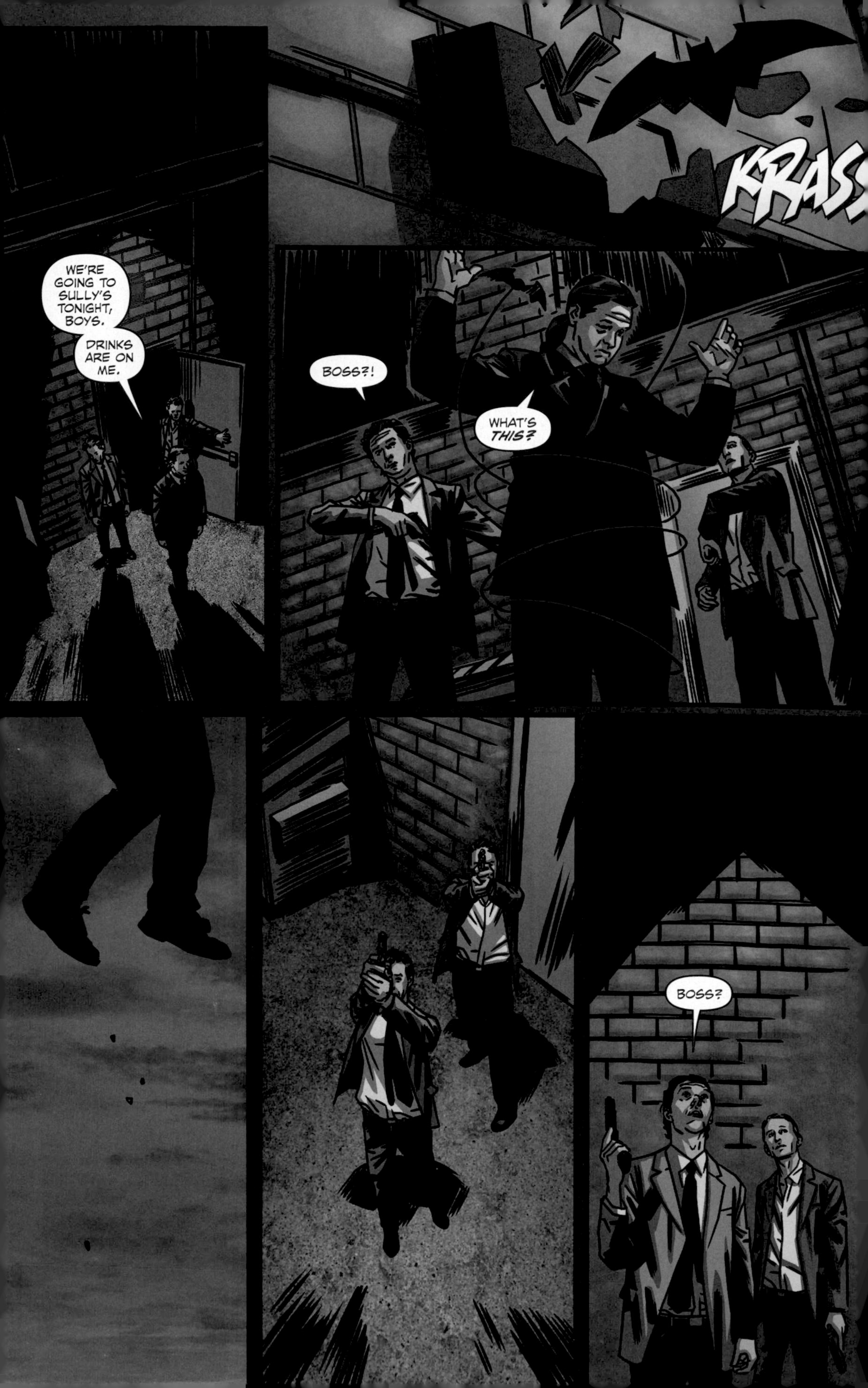
KRASS
WE'RE GOING TO SULLY'S TONIGHT, BOYS.
DRINKS ARE ON ME.
BOSS?!
WHAT'S *THIS?*
BOSS?

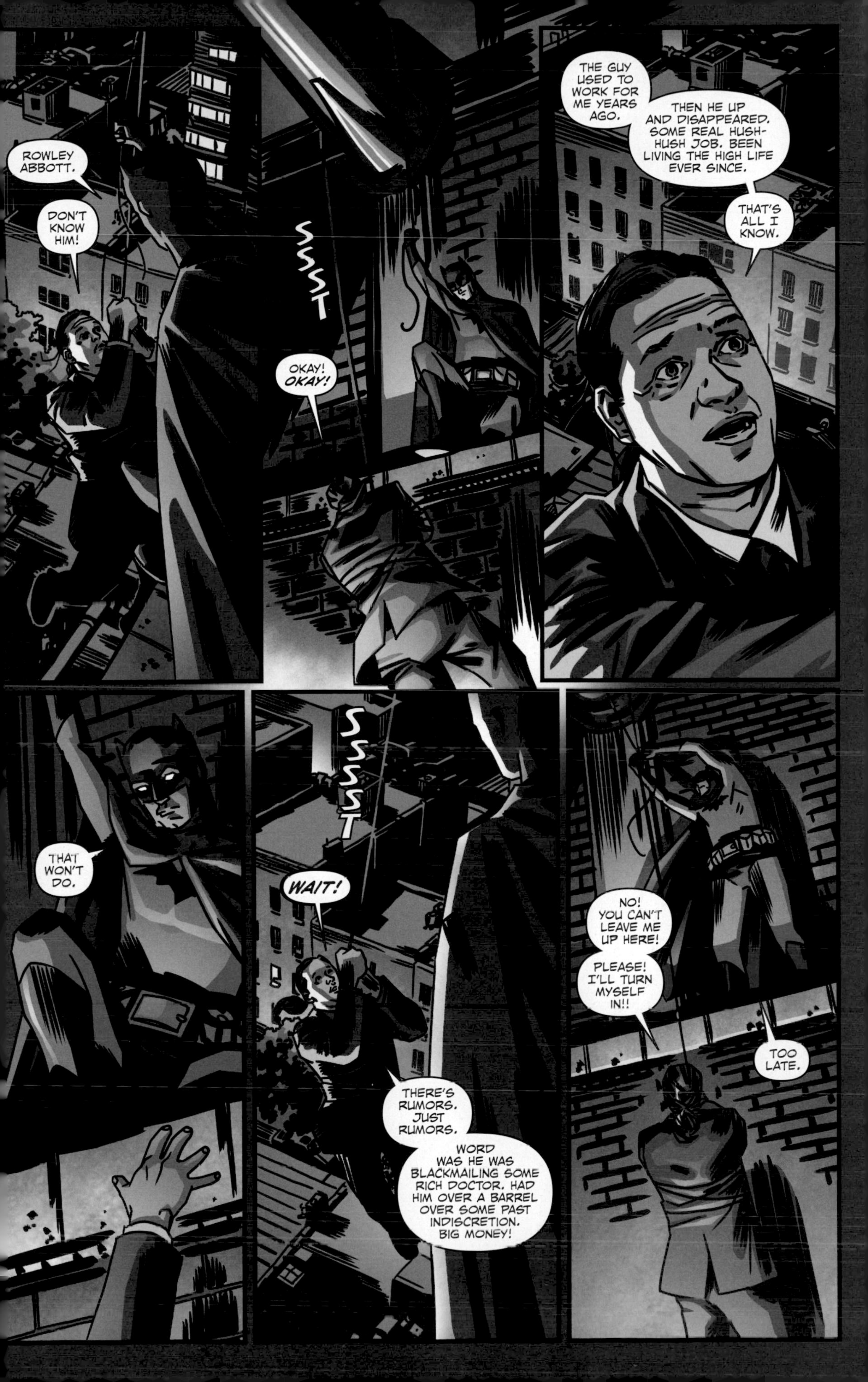
ROWLEY ABBOTT.
DON'T KNOW HIM!
SSSST
OKAY! OKAY!
THE GUY USED TO WORK FOR ME YEARS AGO.
THEN HE UP AND DISAPPEARED. SOME REAL HUSH-HUSH JOB. BEEN LIVING THE HIGH LIFE EVER SINCE.
THAT'S ALL I KNOW.
THAT WON'T DO.
SSSST
WAIT!
THERE'S RUMORS. JUST RUMORS.
WORD WAS HE WAS BLACKMAILING SOME RICH DOCTOR. HAD HIM OVER A BARREL OVER SOME PAST INDISCRETION. BIG MONEY!
NO! YOU CAN'T LEAVE ME UP HERE!
PLEASE! I'LL TURN MYSELF IN!!
TOO LATE.

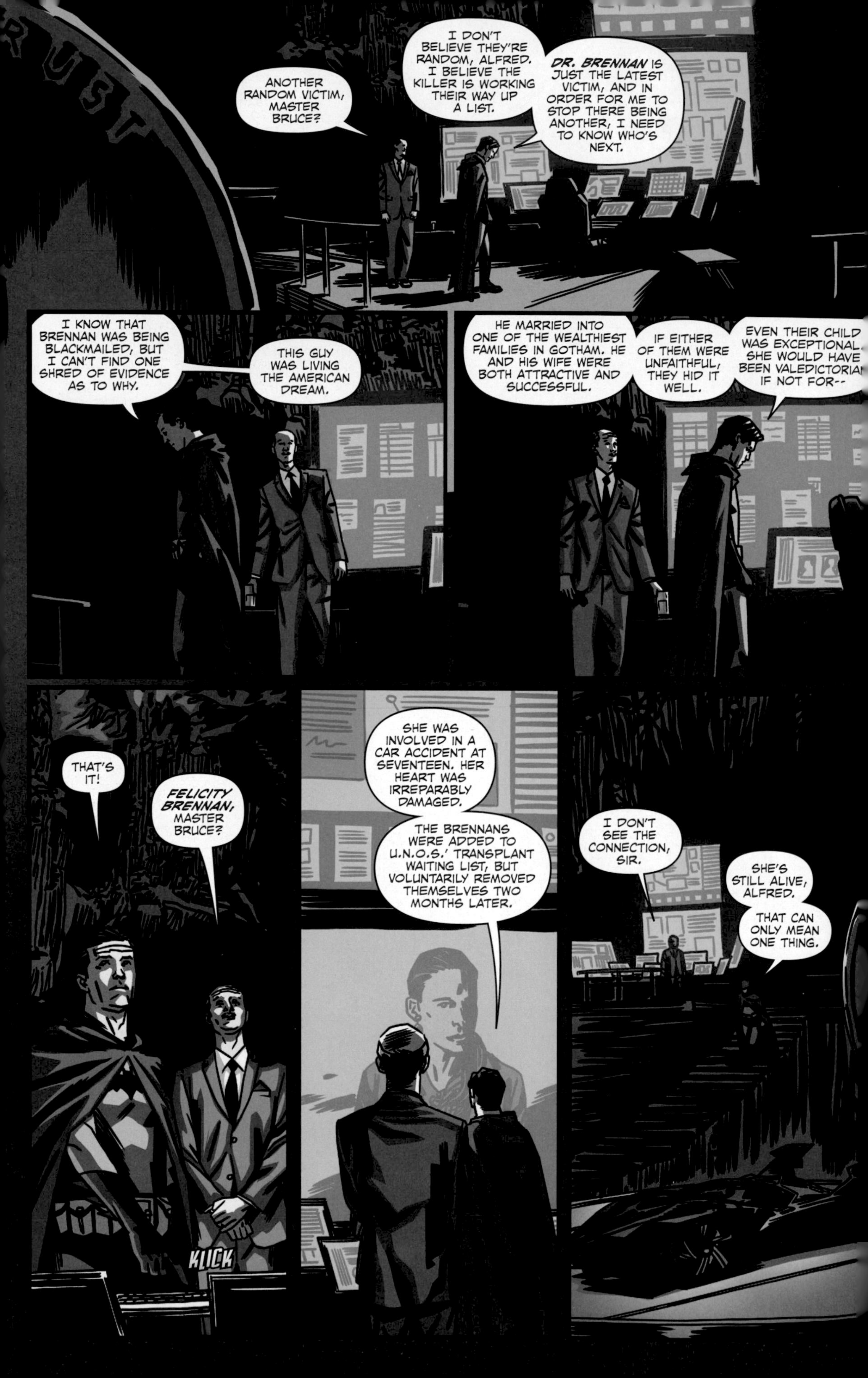
ANOTHER RANDOM VICTIM, MASTER BRUCE?
I DON'T BELIEVE THEY'RE RANDOM, ALFRED. I BELIEVE THE KILLER IS WORKING THEIR WAY UP A LIST.
DR. BRENNAN IS JUST THE LATEST VICTIM, AND IN ORDER FOR ME TO STOP THERE BEING ANOTHER, I NEED TO KNOW WHO'S NEXT.
I KNOW THAT BRENNAN WAS BEING BLACKMAILED, BUT I CAN'T FIND ONE SHRED OF EVIDENCE AS TO WHY.
THIS GUY WAS LIVING THE AMERICAN DREAM.
HE MARRIED INTO ONE OF THE WEALTHIEST FAMILIES IN GOTHAM. HE AND HIS WIFE WERE BOTH ATTRACTIVE AND SUCCESSFUL.
IF EITHER OF THEM WERE UNFAITHFUL, THEY HID IT WELL.
EVEN THEIR CHILD WAS EXCEPTIONAL. SHE WOULD HAVE BEEN VALEDICTORIAN IF NOT FOR--
THAT'S IT!
FELICITY BRENNAN, MASTER BRUCE?
KLICK
SHE WAS INVOLVED IN A CAR ACCIDENT AT SEVENTEEN. HER HEART WAS IRREPARABLY DAMAGED.
THE BRENNANS WERE ADDED TO U.N.O.S.' TRANSPLANT WAITING LIST, BUT VOLUNTARILY REMOVED THEMSELVES TWO MONTHS LATER.
I DON'T SEE THE CONNECTION, SIR.
SHE'S STILL ALIVE, ALFRED.
THAT CAN ONLY MEAN ONE THING.

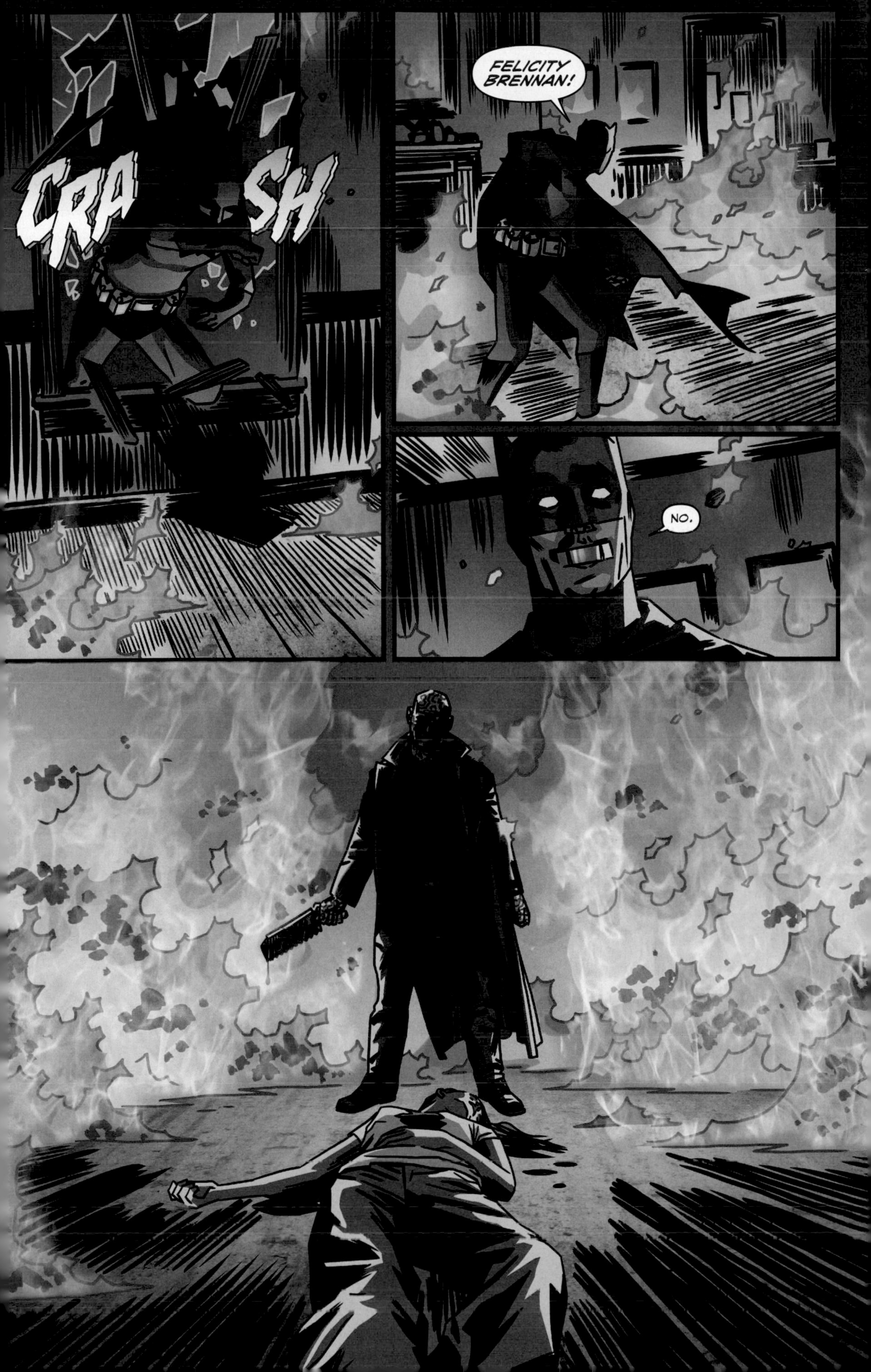
CRASH
FELICITY BRENNAN!
NO.

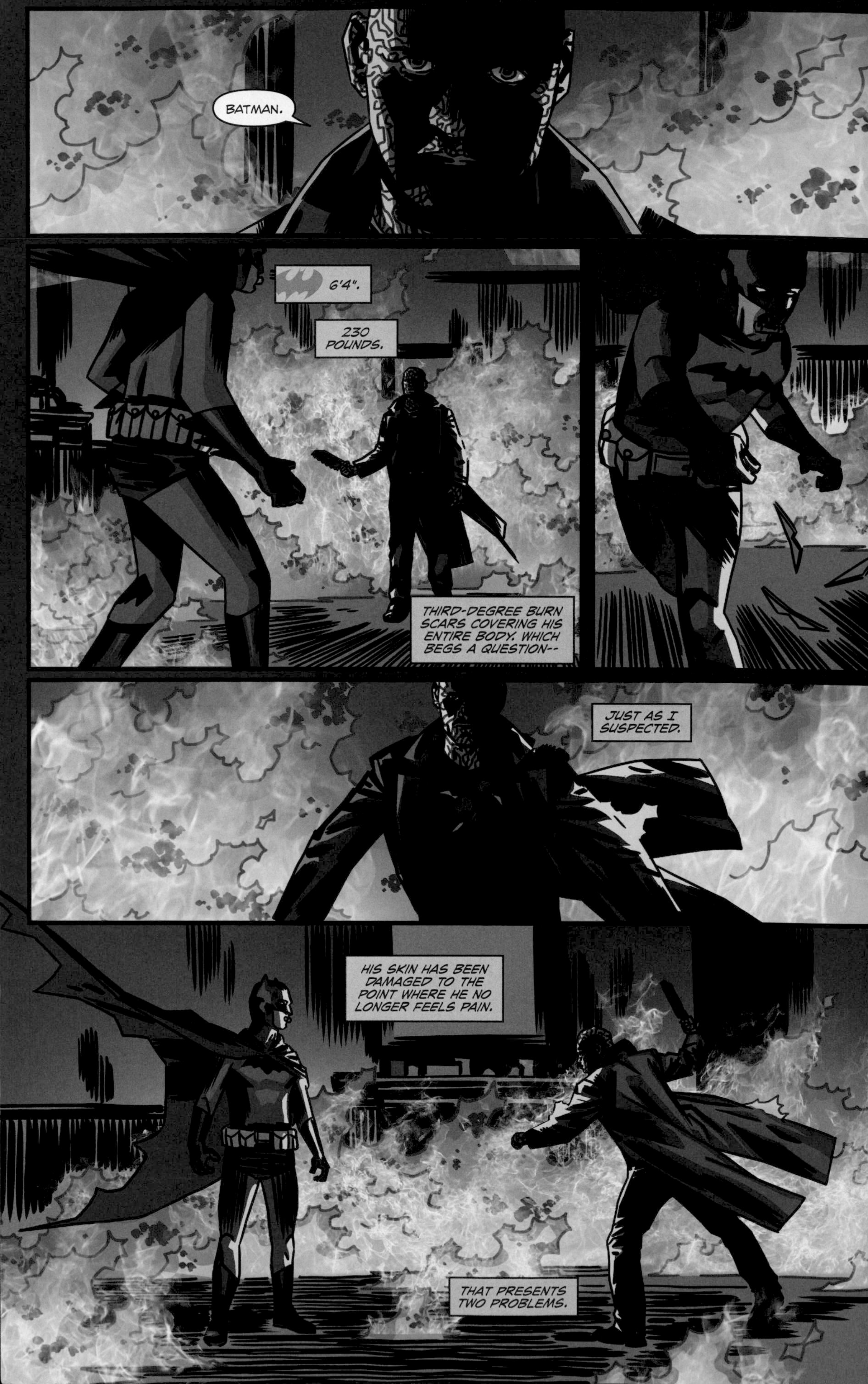
BATMAN.
6'4".
230 POUNDS.
THIRD-DEGREE BURN SCARS COVERING HIS ENTIRE BODY. WHICH BEGS A QUESTION--
JUST AS I SUSPECTED.
HIS SKIN HAS BEEN DAMAGED TO THE POINT WHERE HE NO LONGER FEELS PAIN.
THAT PRESENTS TWO PROBLEMS.

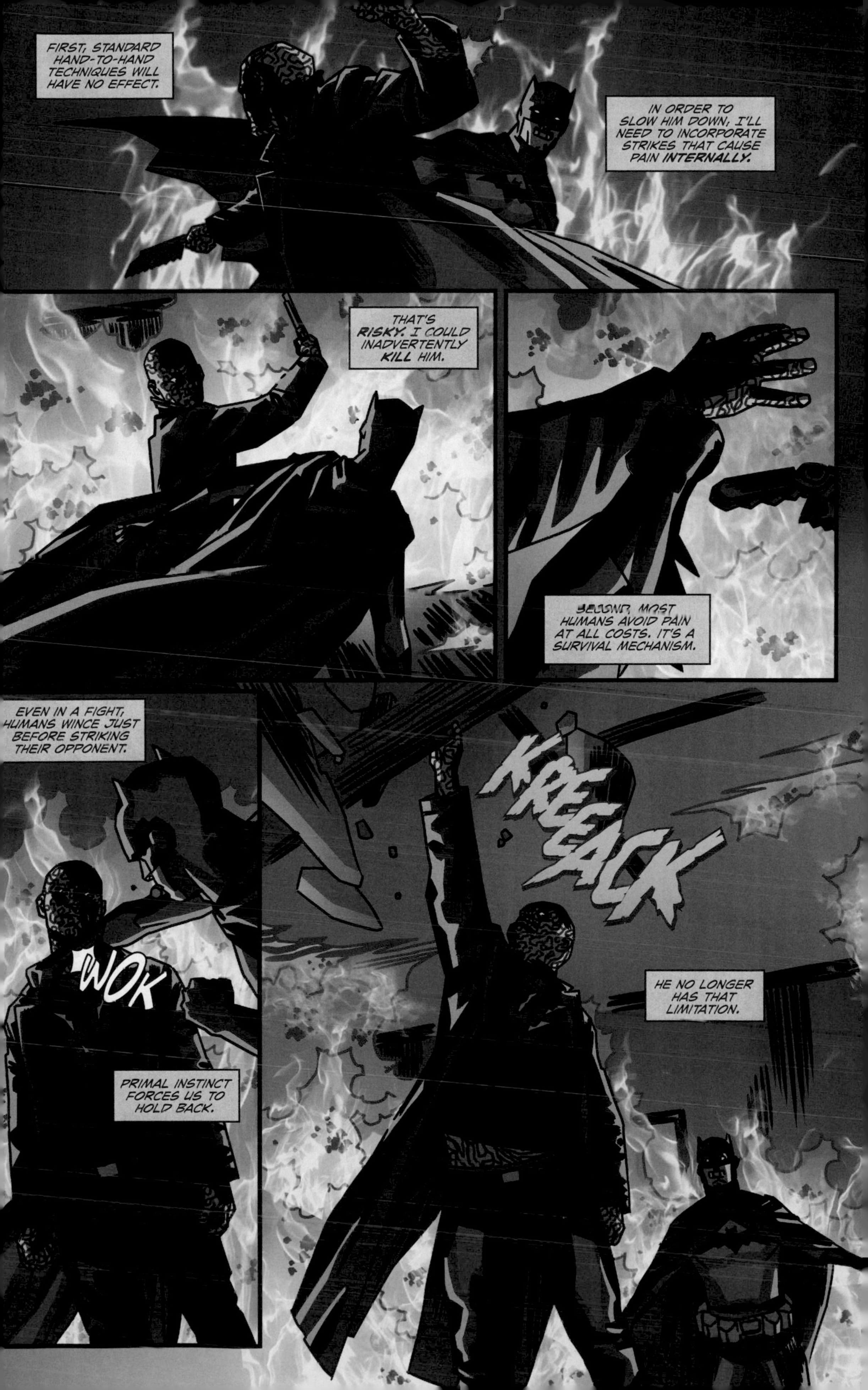
FIRST, STANDARD HAND-TO-HAND TECHNIQUES WILL HAVE NO EFFECT.
IN ORDER TO SLOW HIM DOWN, I'LL NEED TO INCORPORATE STRIKES THAT CAUSE PAIN INTERNALLY.
THAT'S RISKY. I COULD INADVERTENTLY KILL HIM.
SECOND, MOST HUMANS AVOID PAIN AT ALL COSTS. IT'S A SURVIVAL MECHANISM.
EVEN IN A FIGHT, HUMANS WINCE JUST BEFORE STRIKING THEIR OPPONENT.
WOK
PRIMAL INSTINCT FORCES US TO HOLD BACK.
KREEACK
HE NO LONGER HAS THAT LIMITATION.

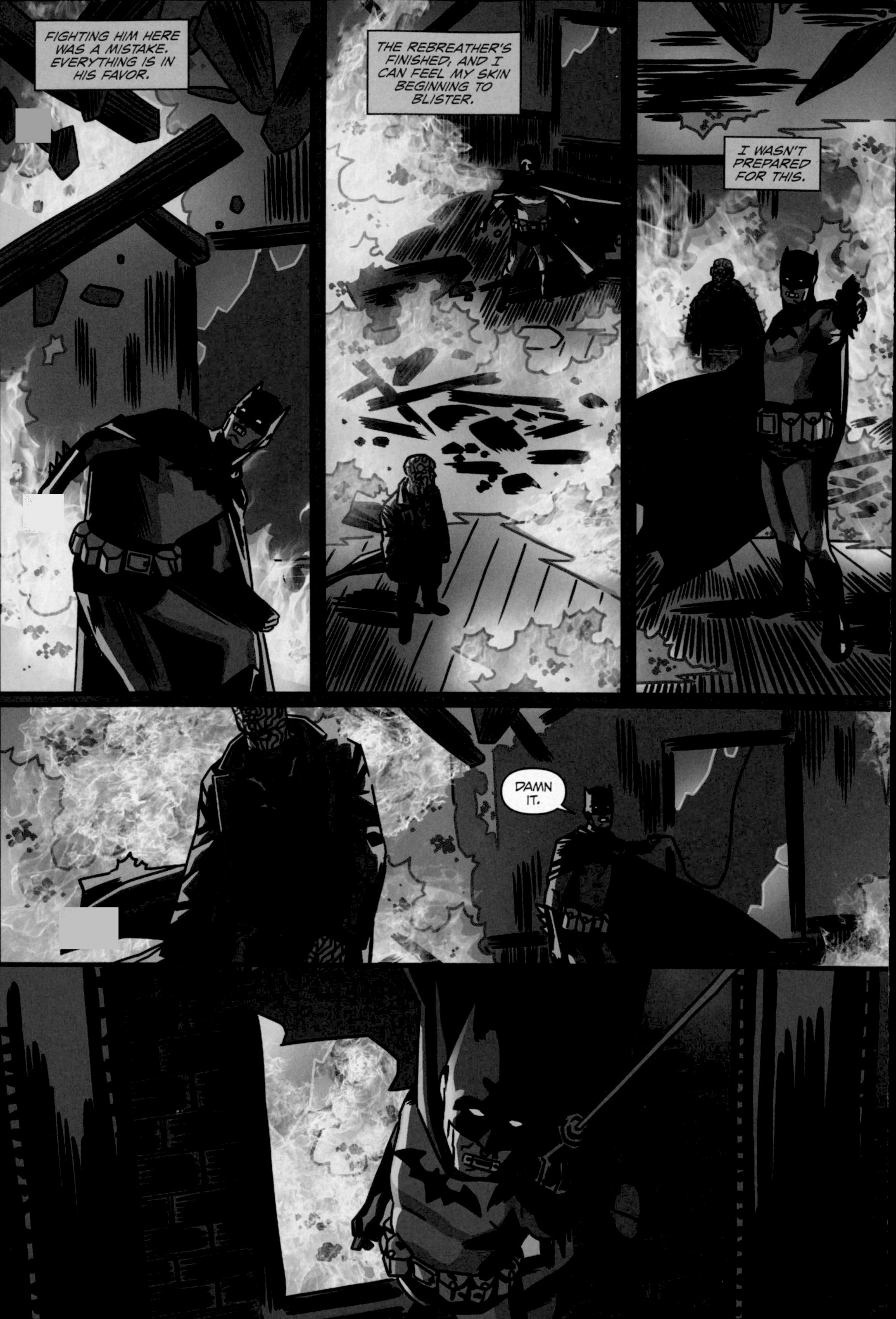
FIGHTING HIM HERE WAS A MISTAKE. EVERYTHING IS IN HIS FAVOR.
THE REBREATHER'S FINISHED, AND I CAN FEEL MY SKIN BEGINNING TO BLISTER.
I WASN'T PREPARED FOR THIS.
DAMN IT.

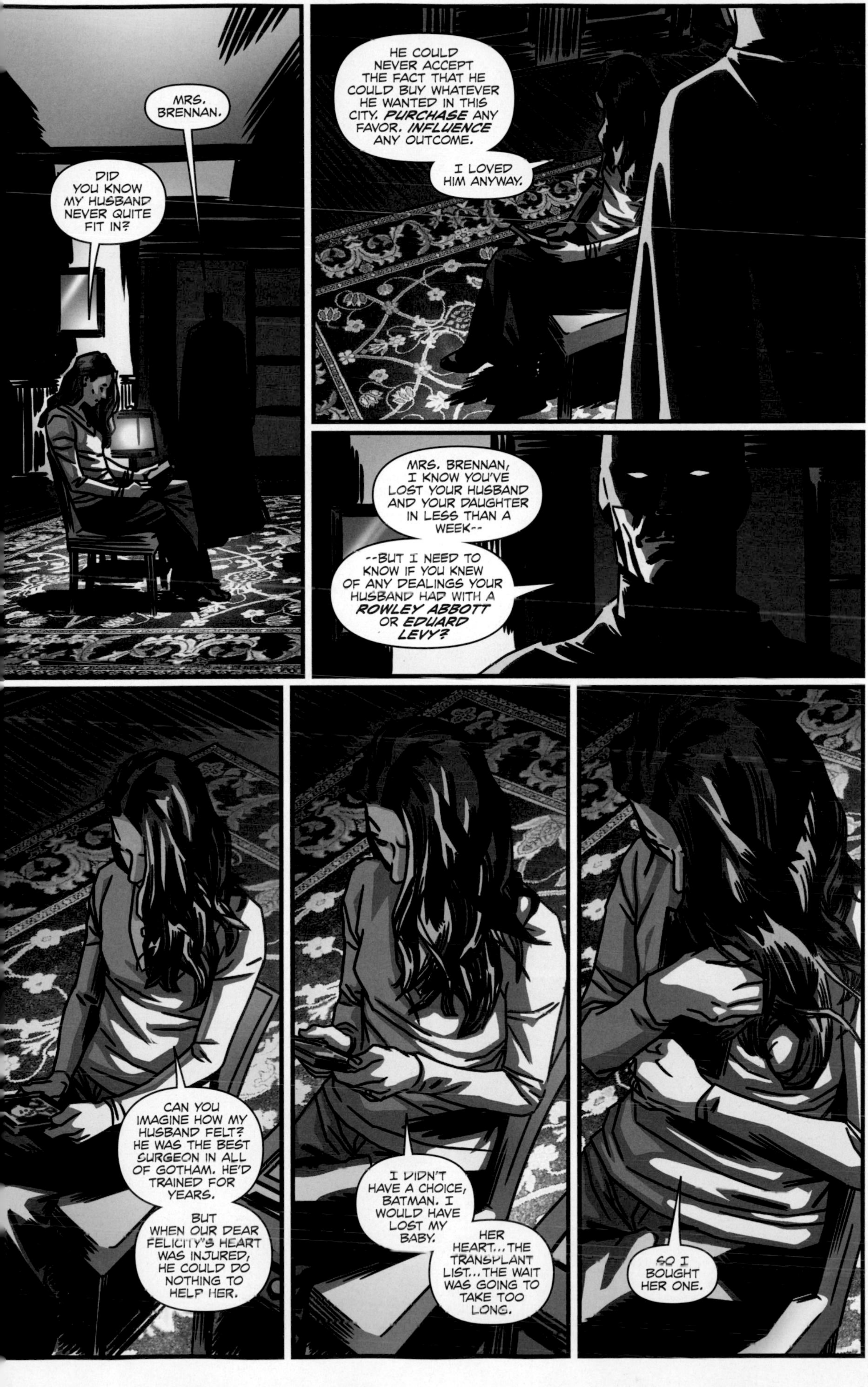
MRS. BRENNAN.
DID YOU KNOW MY HUSBAND NEVER QUITE FIT IN?
HE COULD NEVER ACCEPT THE FACT THAT HE COULD BUY WHATEVER HE WANTED IN THIS CITY. PURCHASE ANY FAVOR. INFLUENCE ANY OUTCOME.
I LOVED HIM ANYWAY.
MRS. BRENNAN, I KNOW YOU'VE LOST YOUR HUSBAND AND YOUR DAUGHTER IN LESS THAN A WEEK--
--BUT I NEED TO KNOW IF YOU KNEW OF ANY DEALINGS YOUR HUSBAND HAD WITH A ROWLEY ABBOTT OR EDUARD LEVY?
CAN YOU IMAGINE HOW MY HUSBAND FELT? HE WAS THE BEST SURGEON IN ALL OF GOTHAM. HE'D TRAINED FOR YEARS.
BUT WHEN OUR DEAR FELICITY'S HEART WAS INJURED, HE COULD DO NOTHING TO HELP HER.
I DIDN'T HAVE A CHOICE, BATMAN. I WOULD HAVE LOST MY BABY.
HER HEART... THE TRANSPLANT LIST... THE WAIT WAS GOING TO TAKE TOO LONG.
SO I BOUGHT HER ONE.

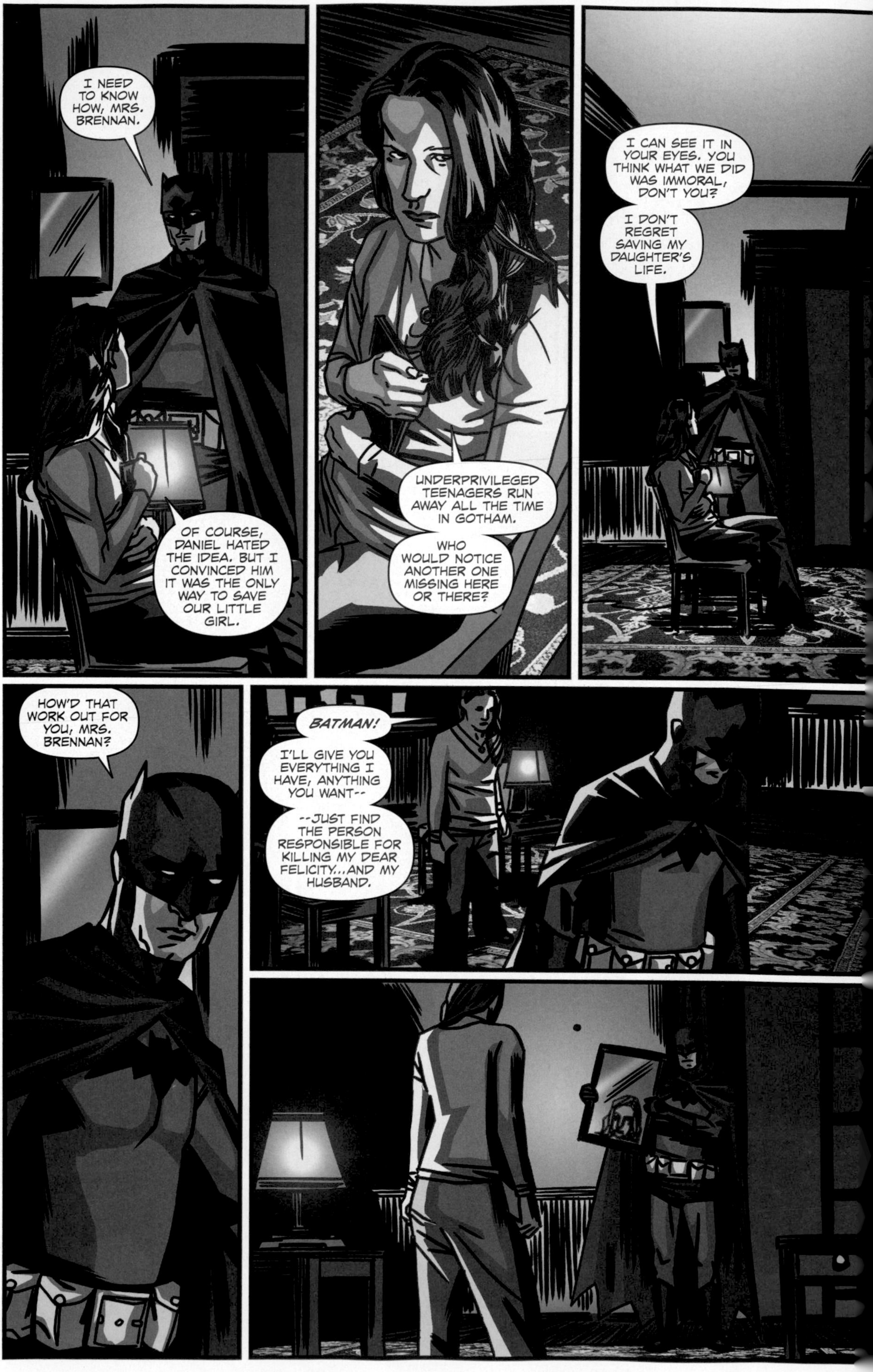

I NEED TO KNOW HOW, MRS. BRENNAN.
OF COURSE, DANIEL HATED THE IDEA. BUT I CONVINCED HIM IT WAS THE ONLY WAY TO SAVE OUR LITTLE GIRL.
UNDERPRIVILEGED TEENAGERS RUN AWAY ALL THE TIME IN GOTHAM.
WHO WOULD NOTICE ANOTHER ONE MISSING HERE OR THERE?
I CAN SEE IT IN YOUR EYES. YOU THINK WHAT WE DID WAS IMMORAL, DON'T YOU?
I DON'T REGRET SAVING MY DAUGHTER'S LIFE.
HOW'D THAT WORK OUT FOR YOU, MRS. BRENNAN?
BATMAN!
I'LL GIVE YOU EVERYTHING I HAVE, ANYTHING YOU WANT--
--JUST FIND THE PERSON RESPONSIBLE FOR KILLING MY DEAR FELICITY...AND MY HUSBAND.

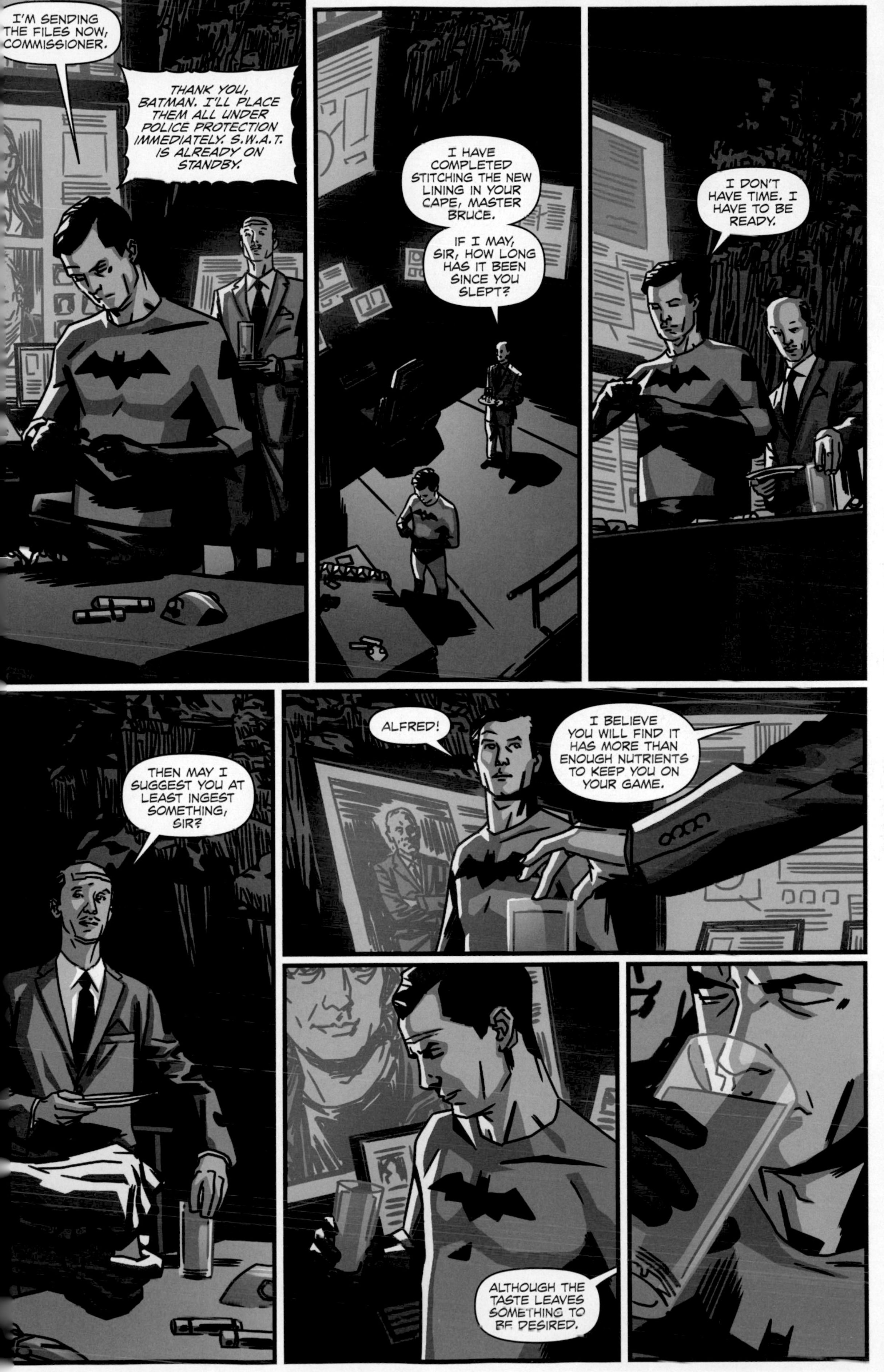
I'M SENDING THE FILES NOW, COMMISSIONER.
THANK YOU, BATMAN. I'LL PLACE THEM ALL UNDER POLICE PROTECTION IMMEDIATELY. S.W.A.T. IS ALREADY ON STANDBY.
I HAVE COMPLETED STITCHING THE NEW LINING IN YOUR CAPE, MASTER BRUCE.
IF I MAY, SIR, HOW LONG HAS IT BEEN SINCE YOU SLEPT?
I DON'T HAVE TIME. I HAVE TO BE READY.
THEN MAY I SUGGEST YOU AT LEAST INGEST SOMETHING, SIR?
ALFRED!
I BELIEVE YOU WILL FIND IT HAS MORE THAN ENOUGH NUTRIENTS TO KEEP YOU ON YOUR GAME.
ALTHOUGH THE TASTE LEAVES SOMETHING TO BE DESIRED.

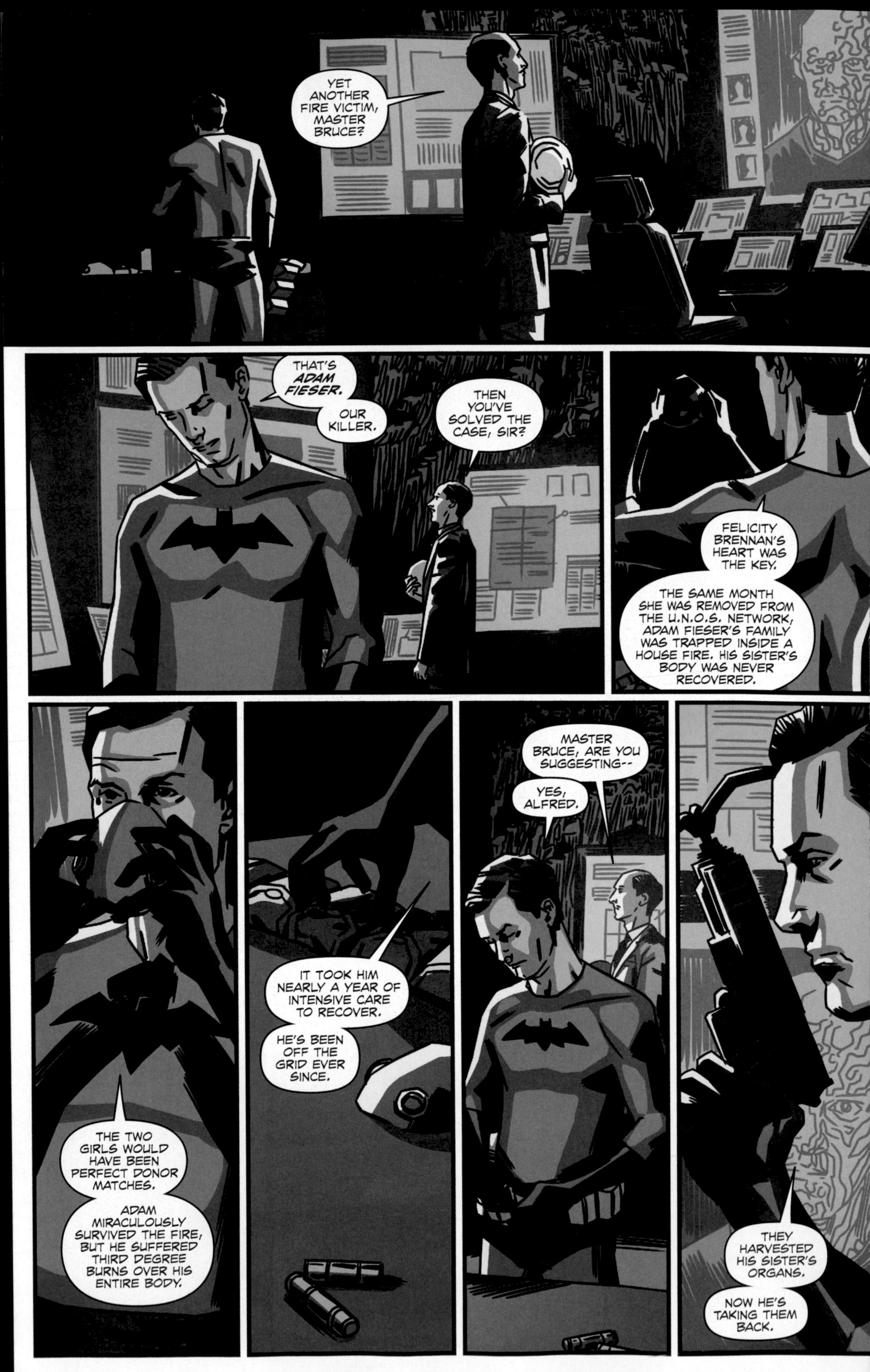
YET ANOTHER FIRE VICTIM, MASTER BRUCE?
THAT'S *ADAM FIESER.*
OUR KILLER.
THEN YOU'VE SOLVED THE CASE, SIR?
FELICITY BRENNAN'S HEART WAS THE KEY.
THE SAME MONTH SHE WAS REMOVED FROM THE U.N.O.S. NETWORK, ADAM FIESER'S FAMILY WAS TRAPPED INSIDE A HOUSE FIRE. HIS SISTER'S BODY WAS NEVER RECOVERED.
THE TWO GIRLS WOULD HAVE BEEN PERFECT DONOR MATCHES.
ADAM MIRACULOUSLY SURVIVED THE FIRE, BUT HE SUFFERED THIRD DEGREE BURNS OVER HIS ENTIRE BODY.
IT TOOK HIM NEARLY A YEAR OF INTENSIVE CARE TO RECOVER.
HE'S BEEN OFF THE GRID EVER SINCE.
MASTER BRUCE, ARE YOU SUGGESTING--
YES, ALFRED.
THEY HARVESTED HIS SISTER'S ORGANS.
NOW HE'S TAKING THEM BACK.

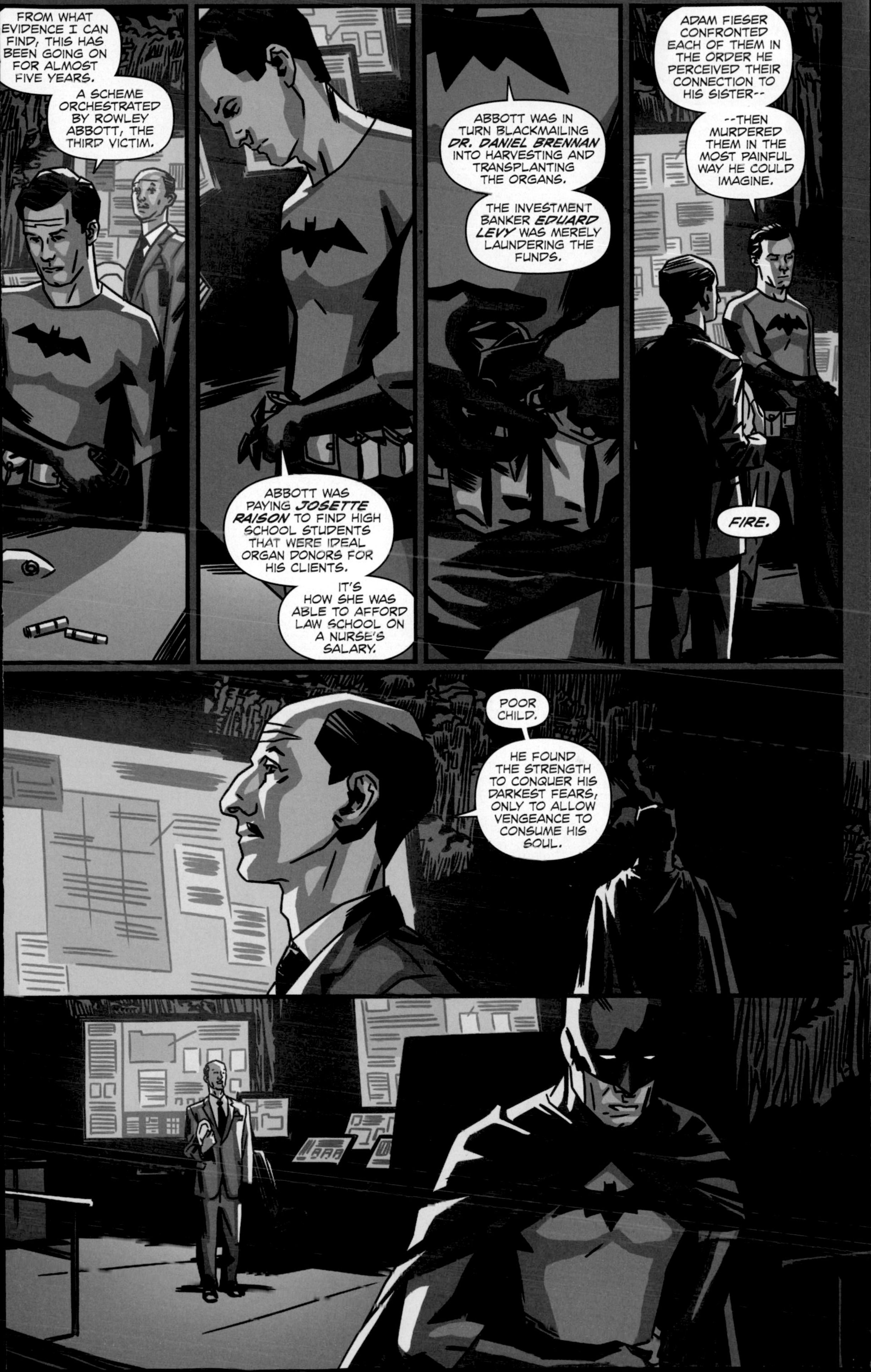
FROM WHAT EVIDENCE I CAN FIND, THIS HAS BEEN GOING ON FOR ALMOST FIVE YEARS.
A SCHEME ORCHESTRATED BY ROWLEY ABBOTT, THE THIRD VICTIM.
ABBOTT WAS PAYING JOSETTE RAISON TO FIND HIGH SCHOOL STUDENTS THAT WERE IDEAL ORGAN DONORS FOR HIS CLIENTS.
IT'S HOW SHE WAS ABLE TO AFFORD LAW SCHOOL ON A NURSE'S SALARY.
ABBOTT WAS IN TURN BLACKMAILING DR. DANIEL BRENNAN INTO HARVESTING AND TRANSPLANTING THE ORGANS.
THE INVESTMENT BANKER EDUARD LEVY WAS MERELY LAUNDERING THE FUNDS.
ADAM FIESER CONFRONTED EACH OF THEM IN THE ORDER HE PERCEIVED THEIR CONNECTION TO HIS SISTER--
--THEN MURDERED THEM IN THE MOST PAINFUL WAY HE COULD IMAGINE.
FIRE.
POOR CHILD.
HE FOUND THE STRENGTH TO CONQUER HIS DARKEST FEARS, ONLY TO ALLOW VENGEANCE TO CONSUME HIS SOUL.

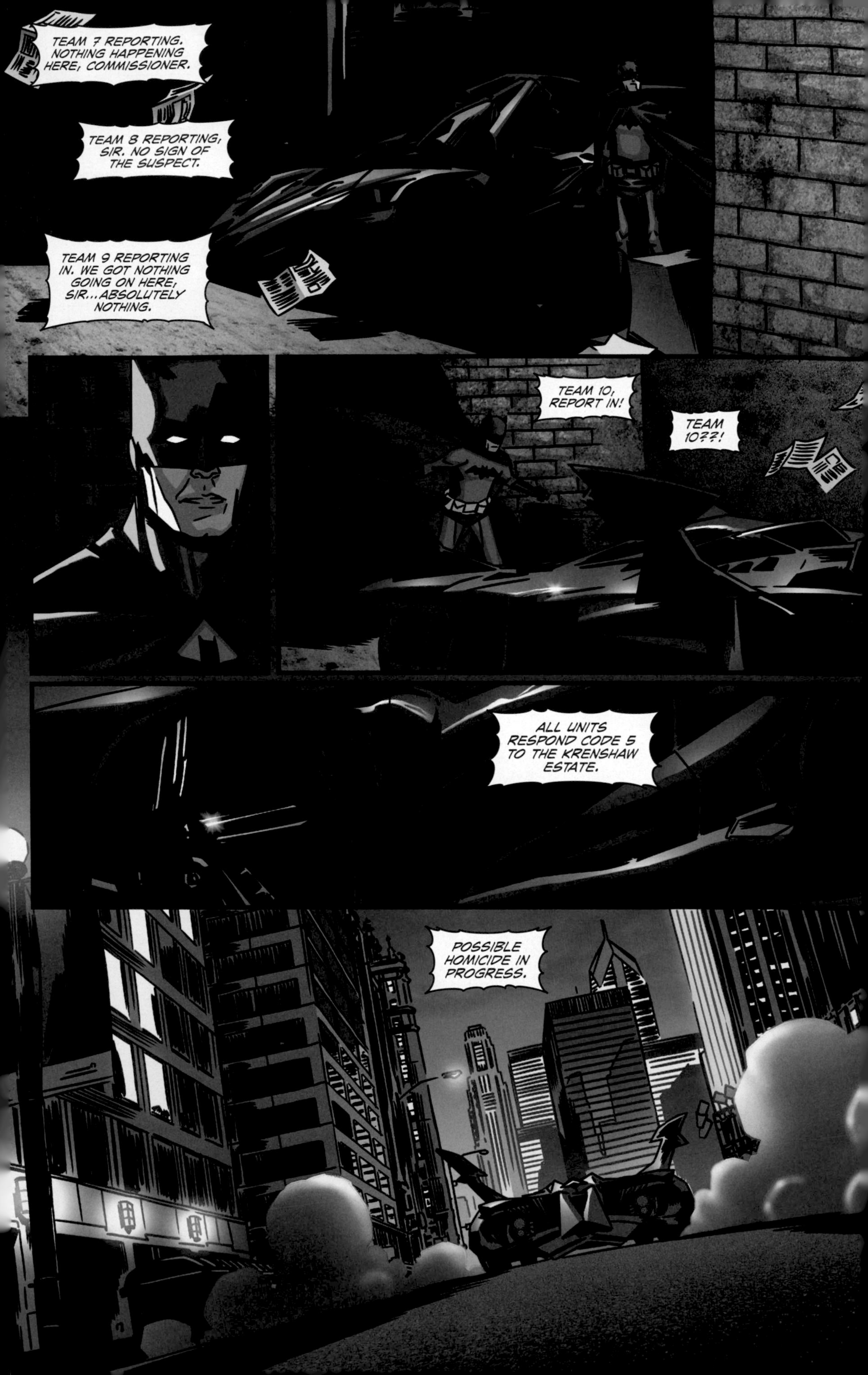
TEAM 7 REPORTING. NOTHING HAPPENING HERE, COMMISSIONER.
TEAM 8 REPORTING, SIR. NO SIGN OF THE SUSPECT.
TEAM 9 REPORTING IN. WE GOT NOTHING GOING ON HERE, SIR...ABSOLUTELY NOTHING.
TEAM 10, REPORT IN!
TEAM 10??!
ALL UNITS RESPOND CODE 5 TO THE KRENSHAW ESTATE.
POSSIBLE HOMICIDE IN PROGRESS.

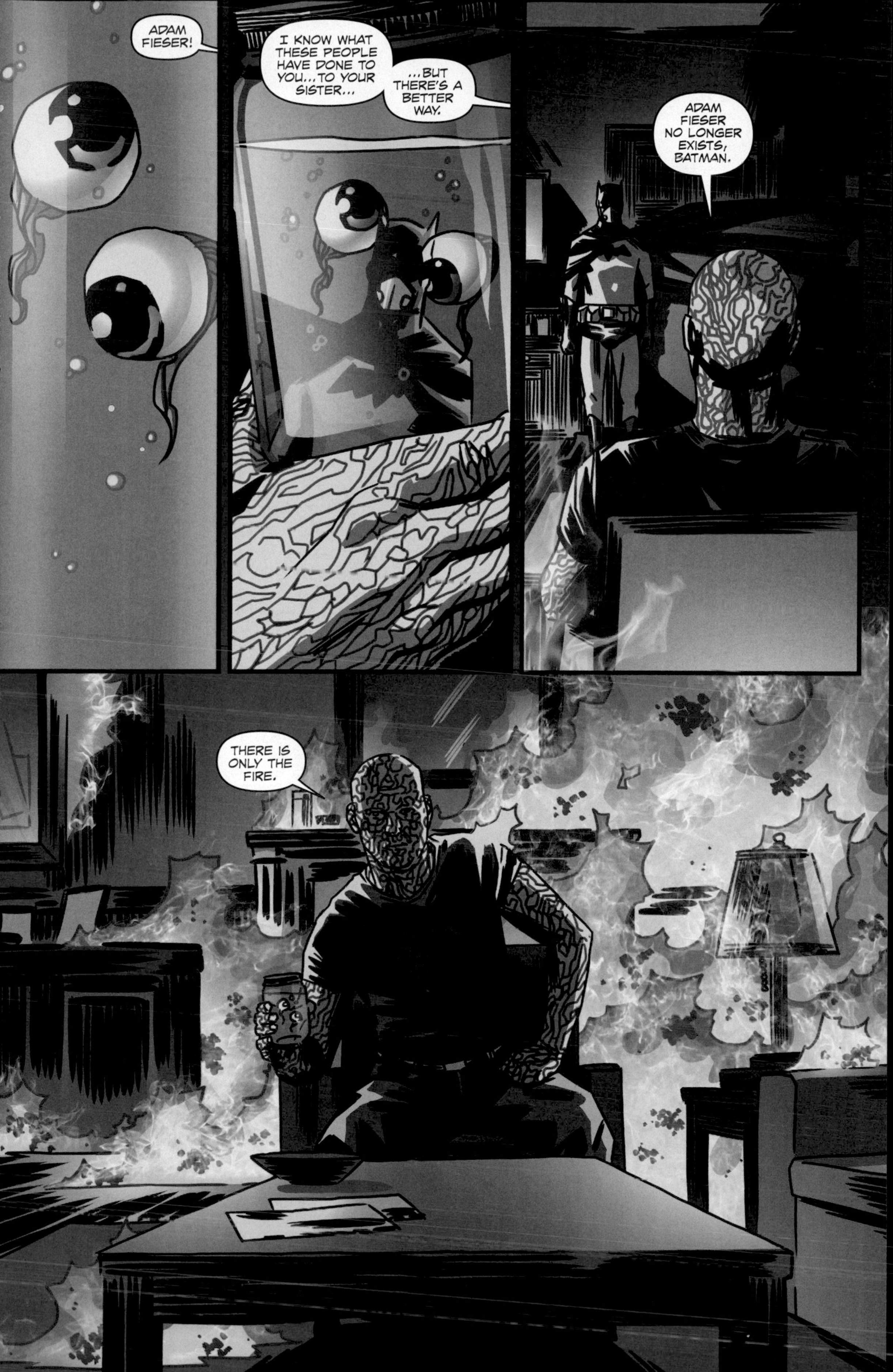
ADAM FIESER!
I KNOW WHAT THESE PEOPLE HAVE DONE TO YOU...TO YOUR SISTER...
...BUT THERE'S A BETTER WAY.
ADAM FIESER NO LONGER EXISTS, BATMAN.
THERE IS ONLY THE FIRE.

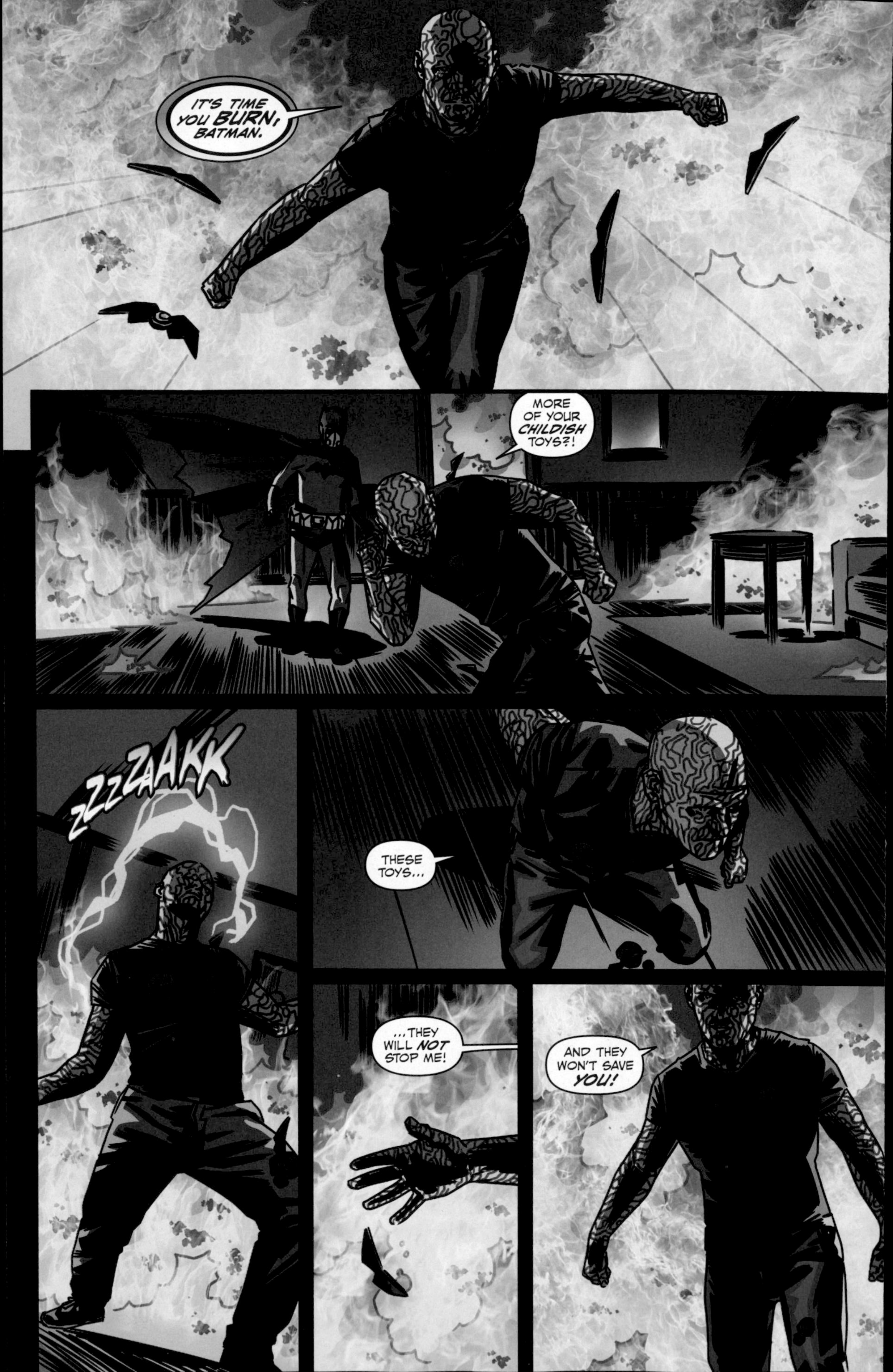
IT'S TIME YOU BURN, BATMAN.
MORE OF YOUR CHILDISH TOYS?!
ZZZZAAKK
THESE TOYS...
...THEY WILL NOT STOP ME!
AND THEY WON'T SAVE YOU!

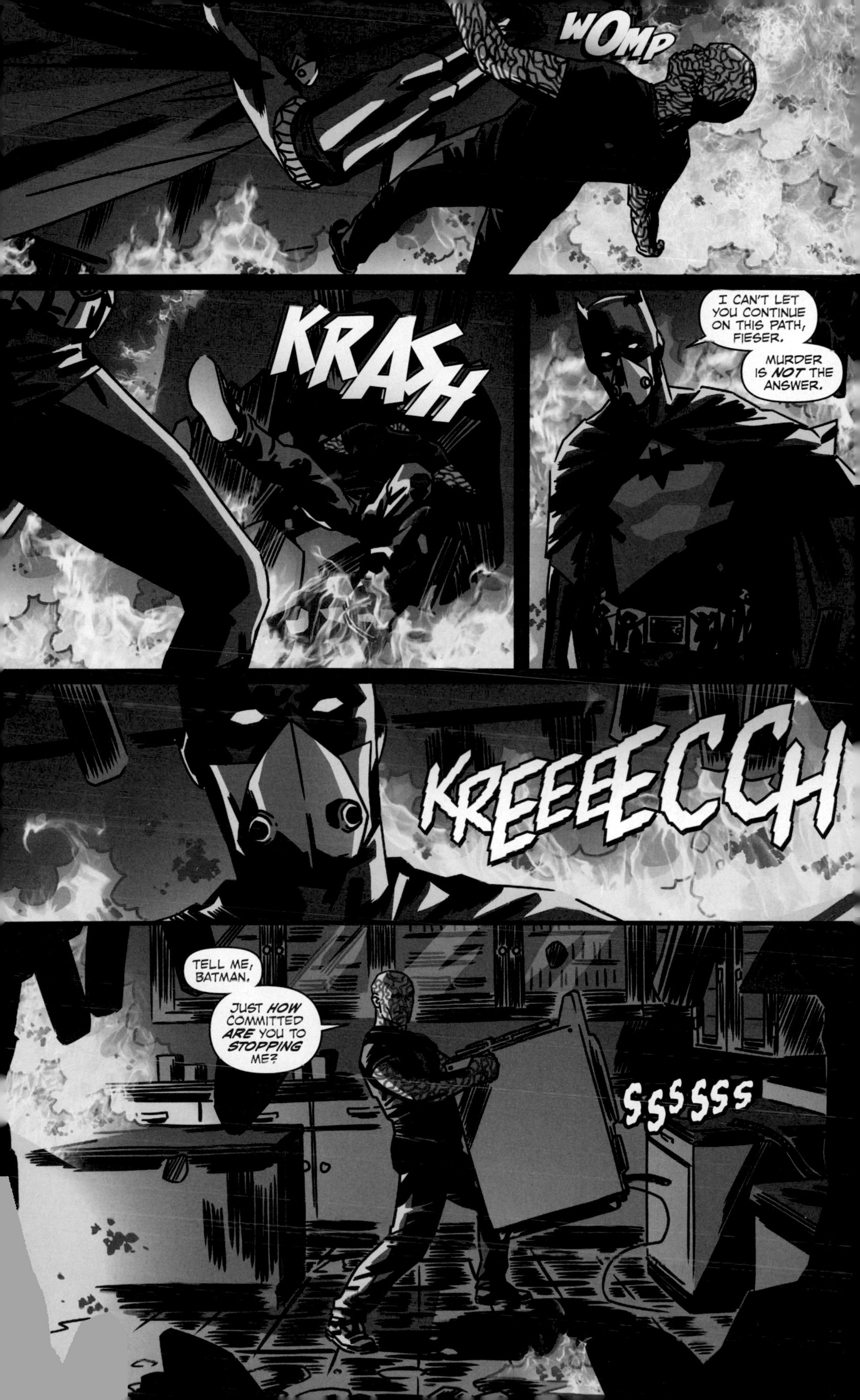
WOMP
KRASH
I CAN'T LET YOU CONTINUE ON THIS PATH, FIESER.
MURDER IS *NOT* THE ANSWER.
KREEEECCH
TELL ME, BATMAN.
JUST *HOW* COMMITTED *ARE* YOU TO *STOPPING* ME?
SSSSSS

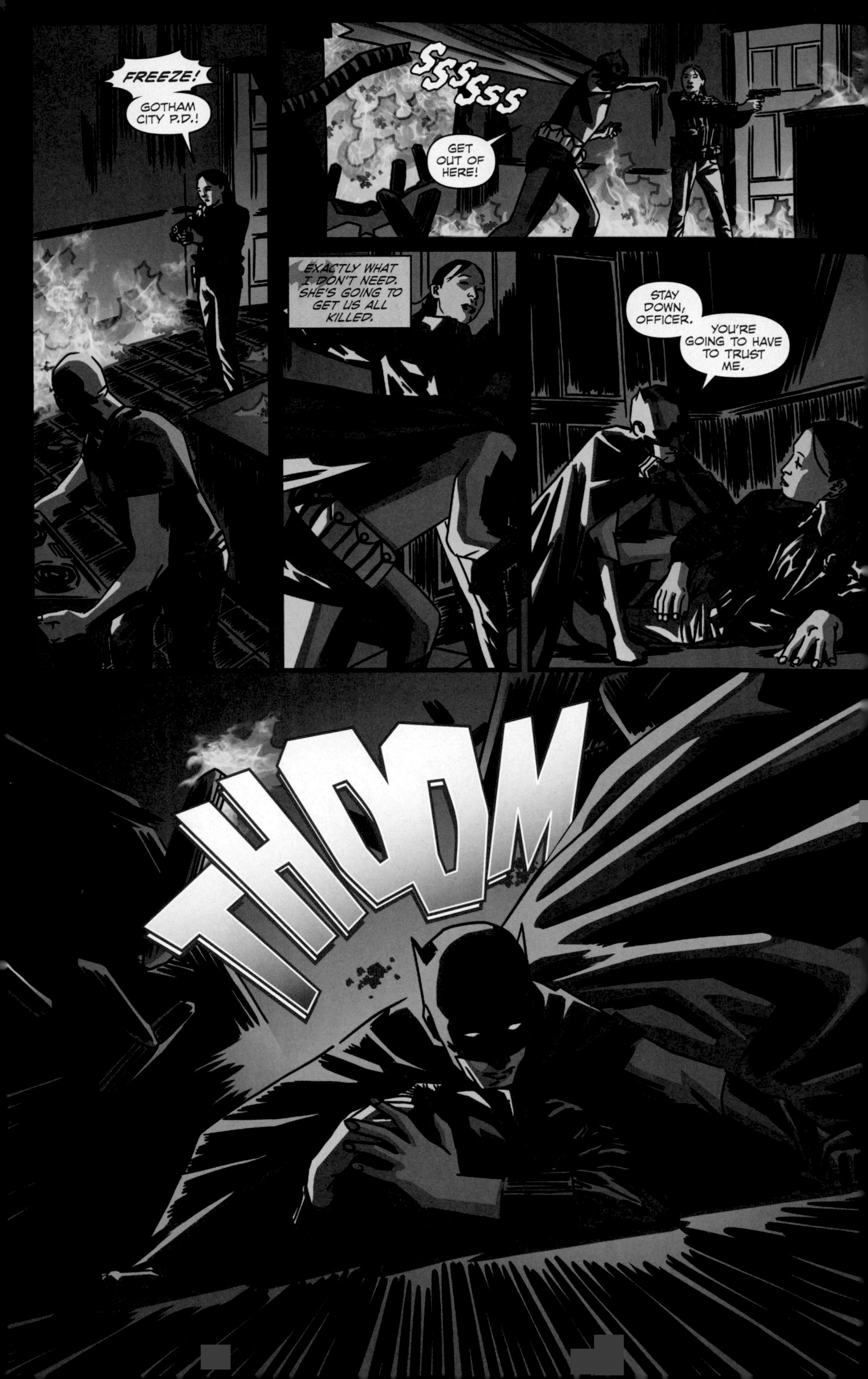
FREEZE!
GOTHAM CITY P.D.!
SSSSSS
GET OUT OF HERE!
EXACTLY WHAT I DON'T NEED. SHE'S GOING TO GET US ALL KILLED.
STAY DOWN, OFFICER.
YOU'RE GOING TO HAVE TO TRUST ME.
THOOM

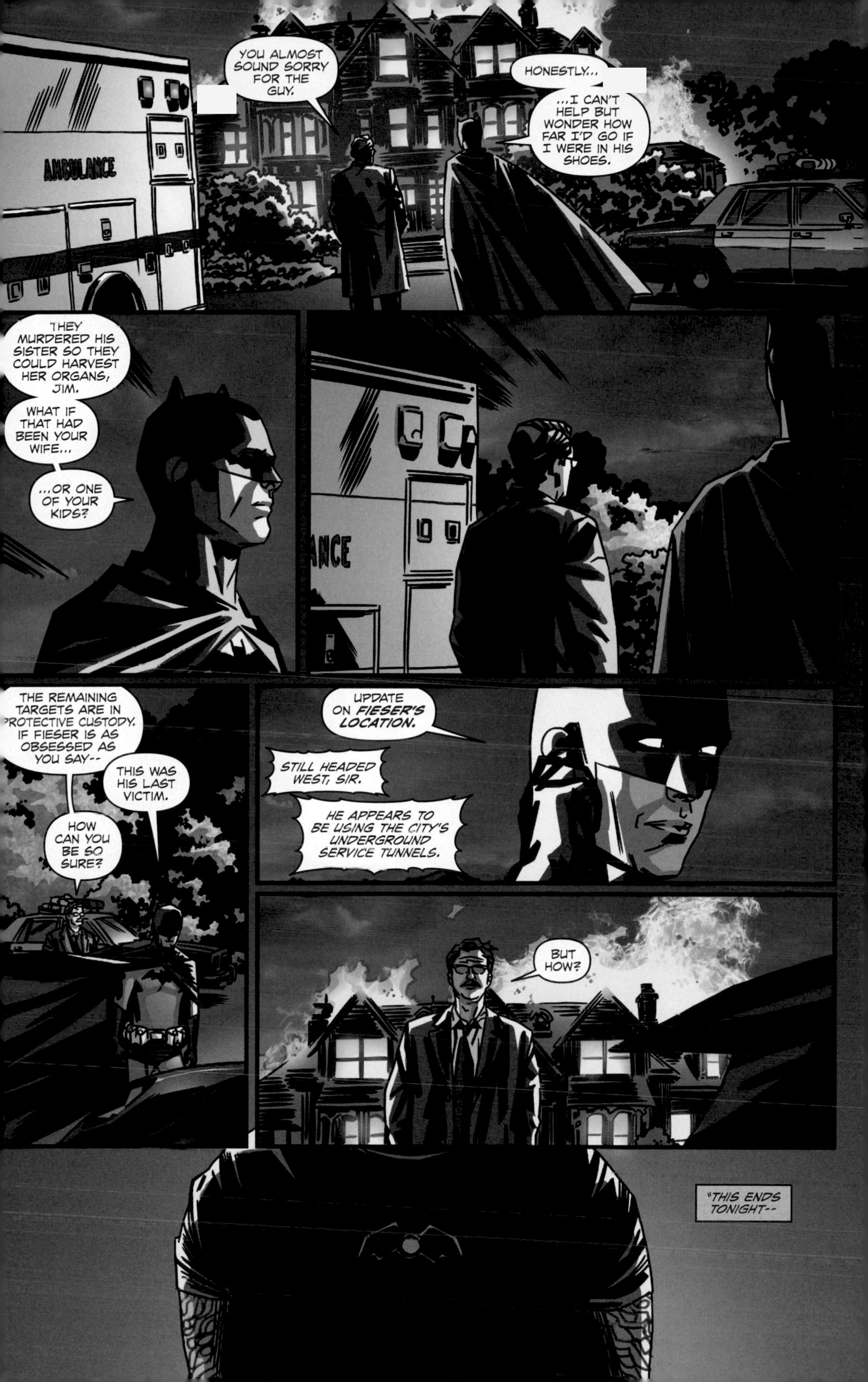
YOU ALMOST SOUND SORRY FOR THE GUY.
HONESTLY...
...I CAN'T HELP BUT WONDER HOW FAR I'D GO IF I WERE IN HIS SHOES.
AMBULANCE
THEY MURDERED HIS SISTER SO THEY COULD HARVEST HER ORGANS, JIM.
WHAT IF THAT HAD BEEN YOUR WIFE...
...OR ONE OF YOUR KIDS?
THE REMAINING TARGETS ARE IN PROTECTIVE CUSTODY. IF FIESER IS AS OBSESSED AS YOU SAY--
THIS WAS HIS LAST VICTIM.
HOW CAN YOU BE SO SURE?
UPDATE ON FIESER'S LOCATION.
STILL HEADED WEST, SIR.
HE APPEARS TO BE USING THE CITY'S UNDERGROUND SERVICE TUNNELS.
BUT HOW?
"THIS ENDS TONIGHT--

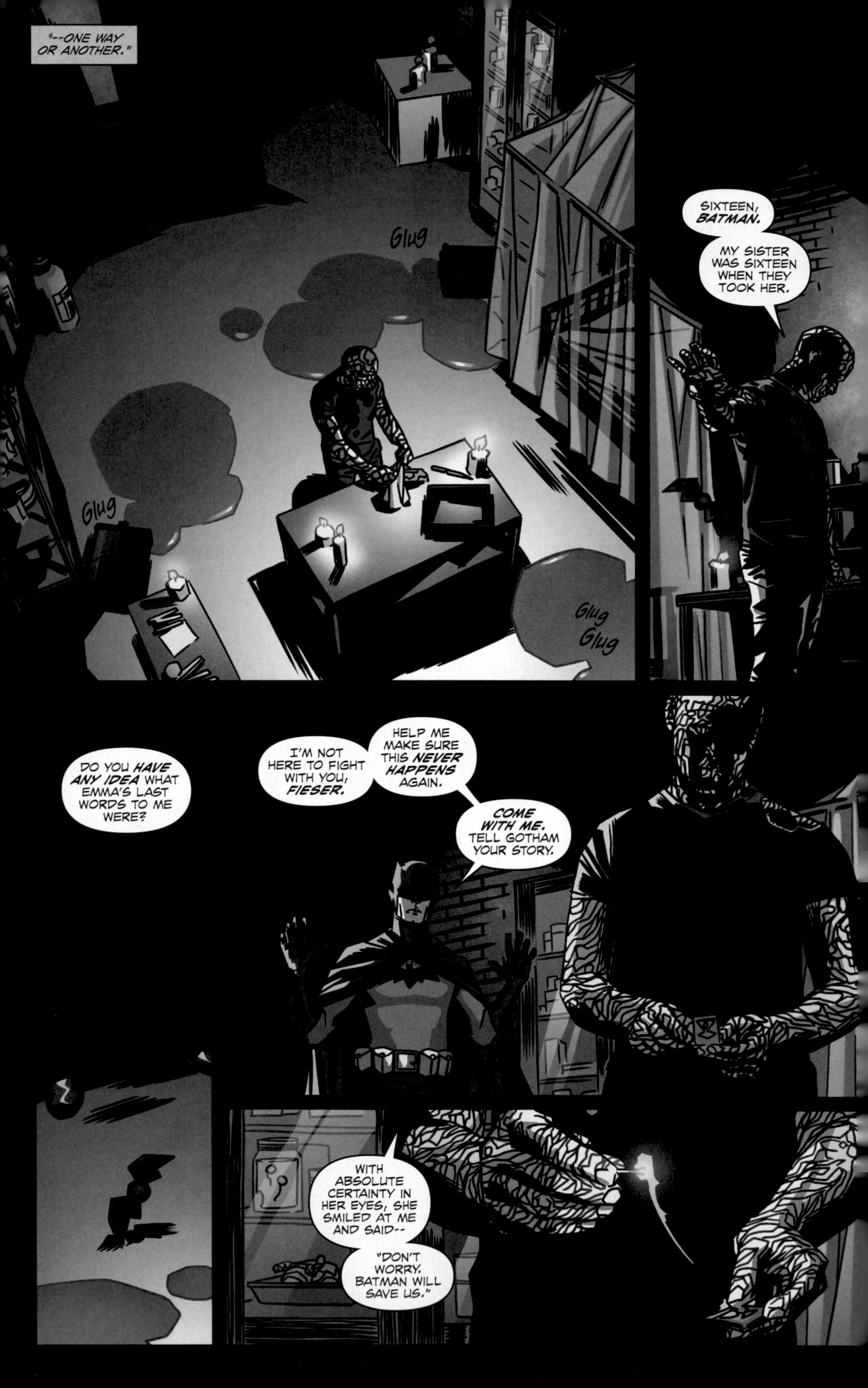
"--ONE WAY OR ANOTHER."
Glug
Glug
Glug Glug
SIXTEEN, BATMAN.
MY SISTER WAS SIXTEEN WHEN THEY TOOK HER.
DO YOU HAVE ANY IDEA WHAT EMMA'S LAST WORDS TO ME WERE?
I'M NOT HERE TO FIGHT WITH YOU, FIESER.
HELP ME MAKE SURE THIS NEVER HAPPENS AGAIN.
COME WITH ME. TELL GOTHAM YOUR STORY.
WITH ABSOLUTE CERTAINTY IN HER EYES, SHE SMILED AT ME AND SAID--
"DON'T WORRY. BATMAN WILL SAVE US."

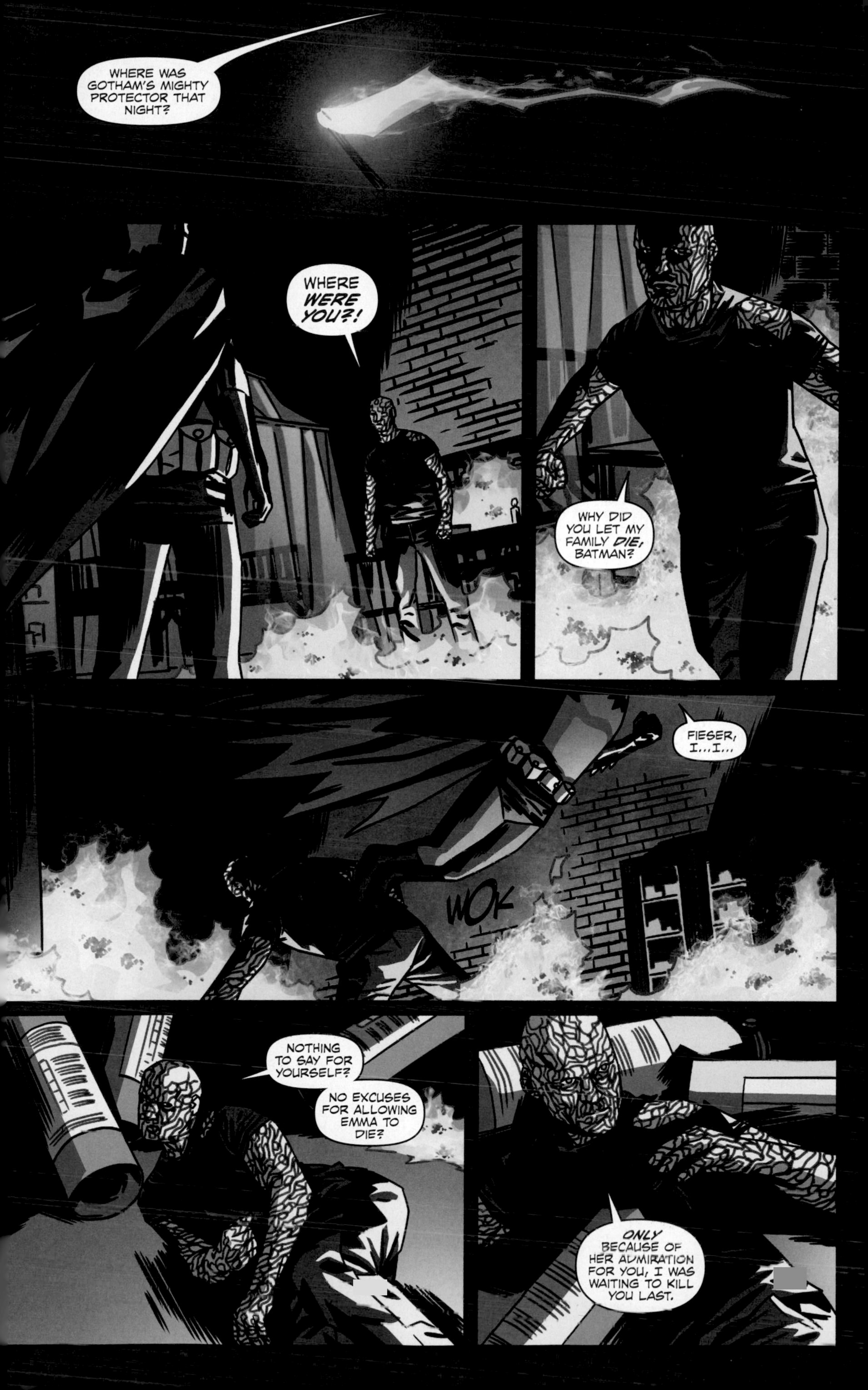
WHERE WAS GOTHAM'S MIGHTY PROTECTOR THAT NIGHT?
WHERE WERE YOU?!
WHY DID YOU LET MY FAMILY DIE, BATMAN?
FIESER, I...I...
WOK
NOTHING TO SAY FOR YOURSELF?
NO EXCUSES FOR ALLOWING EMMA TO DIE?
ONLY BECAUSE OF HER ADMIRATION FOR YOU, I WAS WAITING TO KILL YOU LAST.

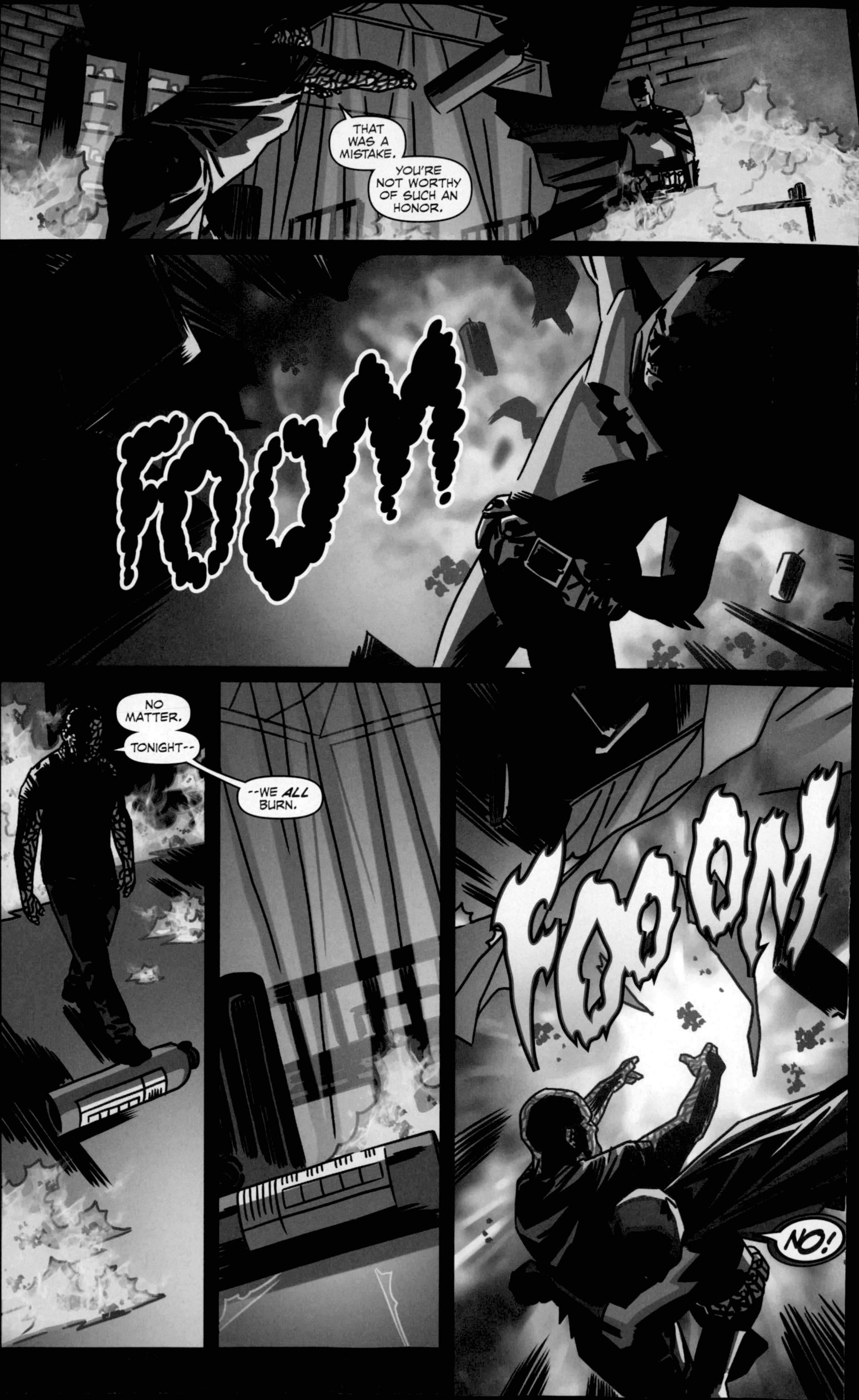
THAT WAS A MISTAKE.
YOU'RE NOT WORTHY OF SUCH AN HONOR.
FOOM!
NO MATTER.
TONIGHT--
--WE ALL BURN.
FOOOM
NO!

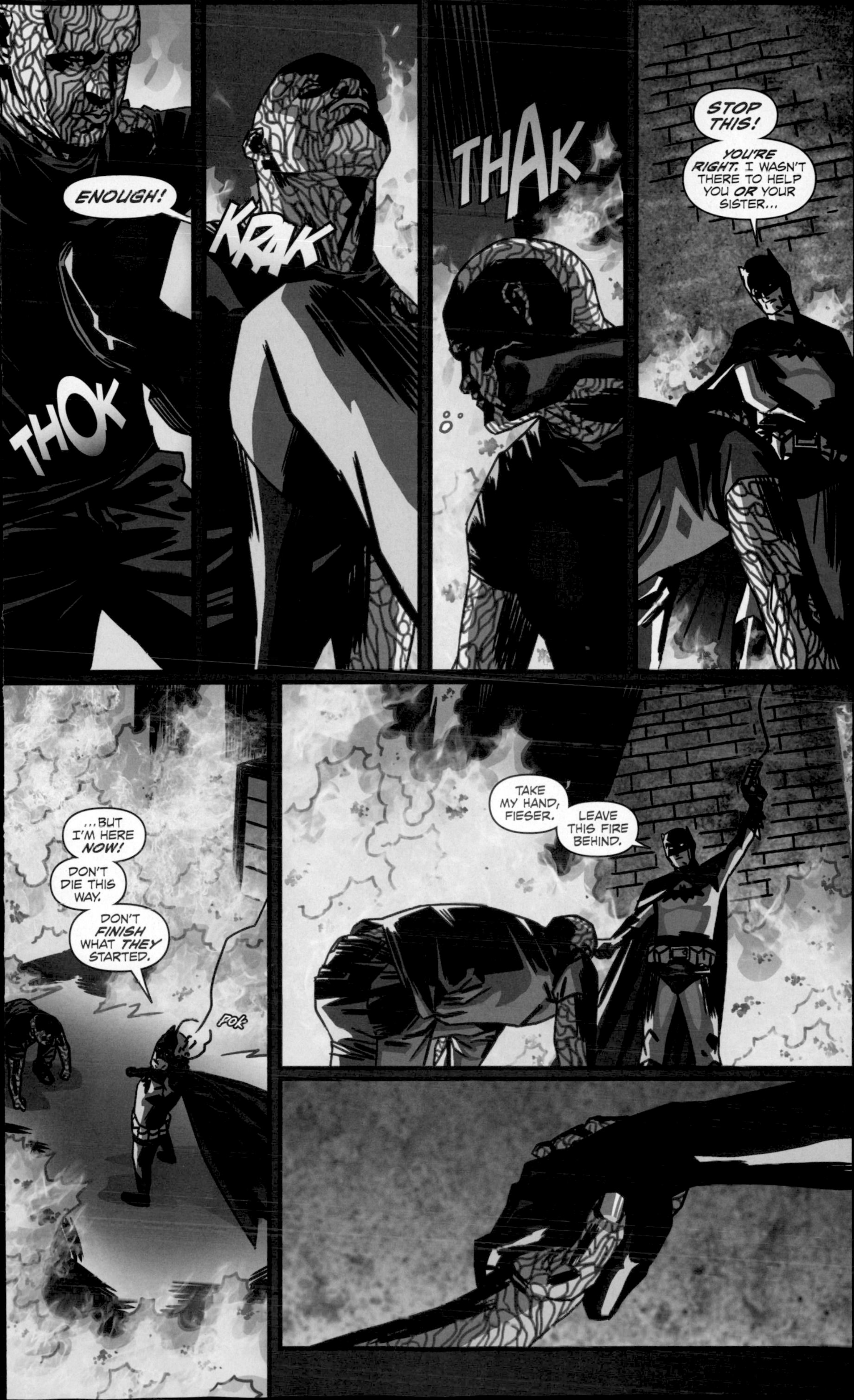
ENOUGH!
THOK
KRAK
THAK
STOP THIS!
YOU'RE RIGHT. I WASN'T THERE TO HELP YOU OR YOUR SISTER...
...BUT I'M HERE NOW!
DON'T DIE THIS WAY.
DON'T FINISH WHAT THEY STARTED.
POK
TAKE MY HAND, FIESER.
LEAVE THIS FIRE BEHIND.

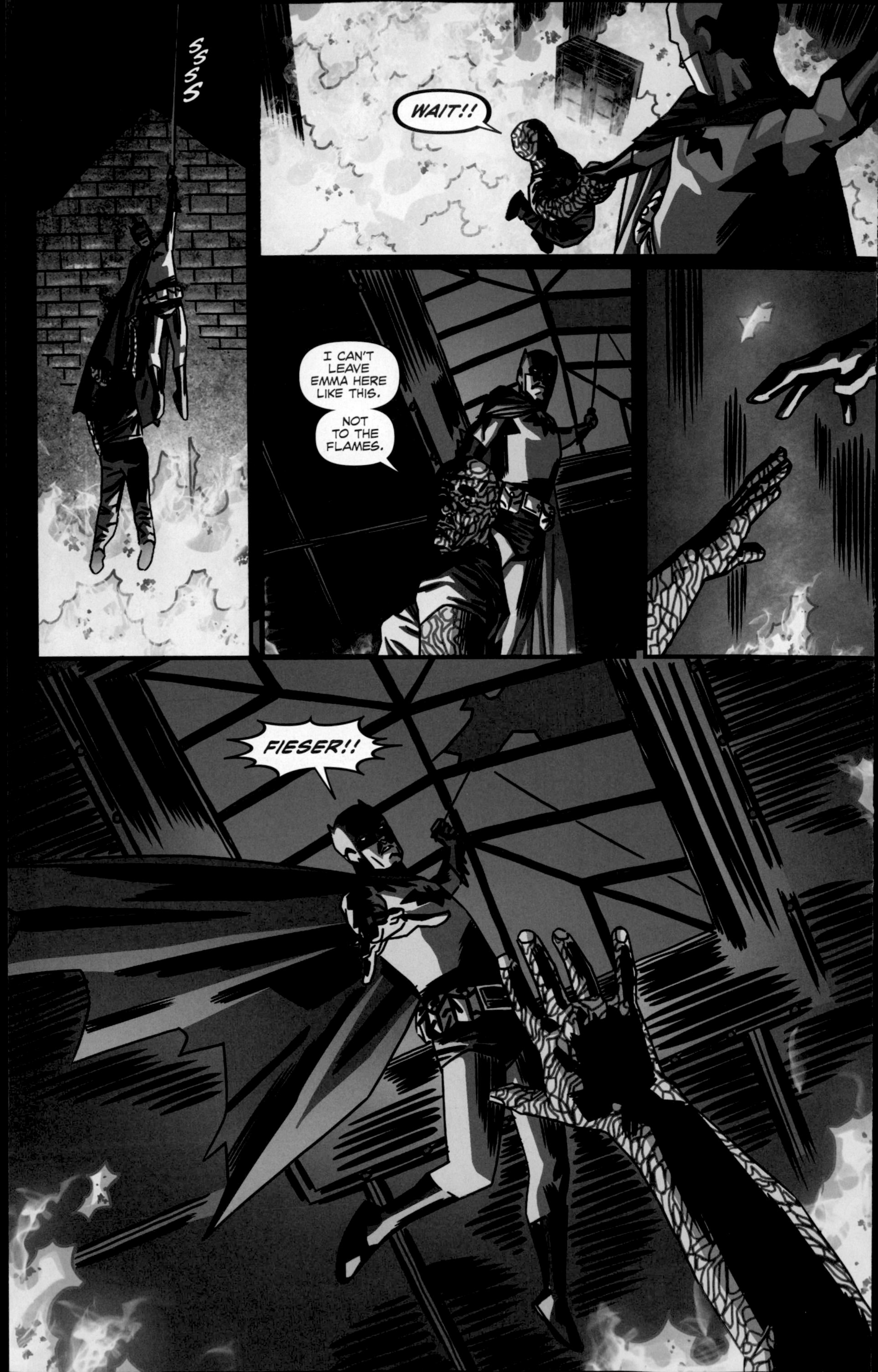
SSSS
WAIT!!
I CAN'T LEAVE EMMA HERE LIKE THIS.
NOT TO THE FLAMES.
FIESER!!

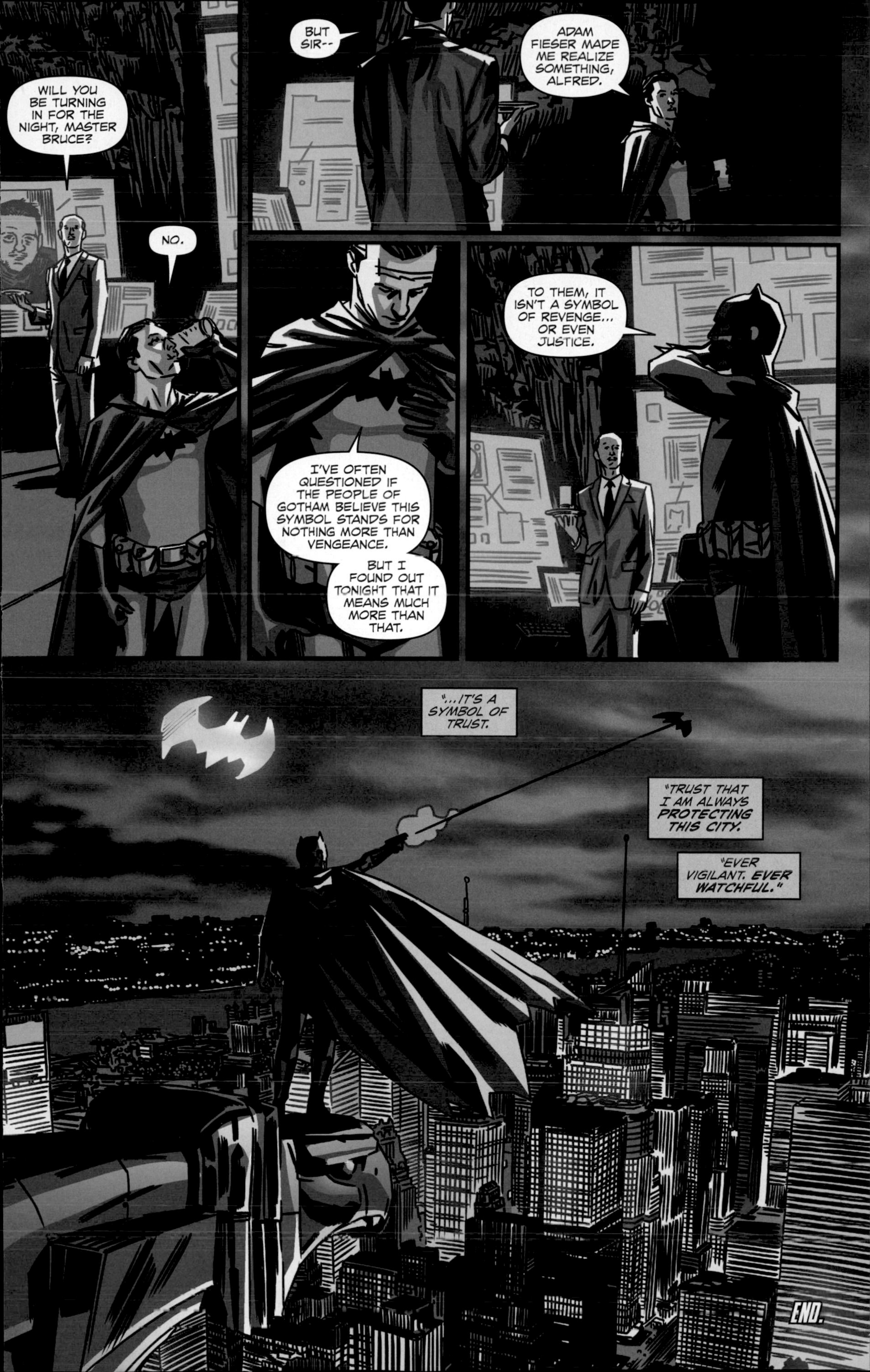
WILL YOU BE TURNING IN FOR THE NIGHT, MASTER BRUCE?
NO.
BUT SIR--
ADAM FIESER MADE ME REALIZE SOMETHING, ALFRED.
I'VE OFTEN QUESTIONED IF THE PEOPLE OF GOTHAM BELIEVE THIS SYMBOL STANDS FOR NOTHING MORE THAN VENGEANCE.
BUT I FOUND OUT TONIGHT THAT IT MEANS MUCH MORE THAN THAT.
TO THEM, IT ISN'T A SYMBOL OF REVENGE... OR EVEN JUSTICE.
"...IT'S A SYMBOL OF TRUST.
"TRUST THAT I AM ALWAYS PROTECTING THIS CITY.
"EVER VIGILANT. EVER WATCHFUL."
END.

HERDED LIMITS

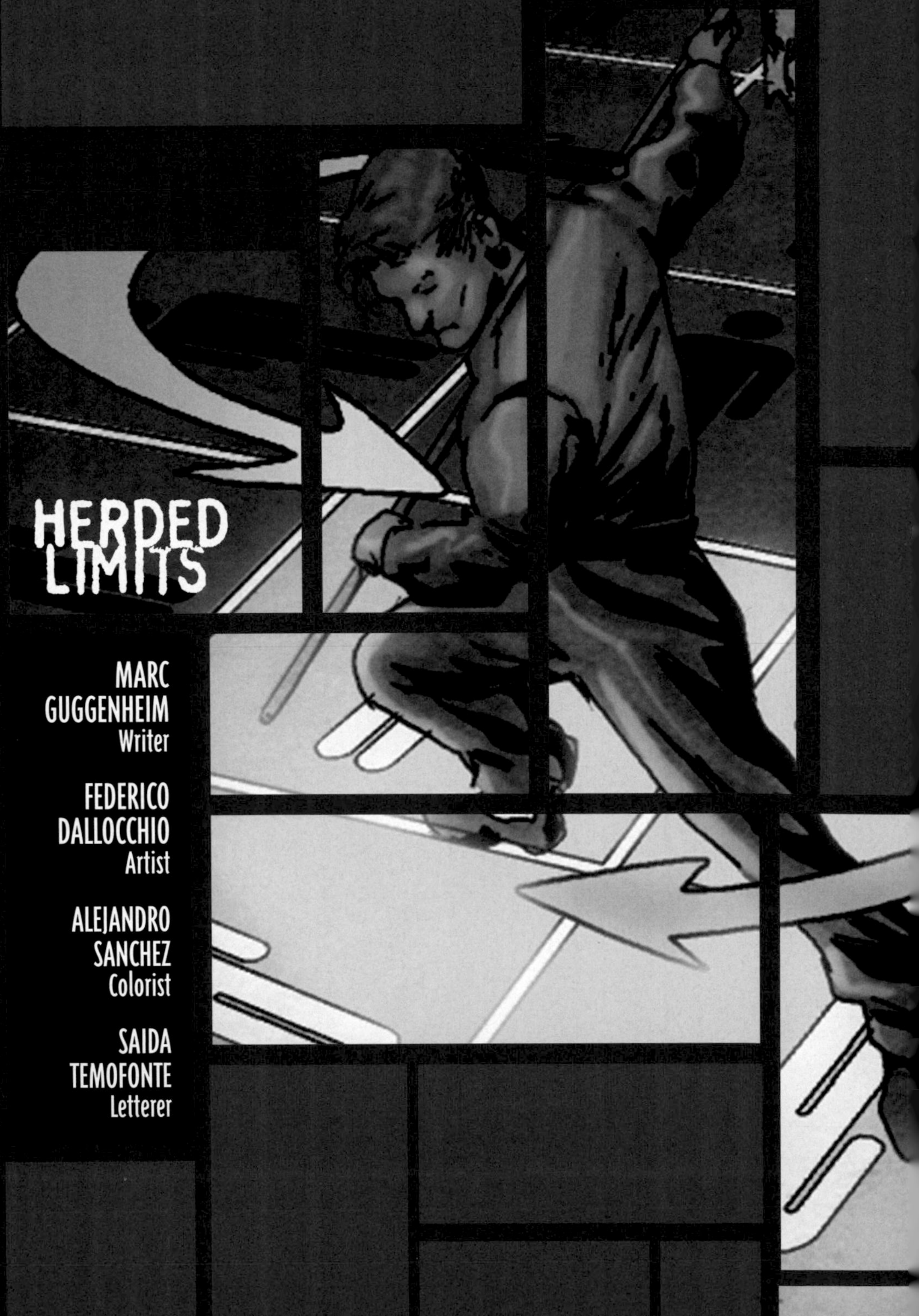

MARC GUGGENHEIM
Writer

FEDERICO DALLOCCHIO
Artist

ALEJANDRO SANCHEZ
Colorist

SAIDA TEMOFONTE
Letterer

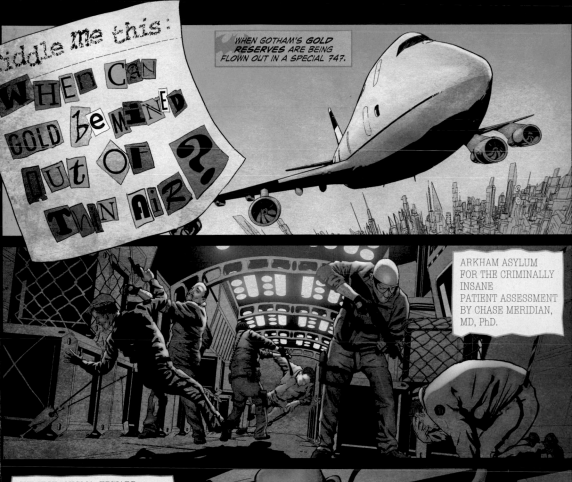

Riddle me this:

WHEN CAN GOLD BE MINED OUT OF THIN AIR?

WHEN GOTHAM'S *GOLD RESERVES* ARE BEING FLOWN OUT IN A SPECIAL 747.

ARKHAM ASYLUM FOR THE CRIMINALLY INSANE
PATIENT ASSESSMENT BY CHASE MERIDIAN, MD, PhD.

SUBJECT: NIGMA, EDWARD
*** SOME PORTIONS REDACTED ***

The DSM-IV defines Obsessive Compulsive Disorder (OCD) in relevant part as "repetitive behaviors ... that the person feels driven to perform in response to an obsession, or according to rules that must be applied rigidly."

In the case of the subject, Edward Nigma, this repetitive behavior is limited to a drive to inform law enforcement of crimes he intends to commit.

...certain vigilante elements.

Note that I'm referring here to "law enforcement" to include not just the GCPD, but also...

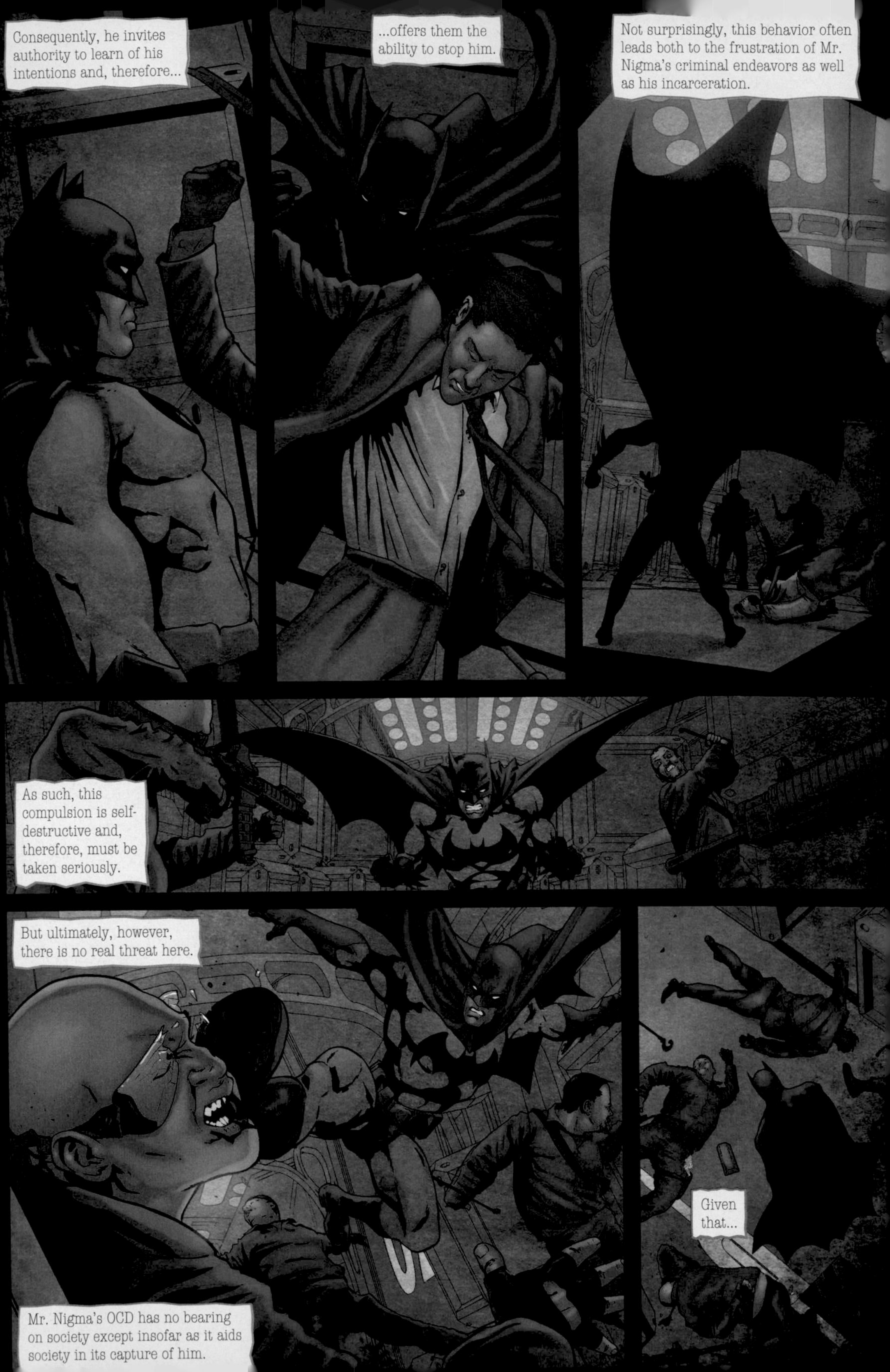
Consequently, he invites authority to learn of his intentions and, therefore...
...offers them the ability to stop him.
Not surprisingly, this behavior often leads both to the frustration of Mr. Nigma's criminal endeavors as well as his incarceration.
As such, this compulsion is self-destructive and, therefore, must be taken seriously.
But ultimately, however, there is no real threat here.
Mr. Nigma's OCD has no bearing on society except insofar as it aids society in its capture of him.
Given that...

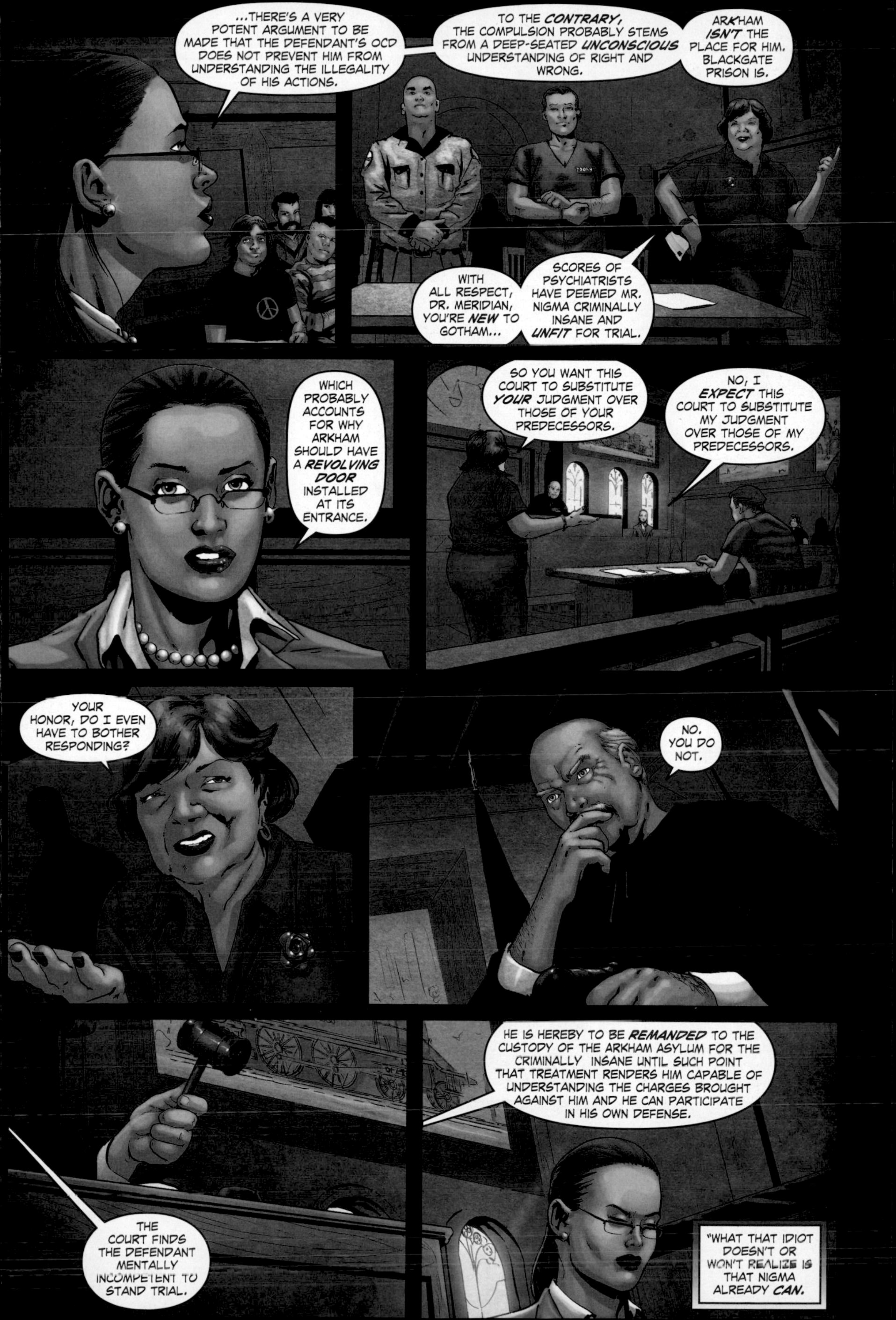

...THERE'S A VERY POTENT ARGUMENT TO BE MADE THAT THE DEFENDANT'S OCD DOES NOT PREVENT HIM FROM UNDERSTANDING THE ILLEGALITY OF HIS ACTIONS.
TO THE CONTRARY, THE COMPULSION PROBABLY STEMS FROM A DEEP-SEATED UNCONSCIOUS UNDERSTANDING OF RIGHT AND WRONG.
ARKHAM ISN'T THE PLACE FOR HIM. BLACKGATE PRISON IS.
WITH ALL RESPECT, DR. MERIDIAN, YOU'RE NEW TO GOTHAM...
SCORES OF PSYCHIATRISTS HAVE DEEMED MR. NIGMA CRIMINALLY INSANE AND UNFIT FOR TRIAL.
WHICH PROBABLY ACCOUNTS FOR WHY ARKHAM SHOULD HAVE A REVOLVING DOOR INSTALLED AT ITS ENTRANCE.
SO YOU WANT THIS COURT TO SUBSTITUTE YOUR JUDGMENT OVER THOSE OF YOUR PREDECESSORS.
NO, I EXPECT THIS COURT TO SUBSTITUTE MY JUDGMENT OVER THOSE OF MY PREDECESSORS.
YOUR HONOR, DO I EVEN HAVE TO BOTHER RESPONDING?
NO. YOU DO NOT.
THE COURT FINDS THE DEFENDANT MENTALLY INCOMPETENT TO STAND TRIAL.
HE IS HEREBY TO BE REMANDED TO THE CUSTODY OF THE ARKHAM ASYLUM FOR THE CRIMINALLY INSANE UNTIL SUCH POINT THAT TREATMENT RENDERS HIM CAPABLE OF UNDERSTANDING THE CHARGES BROUGHT AGAINST HIM AND HE CAN PARTICIPATE IN HIS OWN DEFENSE.
"WHAT THAT IDIOT DOESN'T OR WON'T REALIZE IS THAT NIGMA ALREADY CAN.

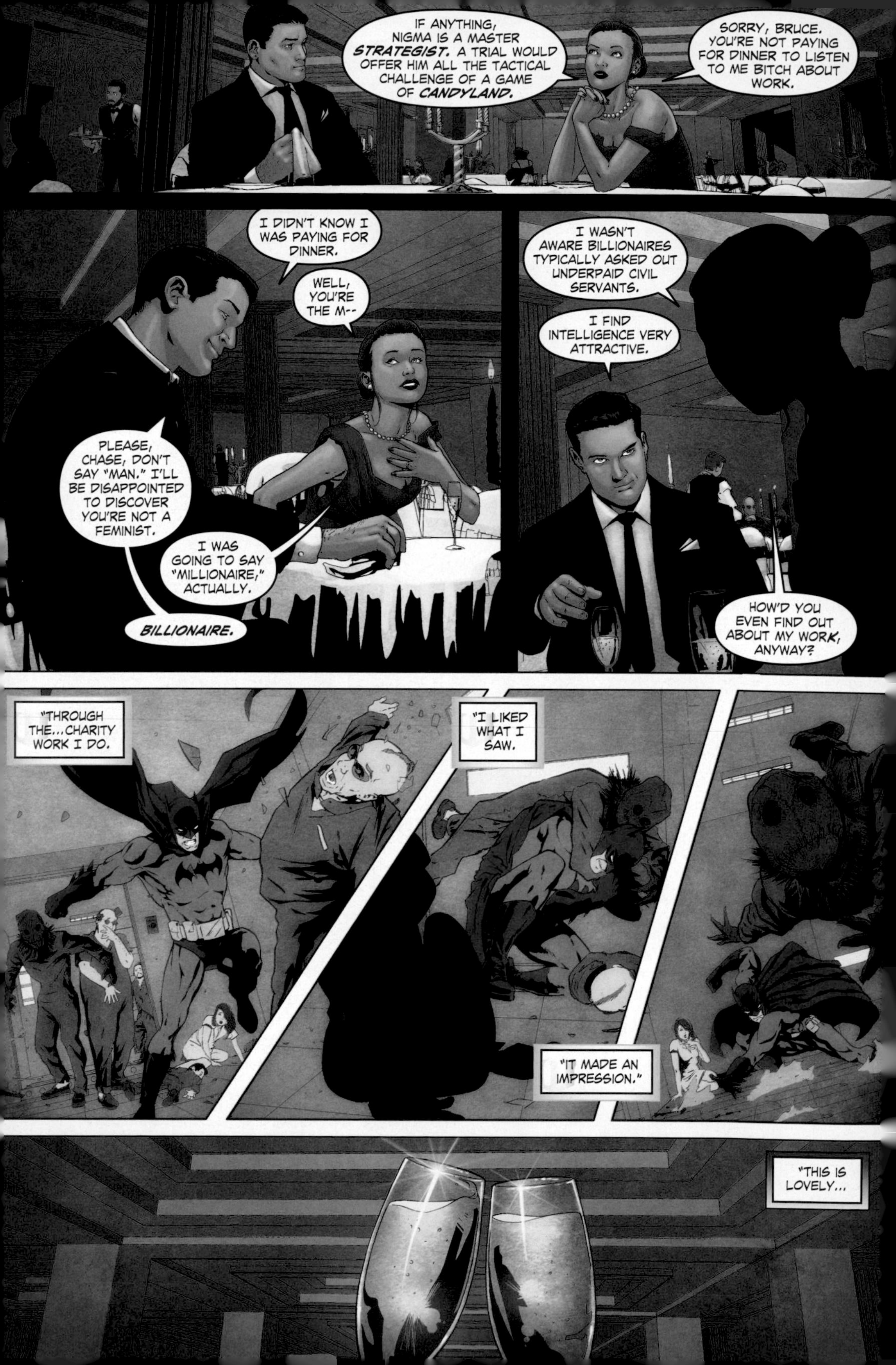
IF ANYTHING, NIGMA IS A MASTER STRATEGIST. A TRIAL WOULD OFFER HIM ALL THE TACTICAL CHALLENGE OF A GAME OF CANDYLAND.
SORRY, BRUCE. YOU'RE NOT PAYING FOR DINNER TO LISTEN TO ME BITCH ABOUT WORK.
I DIDN'T KNOW I WAS PAYING FOR DINNER.
WELL, YOU'RE THE M--
PLEASE, CHASE, DON'T SAY "MAN." I'LL BE DISAPPOINTED TO DISCOVER YOU'RE NOT A FEMINIST.
I WAS GOING TO SAY "MILLIONAIRE," ACTUALLY.
BILLIONAIRE.
I WASN'T AWARE BILLIONAIRES TYPICALLY ASKED OUT UNDERPAID CIVIL SERVANTS.
I FIND INTELLIGENCE VERY ATTRACTIVE.
HOW'D YOU EVEN FIND OUT ABOUT MY WORK, ANYWAY?
"THROUGH THE...CHARITY WORK I DO.
"I LIKED WHAT I SAW.
"IT MADE AN IMPRESSION."
"THIS IS LOVELY...

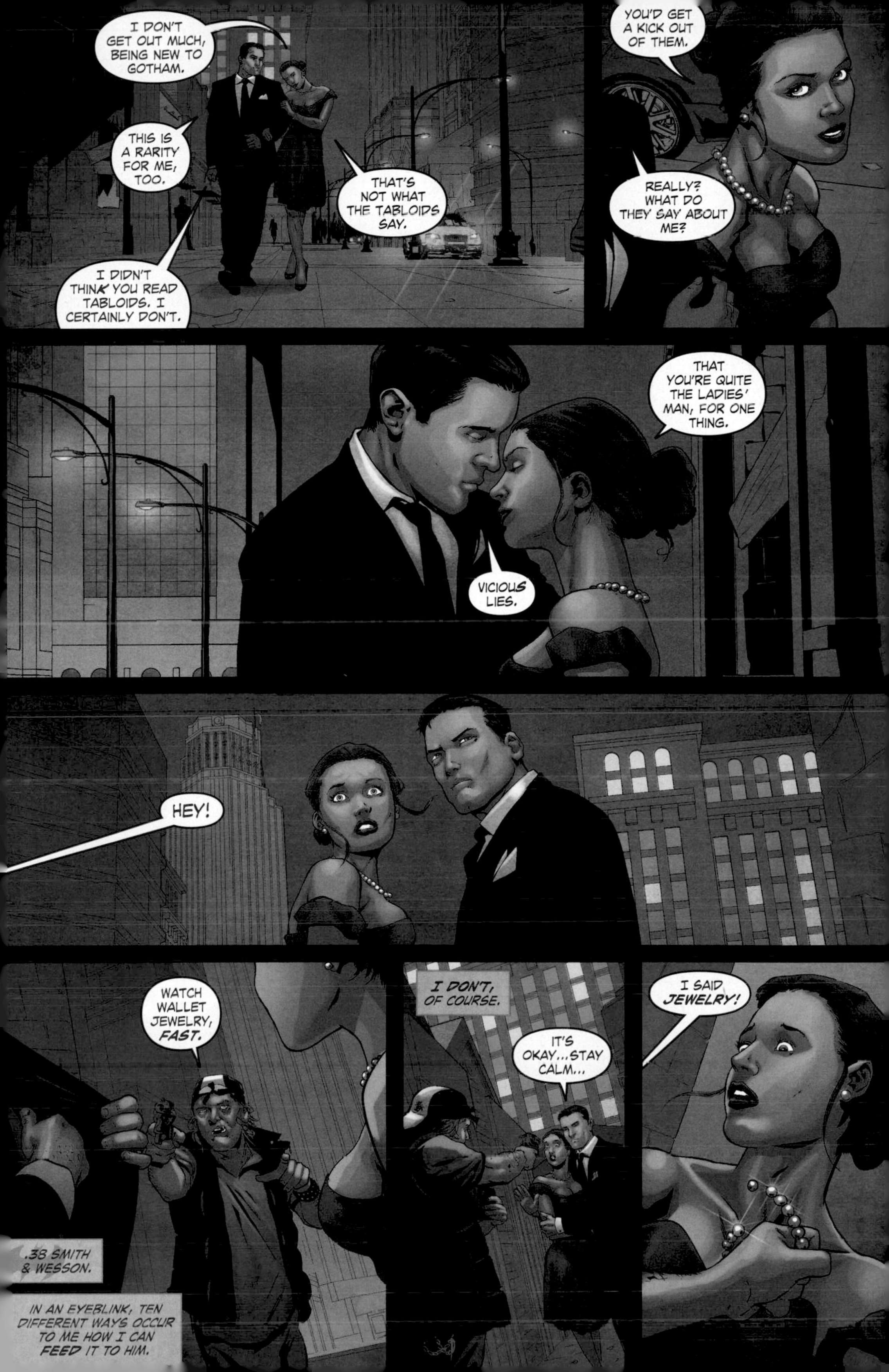
I DON'T GET OUT MUCH, BEING NEW TO GOTHAM.
THIS IS A RARITY FOR ME, TOO.
THAT'S NOT WHAT THE TABLOIDS SAY.
I DIDN'T THINK YOU READ TABLOIDS. I CERTAINLY DON'T.
YOU'D GET A KICK OUT OF THEM.
REALLY? WHAT DO THEY SAY ABOUT ME?
THAT YOU'RE QUITE THE LADIES' MAN, FOR ONE THING.
VICIOUS LIES.
HEY!
WATCH WALLET JEWELRY, FAST.
.38 SMITH & WESSON.
IN AN EYEBLINK, TEN DIFFERENT WAYS OCCUR TO ME HOW I CAN FEED IT TO HIM.
I DON'T, OF COURSE.
IT'S OKAY...STAY CALM...
I SAID JEWELRY!

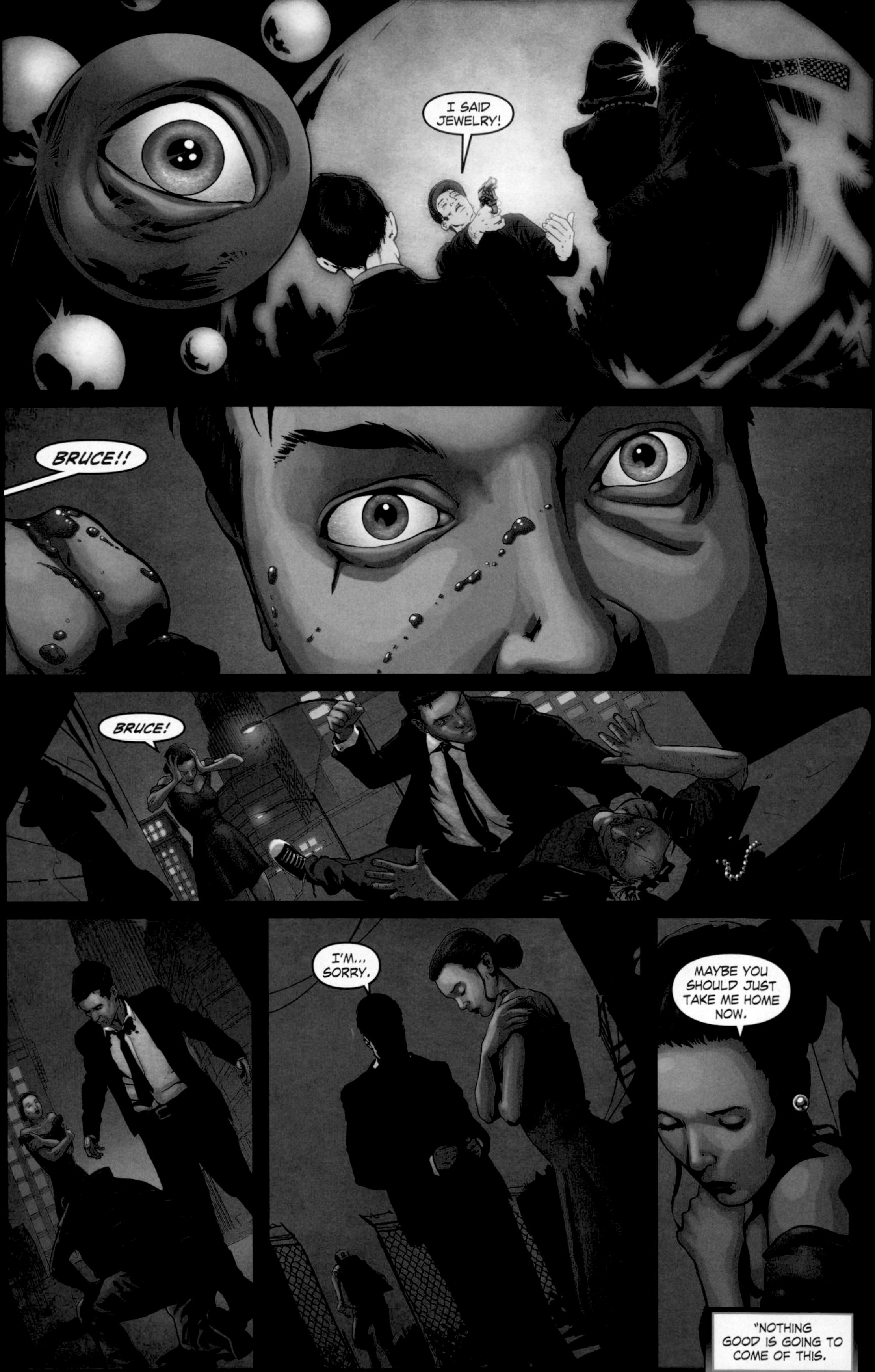
I SAID JEWELRY!
BRUCE!!
BRUCE!
I'M... SORRY.
MAYBE YOU SHOULD JUST TAKE ME HOME NOW.
"NOTHING GOOD IS GOING TO COME OF THIS.

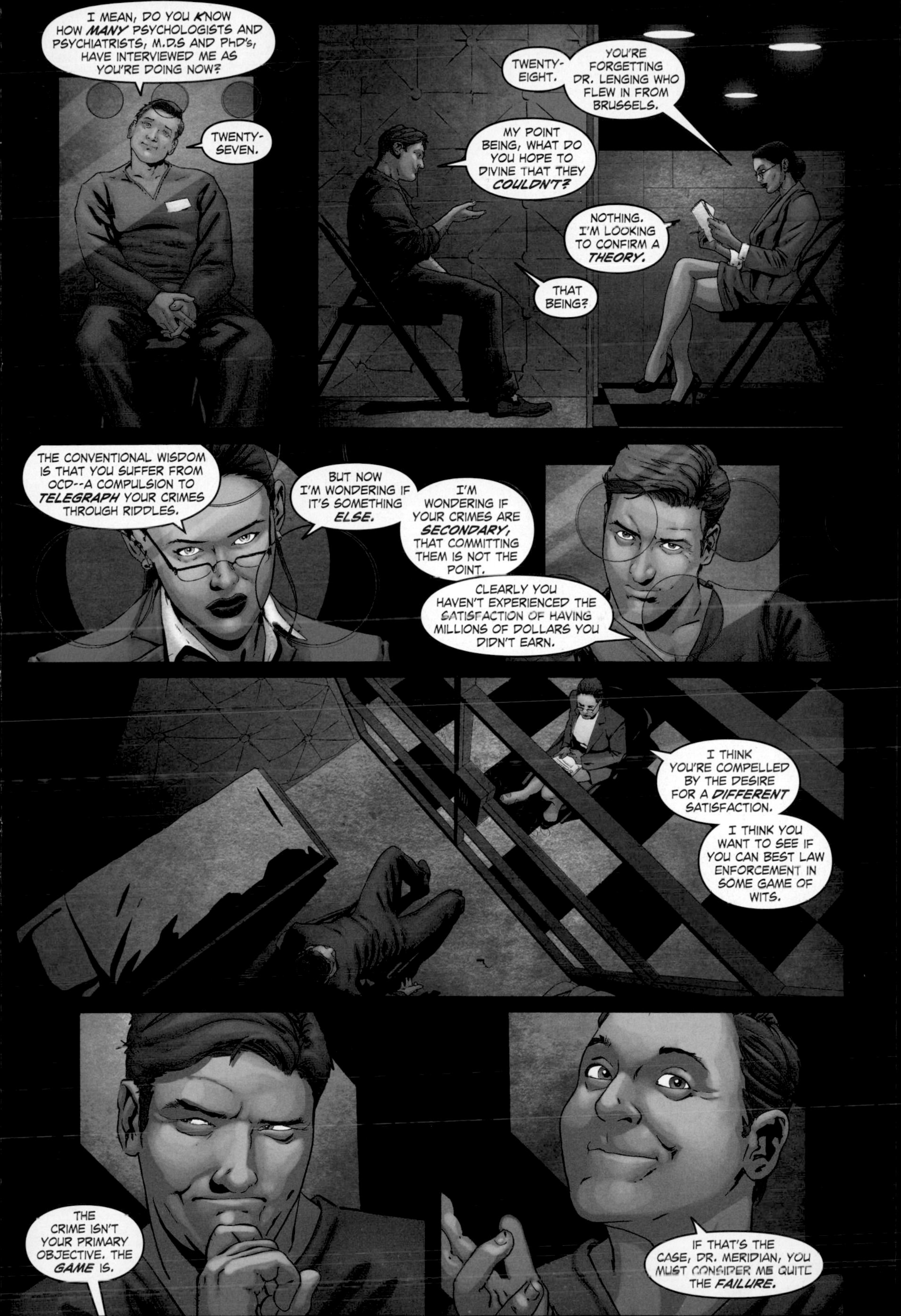
I MEAN, DO YOU KNOW HOW MANY PSYCHOLOGISTS AND PSYCHIATRISTS, M.D.S AND PhD's, HAVE INTERVIEWED ME AS YOU'RE DOING NOW?
TWENTY-SEVEN.
TWENTY-EIGHT.
YOU'RE FORGETTING DR. LENGING WHO FLEW IN FROM BRUSSELS.
MY POINT BEING, WHAT DO YOU HOPE TO DIVINE THAT THEY COULDN'T?
NOTHING. I'M LOOKING TO CONFIRM A THEORY.
THAT BEING?
THE CONVENTIONAL WISDOM IS THAT YOU SUFFER FROM OCD--A COMPULSION TO TELEGRAPH YOUR CRIMES THROUGH RIDDLES.
BUT NOW I'M WONDERING IF IT'S SOMETHING ELSE.
I'M WONDERING IF YOUR CRIMES ARE SECONDARY, THAT COMMITTING THEM IS NOT THE POINT.
CLEARLY YOU HAVEN'T EXPERIENCED THE SATISFACTION OF HAVING MILLIONS OF DOLLARS YOU DIDN'T EARN.
I THINK YOU'RE COMPELLED BY THE DESIRE FOR A DIFFERENT SATISFACTION.
I THINK YOU WANT TO SEE IF YOU CAN BEST LAW ENFORCEMENT IN SOME GAME OF WITS.
THE CRIME ISN'T YOUR PRIMARY OBJECTIVE. THE GAME IS.
IF THAT'S THE CASE, DR. MERIDIAN, YOU MUST CONSIDER ME QUITE THE FAILURE.

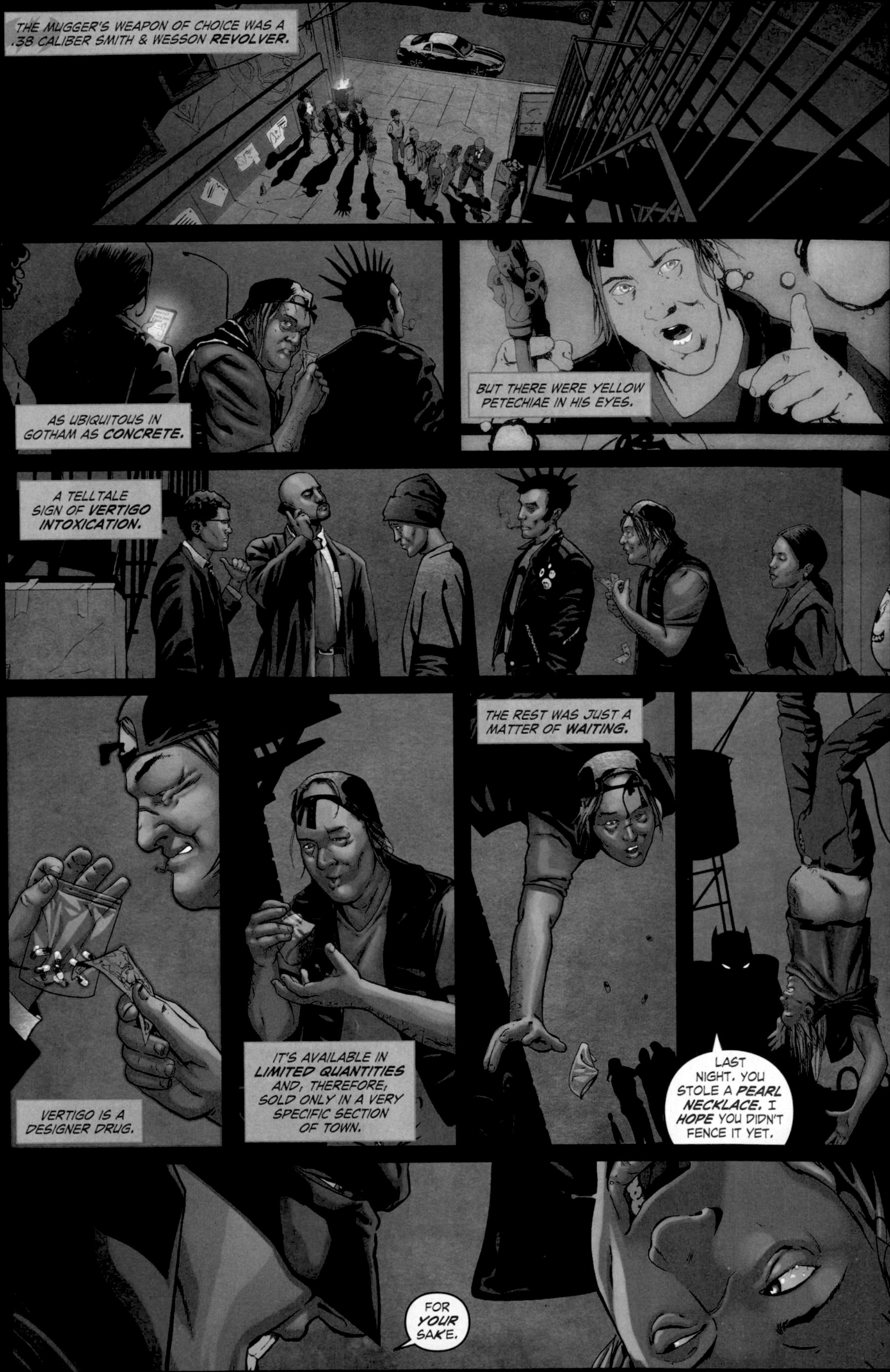
THE MUGGER'S WEAPON OF CHOICE WAS A .38 CALIBER SMITH & WESSON REVOLVER.
AS UBIQUITOUS IN GOTHAM AS CONCRETE.
BUT THERE WERE YELLOW PETECHIAE IN HIS EYES.
A TELLTALE SIGN OF VERTIGO INTOXICATION.
VERTIGO IS A DESIGNER DRUG.
IT'S AVAILABLE IN LIMITED QUANTITIES AND, THEREFORE, SOLD ONLY IN A VERY SPECIFIC SECTION OF TOWN.
THE REST WAS JUST A MATTER OF WAITING.
LAST NIGHT, YOU STOLE A PEARL NECKLACE. I HOPE YOU DIDN'T FENCE IT YET.
FOR YOUR SAKE.

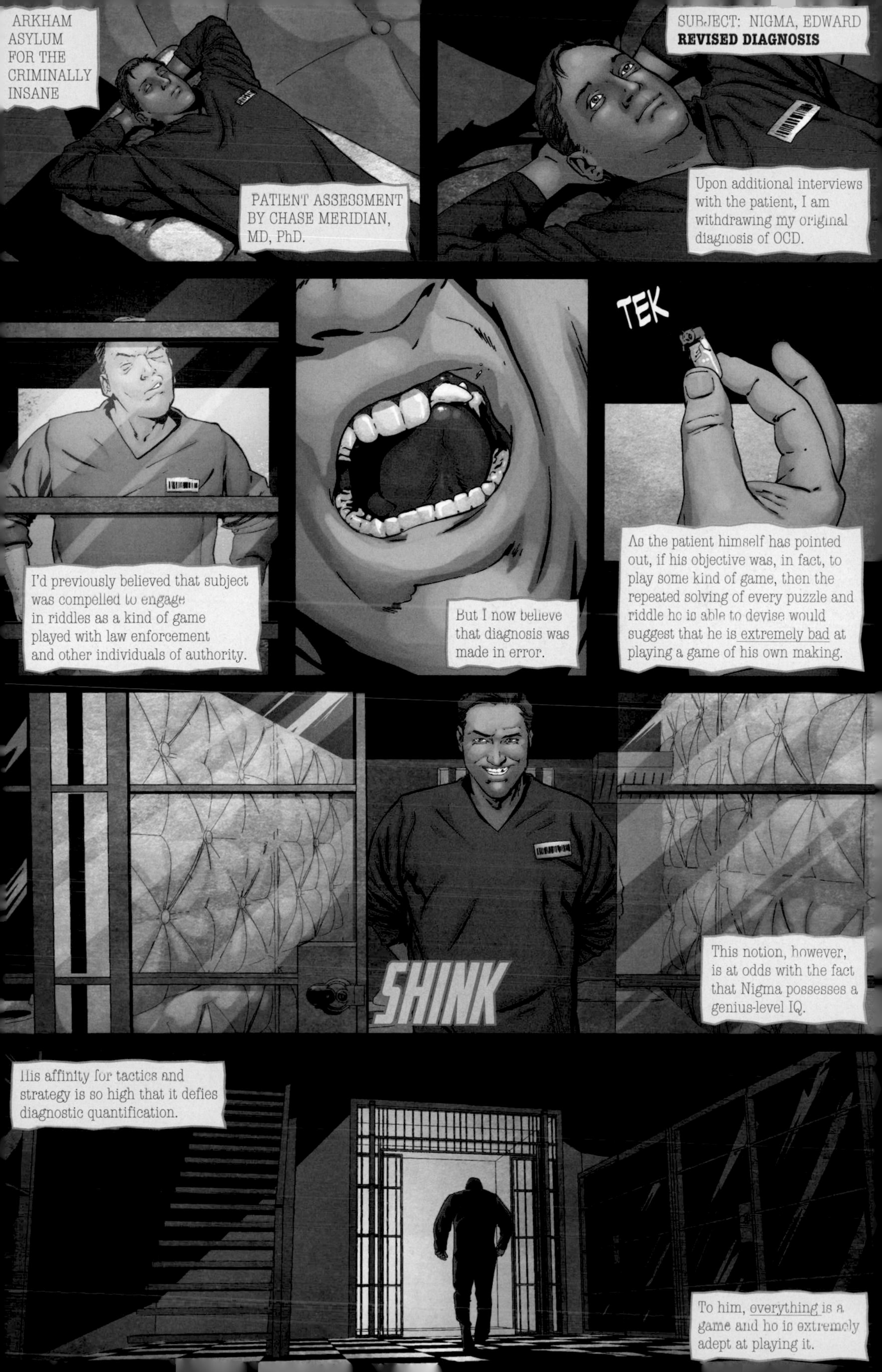
ARKHAM ASYLUM FOR THE CRIMINALLY INSANE
PATIENT ASSESSMENT BY CHASE MERIDIAN, MD, PhD.
SUBJECT: NIGMA, EDWARD
REVISED DIAGNOSIS
Upon additional interviews with the patient, I am withdrawing my original diagnosis of OCD.
I'd previously believed that subject was compelled to engage in riddles as a kind of game played with law enforcement and other individuals of authority.
But I now believe that diagnosis was made in error.
TEK
As the patient himself has pointed out, if his objective was, in fact, to play some kind of game, then the repeated solving of every puzzle and riddle he is able to devise would suggest that he is extremely bad at playing a game of his own making.
SHINK
This notion, however, is at odds with the fact that Nigma possesses a genius-level IQ.
His affinity for tactics and strategy is so high that it defies diagnostic quantification.
To him, everything is a game and he is extremely adept at playing it.

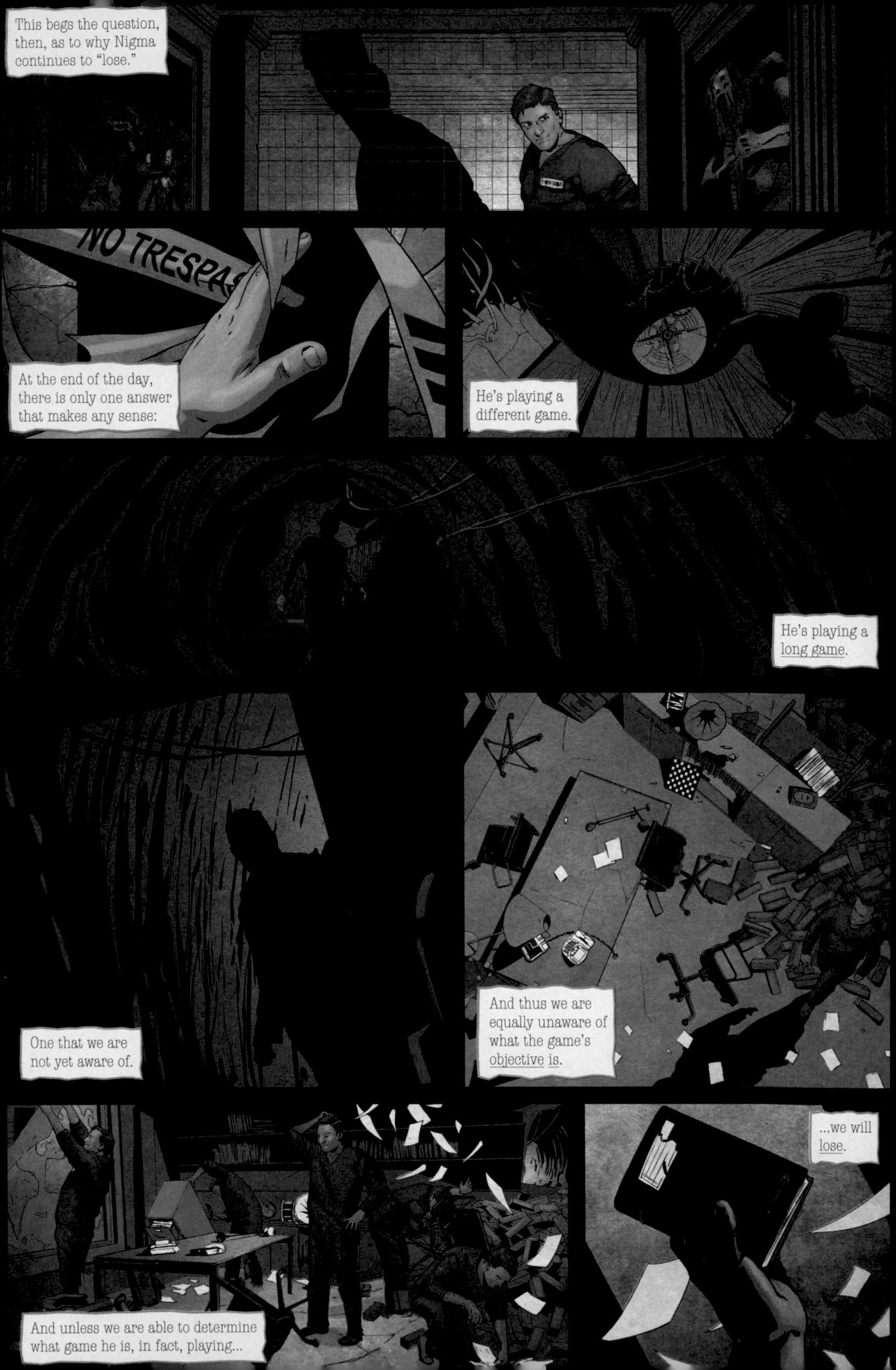

This begs the question, then, as to why Nigma continues to "lose."
NO TRESPAS
At the end of the day, there is only one answer that makes any sense:
He's playing a different game.
He's playing a long game.
One that we are not yet aware of.
And thus we are equally unaware of what the game's objective is.
And unless we are able to determine what game he is, in fact, playing...
...we will lose.

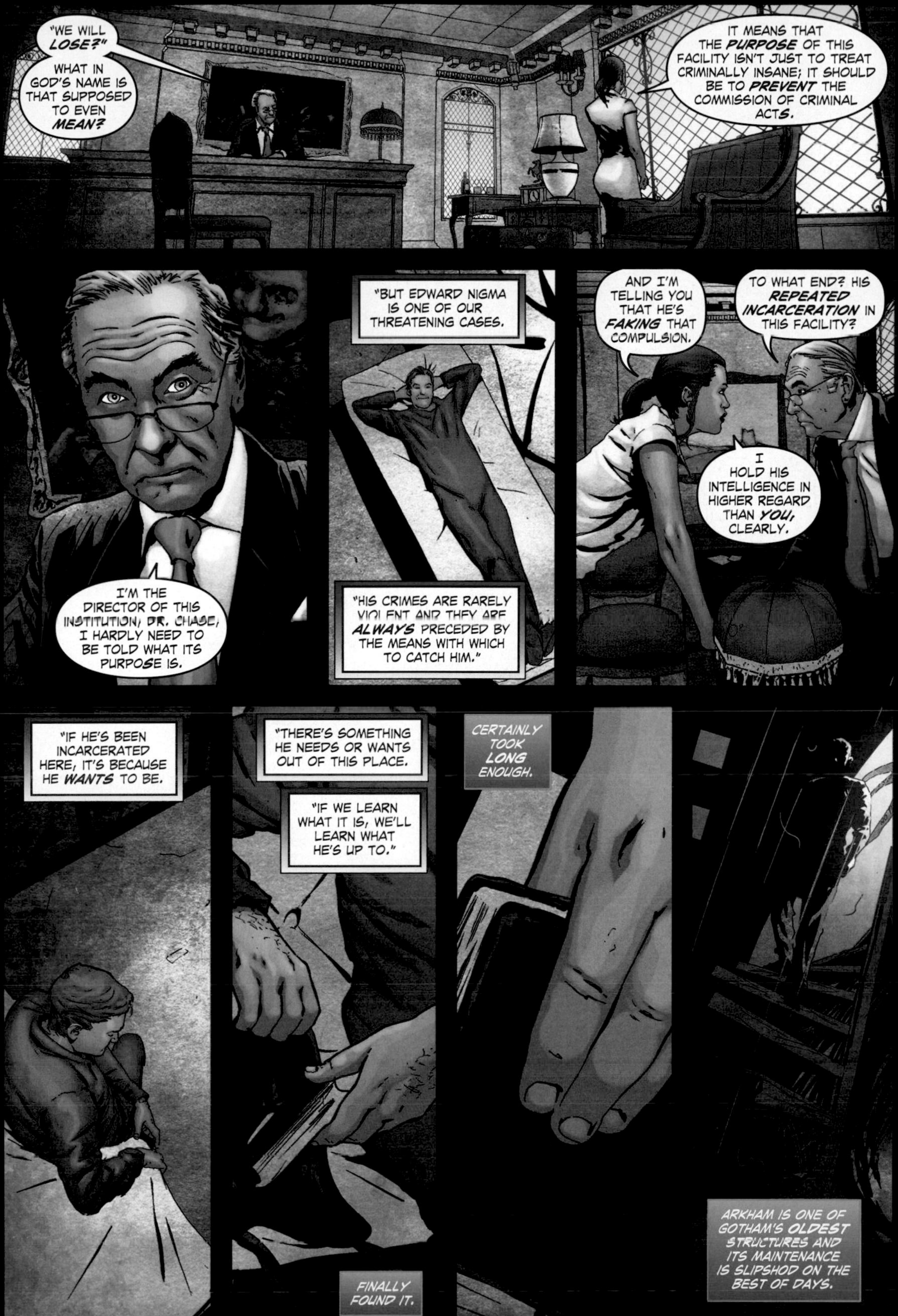
"WE WILL LOSE?" WHAT IN GOD'S NAME IS THAT SUPPOSED TO EVEN MEAN?
IT MEANS THAT THE PURPOSE OF THIS FACILITY ISN'T JUST TO TREAT CRIMINALLY INSANE; IT SHOULD BE TO PREVENT THE COMMISSION OF CRIMINAL ACTS.
I'M THE DIRECTOR OF THIS INSTITUTION, DR. CHASE, I HARDLY NEED TO BE TOLD WHAT ITS PURPOSE IS.
"BUT EDWARD NIGMA IS ONE OF OUR THREATENING CASES.
"HIS CRIMES ARE RARELY VIOLENT AND THEY ARE ALWAYS PRECEDED BY THE MEANS WITH WHICH TO CATCH HIM."
AND I'M TELLING YOU THAT HE'S FAKING THAT COMPULSION.
TO WHAT END? HIS REPEATED INCARCERATION IN THIS FACILITY?
I HOLD HIS INTELLIGENCE IN HIGHER REGARD THAN YOU, CLEARLY.
"IF HE'S BEEN INCARCERATED HERE, IT'S BECAUSE HE WANTS TO BE.
"THERE'S SOMETHING HE NEEDS OR WANTS OUT OF THIS PLACE.
"IF WE LEARN WHAT IT IS, WE'LL LEARN WHAT HE'S UP TO."
FINALLY FOUND IT.
CERTAINLY TOOK LONG ENOUGH.
ARKHAM IS ONE OF GOTHAM'S OLDEST STRUCTURES AND ITS MAINTENANCE IS SLIPSHOD ON THE BEST OF DAYS.
BUT I FOUND IT.

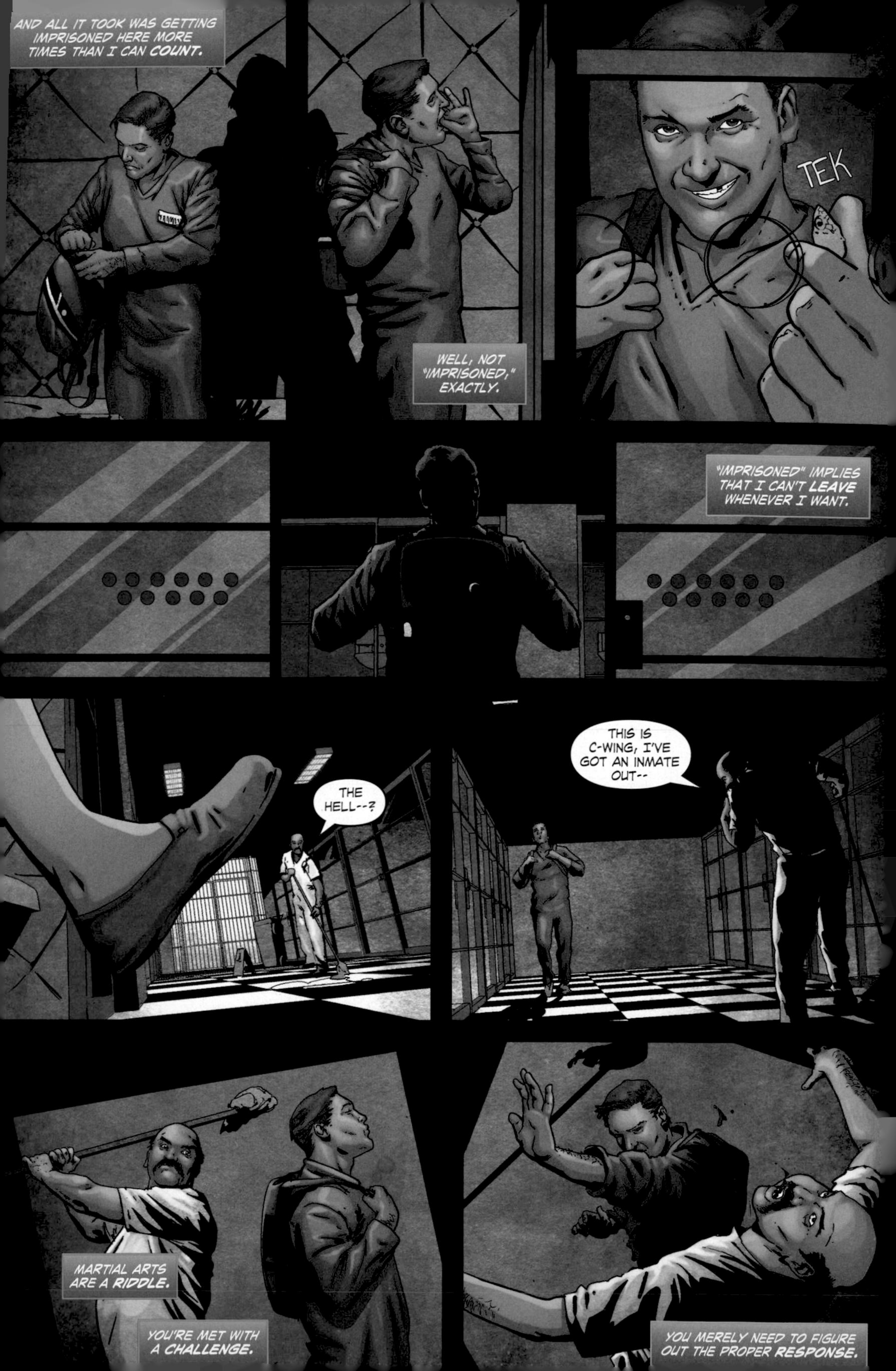

AND ALL IT TOOK WAS GETTING IMPRISONED HERE MORE TIMES THAN I CAN COUNT.
WELL, NOT "IMPRISONED," EXACTLY.
TEK
"IMPRISONED" IMPLIES THAT I CAN'T LEAVE WHENEVER I WANT.
THE HELL--?
THIS IS C-WING, I'VE GOT AN INMATE OUT--
MARTIAL ARTS ARE A RIDDLE.
YOU'RE MET WITH A CHALLENGE.
YOU MERELY NEED TO FIGURE OUT THE PROPER RESPONSE.

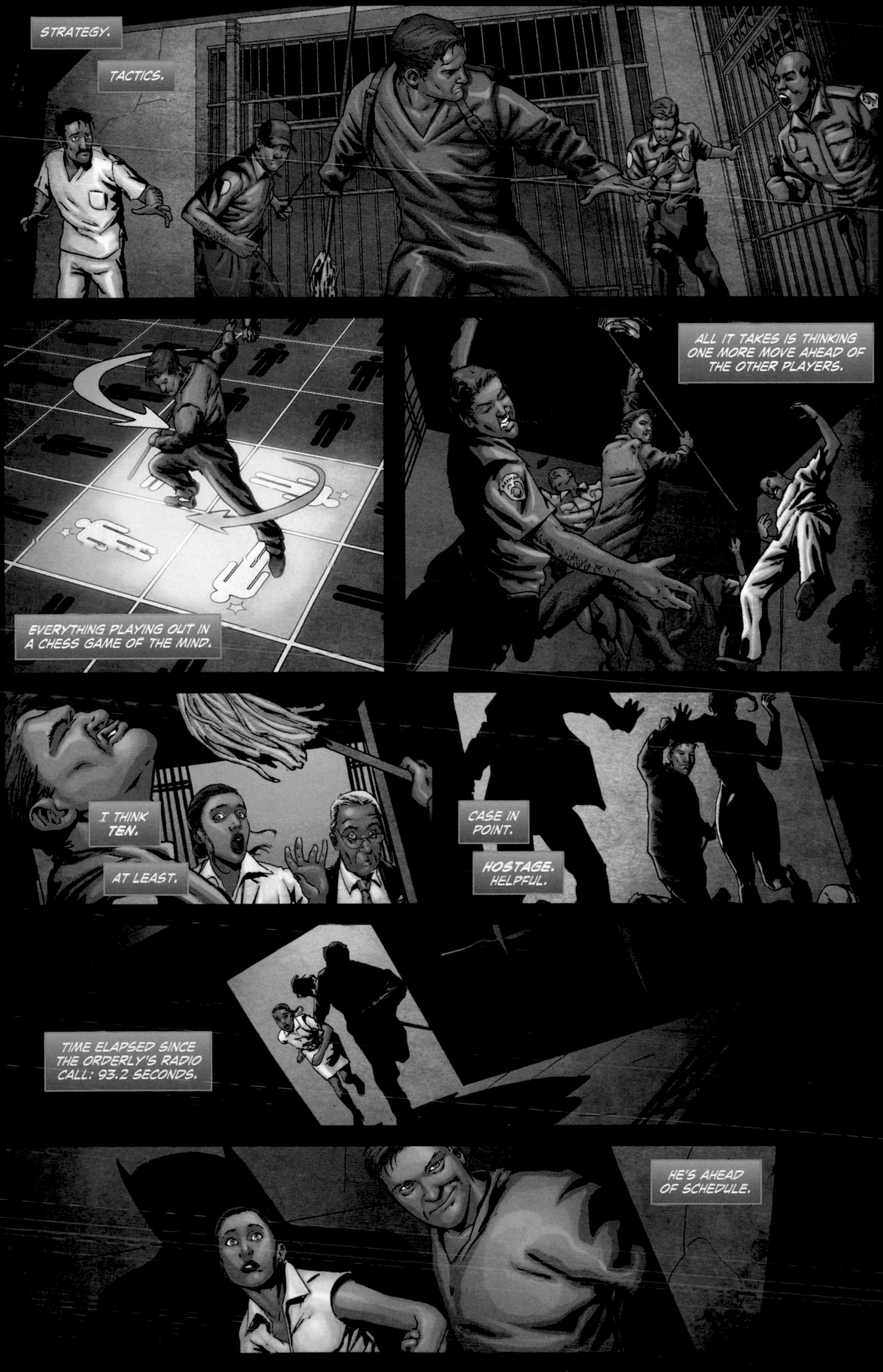
STRATEGY.
TACTICS.
EVERYTHING PLAYING OUT IN A CHESS GAME OF THE MIND.
ALL IT TAKES IS THINKING ONE MORE MOVE AHEAD OF THE OTHER PLAYERS.
I THINK TEN.
AT LEAST.
CASE IN POINT.
HOSTAGE. HELPFUL.
TIME ELAPSED SINCE THE ORDERLY'S RADIO CALL: 93.2 SECONDS.
HE'S AHEAD OF SCHEDULE.

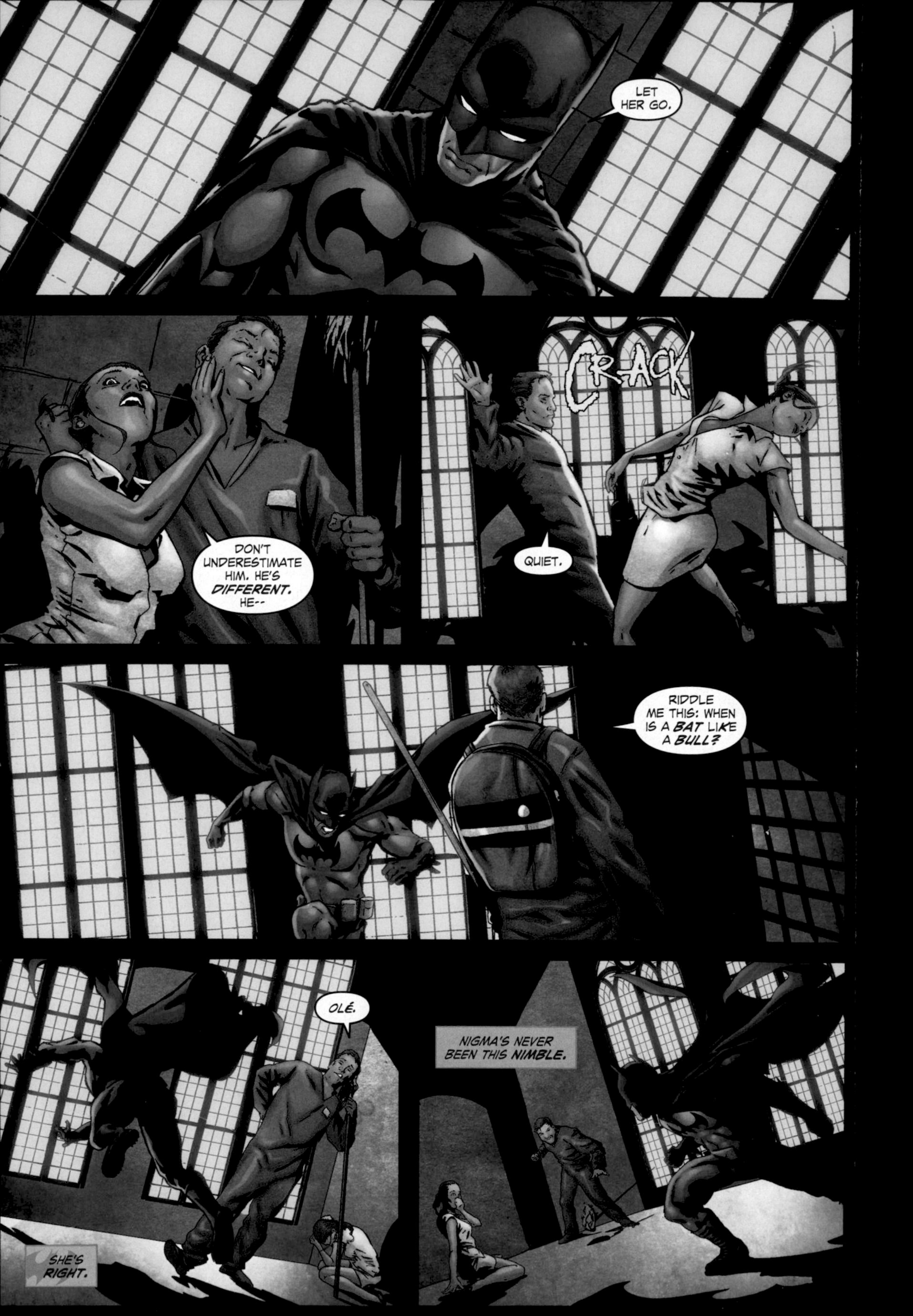
LET HER GO.
DON'T UNDERESTIMATE HIM. HE'S *DIFFERENT.* HE--
CRACK!
QUIET.
RIDDLE ME THIS: WHEN IS A *BAT* LIKE A *BULL?*
OLÉ.
SHE'S RIGHT.
NIGMA'S NEVER BEEN THIS NIMBLE.

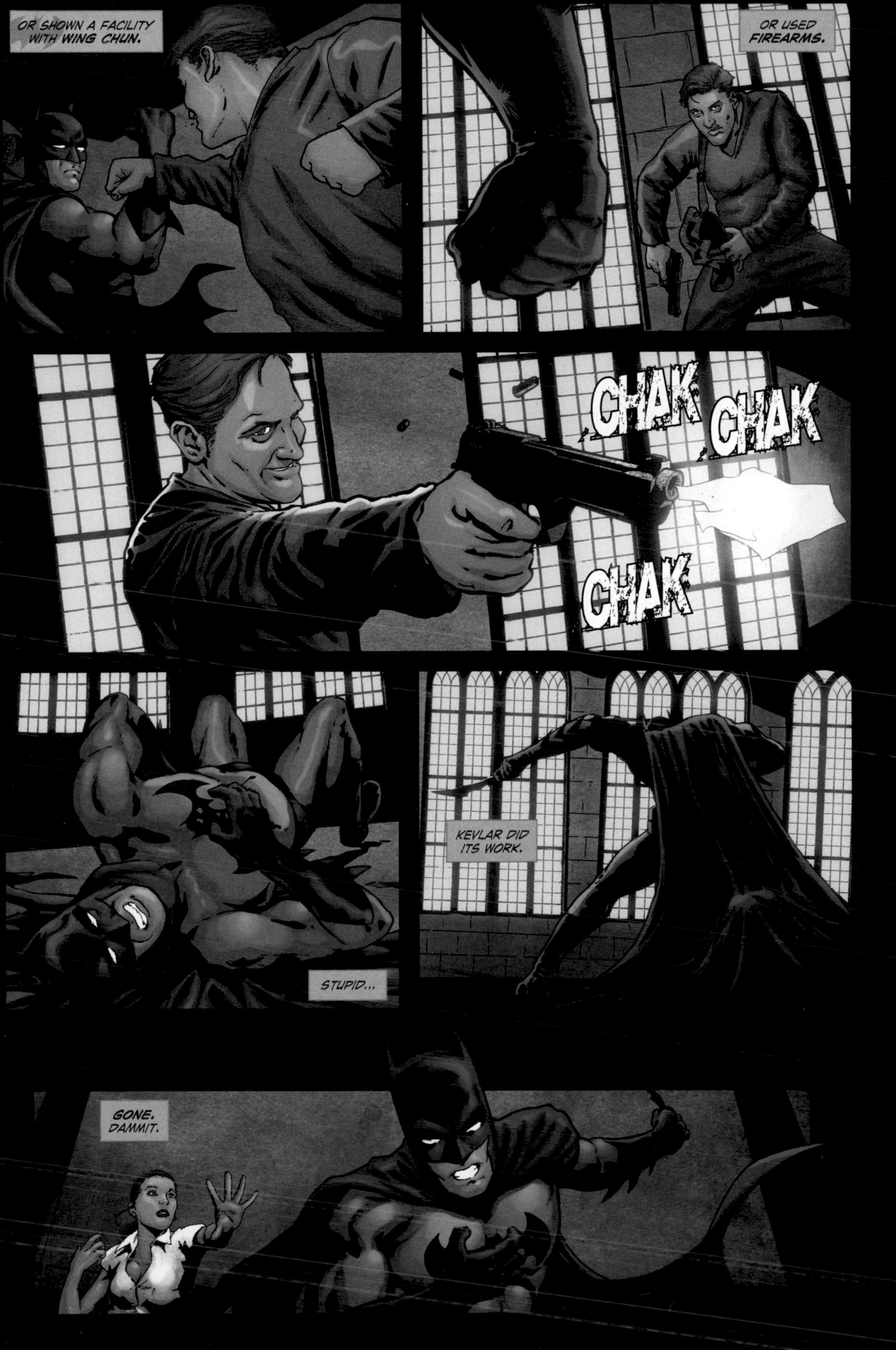
OR SHOWN A FACILITY WITH WING CHUN.
OR USED FIREARMS.
CHAK CHAK
CHAK
STUPID...
KEVLAR DID ITS WORK.
GONE. DAMMIT.

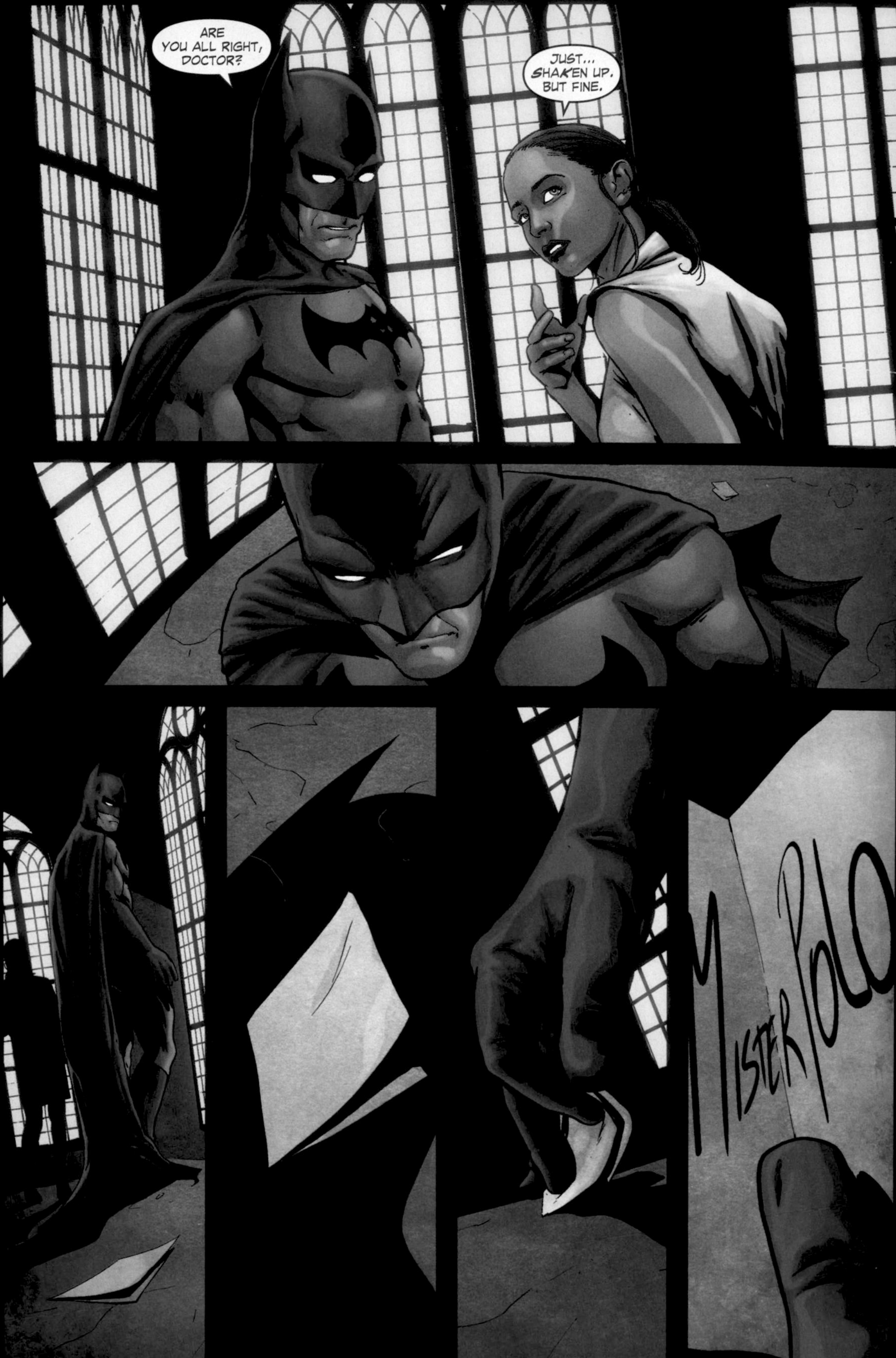
ARE YOU ALL RIGHT, DOCTOR?
JUST... SHAKEN UP. BUT FINE.
MISTER POLO

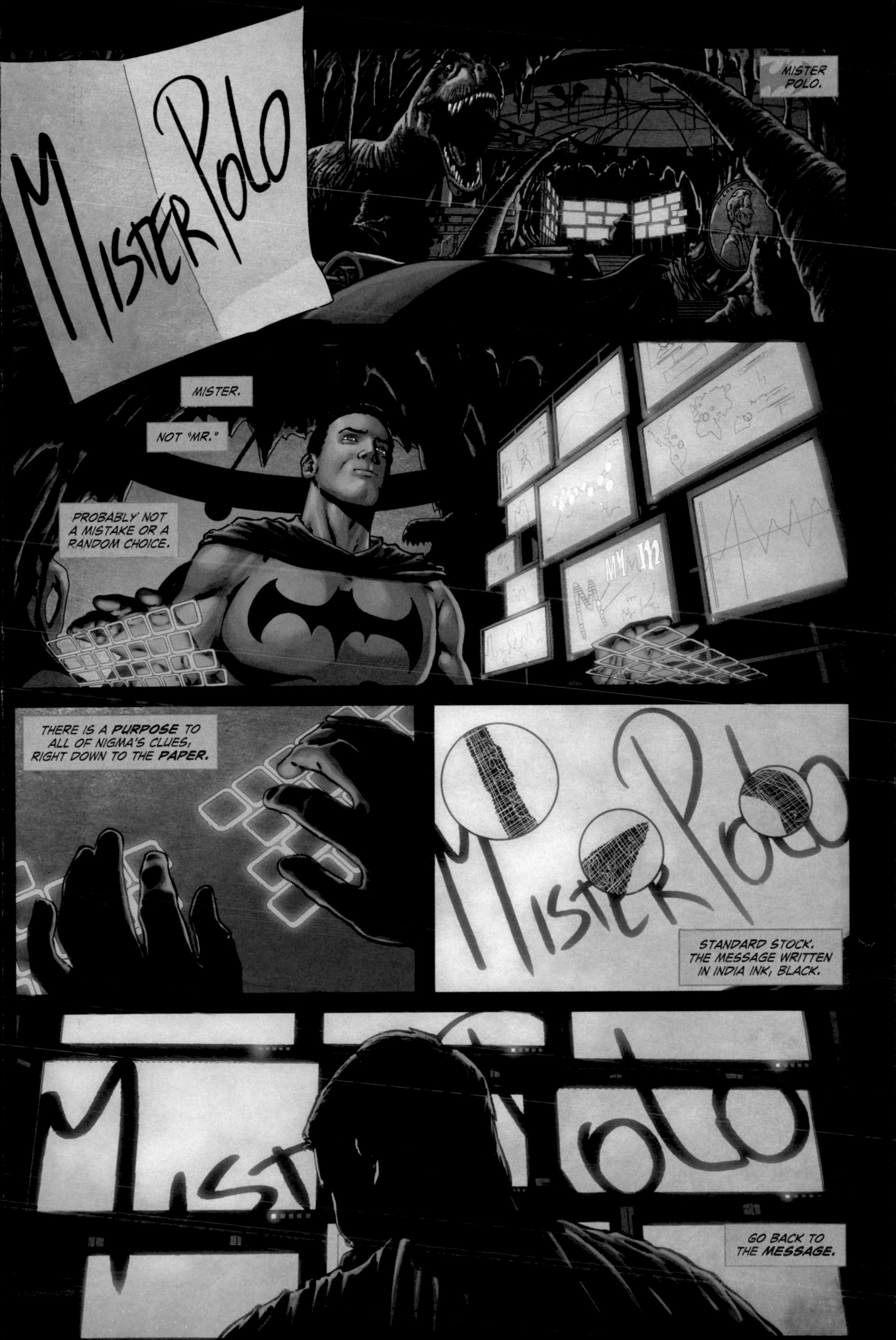
MISTER POLO
MISTER POLO.
MISTER.
NOT "MR."
PROBABLY NOT A MISTAKE OR A RANDOM CHOICE.
THERE IS A PURPOSE TO ALL OF NIGMA'S CLUES, RIGHT DOWN TO THE PAPER.
MISTER POLO
STANDARD STOCK. THE MESSAGE WRITTEN IN INDIA INK, BLACK.
GO BACK TO THE MESSAGE.

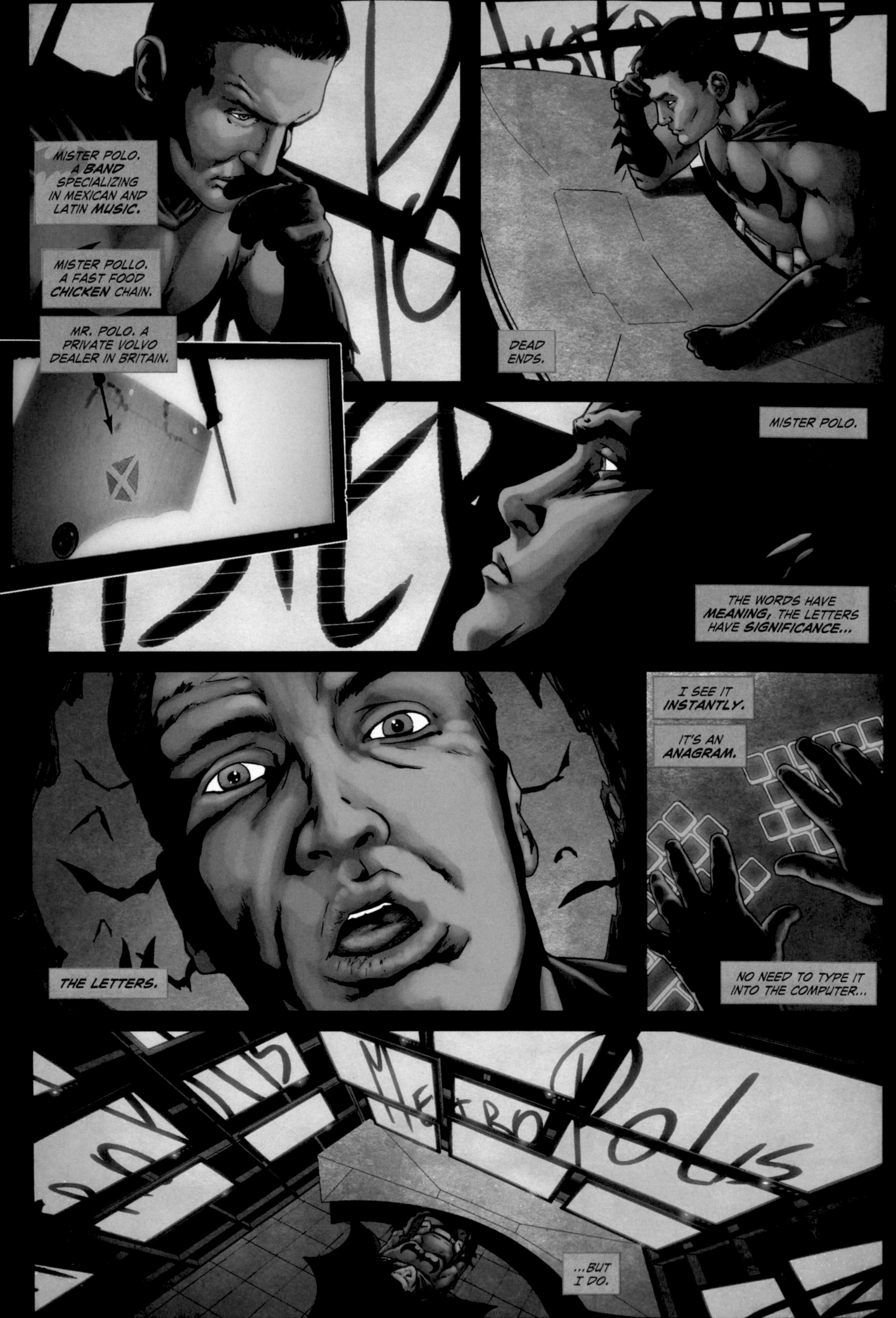

MISTER POLO. A BAND SPECIALIZING IN MEXICAN AND LATIN MUSIC.
MISTER POLLO. A FAST FOOD CHICKEN CHAIN.
MR. POLO. A PRIVATE VOLVO DEALER IN BRITAIN.
DEAD ENDS.
MISTER POLO.
THE WORDS HAVE MEANING, THE LETTERS HAVE SIGNIFICANCE...
THE LETTERS.
I SEE IT INSTANTLY.
IT'S AN ANAGRAM.
NO NEED TO TYPE IT INTO THE COMPUTER...
...BUT I DO.

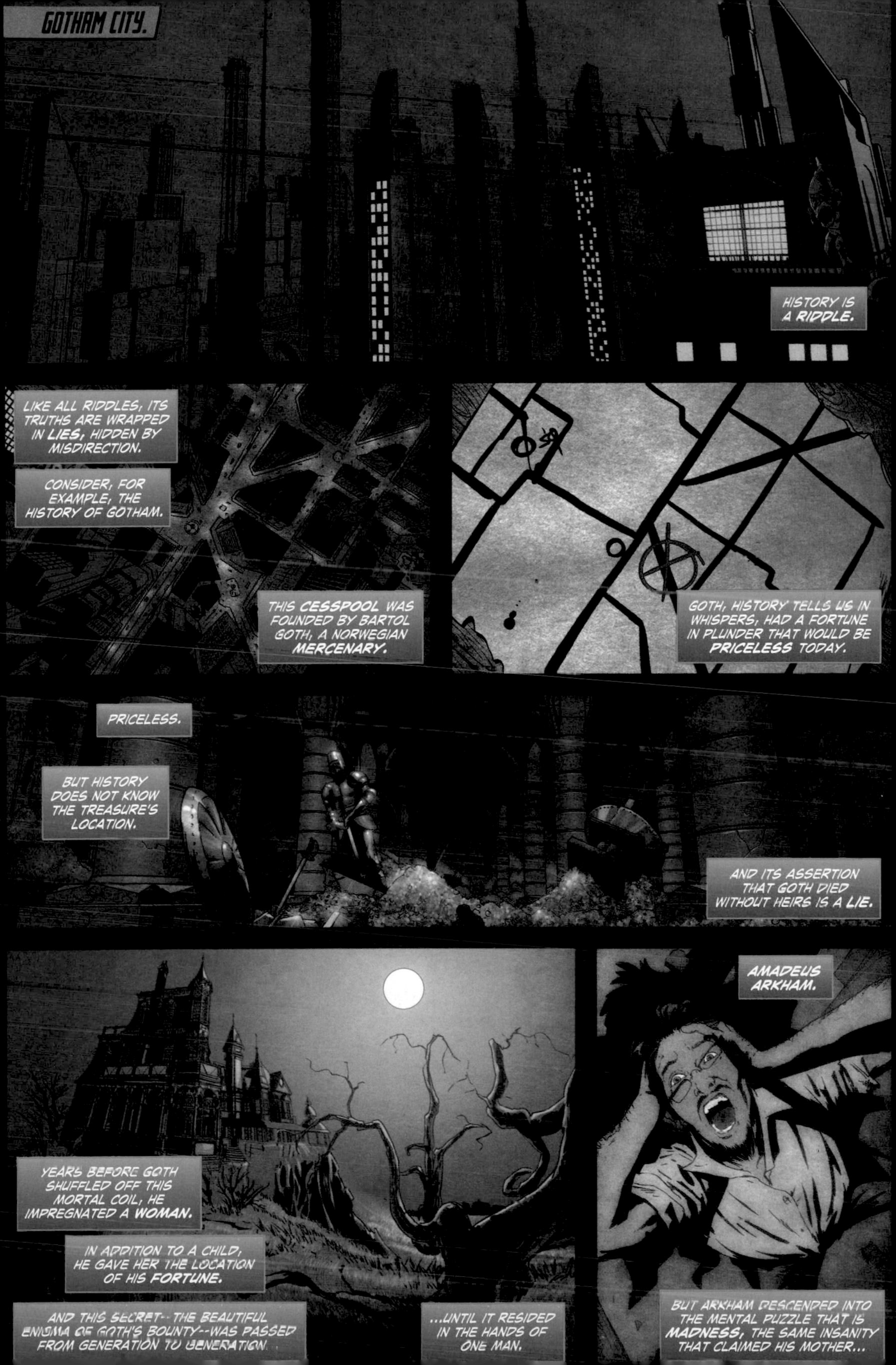
GOTHAM CITY.
HISTORY IS A RIDDLE.
LIKE ALL RIDDLES, ITS TRUTHS ARE WRAPPED IN LIES, HIDDEN BY MISDIRECTION.
CONSIDER, FOR EXAMPLE, THE HISTORY OF GOTHAM.
THIS CESSPOOL WAS FOUNDED BY BARTOL GOTH, A NORWEGIAN MERCENARY.
GOTH, HISTORY TELLS US IN WHISPERS, HAD A FORTUNE IN PLUNDER THAT WOULD BE PRICELESS TODAY.
PRICELESS.
BUT HISTORY DOES NOT KNOW THE TREASURE'S LOCATION.
AND ITS ASSERTION THAT GOTH DIED WITHOUT HEIRS IS A LIE.
YEARS BEFORE GOTH SHUFFLED OFF THIS MORTAL COIL, HE IMPREGNATED A WOMAN.
IN ADDITION TO A CHILD, HE GAVE HER THE LOCATION OF HIS FORTUNE.
AND THIS SECRET--THE BEAUTIFUL ENIGMA OF GOTH'S BOUNTY--WAS PASSED FROM GENERATION TO GENERATION...
...UNTIL IT RESIDED IN THE HANDS OF ONE MAN.
AMADEUS ARKHAM.
BUT ARKHAM DESCENDED INTO THE MENTAL PUZZLE THAT IS MADNESS, THE SAME INSANITY THAT CLAIMED HIS MOTHER...

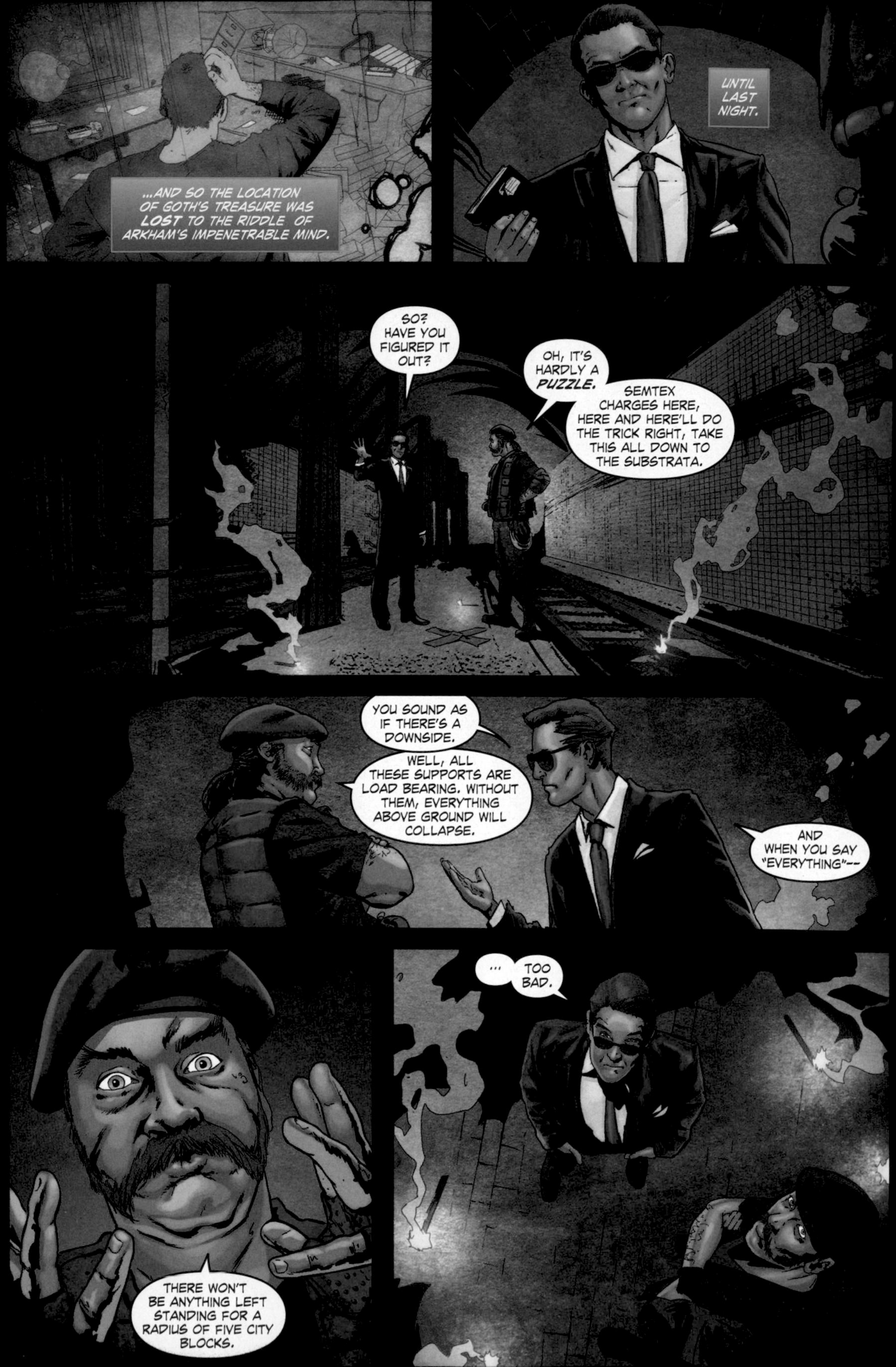
...AND SO THE LOCATION OF GOTH'S TREASURE WAS LOST TO THE RIDDLE OF ARKHAM'S IMPENETRABLE MIND.
UNTIL LAST NIGHT.
SO? HAVE YOU FIGURED IT OUT?
OH, IT'S HARDLY A PUZZLE.
SEMTEX CHARGES HERE, HERE AND HERE'LL DO THE TRICK RIGHT, TAKE THIS ALL DOWN TO THE SUBSTRATA.
YOU SOUND AS IF THERE'S A DOWNSIDE.
WELL, ALL THESE SUPPORTS ARE LOAD BEARING. WITHOUT THEM, EVERYTHING ABOVE GROUND WILL COLLAPSE.
AND WHEN YOU SAY "EVERYTHING"--
THERE WON'T BE ANYTHING LEFT STANDING FOR A RADIUS OF FIVE CITY BLOCKS.
...
TOO BAD.

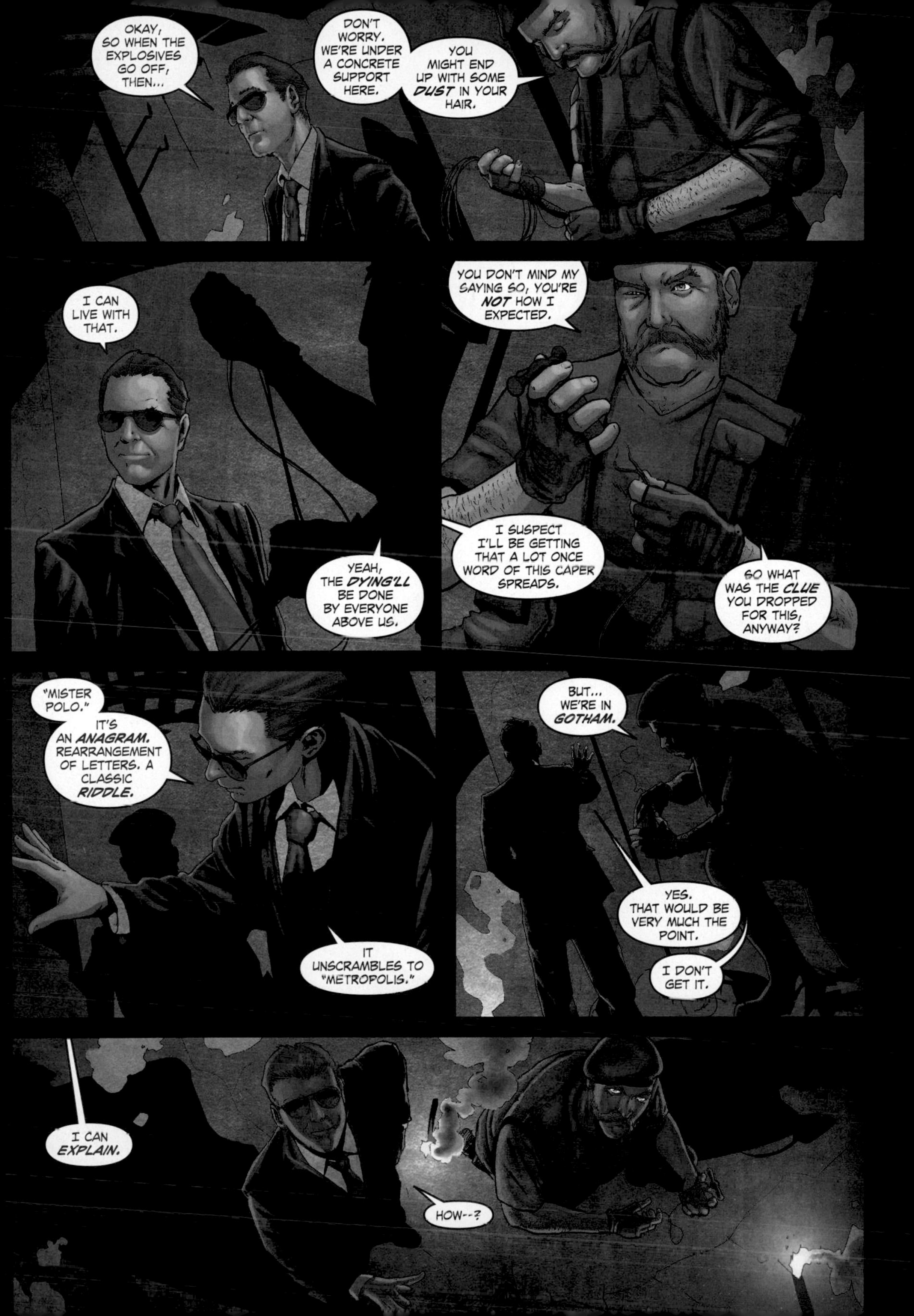
OKAY, SO WHEN THE EXPLOSIVES GO OFF, THEN...
DON'T WORRY. WE'RE UNDER A CONCRETE SUPPORT HERE.
YOU MIGHT END UP WITH SOME DUST IN YOUR HAIR.
I CAN LIVE WITH THAT.
YEAH, THE DYING'LL BE DONE BY EVERYONE ABOVE US.
YOU DON'T MIND MY SAYING SO, YOU'RE NOT HOW I EXPECTED.
I SUSPECT I'LL BE GETTING THAT A LOT ONCE WORD OF THIS CAPER SPREADS.
SO WHAT WAS THE CLUE YOU DROPPED FOR THIS, ANYWAY?
"MISTER POLO."
IT'S AN ANAGRAM. REARRANGEMENT OF LETTERS. A CLASSIC RIDDLE.
IT UNSCRAMBLES TO "METROPOLIS."
BUT... WE'RE IN GOTHAM.
YES. THAT WOULD BE VERY MUCH THE POINT.
I DON'T GET IT.
I CAN EXPLAIN.
HOW--?

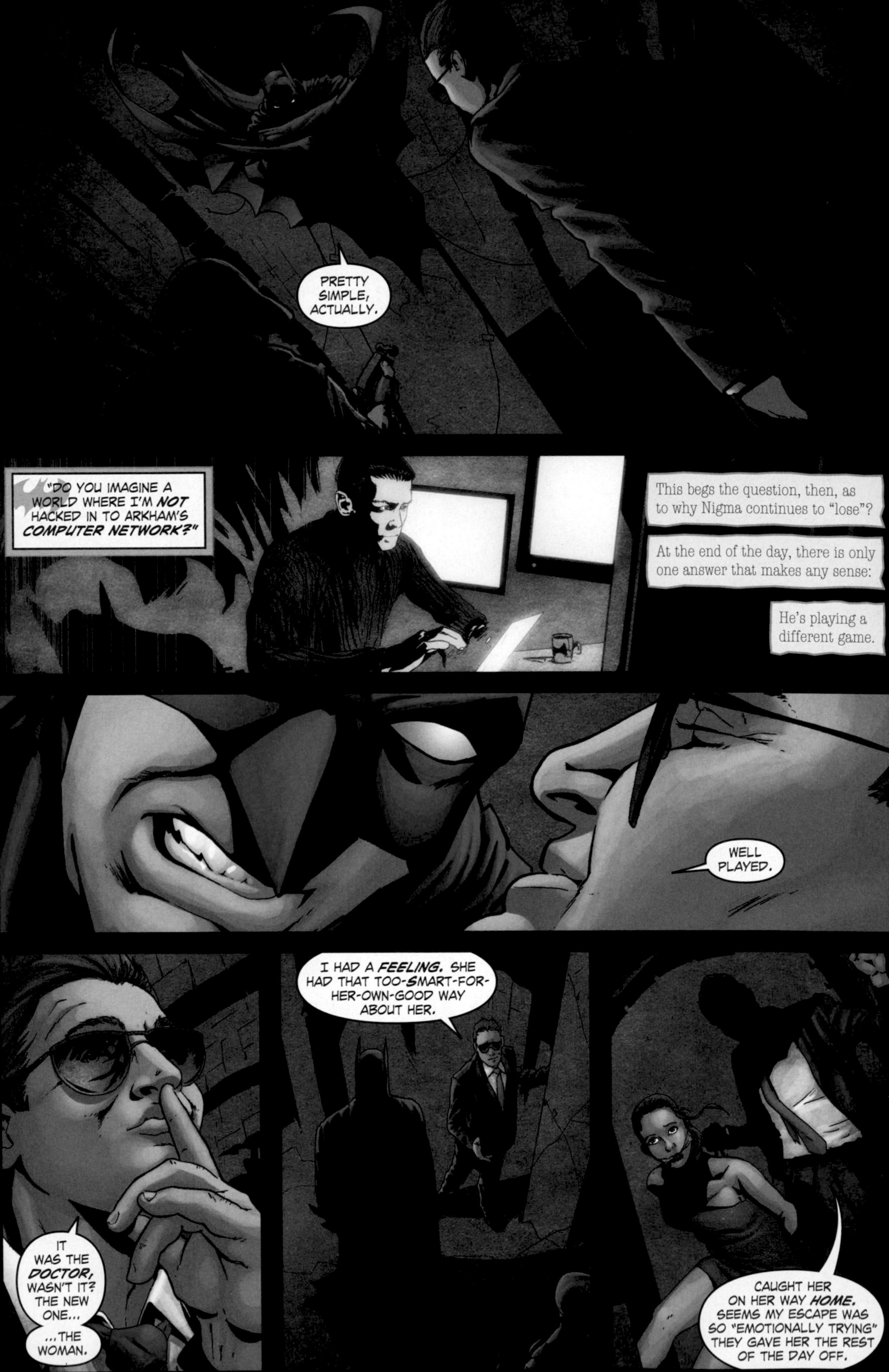
PRETTY SIMPLE, ACTUALLY.
"DO YOU IMAGINE A WORLD WHERE I'M NOT HACKED IN TO ARKHAM'S COMPUTER NETWORK?"
This begs the question, then, as to why Nigma continues to "lose"?
At the end of the day, there is only one answer that makes any sense:
He's playing a different game.
WELL PLAYED.
IT WAS THE DOCTOR, WASN'T IT? THE NEW ONE...
...THE WOMAN.
I HAD A FEELING. SHE HAD THAT TOO-SMART-FOR-HER-OWN-GOOD WAY ABOUT HER.
CAUGHT HER ON HER WAY HOME. SEEMS MY ESCAPE WAS SO "EMOTIONALLY TRYING" THEY GAVE HER THE REST OF THE DAY OFF.

YOU *KNOW* THE KEY TO WINNING AT *CHESS?* IT'S ALWAYS TO SEE THE BOARD AT LEAST *ONE MOVE DEEPER* THAN YOUR OPPONENT.

IN CHESS, THIS WOULD BE CALLED A *PIN.*

BLOW THE CHARGES, PLEASE.

HE'S *BLUFFING.* OR THE REST OF *HER* LIFE WILL BE MEASURED IN *SECONDS.*

HE'S *RIGHT.*

DO IT AND I'LL INTRODUCE YOU TO A NEW *KIND* OF *PAIN* THAT WILL GIVE YOU *NIGHTMARES* FOR THE REST OF YOUR LIFE.

BUT SECONDS ARE ALL I NEED.

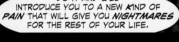

FWOOSH

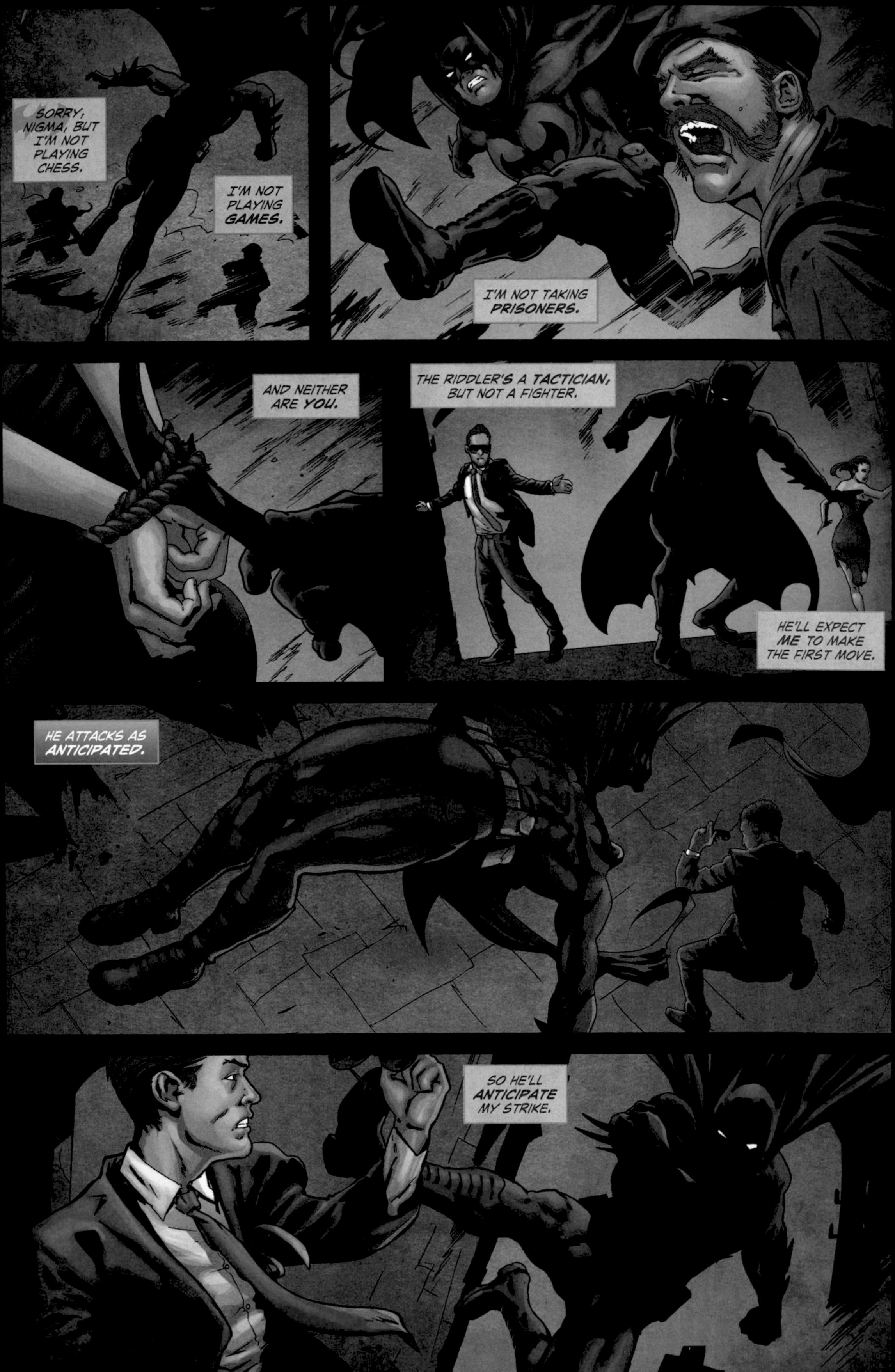
SORRY, NIGMA, BUT I'M NOT PLAYING CHESS.
I'M NOT PLAYING GAMES.
I'M NOT TAKING PRISONERS.
AND NEITHER ARE YOU.
THE RIDDLER'S A TACTICIAN, BUT NOT A FIGHTER.
HE'LL EXPECT ME TO MAKE THE FIRST MOVE.
HE ATTACKS AS ANTICIPATED.
SO HE'LL ANTICIPATE MY STRIKE.

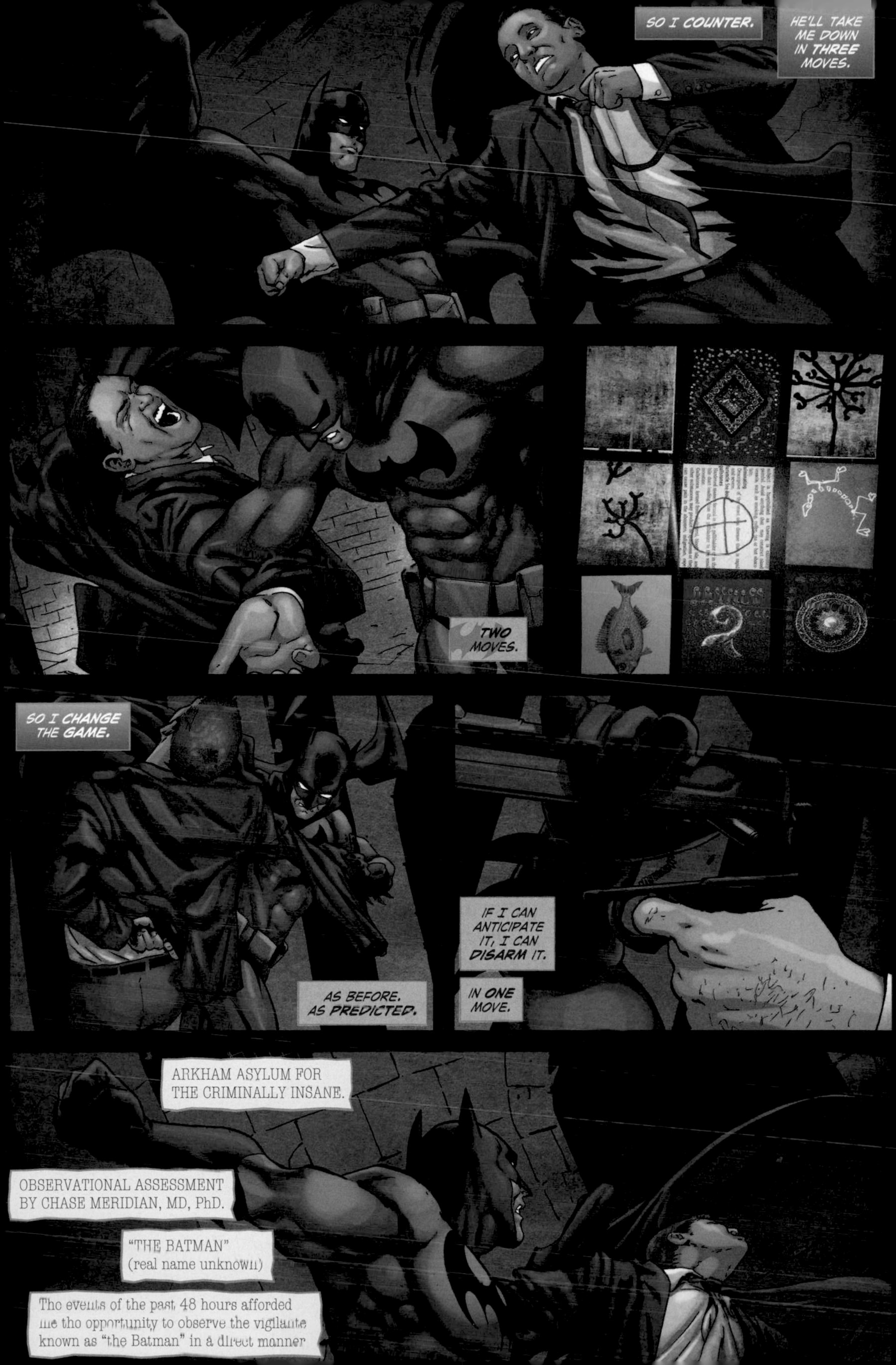
SO I COUNTER.
HE'LL TAKE ME DOWN IN THREE MOVES.
TWO MOVES.
SO I CHANGE THE GAME.
AS BEFORE. AS PREDICTED.
IF I CAN ANTICIPATE IT, I CAN DISARM IT.
IN ONE MOVE.
ARKHAM ASYLUM FOR THE CRIMINALLY INSANE.
OBSERVATIONAL ASSESSMENT BY CHASE MERIDIAN, MD, PhD.
"THE BATMAN" (real name unknown)
The events of the past 48 hours afforded me the opportunity to observe the vigilante known as "the Batman" in a direct manner

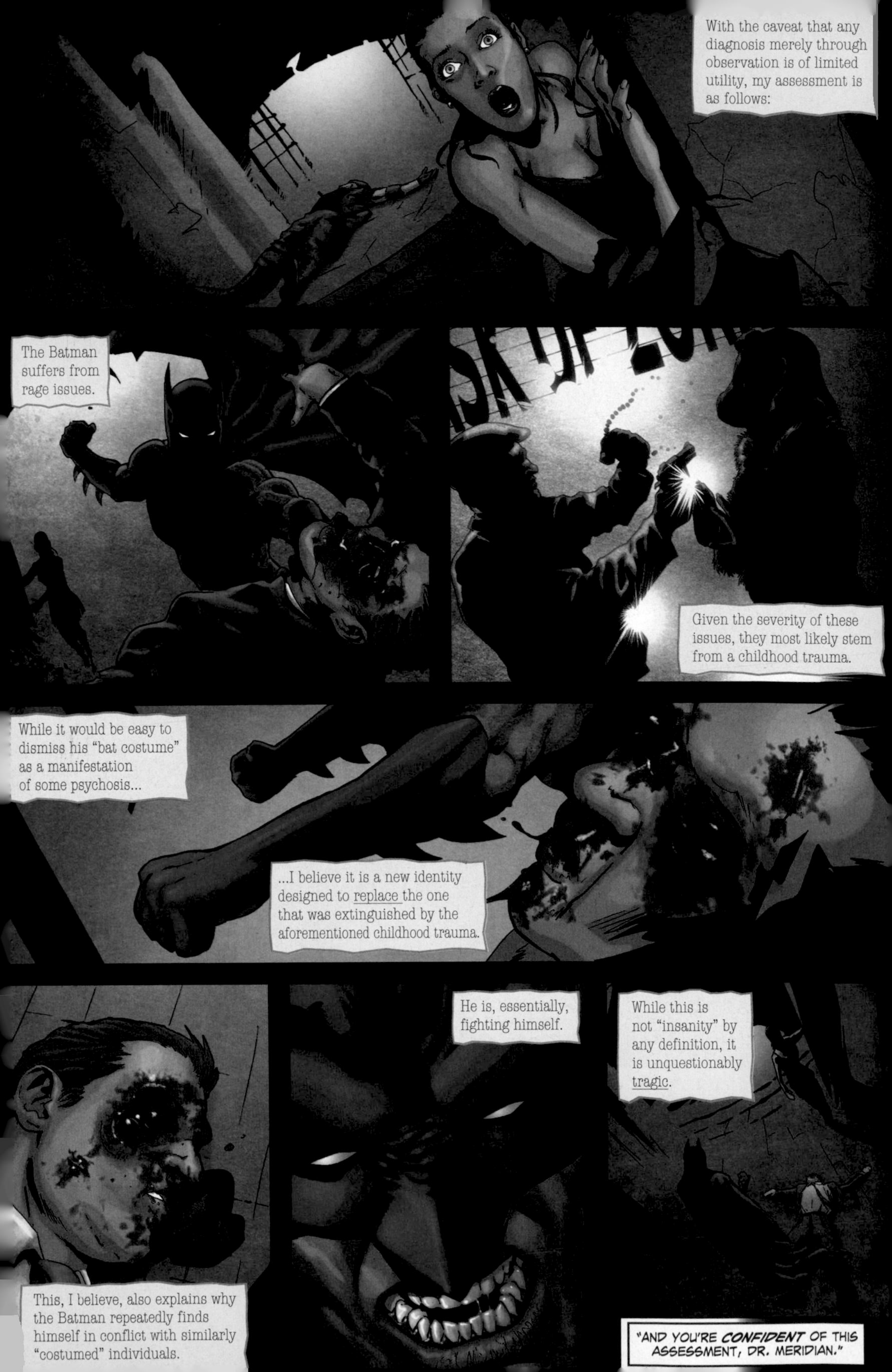
With the caveat that any diagnosis merely through observation is of limited utility, my assessment is as follows:
The Batman suffers from rage issues.
Given the severity of these issues, they most likely stem from a childhood trauma.
While it would be easy to dismiss his "bat costume" as a manifestation of some psychosis...
...I believe it is a new identity designed to replace the one that was extinguished by the aforementioned childhood trauma.
This, I believe, also explains why the Batman repeatedly finds himself in conflict with similarly "costumed" individuals.
He is, essentially, fighting himself.
While this is not "insanity" by any definition, it is unquestionably tragic.
"AND YOU'RE CONFIDENT OF THIS ASSESSMENT, DR. MERIDIAN."

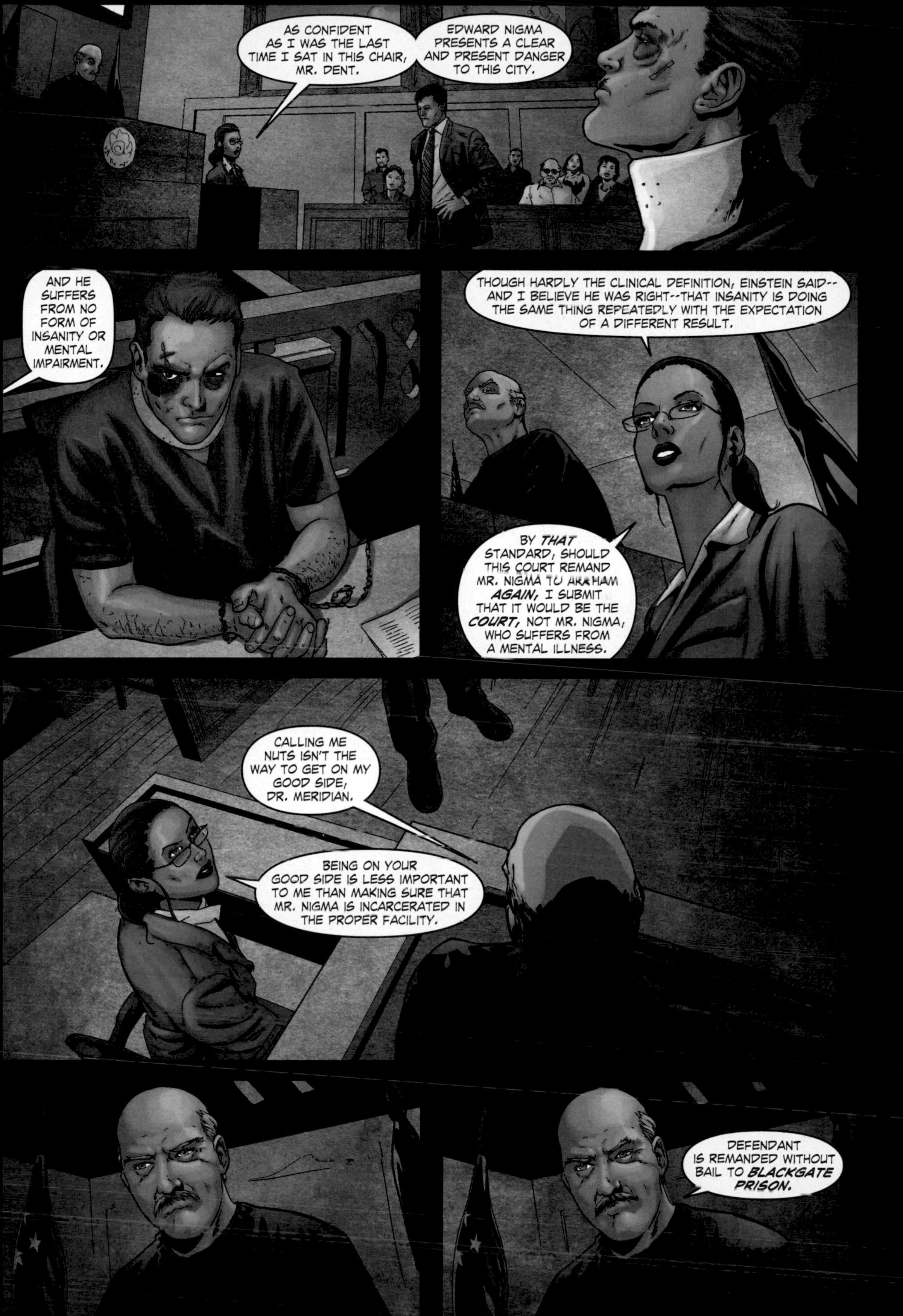
AS CONFIDENT AS I WAS THE LAST TIME I SAT IN THIS CHAIR, MR. DENT.
EDWARD NIGMA PRESENTS A CLEAR AND PRESENT DANGER TO THIS CITY.
AND HE SUFFERS FROM NO FORM OF INSANITY OR MENTAL IMPAIRMENT.
THOUGH HARDLY THE CLINICAL DEFINITION, EINSTEIN SAID--AND I BELIEVE HE WAS RIGHT--THAT INSANITY IS DOING THE SAME THING REPEATEDLY WITH THE EXPECTATION OF A DIFFERENT RESULT.
BY THAT STANDARD, SHOULD THIS COURT REMAND MR. NIGMA TO ARKHAM AGAIN, I SUBMIT THAT IT WOULD BE THE COURT, NOT MR. NIGMA, WHO SUFFERS FROM A MENTAL ILLNESS.
CALLING ME NUTS ISN'T THE WAY TO GET ON MY GOOD SIDE, DR. MERIDIAN.
BEING ON YOUR GOOD SIDE IS LESS IMPORTANT TO ME THAN MAKING SURE THAT MR. NIGMA IS INCARCERATED IN THE PROPER FACILITY.
DEFENDANT IS REMANDED WITHOUT BAIL TO BLACKGATE PRISON.

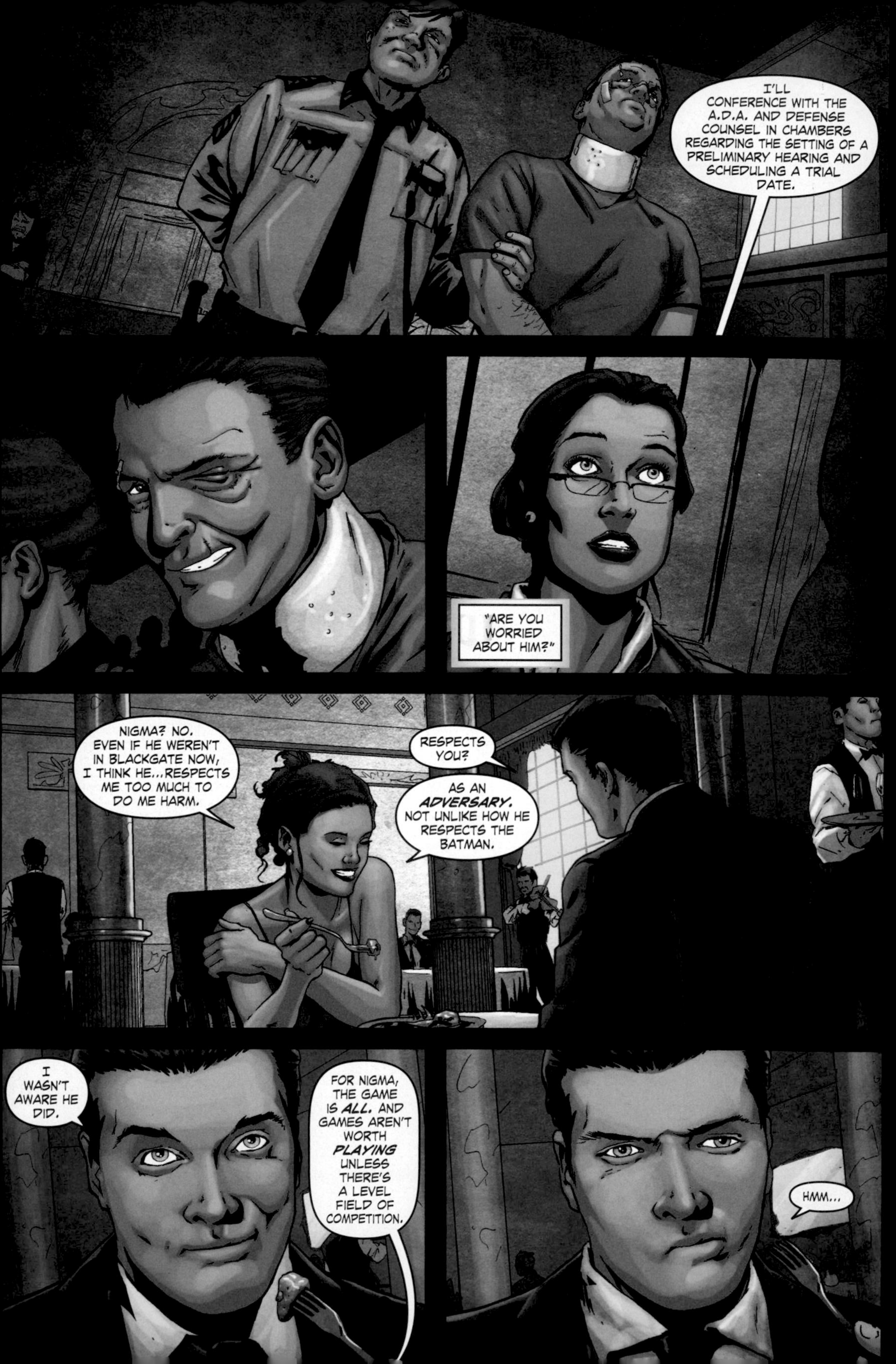
I'LL CONFERENCE WITH THE A.D.A. AND DEFENSE COUNSEL IN CHAMBERS REGARDING THE SETTING OF A PRELIMINARY HEARING AND SCHEDULING A TRIAL DATE.
"ARE YOU WORRIED ABOUT HIM?"
NIGMA? NO. EVEN IF HE WEREN'T IN BLACKGATE NOW, I THINK HE...RESPECTS ME TOO MUCH TO DO ME HARM.
RESPECTS YOU?
AS AN ADVERSARY. NOT UNLIKE HOW HE RESPECTS THE BATMAN.
I WASN'T AWARE HE DID.
FOR NIGMA, THE GAME IS ALL. AND GAMES AREN'T WORTH PLAYING UNLESS THERE'S A LEVEL FIELD OF COMPETITION.
HMM...

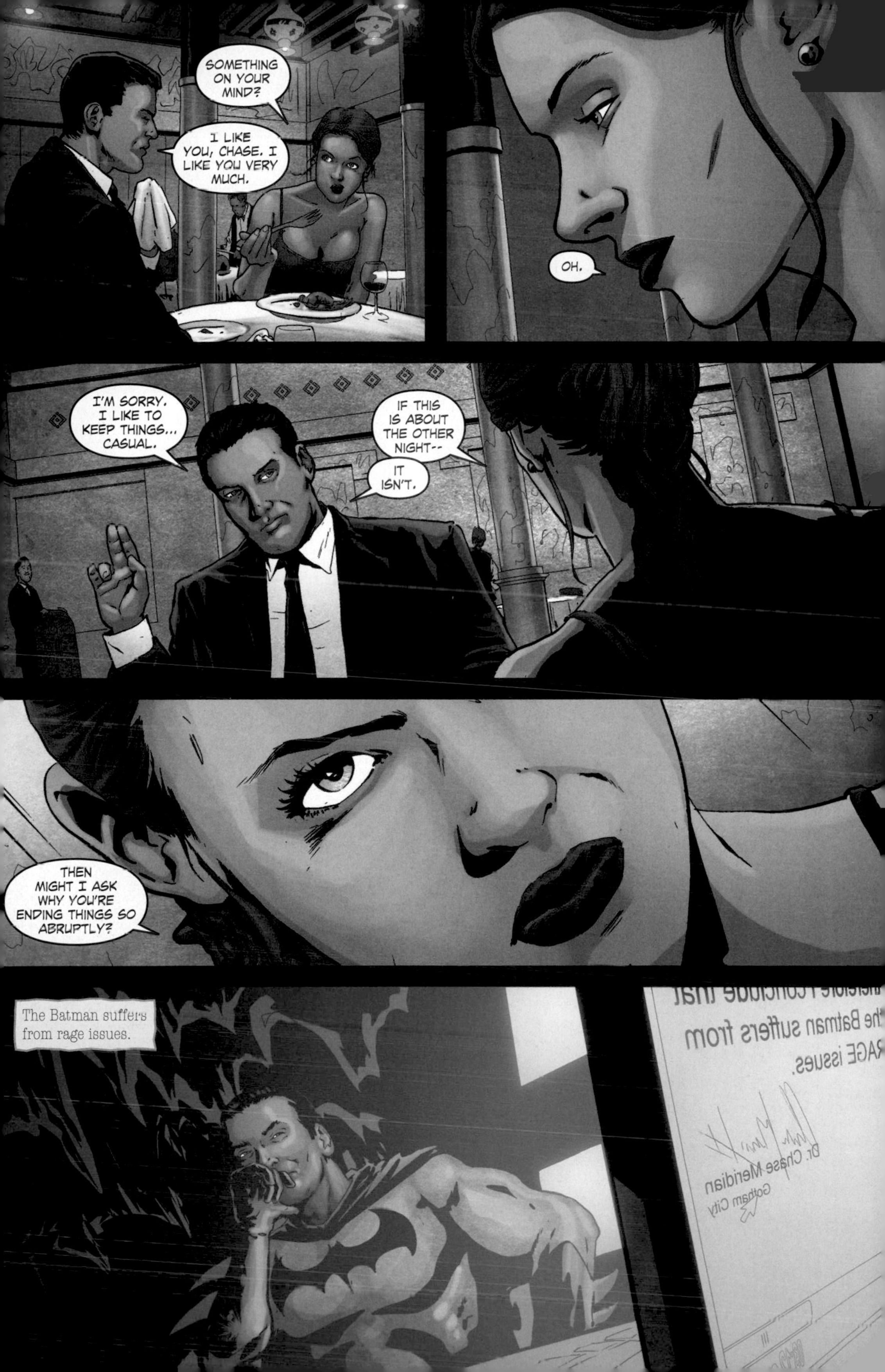
SOMETHING ON YOUR MIND?
I LIKE YOU, CHASE. I LIKE YOU VERY MUCH.
OH.
I'M SORRY. I LIKE TO KEEP THINGS... CASUAL.
IF THIS IS ABOUT THE OTHER NIGHT--
IT ISN'T.
THEN MIGHT I ASK WHY YOU'RE ENDING THINGS SO ABRUPTLY?
The Batman suffers from rage issues.
the Batman suffers from
RAGE issues.
Dr. Chase Meridian
Gotham City

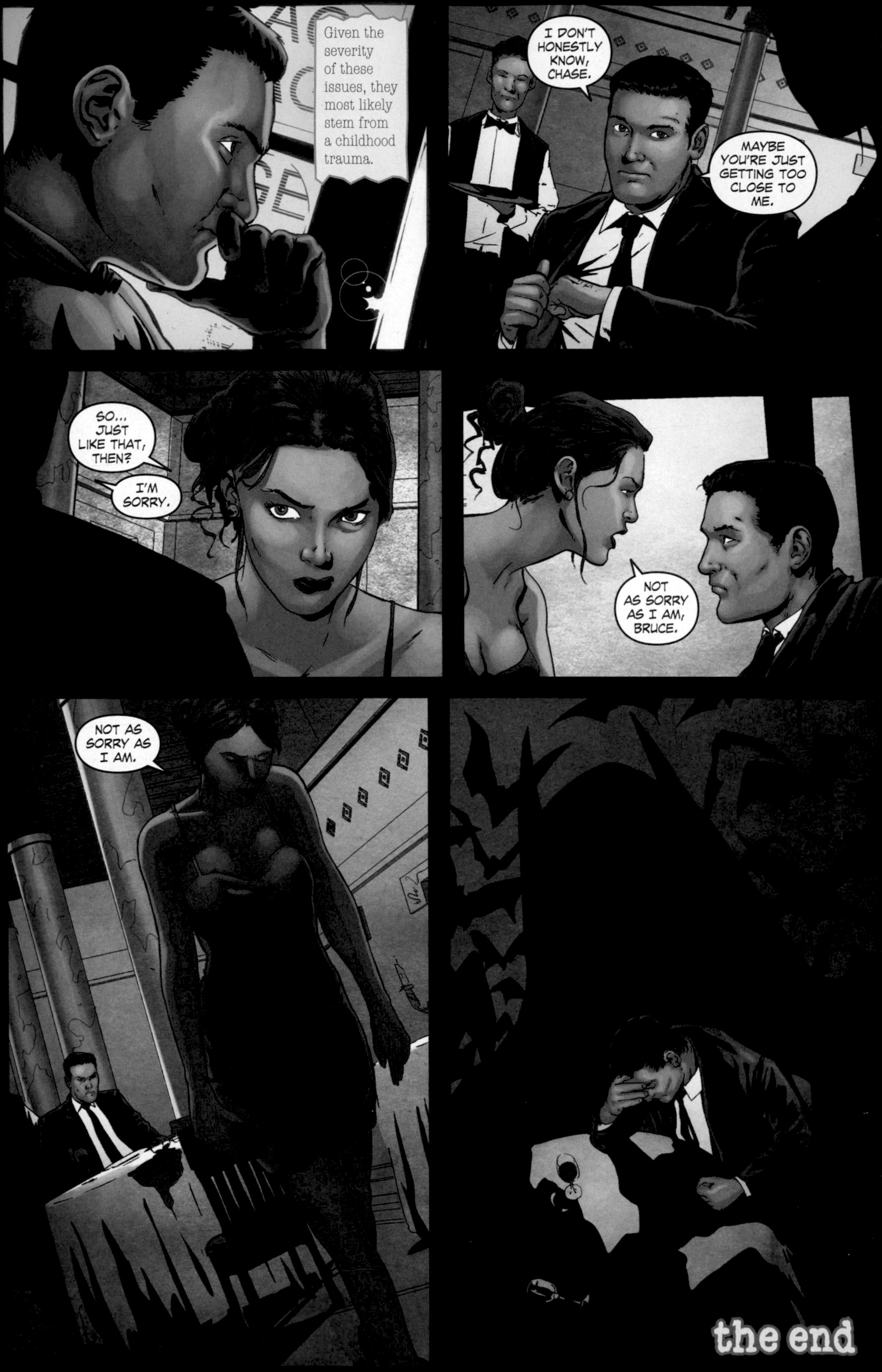
Given the severity of these issues, they most likely stem from a childhood trauma.
I DON'T HONESTLY KNOW, CHASE.
MAYBE YOU'RE JUST GETTING TOO CLOSE TO ME.
SO... JUST LIKE THAT, THEN?
I'M SORRY.
NOT AS SORRY AS I AM, BRUCE.
NOT AS SORRY AS I AM.
the end

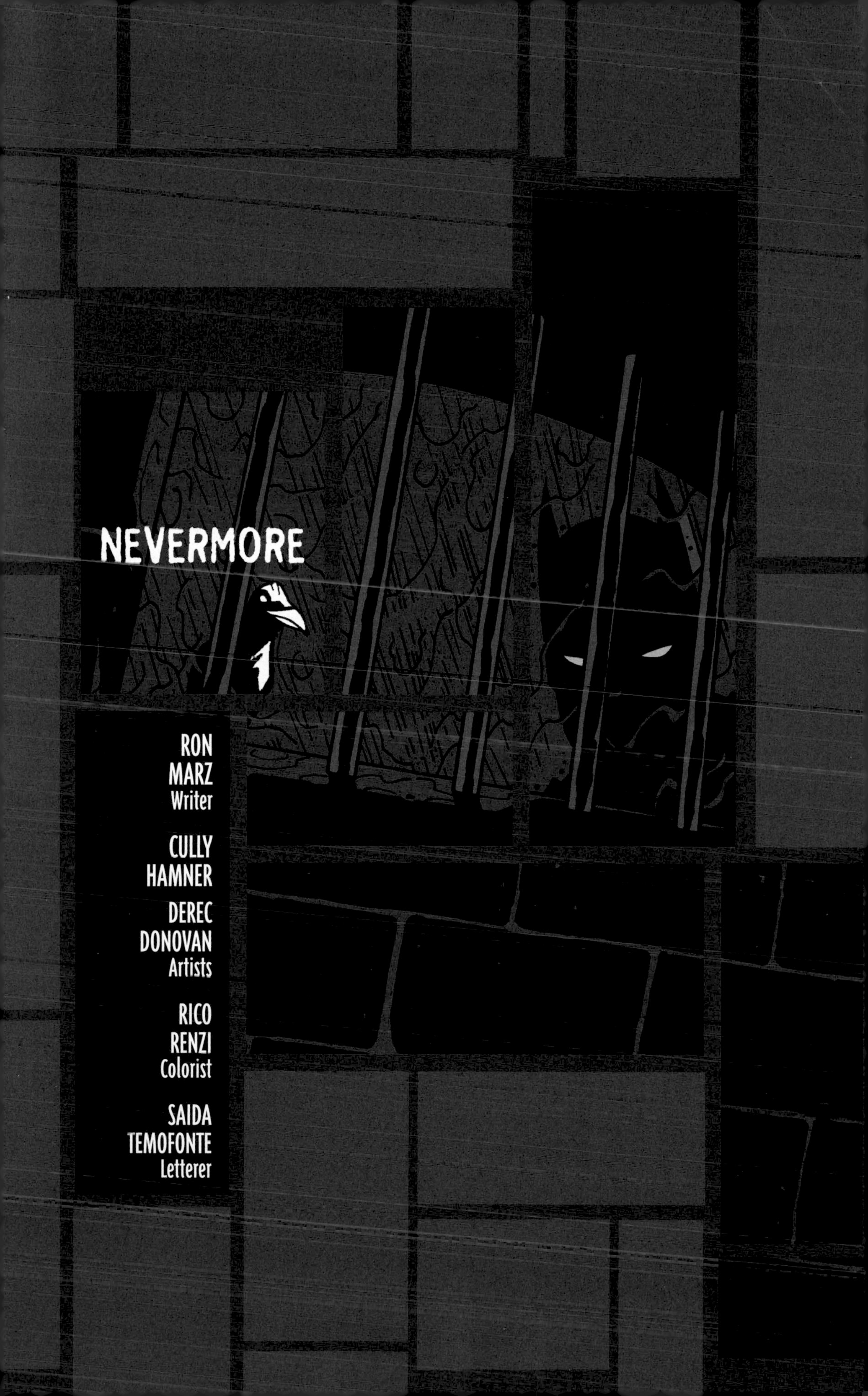
NEVERMORE
RON MARZ Writer
CULLY HAMNER
DEREC DONOVAN Artists
RICO RENZI Colorist
SAIDA TEMOFONTE Letterer

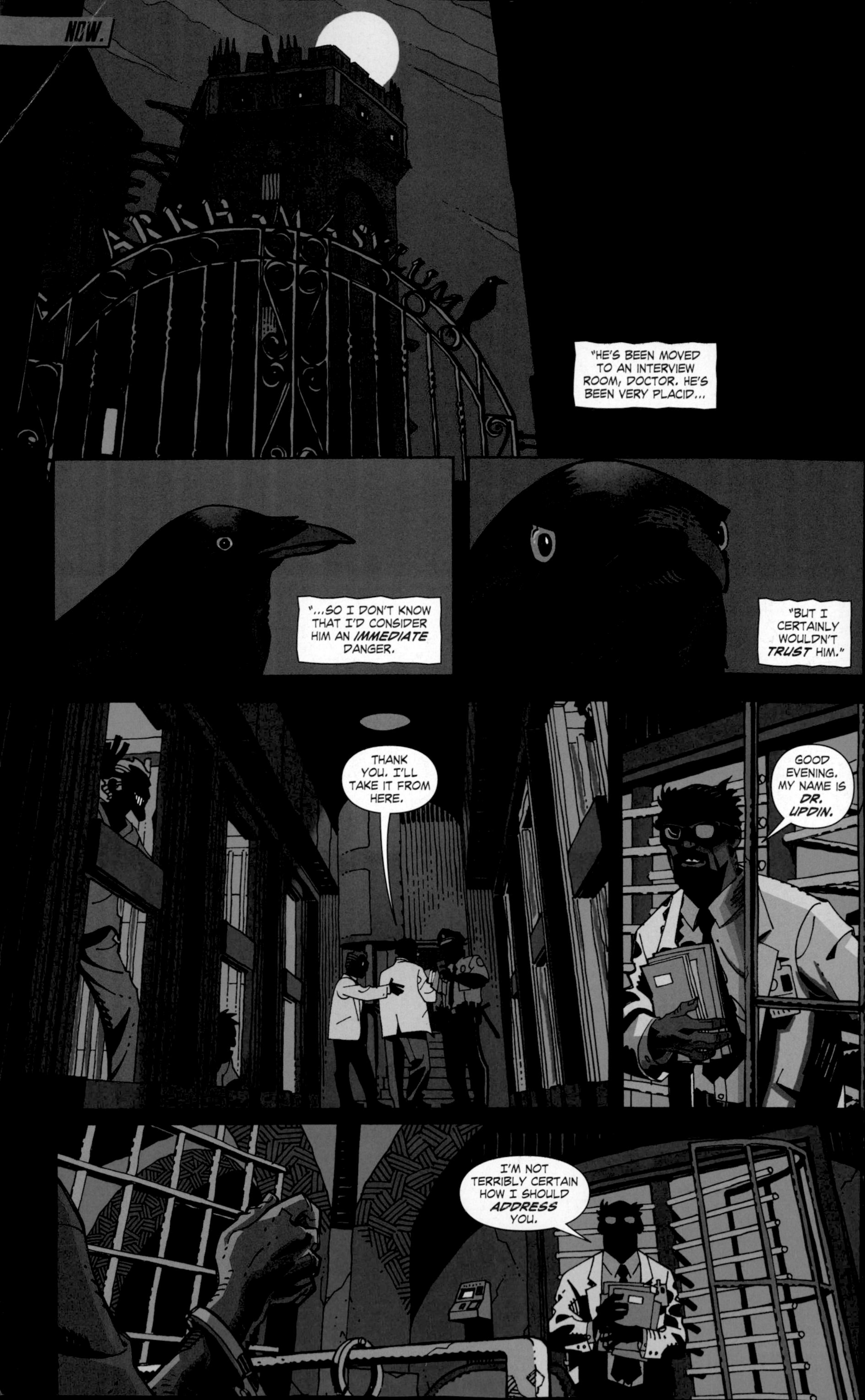
NOW.
"HE'S BEEN MOVED TO AN INTERVIEW ROOM, DOCTOR. HE'S BEEN VERY PLACID...
"...SO I DON'T KNOW THAT I'D CONSIDER HIM AN IMMEDIATE DANGER.
"BUT I CERTAINLY WOULDN'T TRUST HIM."
THANK YOU. I'LL TAKE IT FROM HERE.
GOOD EVENING. MY NAME IS DR. UPDIN.
I'M NOT TERRIBLY CERTAIN HOW I SHOULD ADDRESS YOU.

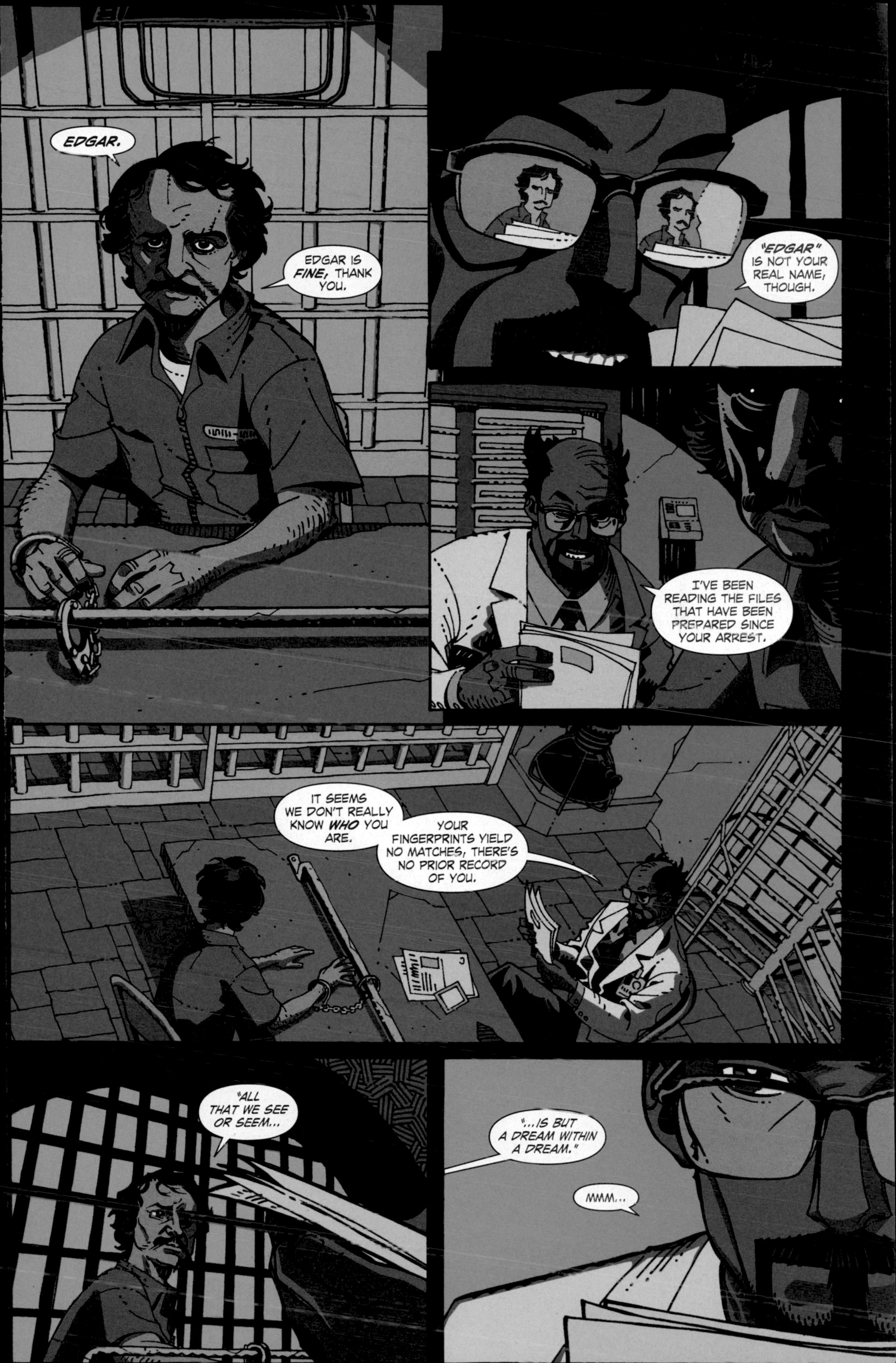
EDGAR.
EDGAR IS FINE, THANK YOU.
"EDGAR" IS NOT YOUR REAL NAME, THOUGH.
I'VE BEEN READING THE FILES THAT HAVE BEEN PREPARED SINCE YOUR ARREST.
IT SEEMS WE DON'T REALLY KNOW WHO YOU ARE.
YOUR FINGERPRINTS YIELD NO MATCHES, THERE'S NO PRIOR RECORD OF YOU.
"ALL THAT WE SEE OR SEEM...
"...IS BUT A DREAM WITHIN A DREAM."
MMM...

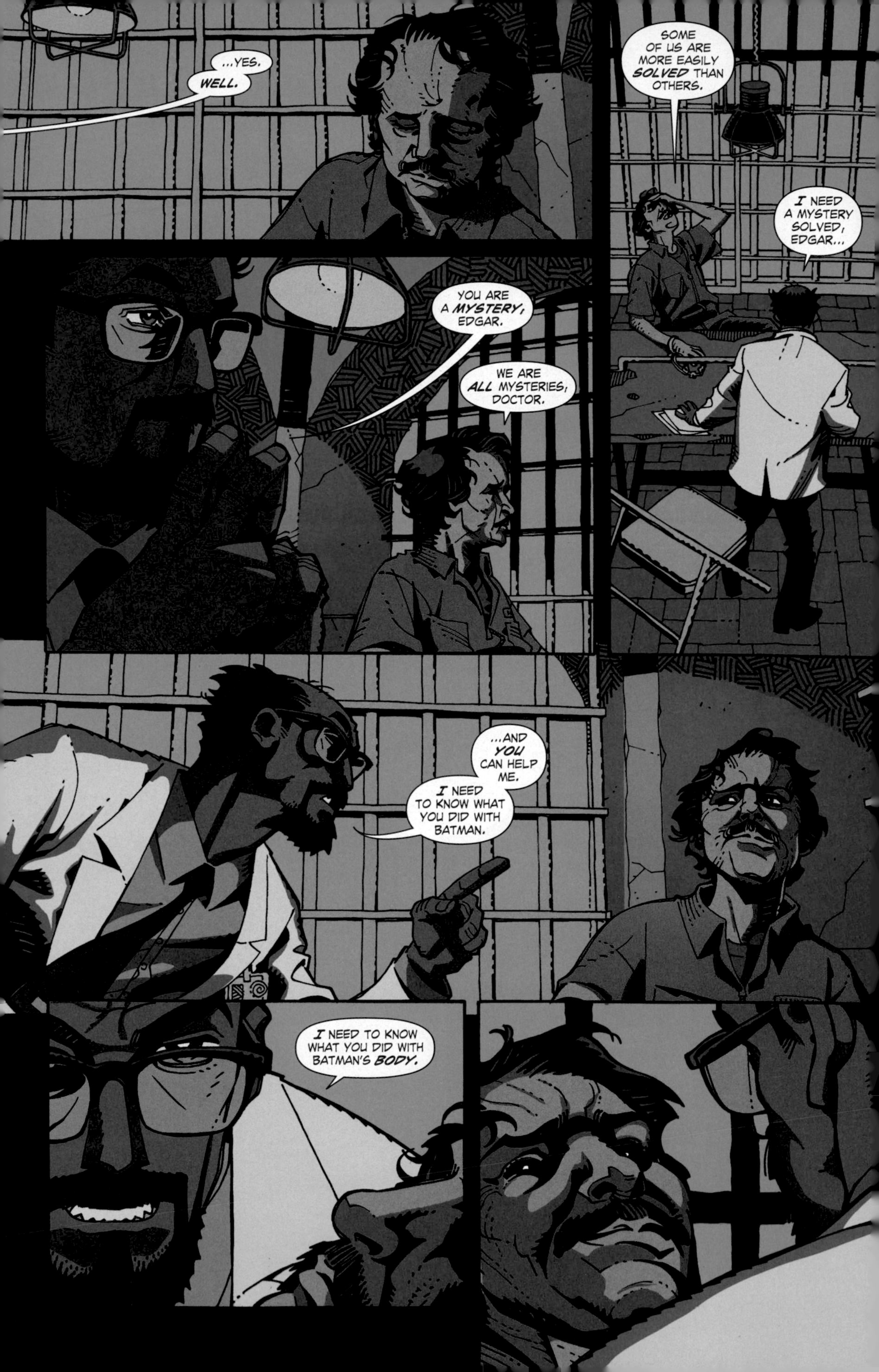
...YES. WELL.
SOME OF US ARE MORE EASILY SOLVED THAN OTHERS.
I NEED A MYSTERY SOLVED, EDGAR...
YOU ARE A MYSTERY, EDGAR.
WE ARE ALL MYSTERIES, DOCTOR.
...AND YOU CAN HELP ME.
I NEED TO KNOW WHAT YOU DID WITH BATMAN.
I NEED TO KNOW WHAT YOU DID WITH BATMAN'S BODY.

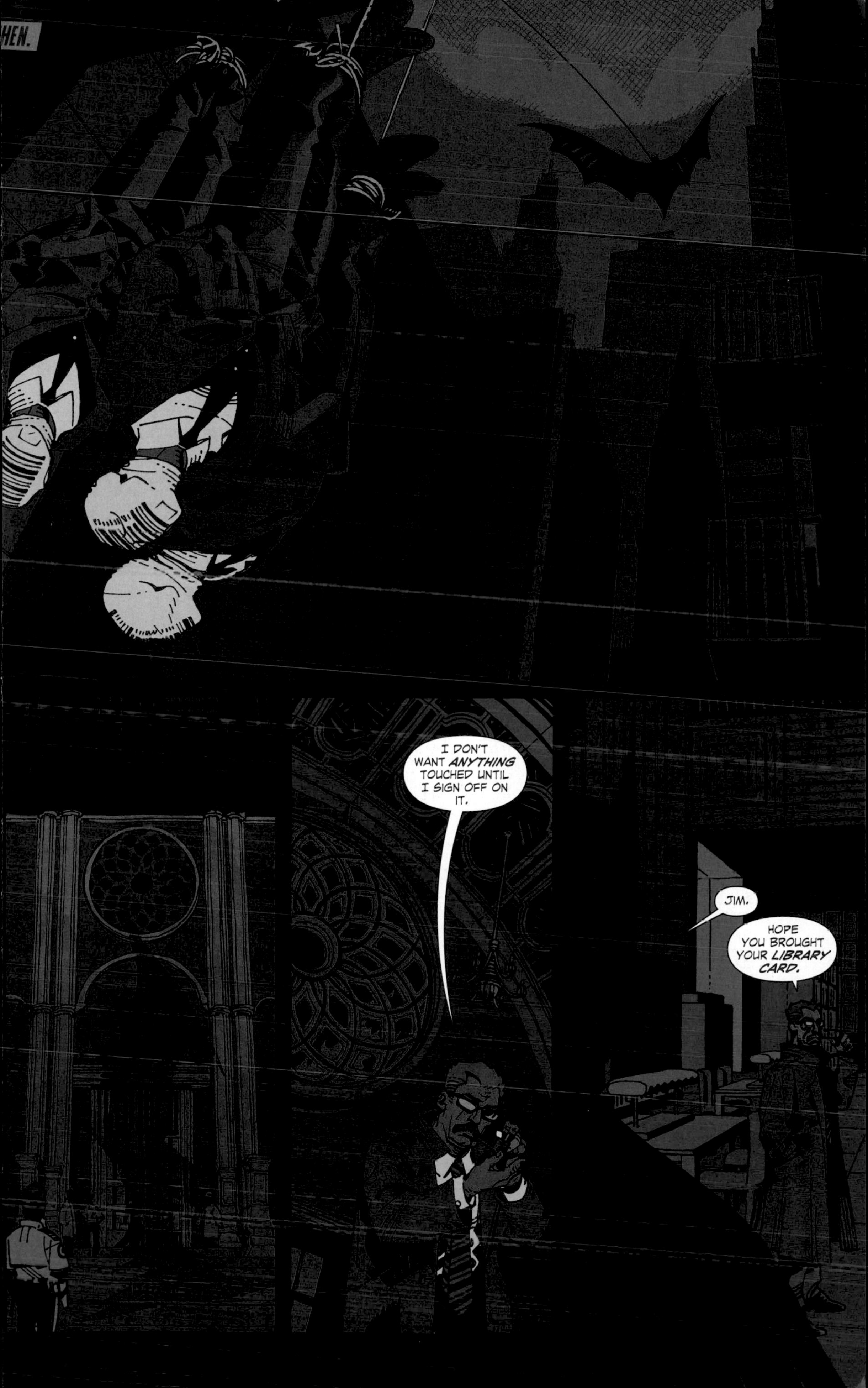
HEN.
I DON'T WANT ANYTHING TOUCHED UNTIL I SIGN OFF ON IT.
JIM.
HOPE YOU BROUGHT YOUR LIBRARY CARD.

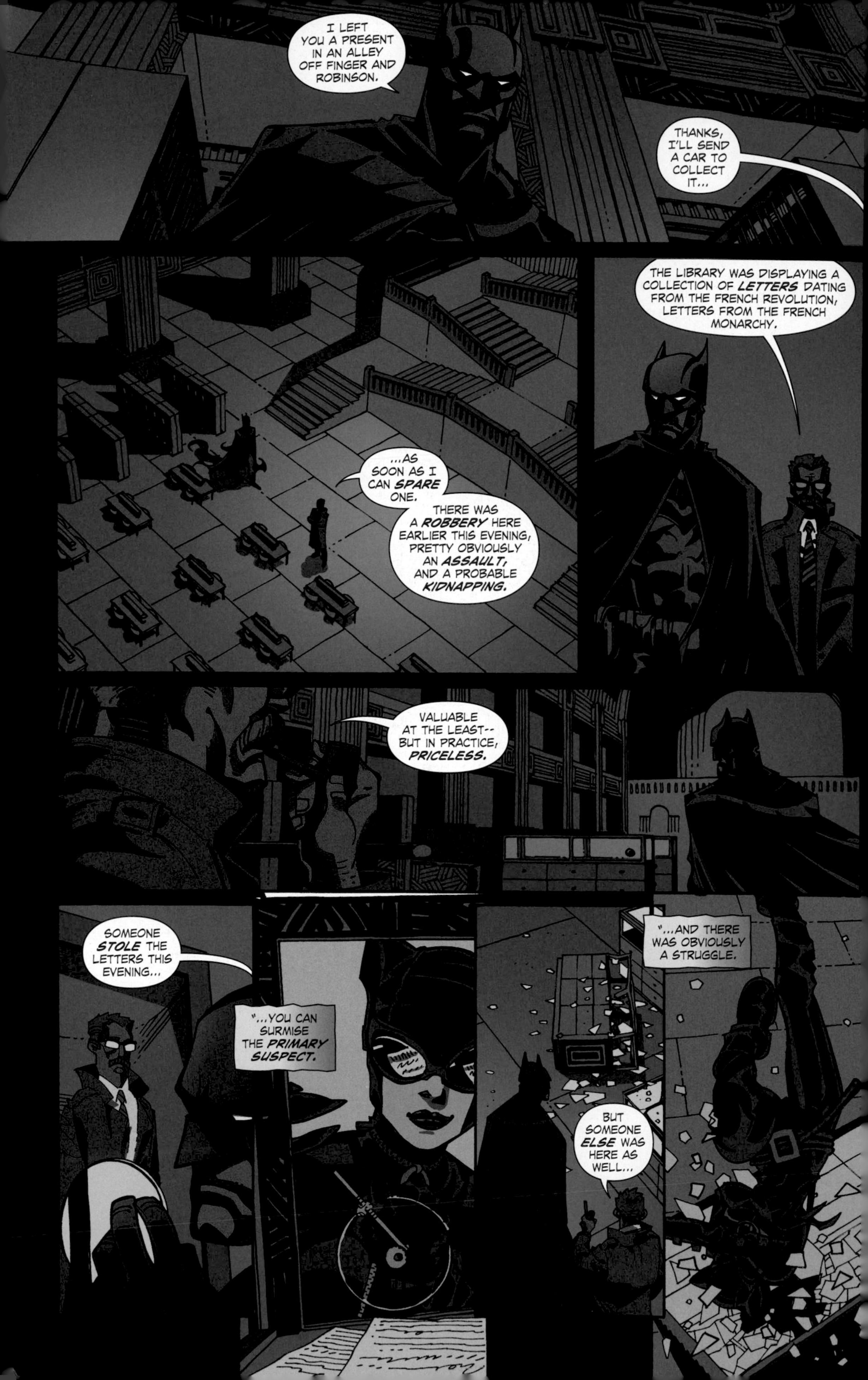
I LEFT YOU A PRESENT IN AN ALLEY OFF FINGER AND ROBINSON.
THANKS, I'LL SEND A CAR TO COLLECT IT...
...AS SOON AS I CAN SPARE ONE.
THERE WAS A ROBBERY HERE EARLIER THIS EVENING, PRETTY OBVIOUSLY AN ASSAULT, AND A PROBABLE KIDNAPPING.
THE LIBRARY WAS DISPLAYING A COLLECTION OF LETTERS DATING FROM THE FRENCH REVOLUTION, LETTERS FROM THE FRENCH MONARCHY.
VALUABLE AT THE LEAST-- BUT IN PRACTICE, PRICELESS.
SOMEONE STOLE THE LETTERS THIS EVENING...
"...YOU CAN SURMISE THE PRIMARY SUSPECT.
"...AND THERE WAS OBVIOUSLY A STRUGGLE.
BUT SOMEONE ELSE WAS HERE AS WELL...

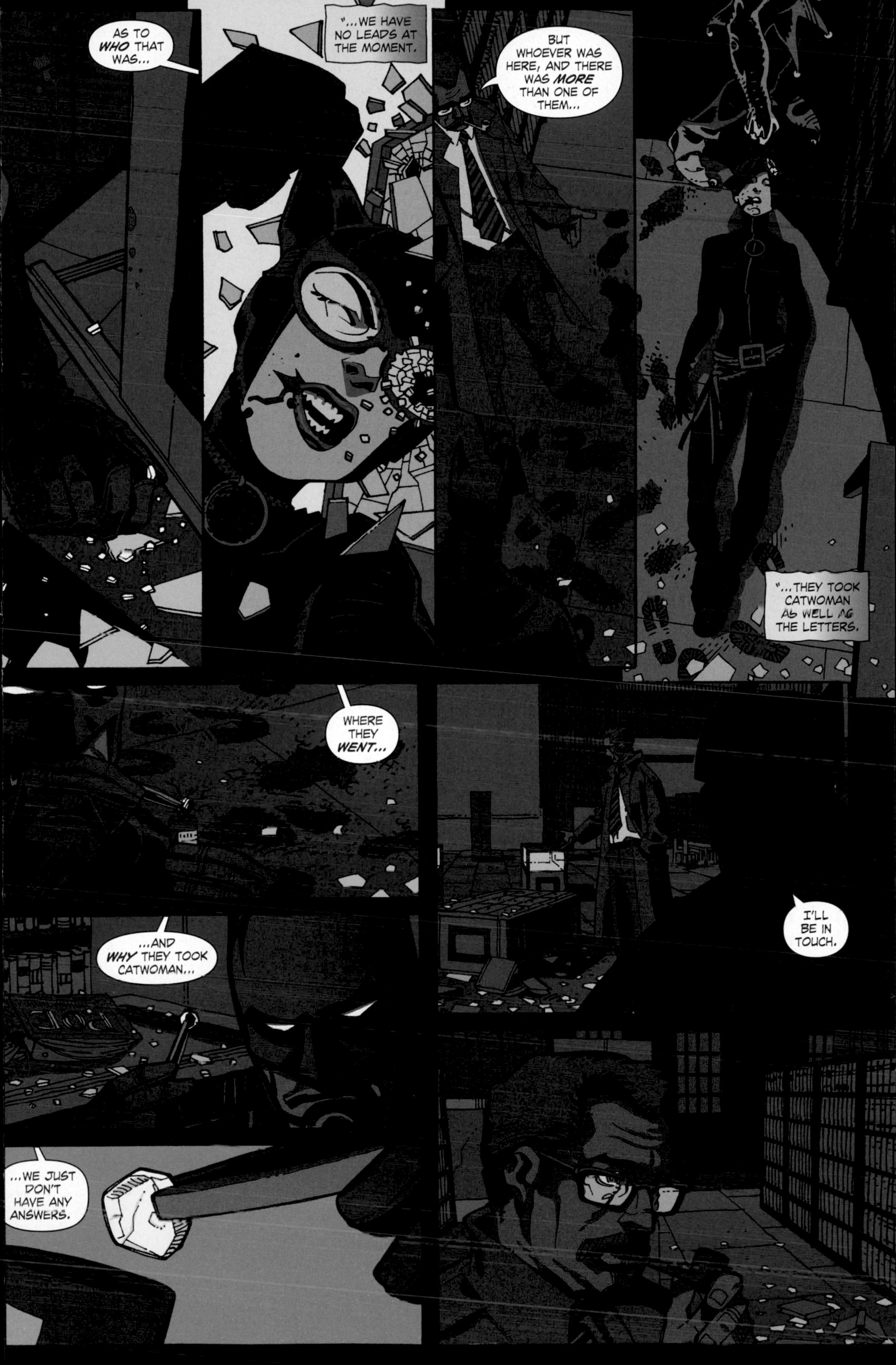

AS TO *WHO* THAT WAS...
"...WE HAVE NO LEADS AT THE MOMENT.
BUT WHOEVER WAS HERE, AND THERE WAS *MORE* THAN ONE OF THEM...
"...THEY TOOK CATWOMAN AS WELL AS THE LETTERS.
WHERE THEY *WENT*...
...AND *WHY* THEY TOOK CATWOMAN...
...WE JUST DON'T HAVE ANY ANSWERS.
I'LL BE IN TOUCH.

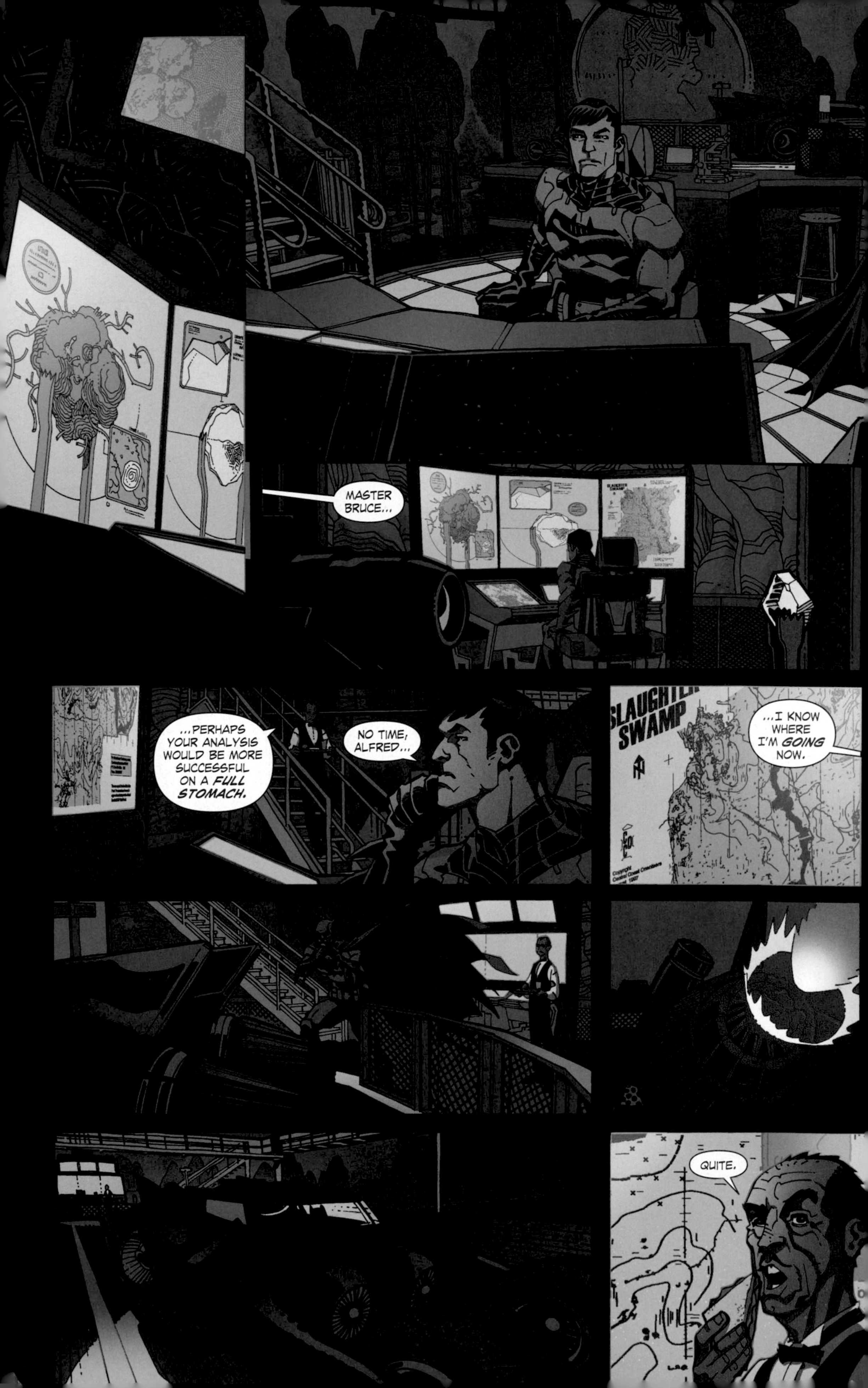
MASTER BRUCE...
...PERHAPS YOUR ANALYSIS WOULD BE MORE SUCCESSFUL ON A *FULL STOMACH.*
NO TIME, ALFRED...
SLAUGHTER SWAMP
...I KNOW WHERE I'M *GOING* NOW.
QUITE.

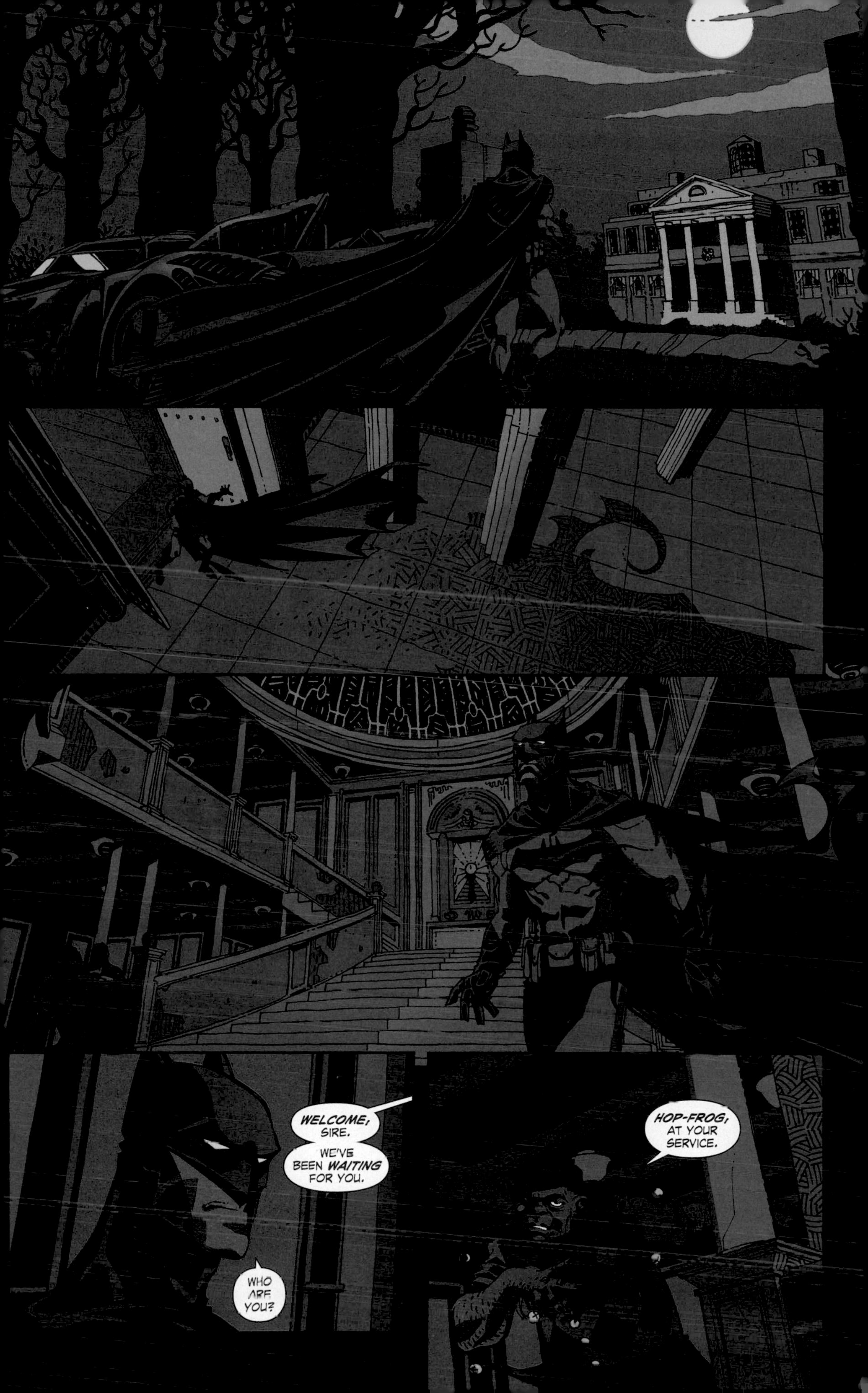
WELCOME, SIRE.
WE'VE BEEN WAITING FOR YOU.
WHO ARE YOU?
HOP-FROG, AT YOUR SERVICE.

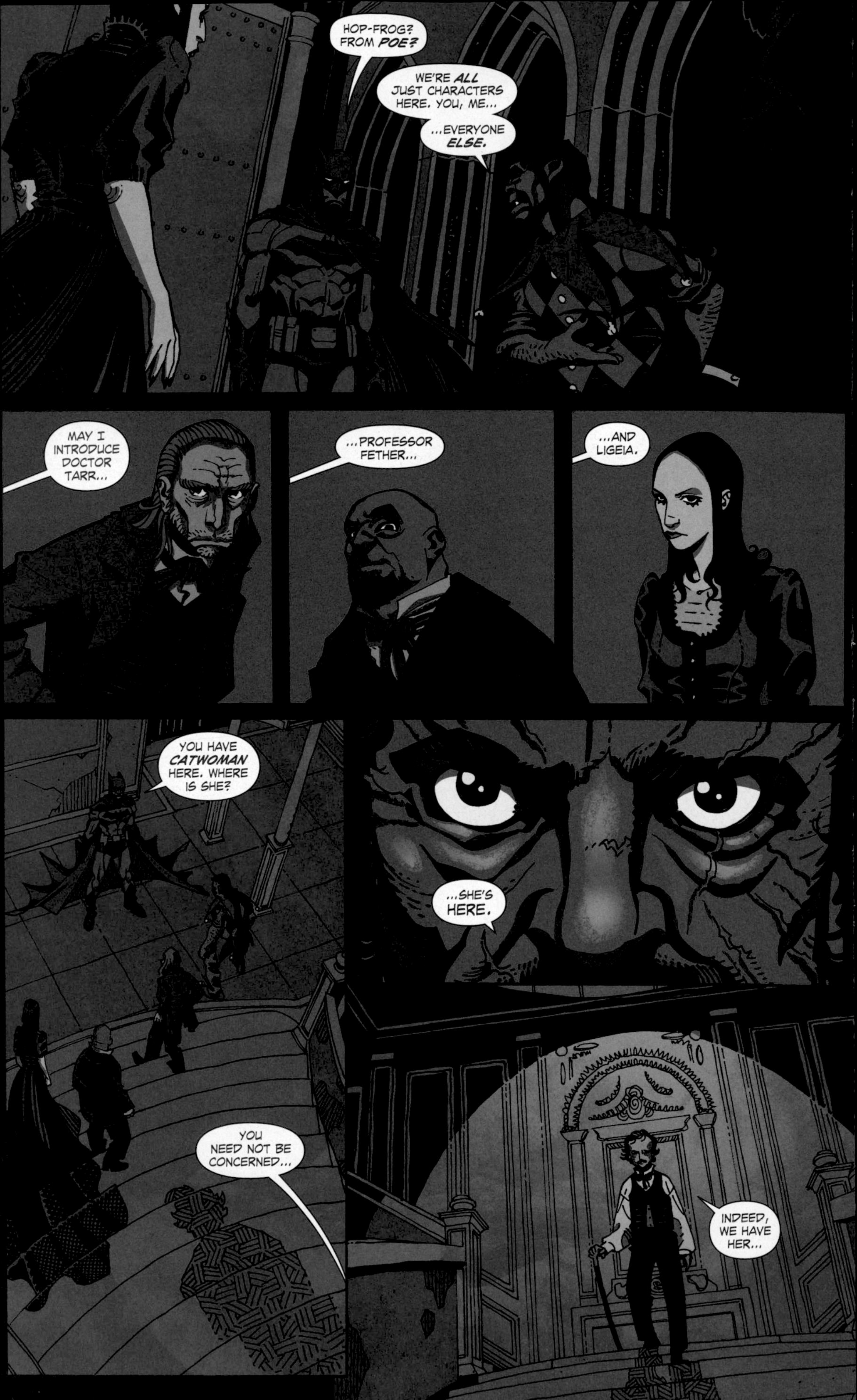
HOP-FROG? FROM POE?
WE'RE ALL JUST CHARACTERS HERE. YOU, ME...
...EVERYONE ELSE.
MAY I INTRODUCE DOCTOR TARR...
...PROFESSOR FETHER...
...AND LIGEIA.
YOU HAVE CATWOMAN HERE. WHERE IS SHE?
...SHE'S HERE.
YOU NEED NOT BE CONCERNED...
INDEED, WE HAVE HER...

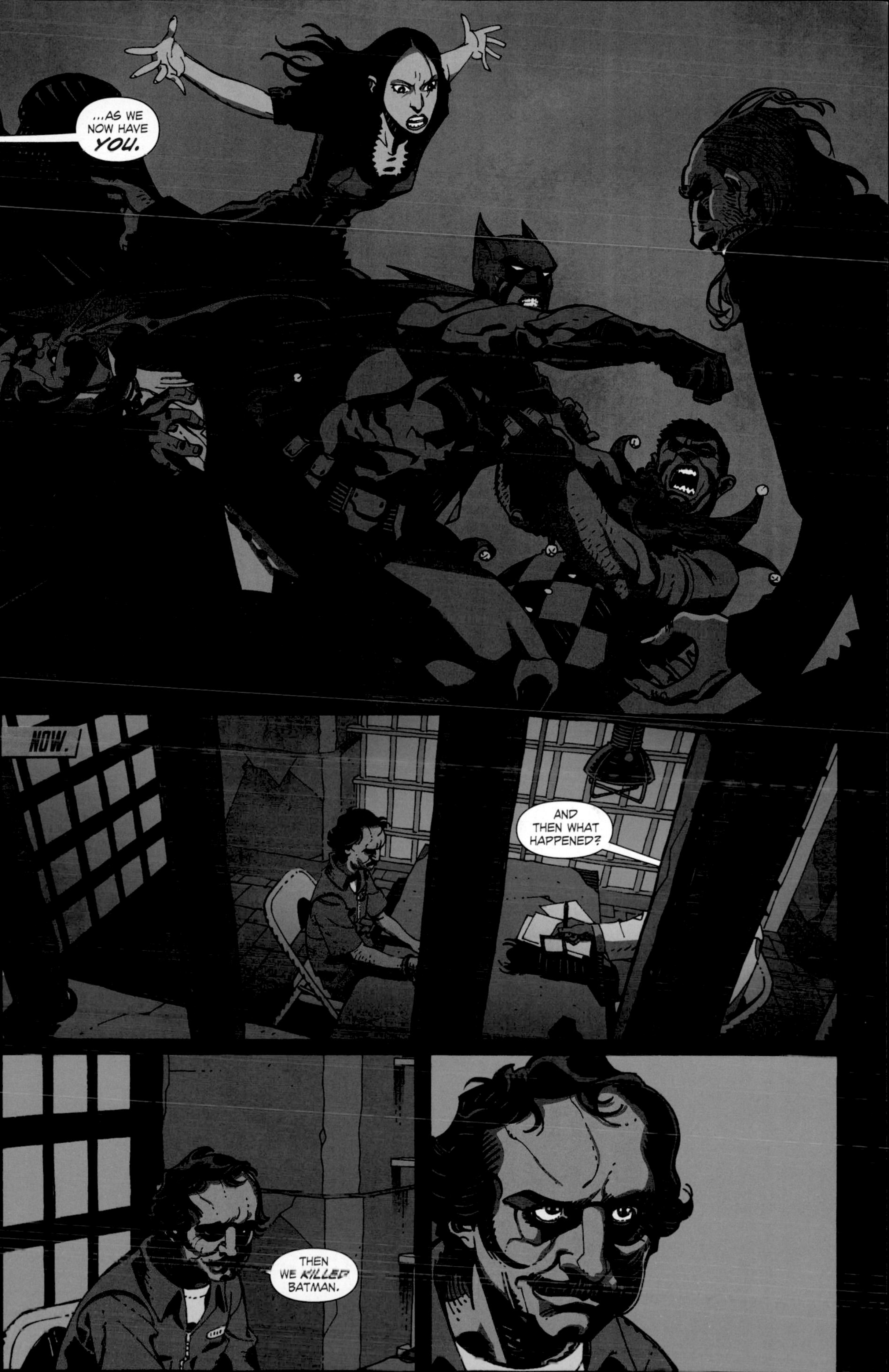
...AS WE NOW HAVE YOU.
NOW.
AND THEN WHAT HAPPENED?
THEN WE KILLED BATMAN.

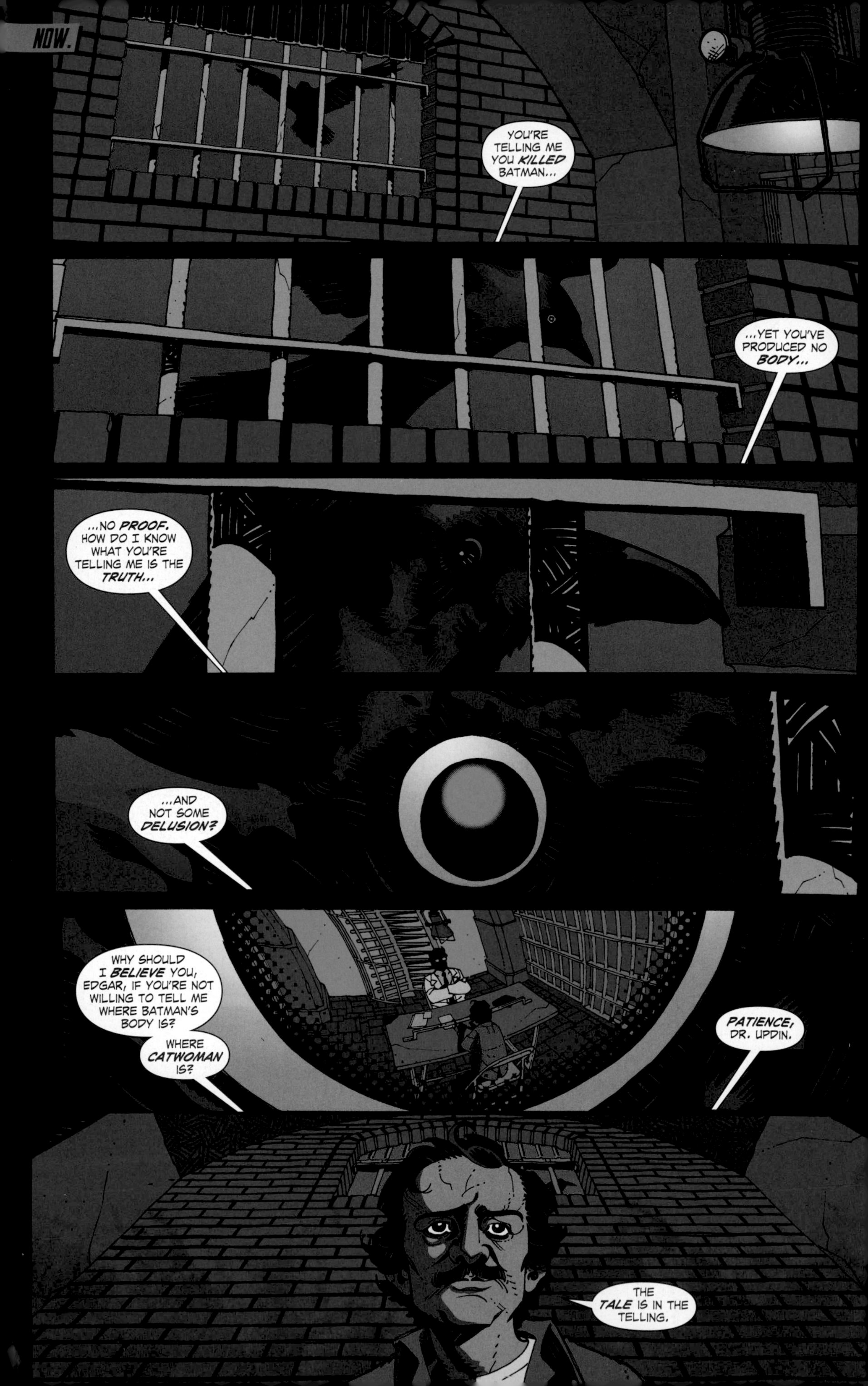
NOW.
YOU'RE TELLING ME YOU KILLED BATMAN...
...YET YOU'VE PRODUCED NO BODY...
...NO PROOF. HOW DO I KNOW WHAT YOU'RE TELLING ME IS THE TRUTH...
...AND NOT SOME DELUSION?
WHY SHOULD I BELIEVE YOU, EDGAR, IF YOU'RE NOT WILLING TO TELL ME WHERE BATMAN'S BODY IS?
WHERE CATWOMAN IS?
PATIENCE, DR. UPDIN.
THE TALE IS IN THE TELLING.

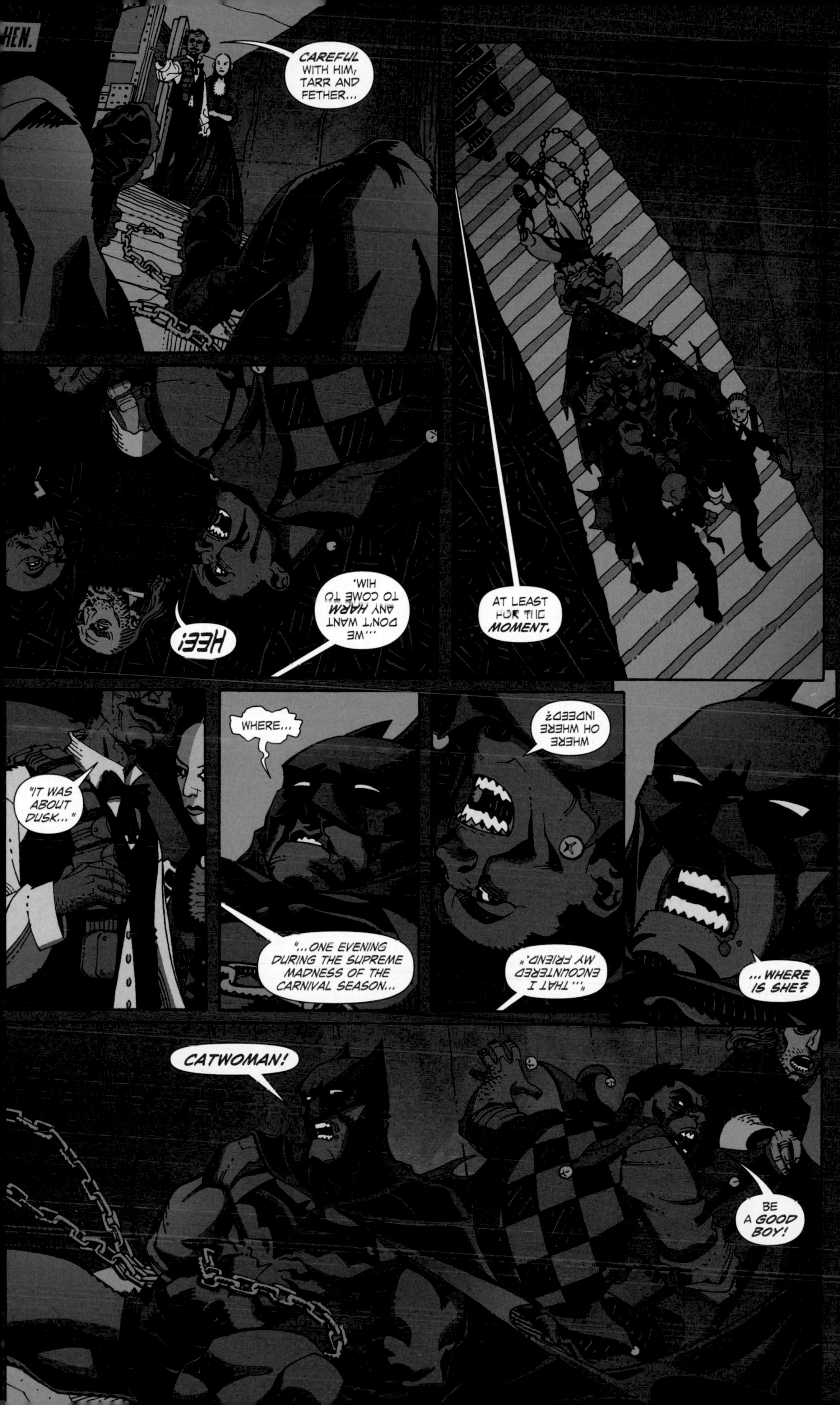

CAREFUL WITH HIM, TARR AND FETHER...
...WE DON'T WANT ANY HARM TO COME TO HIM.
HEE!
AT LEAST FOR THE MOMENT.
"IT WAS ABOUT DUSK..."
WHERE...
"...ONE EVENING DURING THE SUPREME MADNESS OF THE CARNIVAL SEASON...
WHERE OH WHERE INDEED?
"...THAT I ENCOUNTERED MY FRIEND."
...WHERE IS SHE?
CATWOMAN!
BE A GOOD BOY!

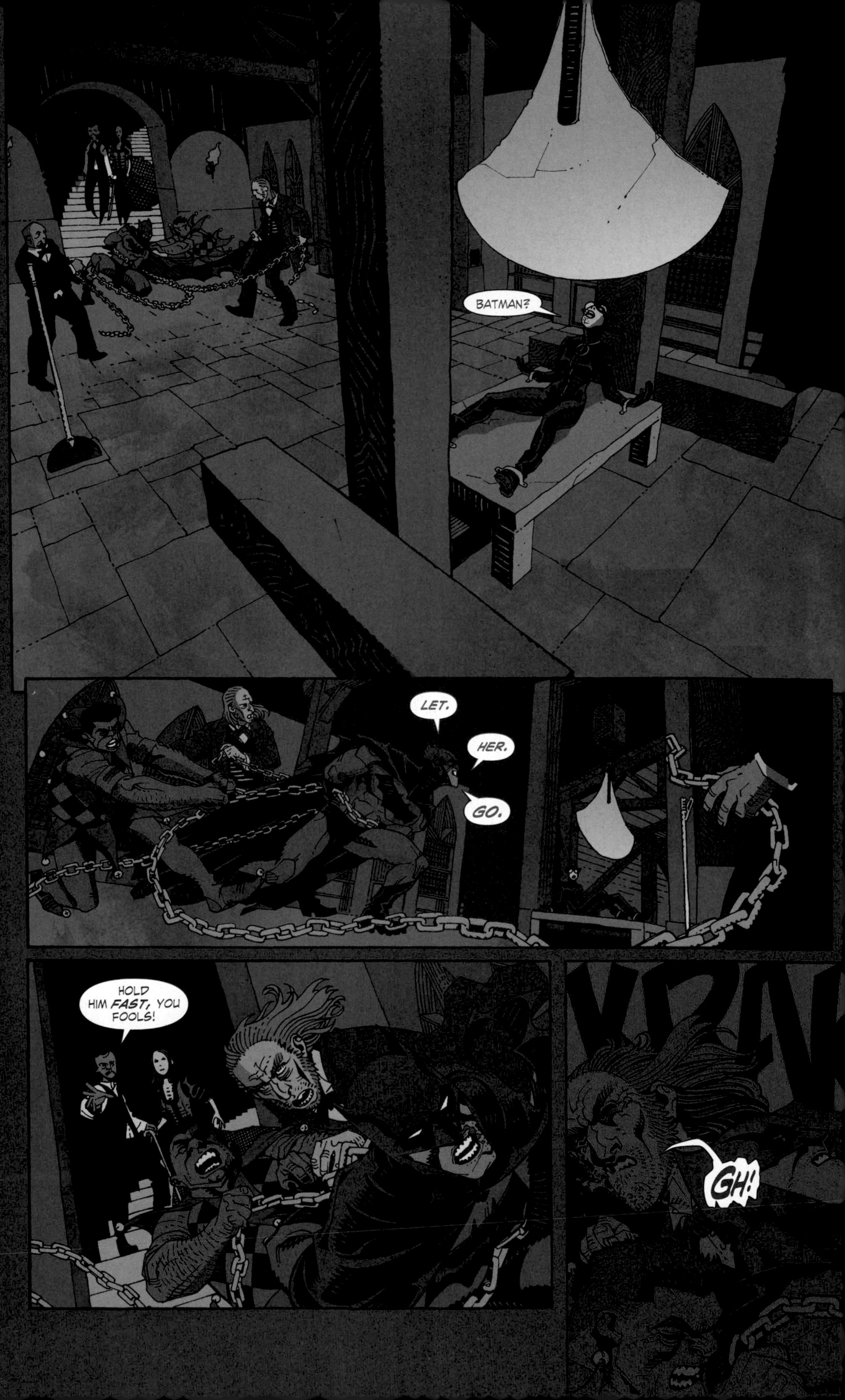
BATMAN?
LET.
HER.
GO.
HOLD HIM FAST, YOU FOOLS!
GH!

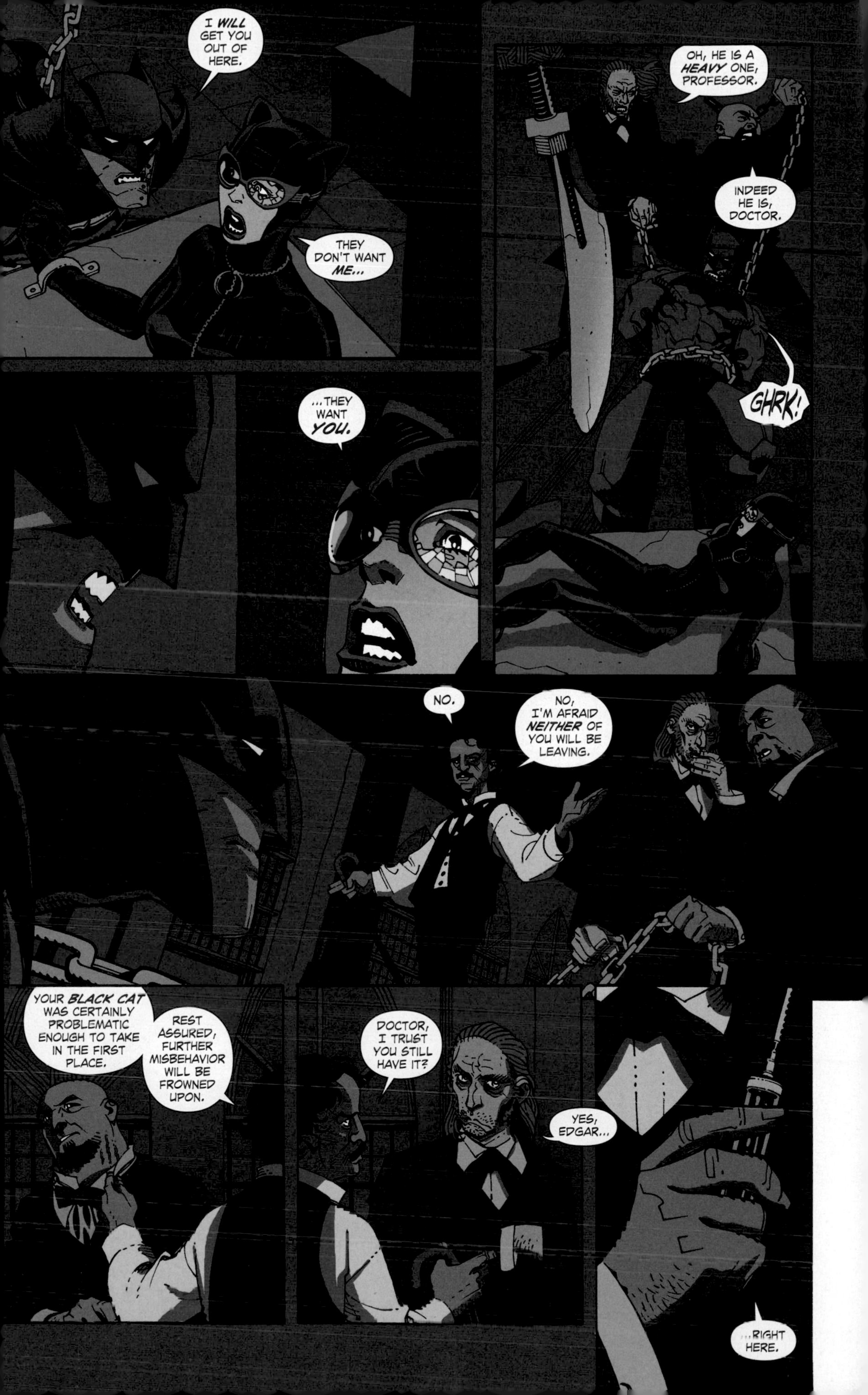

I WILL GET YOU OUT OF HERE.
THEY DON'T WANT ME...
OH, HE IS A HEAVY ONE, PROFESSOR.
INDEED HE IS, DOCTOR.
GHRK!
...THEY WANT YOU.
NO.
NO, I'M AFRAID NEITHER OF YOU WILL BE LEAVING.
YOUR BLACK CAT WAS CERTAINLY PROBLEMATIC ENOUGH TO TAKE IN THE FIRST PLACE.
REST ASSURED, FURTHER MISBEHAVIOR WILL BE FROWNED UPON.
DOCTOR, I TRUST YOU STILL HAVE IT?
YES, EDGAR...
...RIGHT HERE.

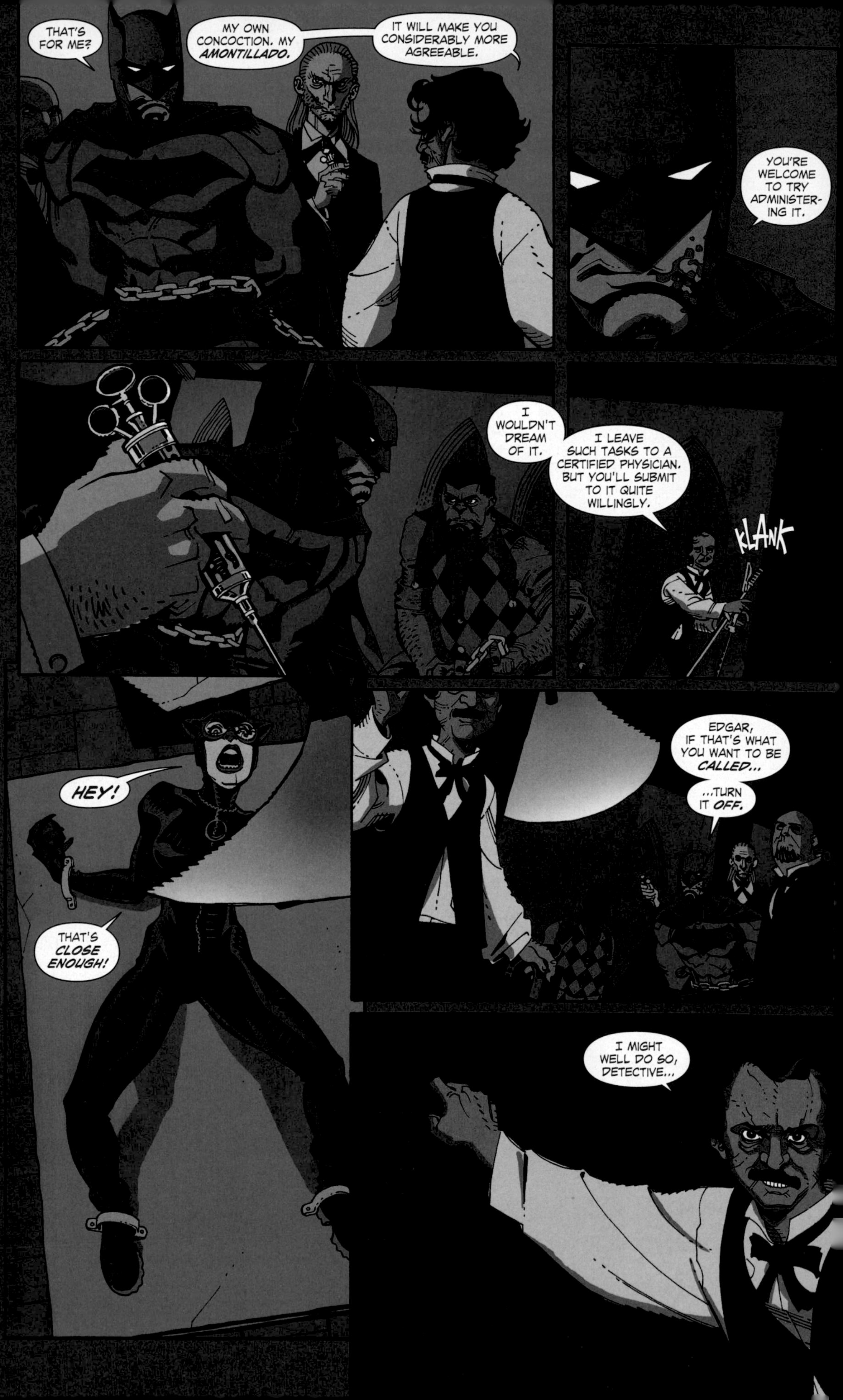

THAT'S FOR ME?
MY OWN CONCOCTION. MY *AMONTILLADO.*
IT WILL MAKE YOU CONSIDERABLY MORE AGREEABLE.
YOU'RE WELCOME TO TRY ADMINISTERING IT.
I WOULDN'T DREAM OF IT.
I LEAVE SUCH TASKS TO A CERTIFIED PHYSICIAN. BUT YOU'LL SUBMIT TO IT QUITE WILLINGLY.
KLANK
HEY!
THAT'S *CLOSE ENOUGH!*
EDGAR, IF THAT'S WHAT YOU WANT TO BE *CALLED...*
...TURN IT *OFF.*
I MIGHT WELL DO SO, DETECTIVE...

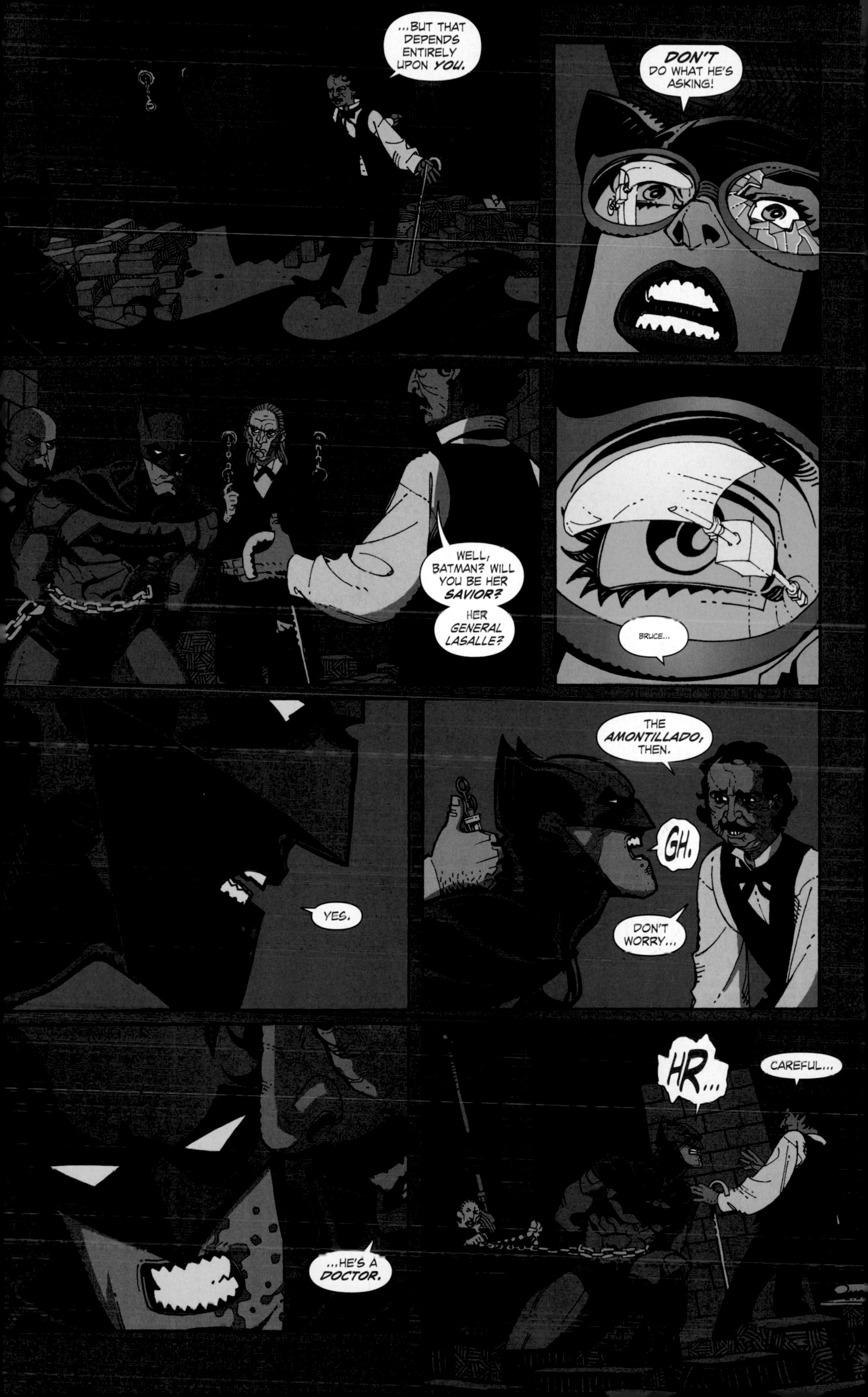
...BUT THAT DEPENDS ENTIRELY UPON *YOU.*
DON'T DO WHAT HE'S ASKING!
WELL, BATMAN? WILL YOU BE HER *SAVIOR?*
HER *GENERAL LASALLE?*
BRUCE...
YES.
THE *AMONTILLADO,* THEN.
GH.
DON'T WORRY...
HR...
CAREFUL...
...HE'S A *DOCTOR.*

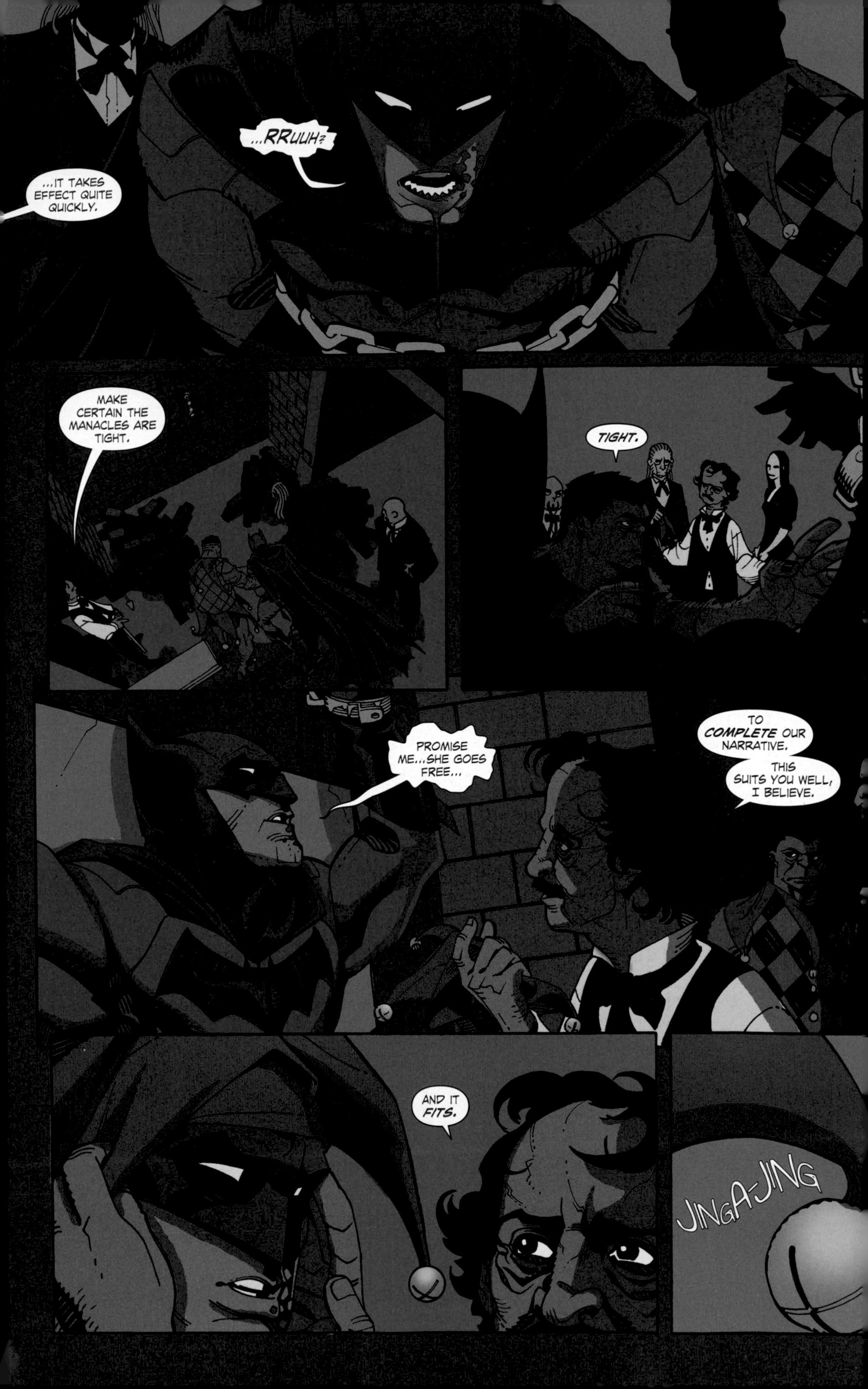
...RRUUH?
...IT TAKES EFFECT QUITE QUICKLY.
MAKE CERTAIN THE MANACLES ARE TIGHT.
TIGHT.
PROMISE ME...SHE GOES FREE...
TO COMPLETE OUR NARRATIVE.
THIS SUITS YOU WELL, I BELIEVE.
AND IT FITS.
JINGA-JING

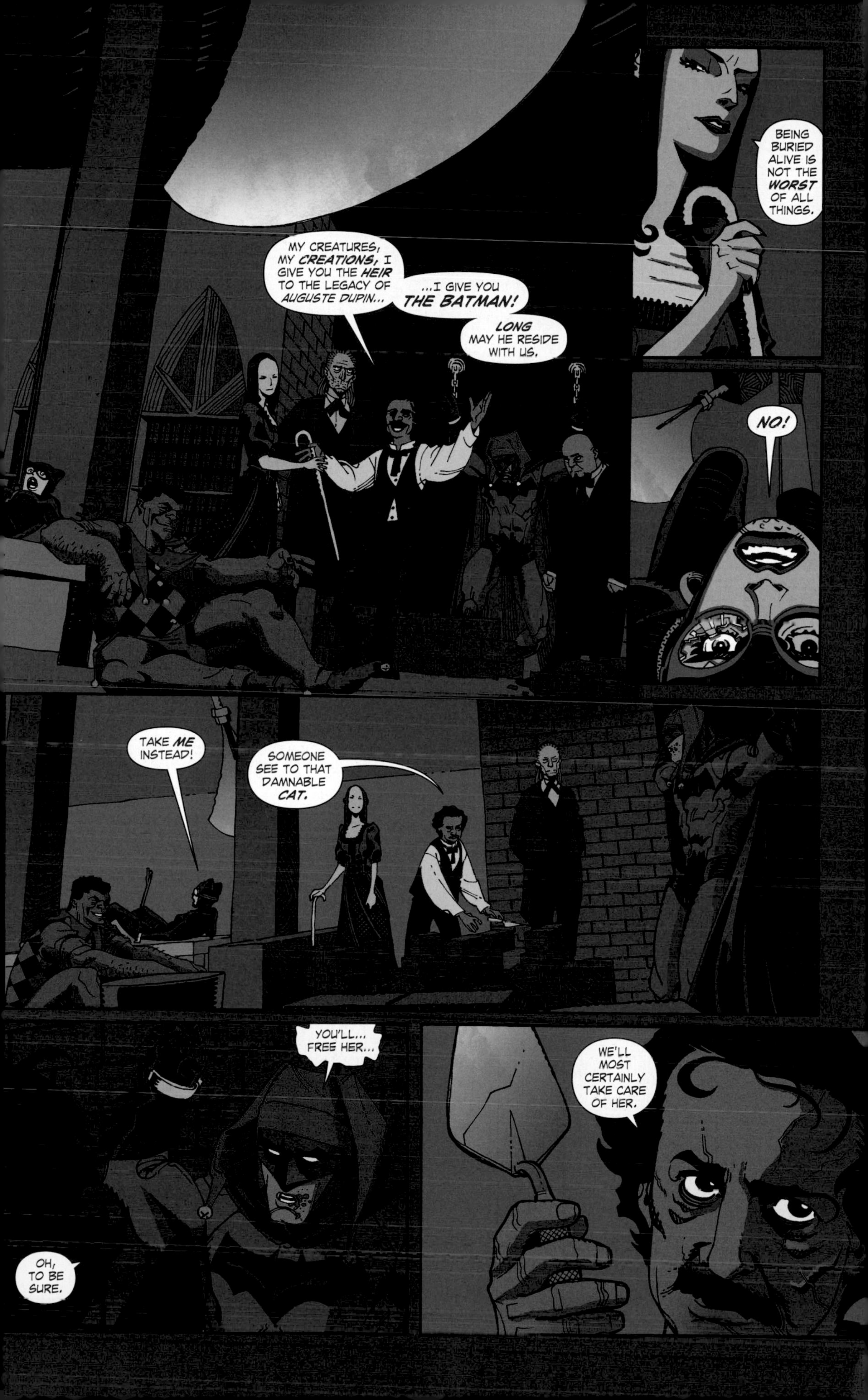
MY CREATURES, MY CREATIONS, I GIVE YOU THE HEIR TO THE LEGACY OF AUGUSTE DUPIN...
...I GIVE YOU THE BATMAN!
LONG MAY HE RESIDE WITH US.
BEING BURIED ALIVE IS NOT THE WORST OF ALL THINGS.
NO!
TAKE ME INSTEAD!
SOMEONE SEE TO THAT DAMNABLE CAT.
YOU'LL... FREE HER...
OH, TO BE SURE.
WE'LL MOST CERTAINLY TAKE CARE OF HER.

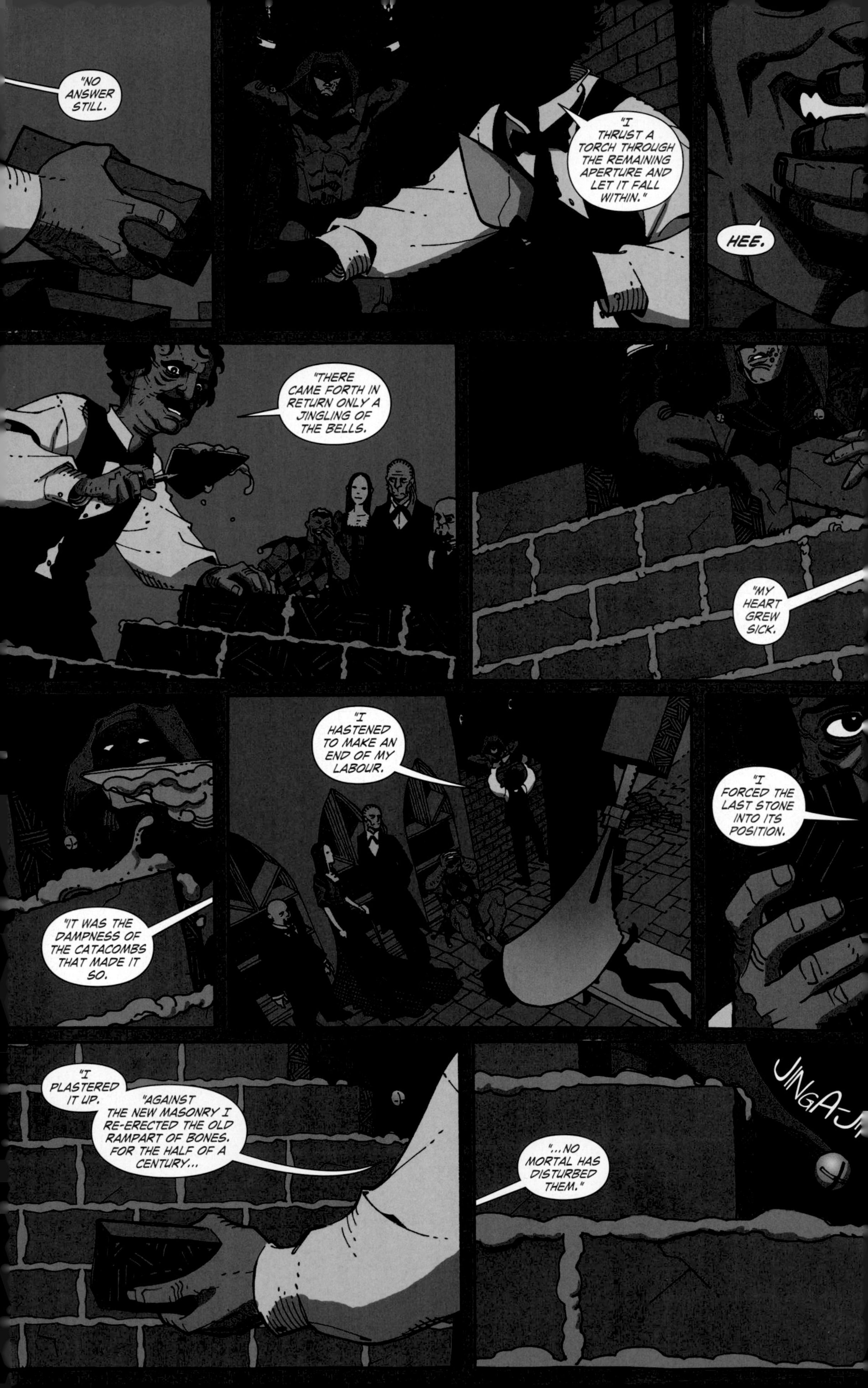
"NO ANSWER STILL.
"I THRUST A TORCH THROUGH THE REMAINING APERTURE AND LET IT FALL WITHIN."
HEE.
"THERE CAME FORTH IN RETURN ONLY A JINGLING OF THE BELLS.
"MY HEART GREW SICK.
"IT WAS THE DAMPNESS OF THE CATACOMBS THAT MADE IT SO.
"I HASTENED TO MAKE AN END OF MY LABOUR.
"I FORCED THE LAST STONE INTO ITS POSITION.
"I PLASTERED IT UP.
"AGAINST THE NEW MASONRY I RE-ERECTED THE OLD RAMPART OF BONES. FOR THE HALF OF A CENTURY...
"...NO MORTAL HAS DISTURBED THEM."

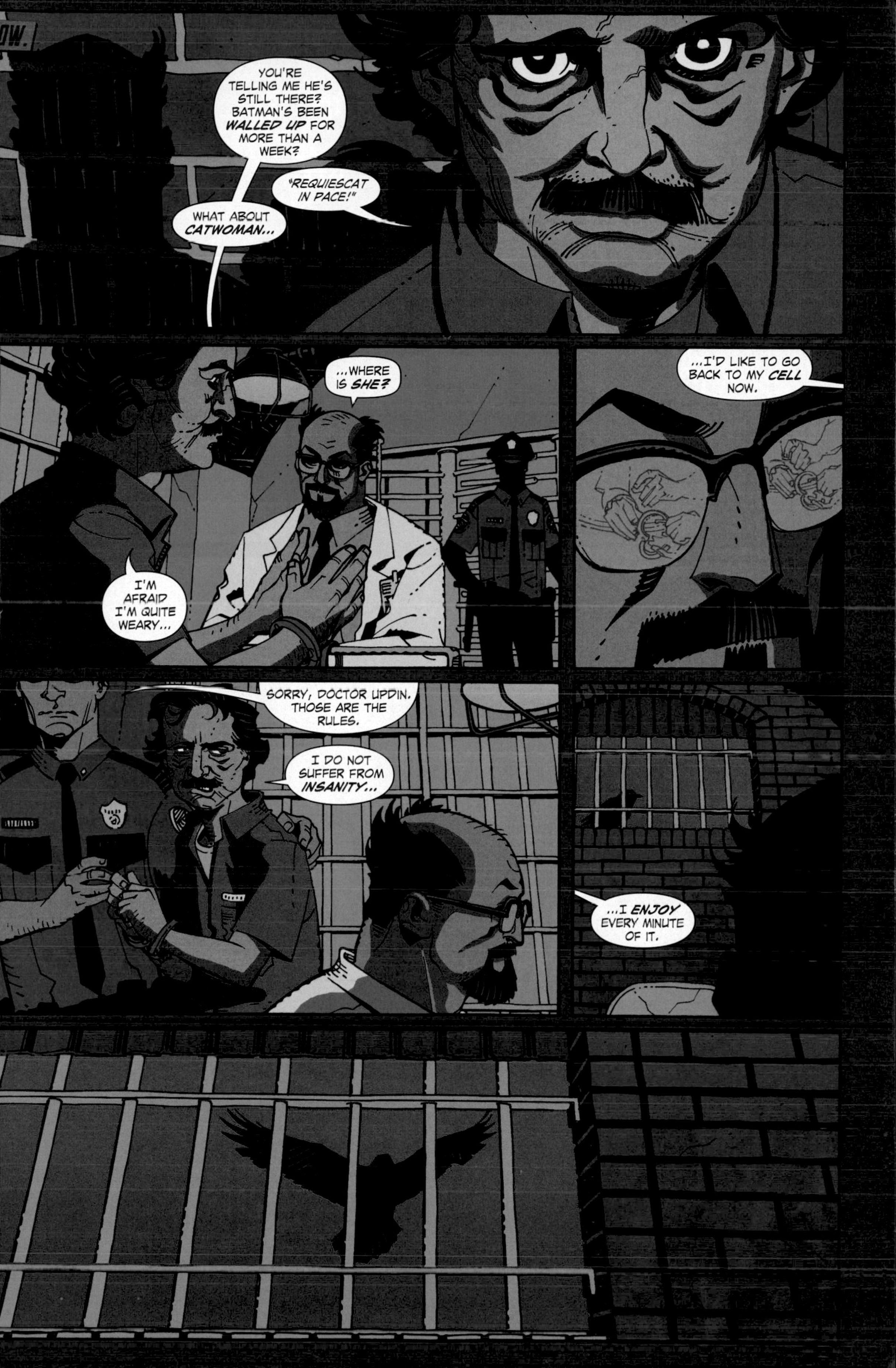
OW.
YOU'RE TELLING ME HE'S STILL THERE? BATMAN'S BEEN WALLED UP FOR MORE THAN A WEEK?
"REQUIESCAT IN PACE!"
WHAT ABOUT CATWOMAN...
...WHERE IS SHE?
I'M AFRAID I'M QUITE WEARY...
...I'D LIKE TO GO BACK TO MY CELL NOW.
SORRY, DOCTOR UPDIN. THOSE ARE THE RULES.
I DO NOT SUFFER FROM INSANITY...
...I ENJOY EVERY MINUTE OF IT.

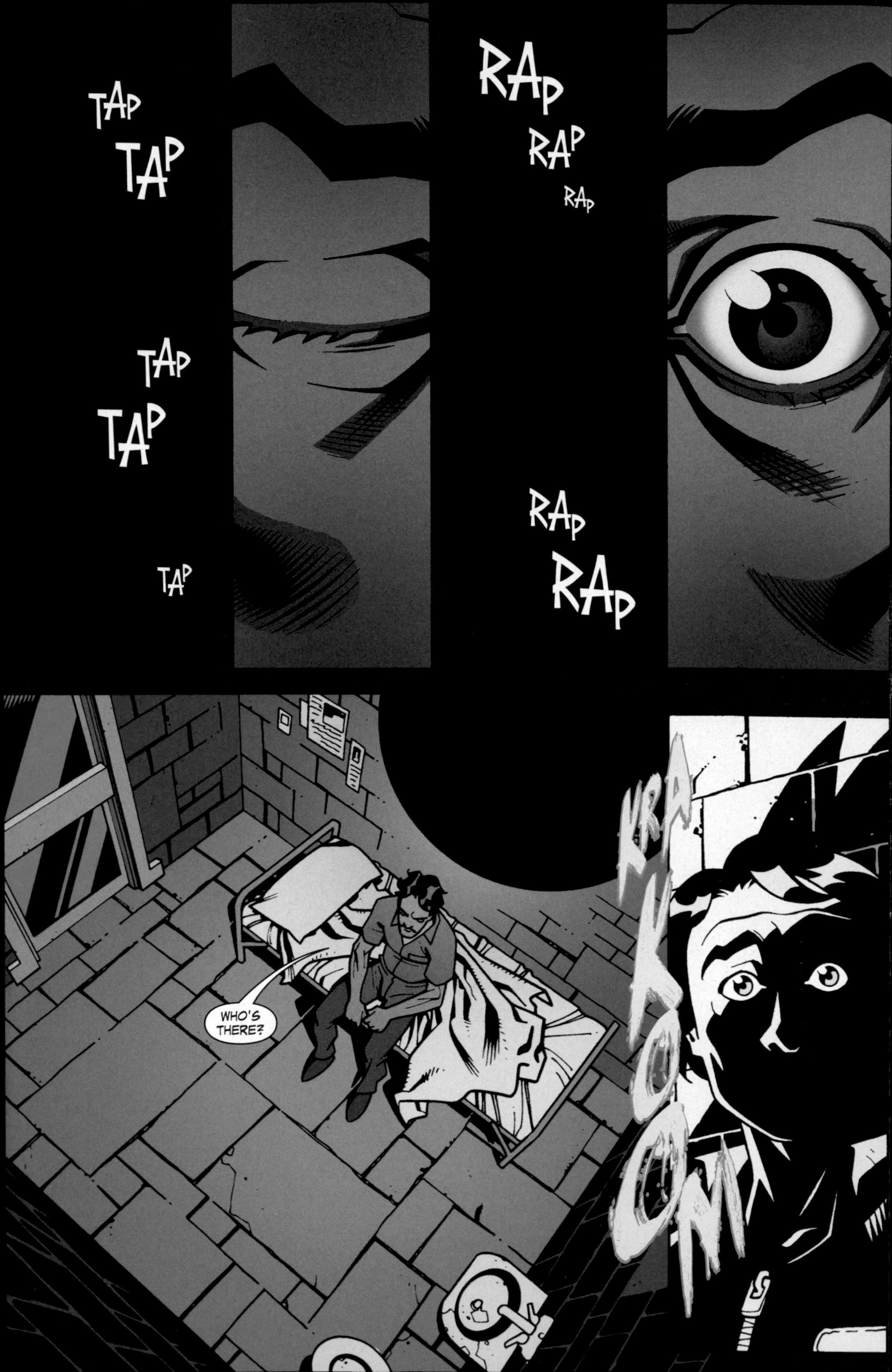
TAP
TAP
TAP
TAP
TAP
RAP
RAP
RAP
RAP
RAP
WHO'S THERE?
KRAKOOM

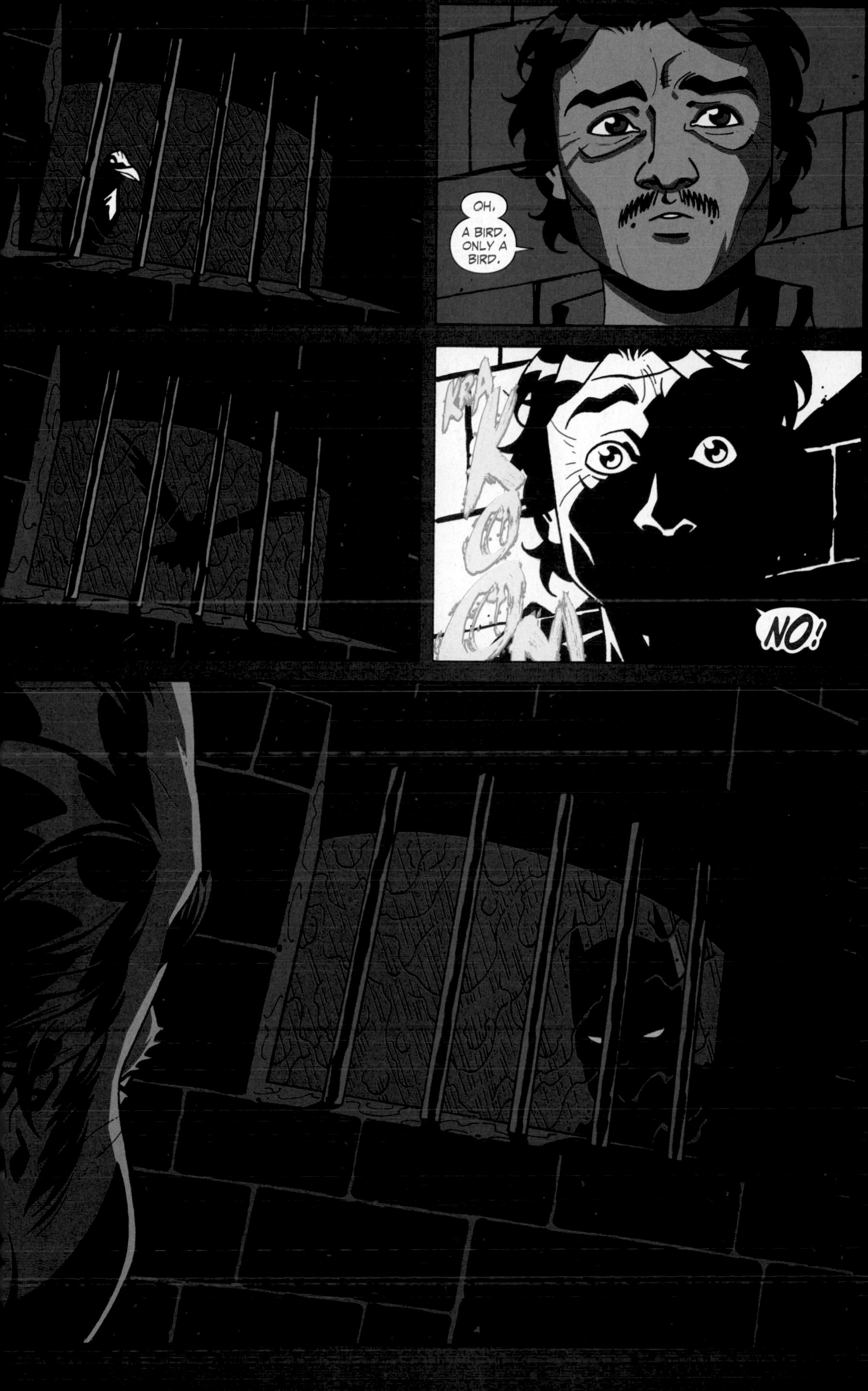
OH, A BIRD. ONLY A BIRD.
KRA-KOOOM
NO!

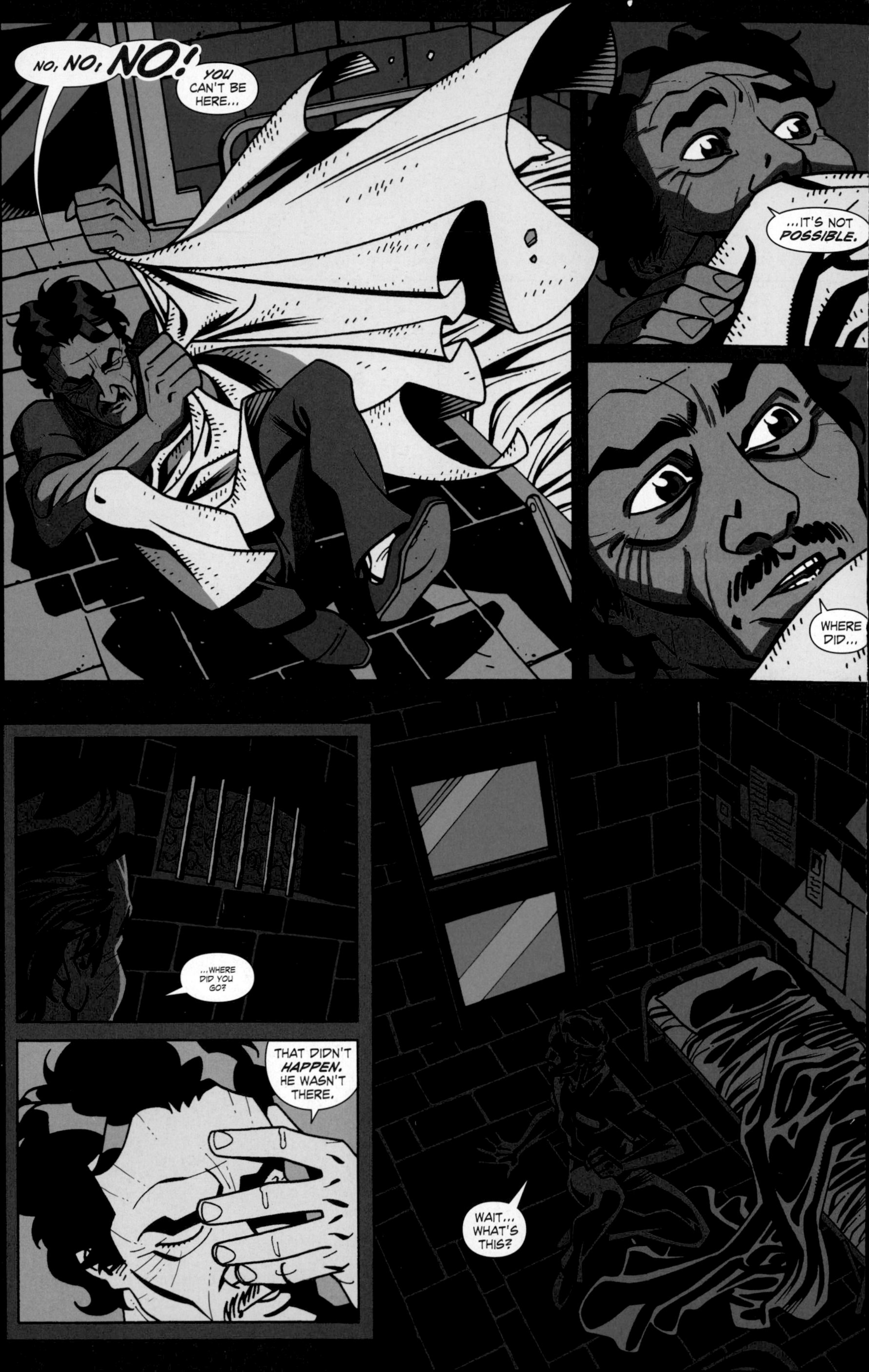
NO, NO, NO! YOU CAN'T BE HERE...
...IT'S NOT POSSIBLE.
WHERE DID...
...WHERE DID YOU GO?
THAT DIDN'T HAPPEN. HE WASN'T THERE.
WAIT... WHAT'S THIS?

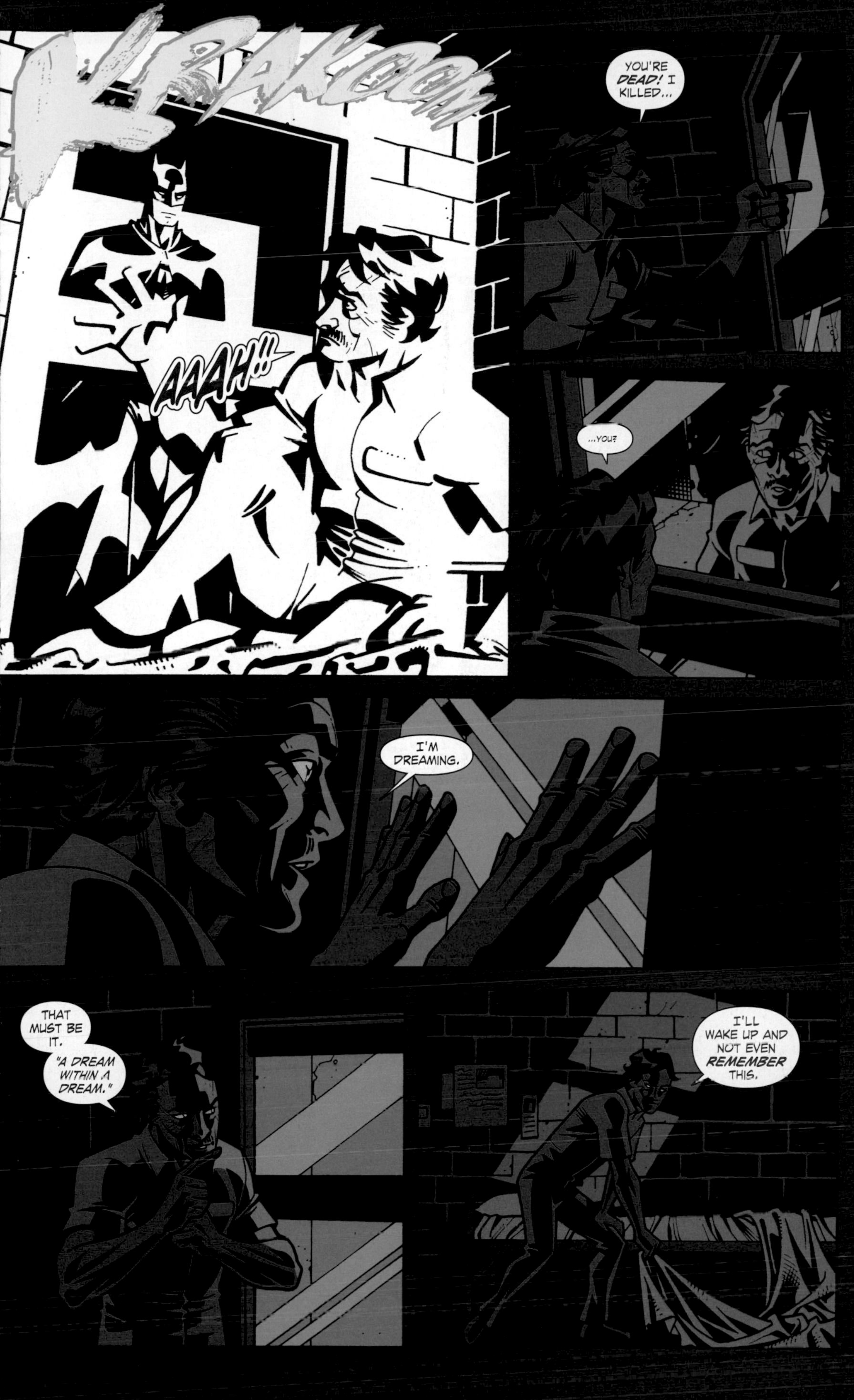
KRAKOOM
AAAH!!
YOU'RE DEAD! I KILLED...
...YOU?
I'M DREAMING.
THAT MUST BE IT. "A DREAM WITHIN A DREAM."
I'LL WAKE UP AND NOT EVEN REMEMBER THIS.

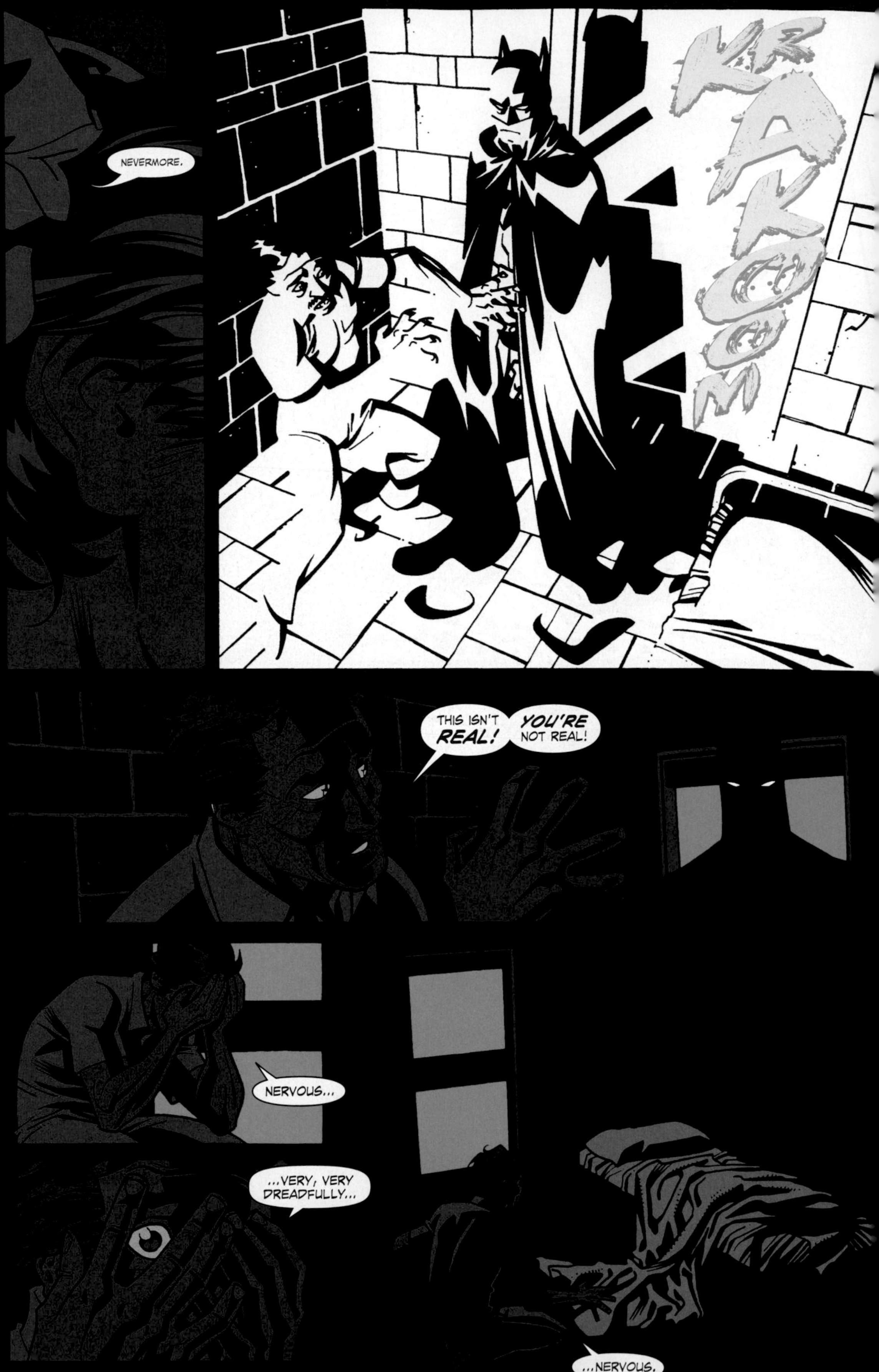
NEVERMORE.
KRAKOOM
THIS ISN'T REAL!
YOU'RE NOT REAL!
NERVOUS...
...VERY, VERY DREADFULLY...
...NERVOUS.

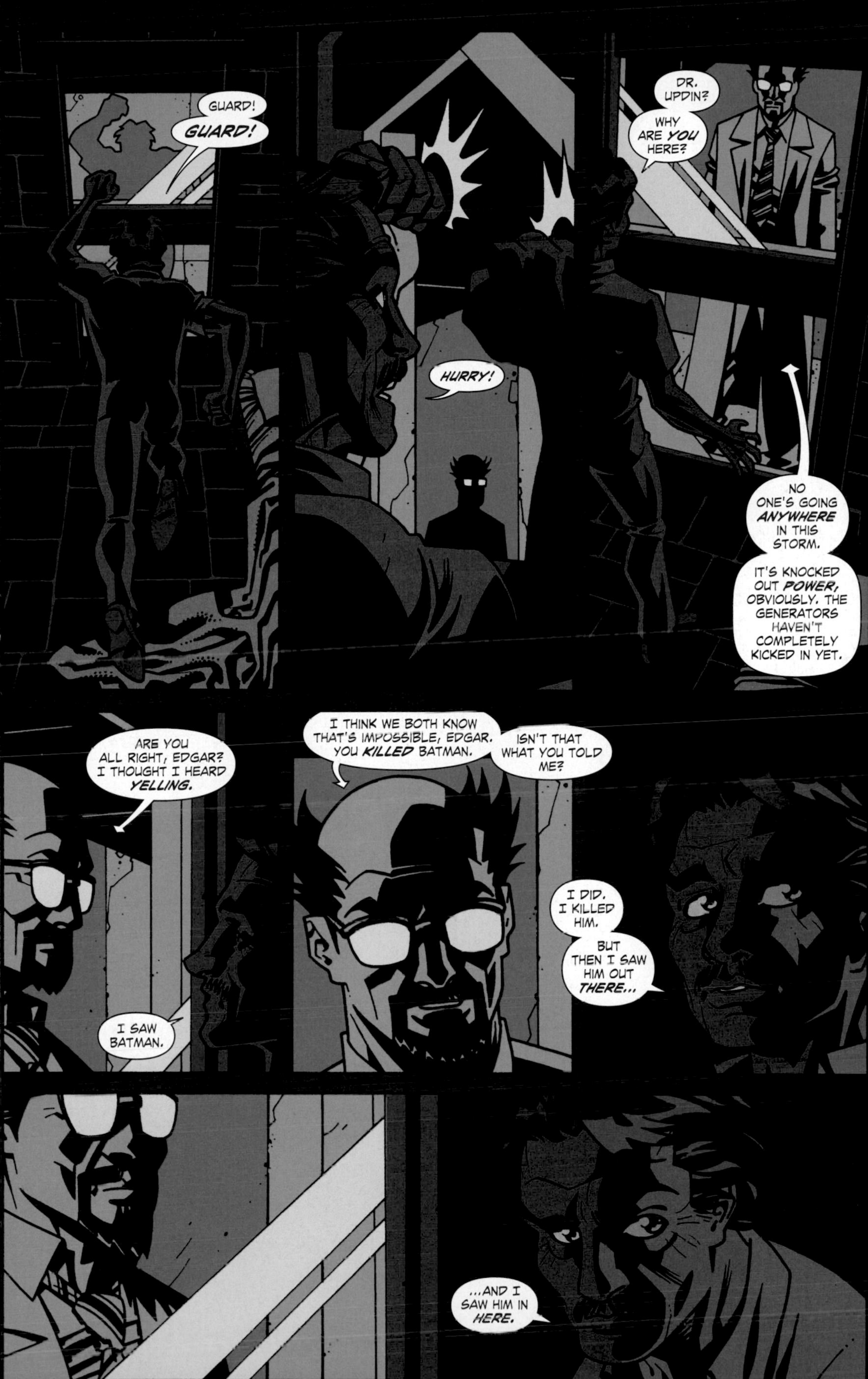
GUARD!
GUARD!
HURRY!
DR. UPDIN?
WHY ARE YOU HERE?
NO ONE'S GOING ANYWHERE IN THIS STORM.
IT'S KNOCKED OUT POWER, OBVIOUSLY. THE GENERATORS HAVEN'T COMPLETELY KICKED IN YET.
ARE YOU ALL RIGHT, EDGAR? I THOUGHT I HEARD YELLING.
I SAW BATMAN.
I THINK WE BOTH KNOW THAT'S IMPOSSIBLE, EDGAR. YOU KILLED BATMAN.
ISN'T THAT WHAT YOU TOLD ME?
I DID. I KILLED HIM.
BUT THEN I SAW HIM OUT THERE...
...AND I SAW HIM IN HERE.

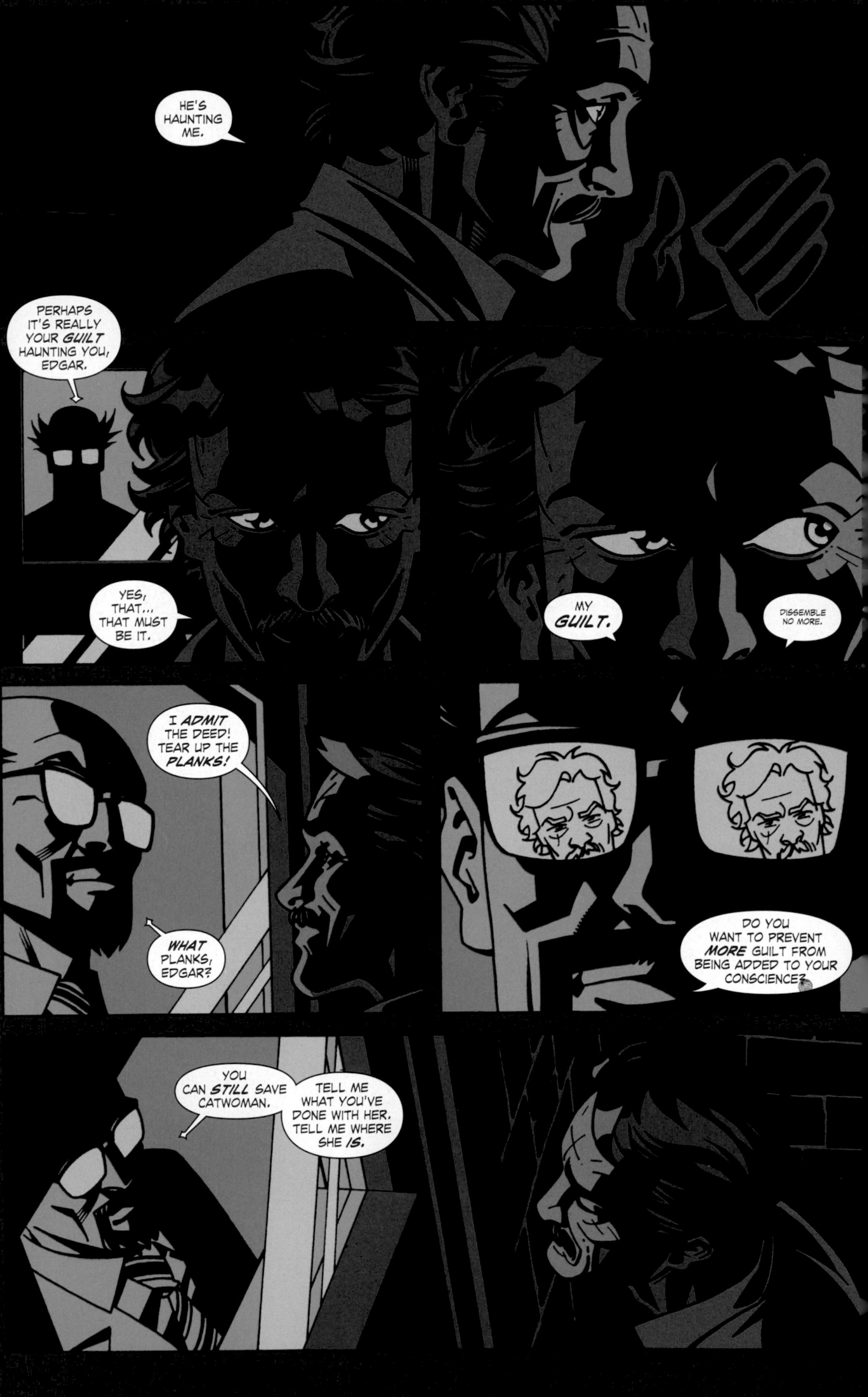
HE'S HAUNTING ME.
PERHAPS IT'S REALLY YOUR GUILT HAUNTING YOU, EDGAR.
YES, THAT... THAT MUST BE IT.
MY GUILT.
DISSEMBLE NO MORE.
I ADMIT THE DEED! TEAR UP THE PLANKS!
WHAT PLANKS, EDGAR?
DO YOU WANT TO PREVENT MORE GUILT FROM BEING ADDED TO YOUR CONSCIENCE?
YOU CAN STILL SAVE CATWOMAN.
TELL ME WHAT YOU'VE DONE WITH HER. TELL ME WHERE SHE IS.

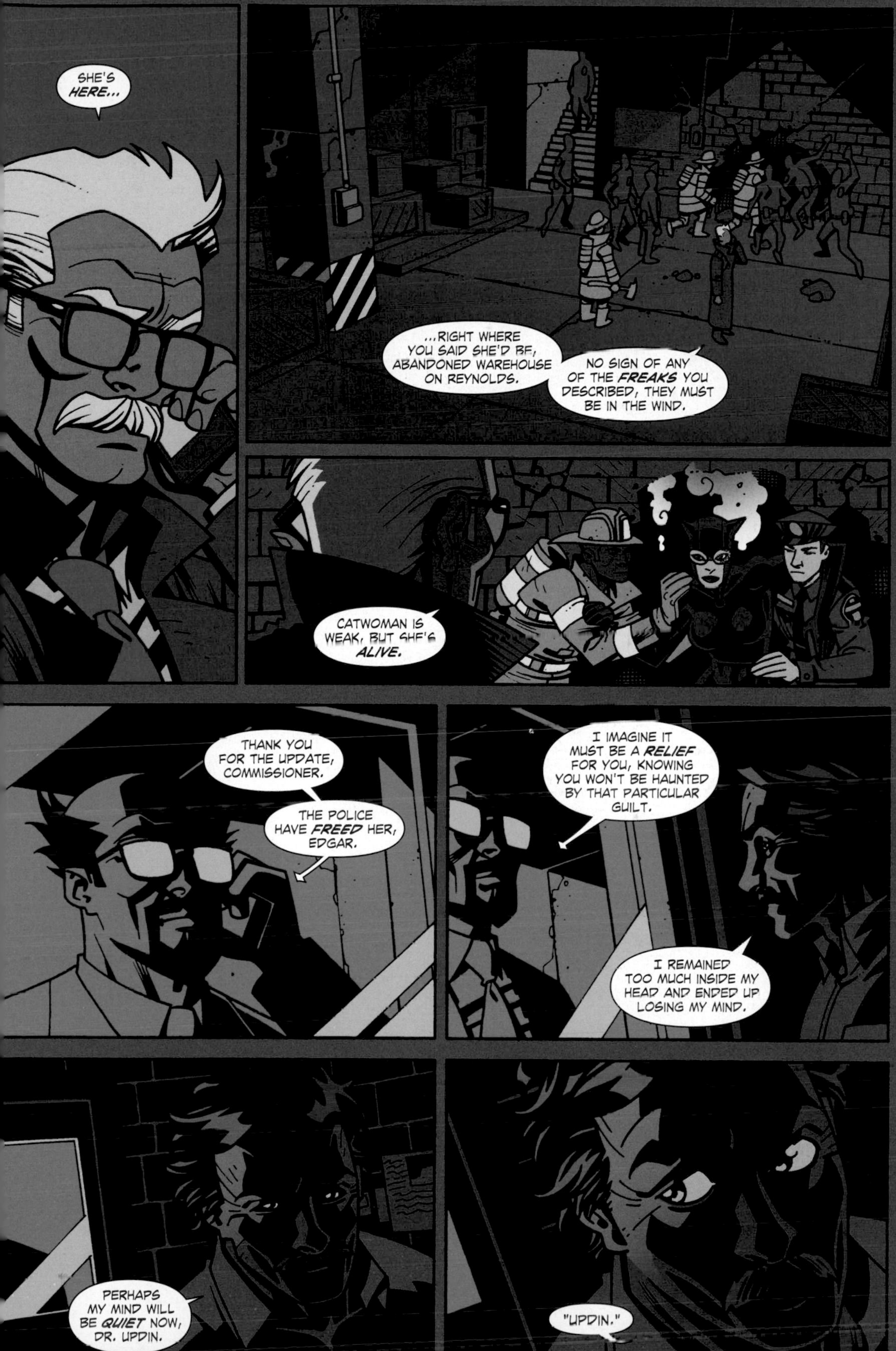

SHE'S HERE...
...RIGHT WHERE YOU SAID SHE'D BE, ABANDONED WAREHOUSE ON REYNOLDS.
NO SIGN OF ANY OF THE FREAKS YOU DESCRIBED, THEY MUST BE IN THE WIND.
CATWOMAN IS WEAK, BUT SHE'S ALIVE.
THANK YOU FOR THE UPDATE, COMMISSIONER.
THE POLICE HAVE FREED HER, EDGAR.
I IMAGINE IT MUST BE A RELIEF FOR YOU, KNOWING YOU WON'T BE HAUNTED BY THAT PARTICULAR GUILT.
I REMAINED TOO MUCH INSIDE MY HEAD AND ENDED UP LOSING MY MIND.
PERHAPS MY MIND WILL BE QUIET NOW, DR. UPDIN.
"UPDIN."

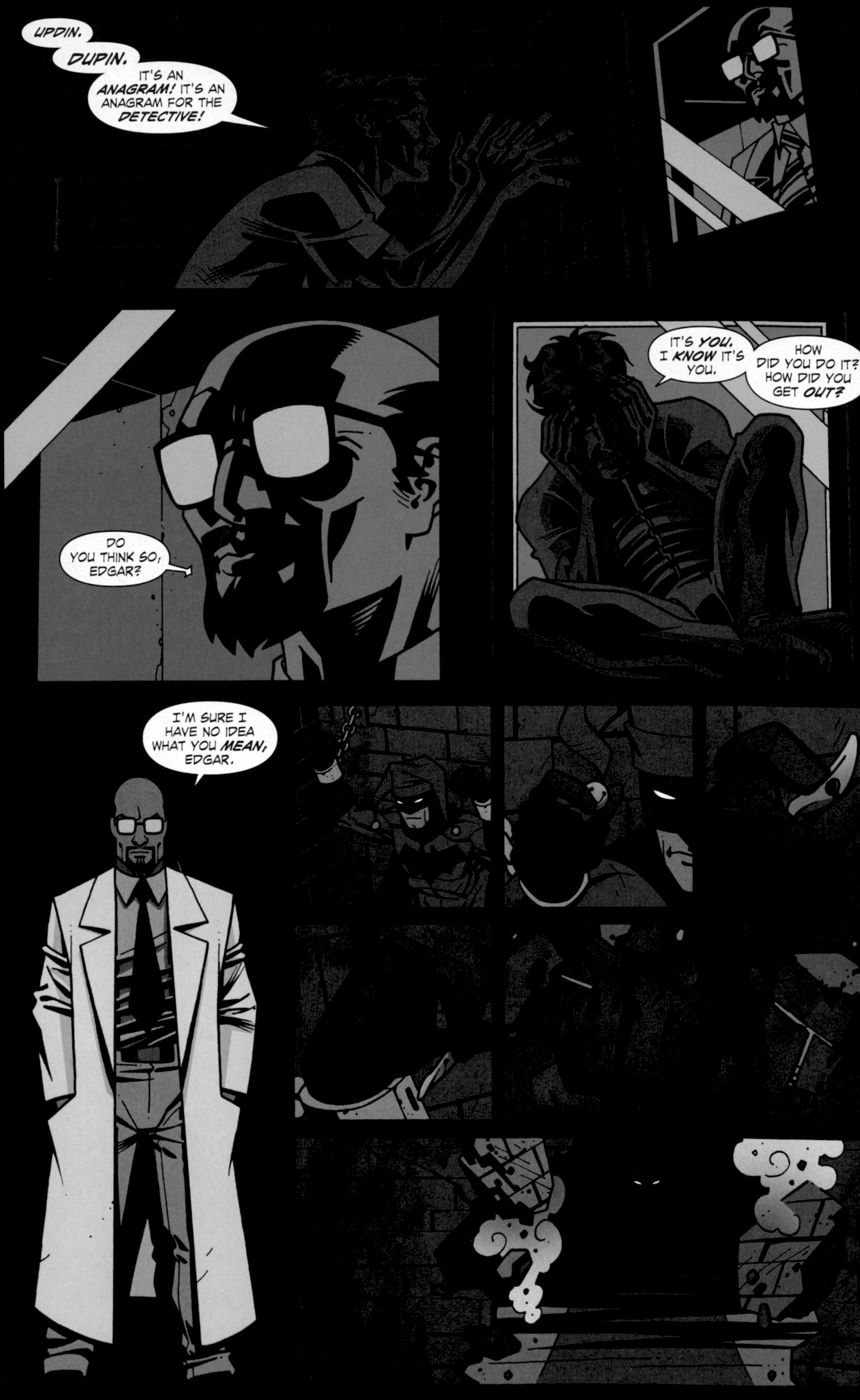
UPDIN.
DUPIN.
IT'S AN ANAGRAM! IT'S AN ANAGRAM FOR THE DETECTIVE!
DO YOU THINK SO, EDGAR?
IT'S YOU. I KNOW IT'S YOU.
HOW DID YOU DO IT? HOW DID YOU GET OUT?
I'M SURE I HAVE NO IDEA WHAT YOU MEAN, EDGAR.

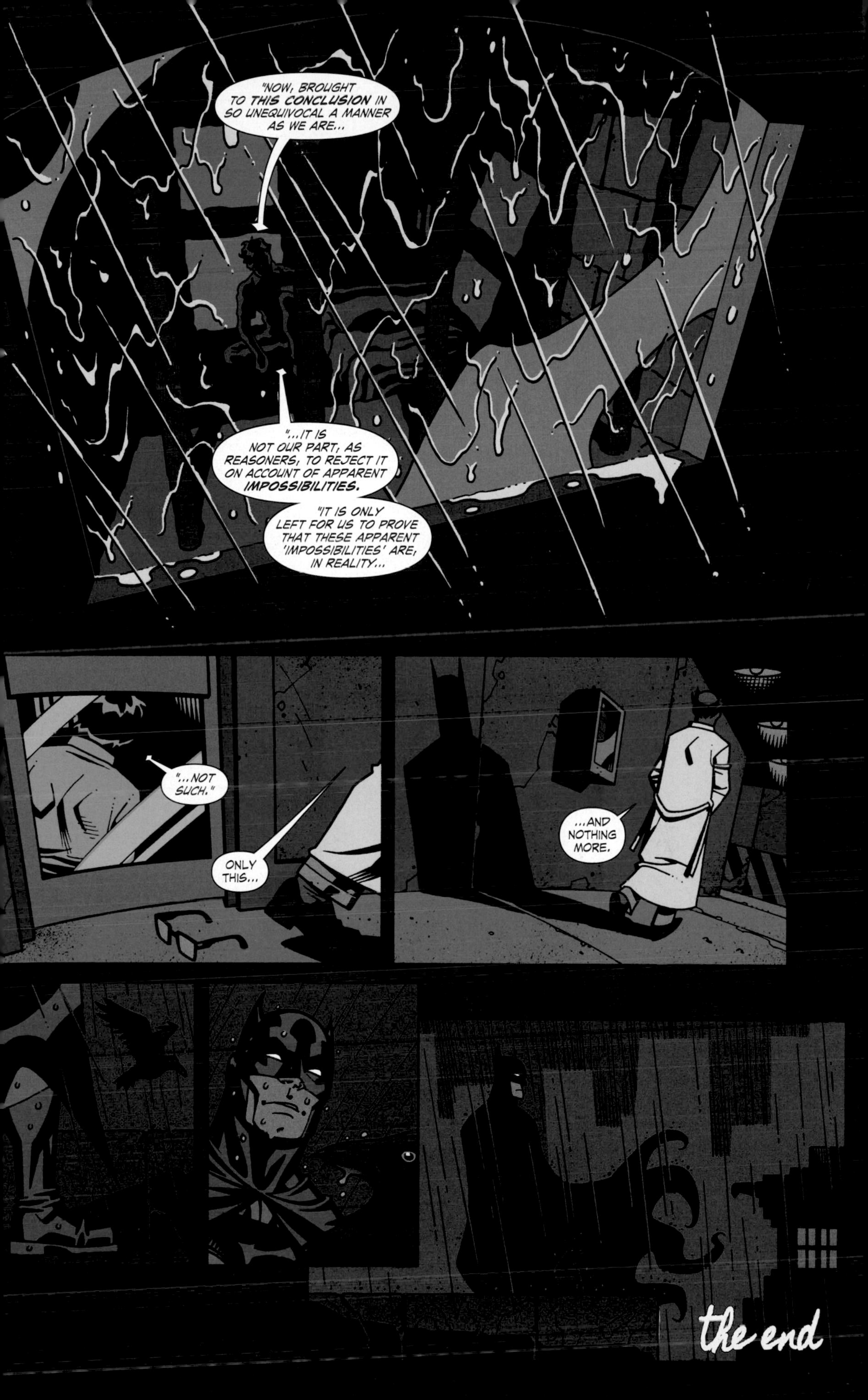
"NOW, BROUGHT TO THIS CONCLUSION IN SO UNEQUIVOCAL A MANNER AS WE ARE...
"...IT IS NOT OUR PART, AS REASONERS, TO REJECT IT ON ACCOUNT OF APPARENT IMPOSSIBILITIES.
"IT IS ONLY LEFT FOR US TO PROVE THAT THESE APPARENT 'IMPOSSIBILITIES' ARE, IN REALITY...
"...NOT SUCH."
ONLY THIS...
...AND NOTHING MORE.
the end

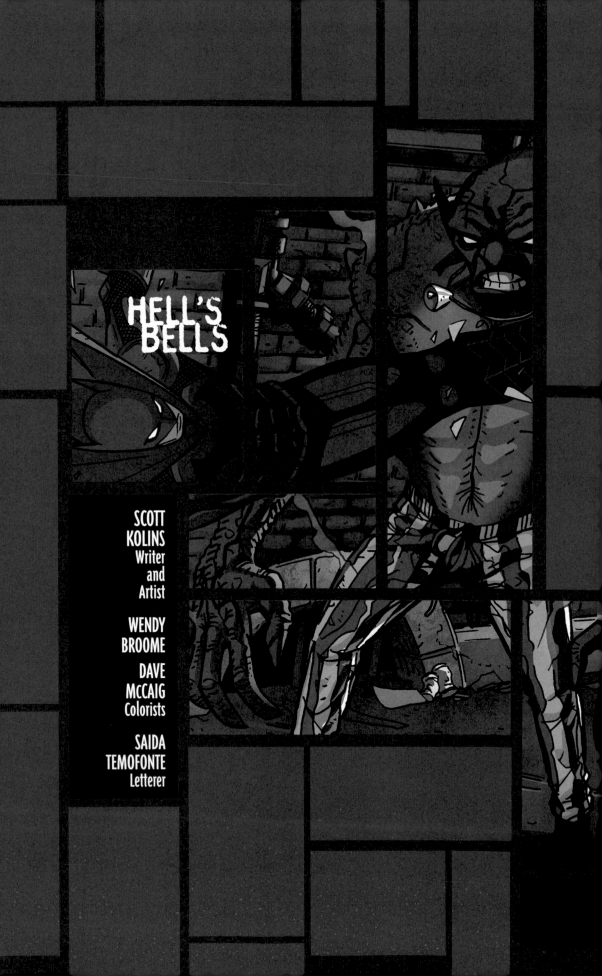

HELL'S BELLS

SCOTT
KOLINS
Writer
and
Artist

WENDY
BROOME

DAVE
McCAIG
Colorists

SAIDA
TEMOFONTE
Letterer

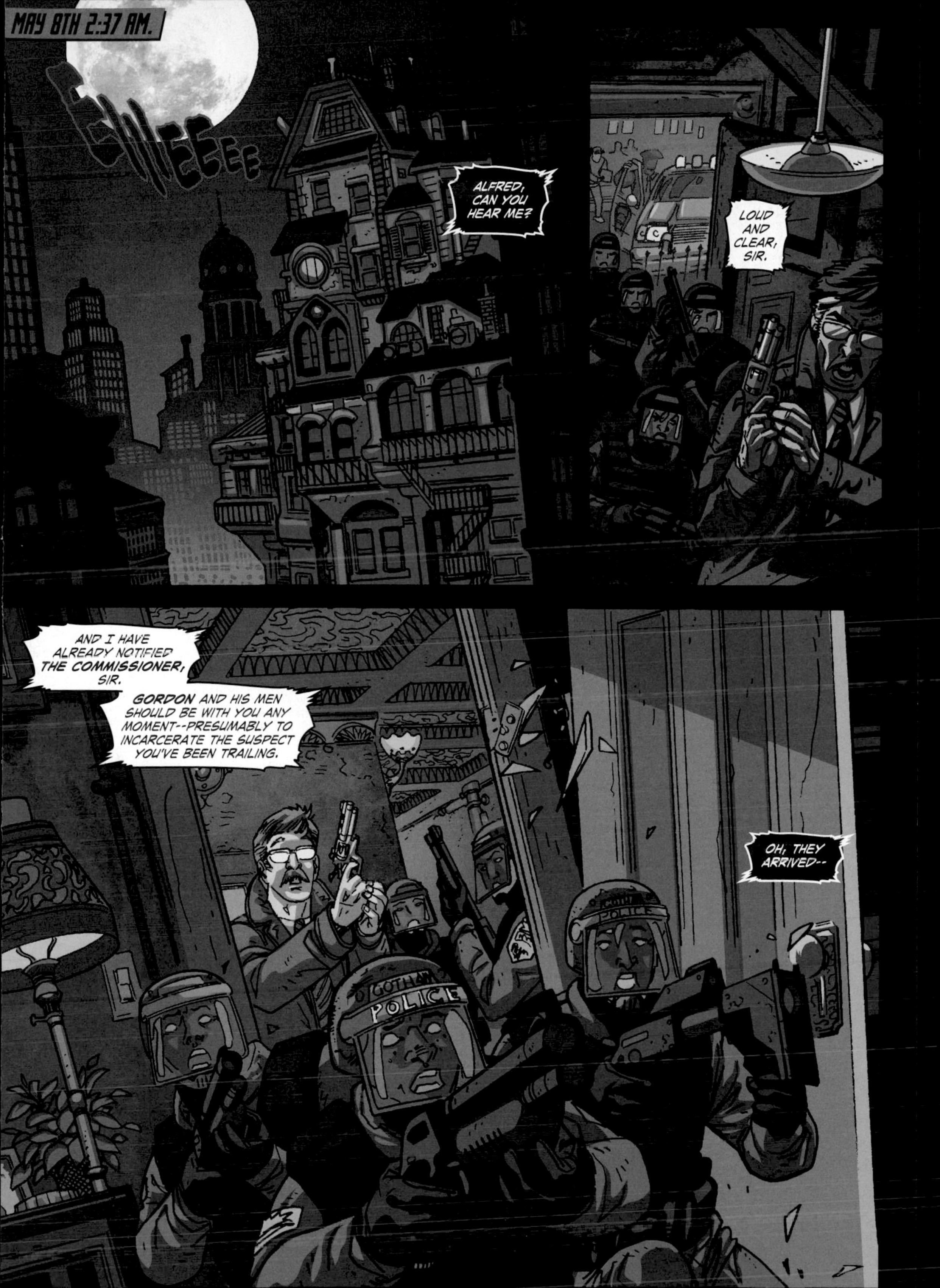
MAY 8TH 2:37 AM.
EEEEEEE
ALFRED, CAN YOU HEAR ME?
LOUD AND CLEAR, SIR.
AND I HAVE ALREADY NOTIFIED THE COMMISSIONER, SIR.
GORDON AND HIS MEN SHOULD BE WITH YOU ANY MOMENT--PRESUMABLY TO INCARCERATE THE SUSPECT YOU'VE BEEN TRAILING.
OH, THEY ARRIVED--
GOTHAM POLICE

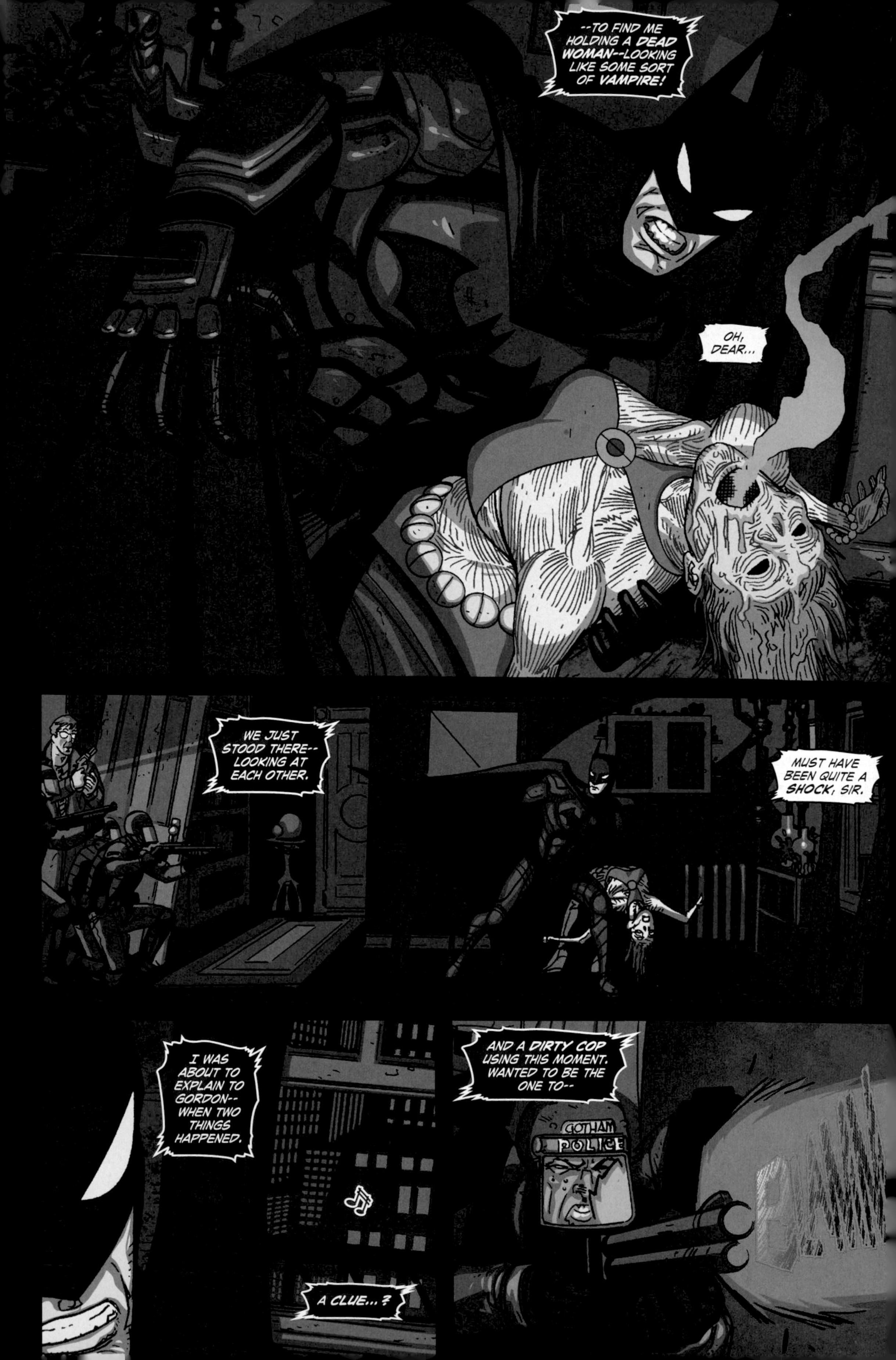
--TO FIND ME HOLDING A DEAD WOMAN--LOOKING LIKE SOME SORT OF VAMPIRE!
OH, DEAR...
WE JUST STOOD THERE--LOOKING AT EACH OTHER.
MUST HAVE BEEN QUITE A SHOCK, SIR.
I WAS ABOUT TO EXPLAIN TO GORDON--WHEN TWO THINGS HAPPENED.
A CLUE...?
AND A DIRTY COP USING THIS MOMENT. WANTED TO BE THE ONE TO--
GOTHAM POLICE

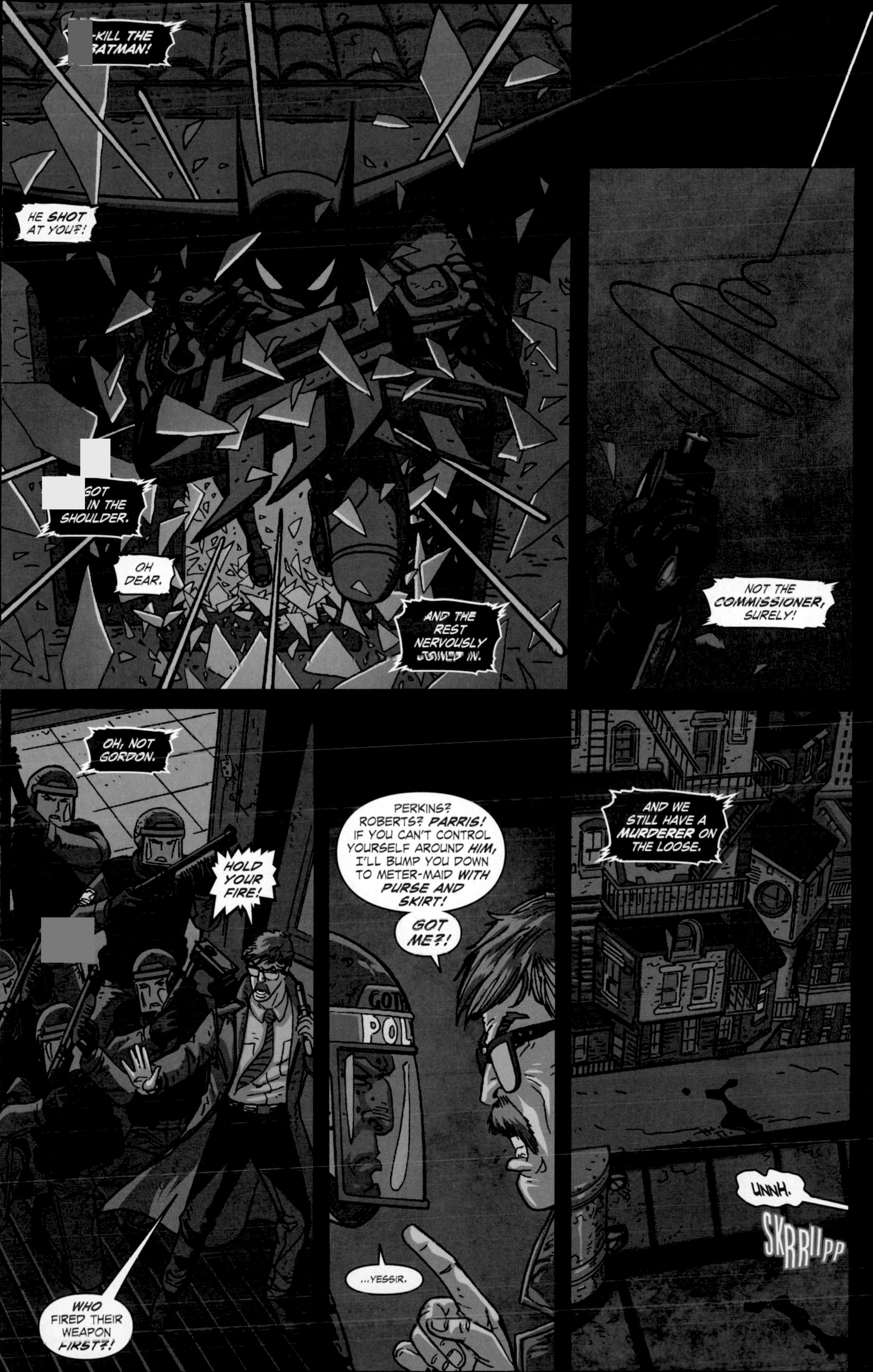

-KILL THE
BATMAN!
HE SHOT AT YOU?!
GOT
IN THE SHOULDER.
OH DEAR.
AND THE REST NERVOUSLY JOINED IN.
NOT THE COMMISSIONER, SURELY!
OH, NOT GORDON.
HOLD YOUR FIRE!
WHO FIRED THEIR WEAPON FIRST?!
PERKINS? ROBERTS? PARRIS! IF YOU CAN'T CONTROL YOURSELF AROUND HIM, I'LL BUMP YOU DOWN TO METER-MAID WITH PURSE AND SKIRT!
GOT ME?!
...YESSIR.
AND WE STILL HAVE A MURDERER ON THE LOOSE.
UNNH.
SKRRIIPP

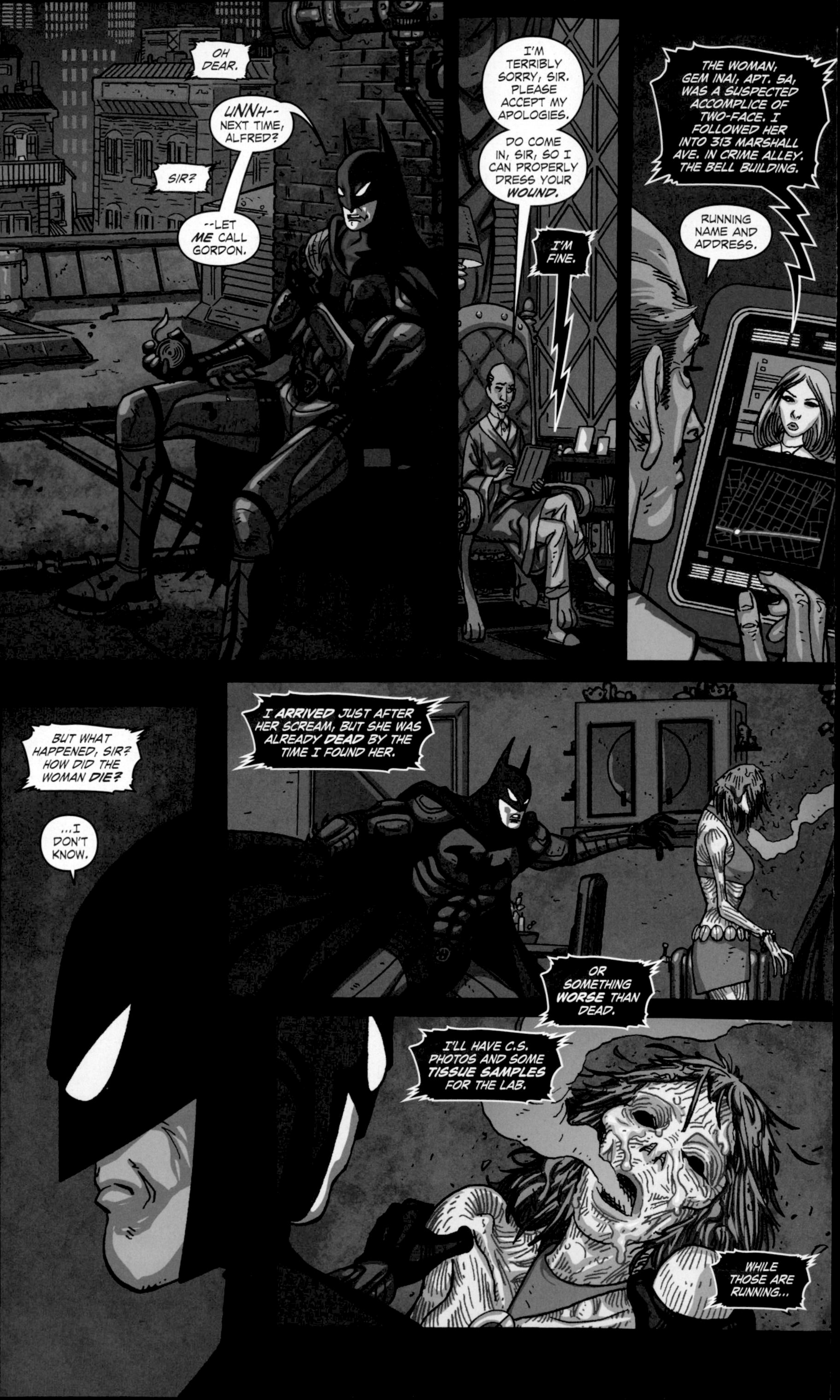
OH DEAR.
UNNH-- NEXT TIME, ALFRED?
SIR?
--LET ME CALL GORDON.
I'M TERRIBLY SORRY, SIR. PLEASE ACCEPT MY APOLOGIES.
DO COME IN, SIR, SO I CAN PROPERLY DRESS YOUR WOUND.
I'M FINE.
THE WOMAN, GEM INAI, APT. 5A, WAS A SUSPECTED ACCOMPLICE OF TWO-FACE. I FOLLOWED HER INTO 313 MARSHALL AVE. IN CRIME ALLEY. THE BELL BUILDING.
RUNNING NAME AND ADDRESS.
BUT WHAT HAPPENED, SIR? HOW DID THE WOMAN DIE?
...I DON'T KNOW.
I ARRIVED JUST AFTER HER SCREAM, BUT SHE WAS ALREADY DEAD BY THE TIME I FOUND HER.
OR SOMETHING WORSE THAN DEAD.
I'LL HAVE C.S. PHOTOS AND SOME TISSUE SAMPLES FOR THE LAB.
WHILE THOSE ARE RUNNING...

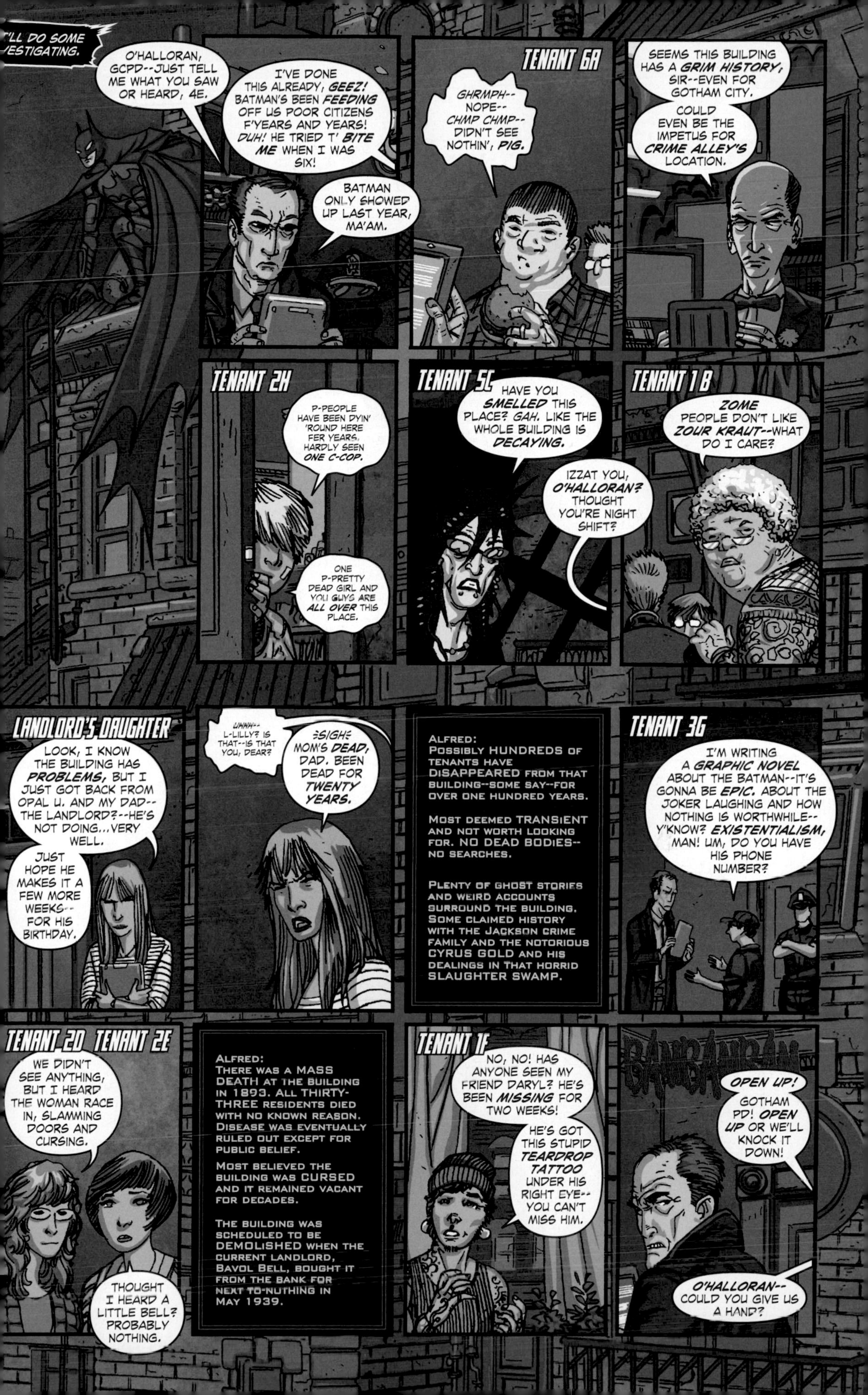
'LL DO SOME
VESTIGATING.
O'HALLORAN, GCPD--JUST TELL ME WHAT YOU SAW OR HEARD, 4E.
I'VE DONE THIS ALREADY, GEEZ! BATMAN'S BEEN FEEDING OFF US POOR CITIZENS F'YEARS AND YEARS! DUH! HE TRIED T' BITE ME WHEN I WAS SIX!
BATMAN ONLY SHOWED UP LAST YEAR, MA'AM.
TENANT 6A
GHRMPH--NOPE--CHMP CHMP--DIDN'T SEE NOTHIN', PIG.
SEEMS THIS BUILDING HAS A GRIM HISTORY, SIR--EVEN FOR GOTHAM CITY.
COULD EVEN BE THE IMPETUS FOR CRIME ALLEY'S LOCATION.
TENANT 2H
P-PEOPLE HAVE BEEN DYIN' 'ROUND HERE FER YEARS. HARDLY SEEN ONE C-COP.
ONE P-PRETTY DEAD GIRL AND YOU GUYS ARE ALL OVER THIS PLACE.
TENANT 5C
HAVE YOU SMELLED THIS PLACE? GAH. LIKE THE WHOLE BUILDING IS DECAYING.
IZZAT YOU, O'HALLORAN? THOUGHT YOU'RE NIGHT SHIFT?
TENANT 1B
ZOME PEOPLE DON'T LIKE ZOUR KRAUT--WHAT DO I CARE?
LANDLORD'S DAUGHTER
LOOK, I KNOW THE BUILDING HAS PROBLEMS, BUT I JUST GOT BACK FROM OPAL U. AND MY DAD--THE LANDLORD?--HE'S NOT DOING...VERY WELL.
JUST HOPE HE MAKES IT A FEW MORE WEEKS--FOR HIS BIRTHDAY.
UHHH--L-LILLY? IS THAT--IS THAT YOU, DEAR?
SIGH MOM'S DEAD, DAD. BEEN DEAD FOR TWENTY YEARS.
ALFRED: POSSIBLY HUNDREDS OF TENANTS HAVE DISAPPEARED FROM THAT BUILDING--SOME SAY--FOR OVER ONE HUNDRED YEARS.
MOST DEEMED TRANSIENT AND NOT WORTH LOOKING FOR. NO DEAD BODIES--NO SEARCHES.
PLENTY OF GHOST STORIES AND WEIRD ACCOUNTS SURROUND THE BUILDING. SOME CLAIMED HISTORY WITH THE JACKSON CRIME FAMILY AND THE NOTORIOUS CYRUS GOLD AND HIS DEALINGS IN THAT HORRID SLAUGHTER SWAMP.
TENANT 3G
I'M WRITING A GRAPHIC NOVEL ABOUT THE BATMAN--IT'S GONNA BE EPIC. ABOUT THE JOKER LAUGHING AND HOW NOTHING IS WORTHWHILE--Y'KNOW? EXISTENTIALISM, MAN! UM, DO YOU HAVE HIS PHONE NUMBER?
TENANT 2D TENANT 2E
WE DIDN'T SEE ANYTHING, BUT I HEARD THE WOMAN RACE IN, SLAMMING DOORS AND CURSING.
THOUGHT I HEARD A LITTLE BELL? PROBABLY NOTHING.
ALFRED: THERE WAS A MASS DEATH AT THE BUILDING IN 1893. ALL THIRTY-THREE RESIDENTS DIED WITH NO KNOWN REASON. DISEASE WAS EVENTUALLY RULED OUT EXCEPT FOR PUBLIC BELIEF.
MOST BELIEVED THE BUILDING WAS CURSED AND IT REMAINED VACANT FOR DECADES.
THE BUILDING WAS SCHEDULED TO BE DEMOLISHED WHEN THE CURRENT LANDLORD, BAVOL BELL, BOUGHT IT FROM THE BANK FOR NEXT TO-NUTHING IN MAY 1939.
TENANT 1F
NO, NO! HAS ANYONE SEEN MY FRIEND DARYL? HE'S BEEN MISSING FOR TWO WEEKS!
HE'S GOT THIS STUPID TEARDROP TATTOO UNDER HIS RIGHT EYE--YOU CAN'T MISS HIM.
BAM BAM BAM
OPEN UP!
GOTHAM PD! OPEN UP OR WE'LL KNOCK IT DOWN!
O'HALLORAN--COULD YOU GIVE US A HAND?

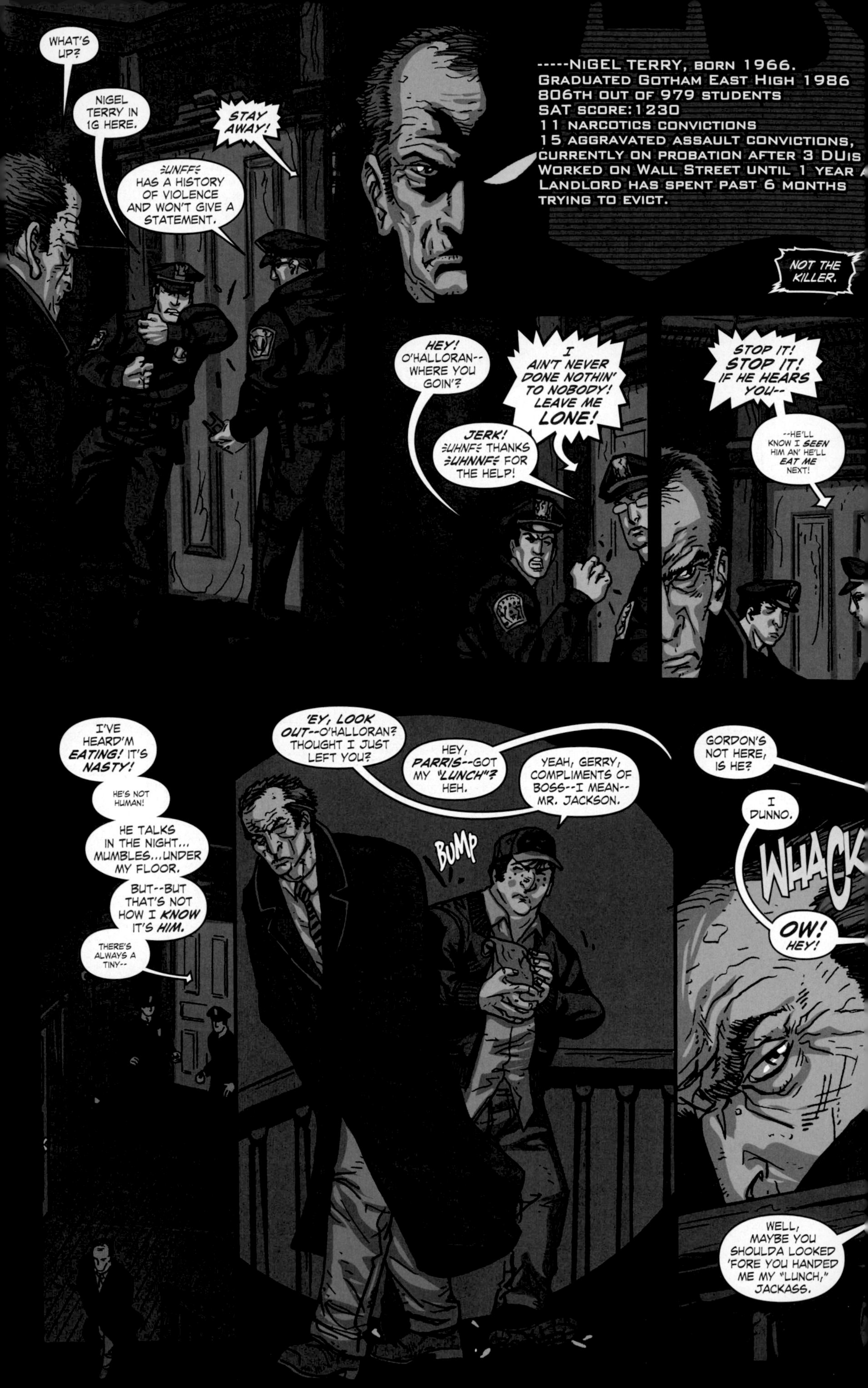

WHAT'S UP?
NIGEL TERRY IN 1G HERE.
=UNFF= HAS A HISTORY OF VIOLENCE AND WON'T GIVE A STATEMENT.
STAY AWAY!
-----NIGEL TERRY, BORN 1966.
GRADUATED GOTHAM EAST HIGH 1986
806TH OUT OF 979 STUDENTS
SAT SCORE:1230
11 NARCOTICS CONVICTIONS
15 AGGRAVATED ASSAULT CONVICTIONS,
CURRENTLY ON PROBATION AFTER 3 DUIS
WORKED ON WALL STREET UNTIL 1 YEAR
LANDLORD HAS SPENT PAST 6 MONTHS
TRYING TO EVICT.
NOT THE KILLER.
HEY! O'HALLORAN--WHERE YOU GOIN'?
I AIN'T NEVER DONE NOTHIN' TO NOBODY! LEAVE ME LONE!
JERK! =UHNF= THANKS =UHHNF= FOR THE HELP!
STOP IT! STOP IT! IF HE HEARS YOU--
--HE'LL KNOW I SEEN HIM AN' HE'LL EAT ME NEXT!
I'VE HEARD'M EATING! IT'S NASTY!
HE'S NOT HUMAN!
HE TALKS IN THE NIGHT... MUMBLES...UNDER MY FLOOR.
BUT--BUT THAT'S NOT HOW I KNOW IT'S HIM.
THERE'S ALWAYS A TINY--
'EY, LOOK OUT--O'HALLORAN? THOUGHT I JUST LEFT YOU?
HEY, PARRIS--GOT MY "LUNCH"? HEH.
YEAH, GERRY, COMPLIMENTS OF BOSS--I MEAN--MR. JACKSON.
BUMP
GORDON'S NOT HERE, IS HE?
I DUNNO.
WHACK
OW! HEY!
WELL, MAYBE YOU SHOULDA LOOKED 'FORE YOU HANDED ME MY "LUNCH," JACKASS.

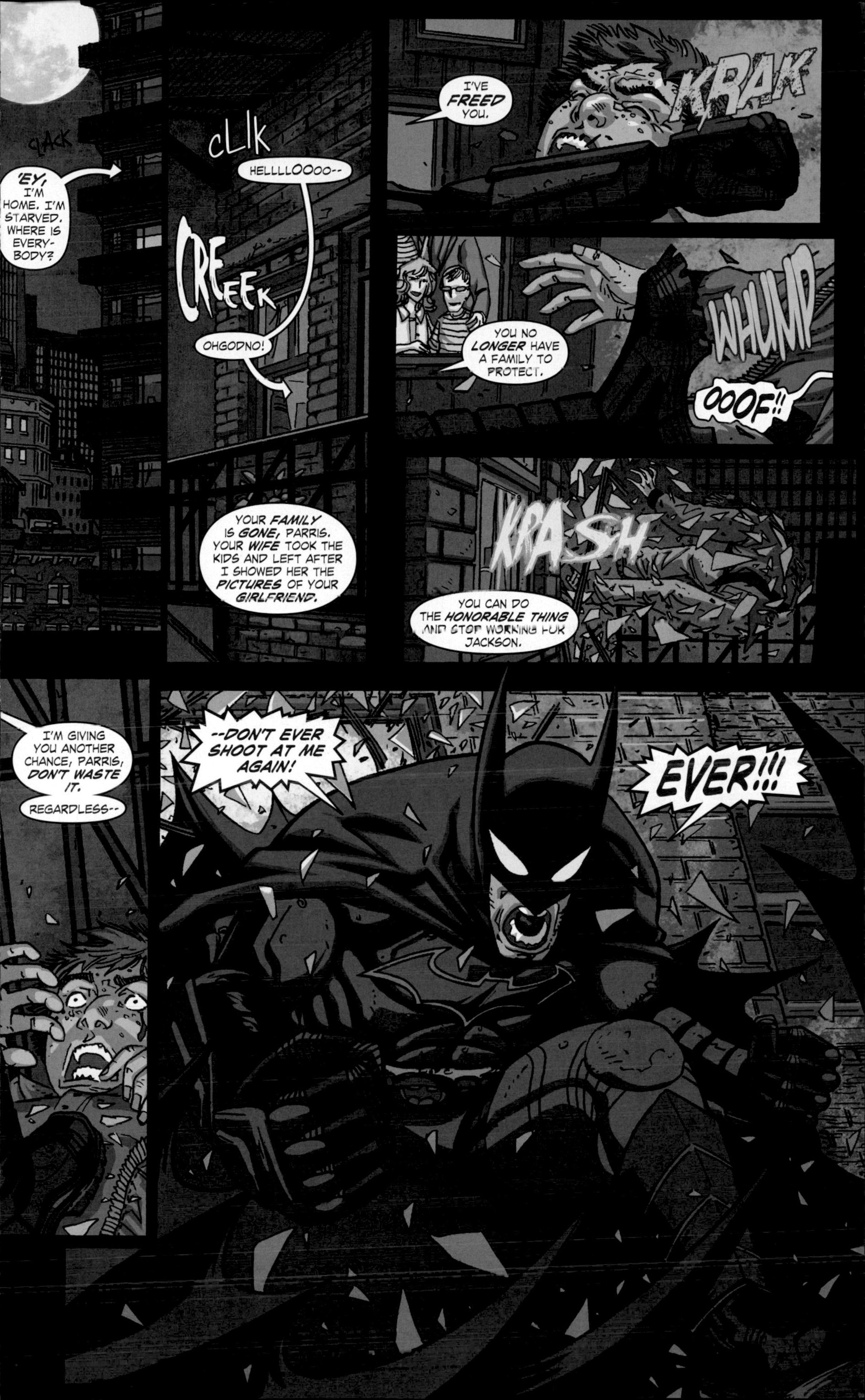
CLACK
'EY, I'M HOME. I'M STARVED. WHERE IS EVERY-BODY?
CLIK
HELLLLOOOO--
CREEEK
OHGODNO!
YOUR FAMILY IS GONE, PARRIS. YOUR WIFE TOOK THE KIDS AND LEFT AFTER I SHOWED HER THE PICTURES OF YOUR GIRLFRIEND.
I'VE FREED YOU.
KRAK
YOU NO LONGER HAVE A FAMILY TO PROTECT.
WHUMP
OOOF!!
KRASH
YOU CAN DO THE HONORABLE THING AND STOP WORKING FOR JACKSON.
I'M GIVING YOU ANOTHER CHANCE, PARRIS, DON'T WASTE IT.
REGARDLESS--
--DON'T EVER SHOOT AT ME AGAIN!
EVER!!!

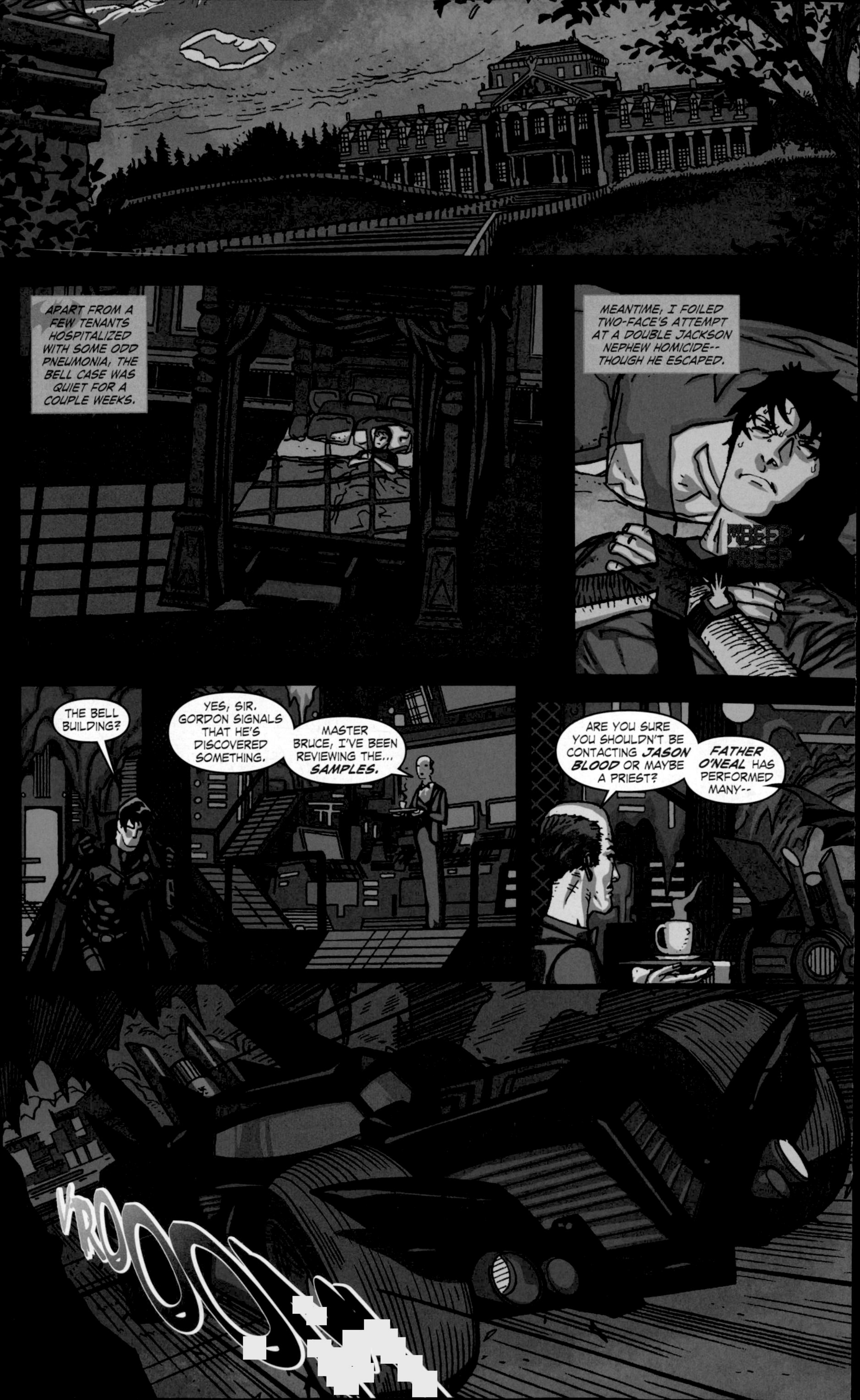
APART FROM A FEW TENANTS HOSPITALIZED WITH SOME ODD PNEUMONIA, THE BELL CASE WAS QUIET FOR A COUPLE WEEKS.
MEANTIME, I FOILED TWO-FACE'S ATTEMPT AT A DOUBLE JACKSON NEPHEW HOMICIDE--THOUGH HE ESCAPED.
BEEP BEEP
MASTER BRUCE, I'VE BEEN REVIEWING THE... SAMPLES.
YES, SIR. GORDON SIGNALS THAT HE'S DISCOVERED SOMETHING.
THE BELL BUILDING?
ARE YOU SURE YOU SHOULDN'T BE CONTACTING JASON BLOOD OR MAYBE A PRIEST?
FATHER O'NEAL HAS PERFORMED MANY--
VROOOOM

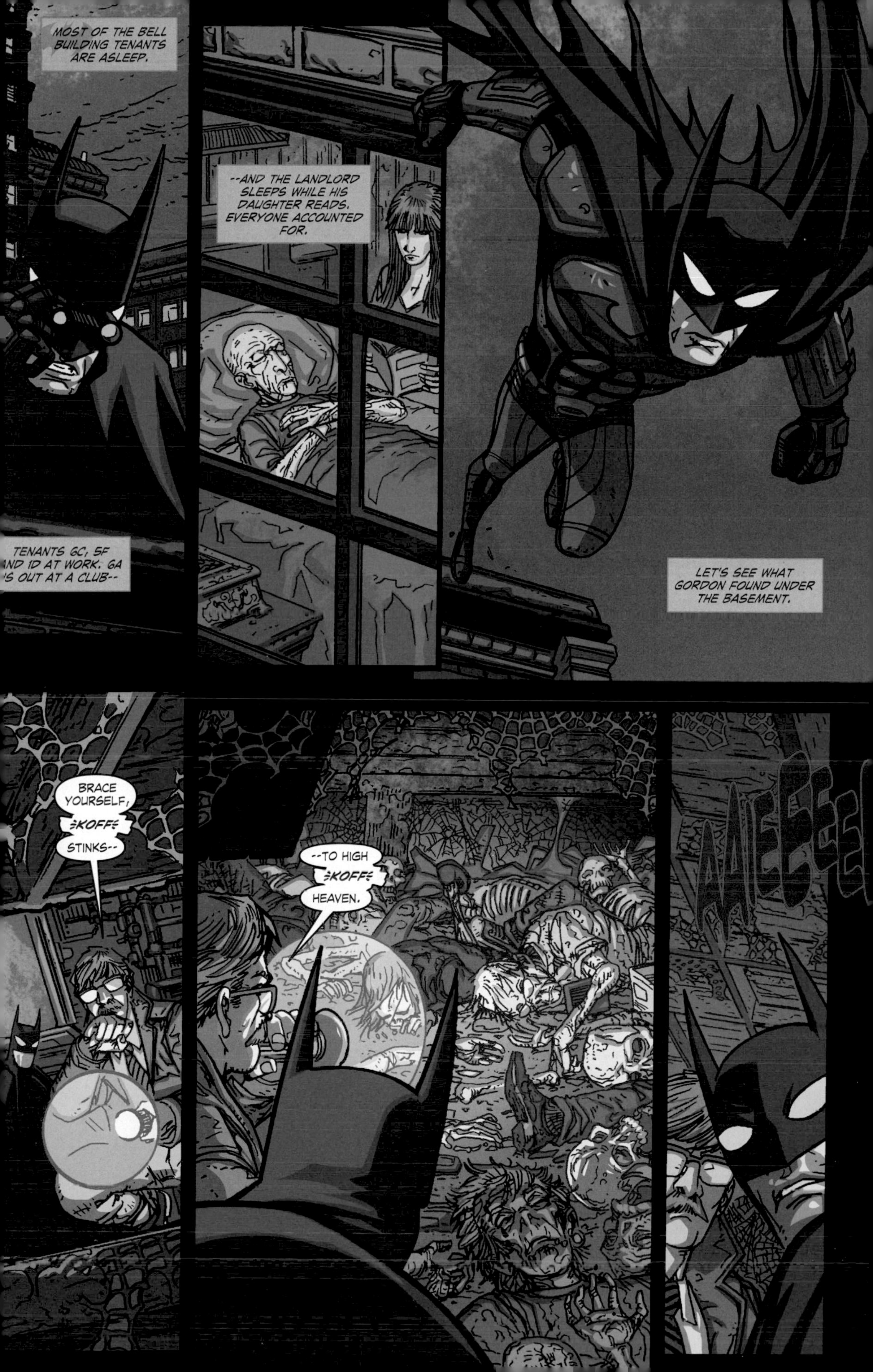
MOST OF THE BELL BUILDING TENANTS ARE ASLEEP.
--AND THE LANDLORD SLEEPS WHILE HIS DAUGHTER READS. EVERYONE ACCOUNTED FOR.
TENANTS 6C, 5F
ND 1D AT WORK. 6A
'S OUT AT A CLUB--
LET'S SEE WHAT GORDON FOUND UNDER THE BASEMENT.
BRACE YOURSELF, *KOFF* STINKS--
--TO HIGH *KOFF* HEAVEN.
AAIEEEE

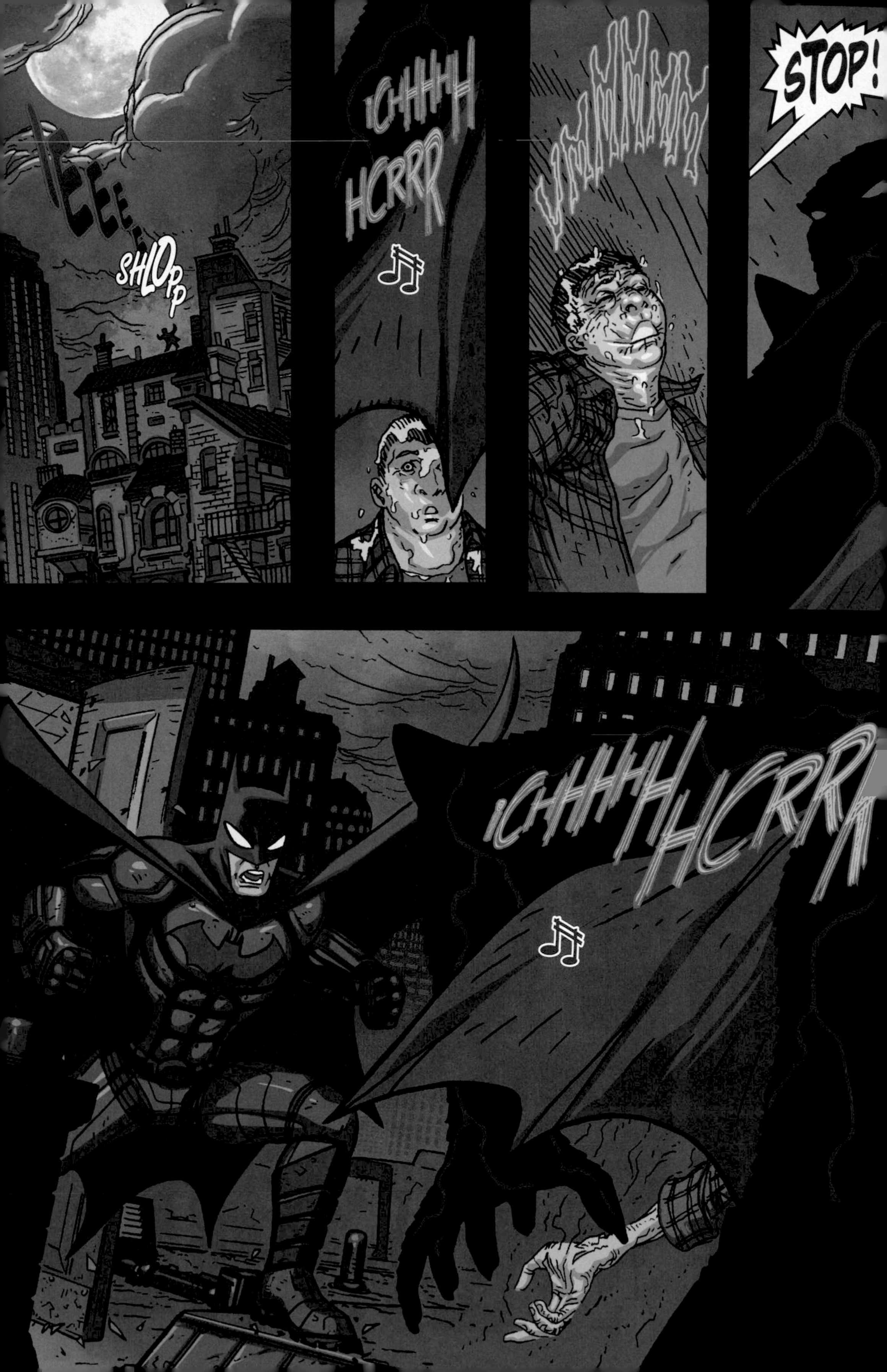
SHLOpp
iCHHHHH
HCRRR
STOP!
iCHHHHHHCRRR

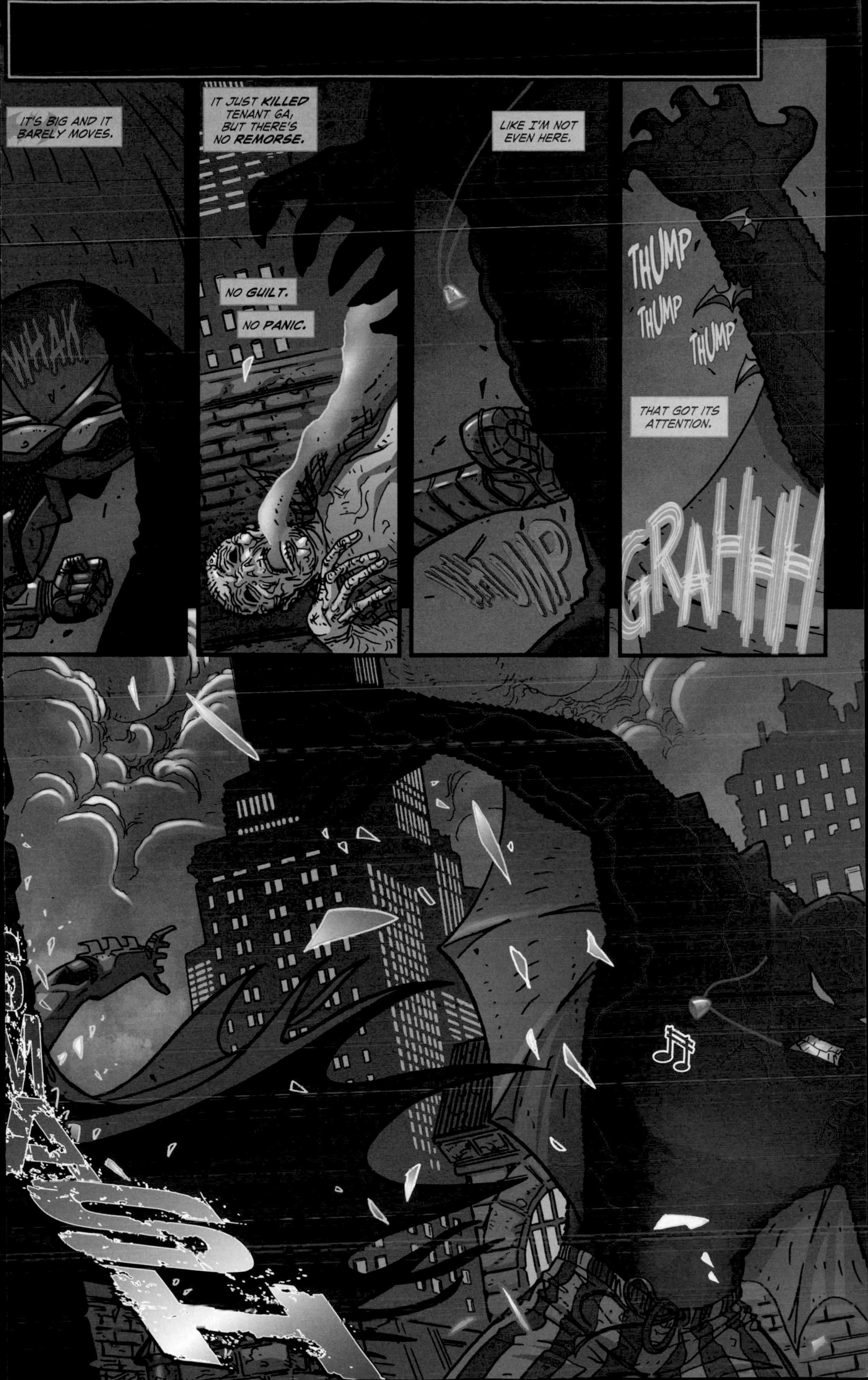
IT'S BIG AND IT BARELY MOVES.
WHAK
IT JUST KILLED TENANT 6A, BUT THERE'S NO REMORSE.
NO GUILT.
NO PANIC.
LIKE I'M NOT EVEN HERE.
THUMP
THUMP
THUMP
THUMP
THAT GOT ITS ATTENTION.
GRAHHH
SMASH

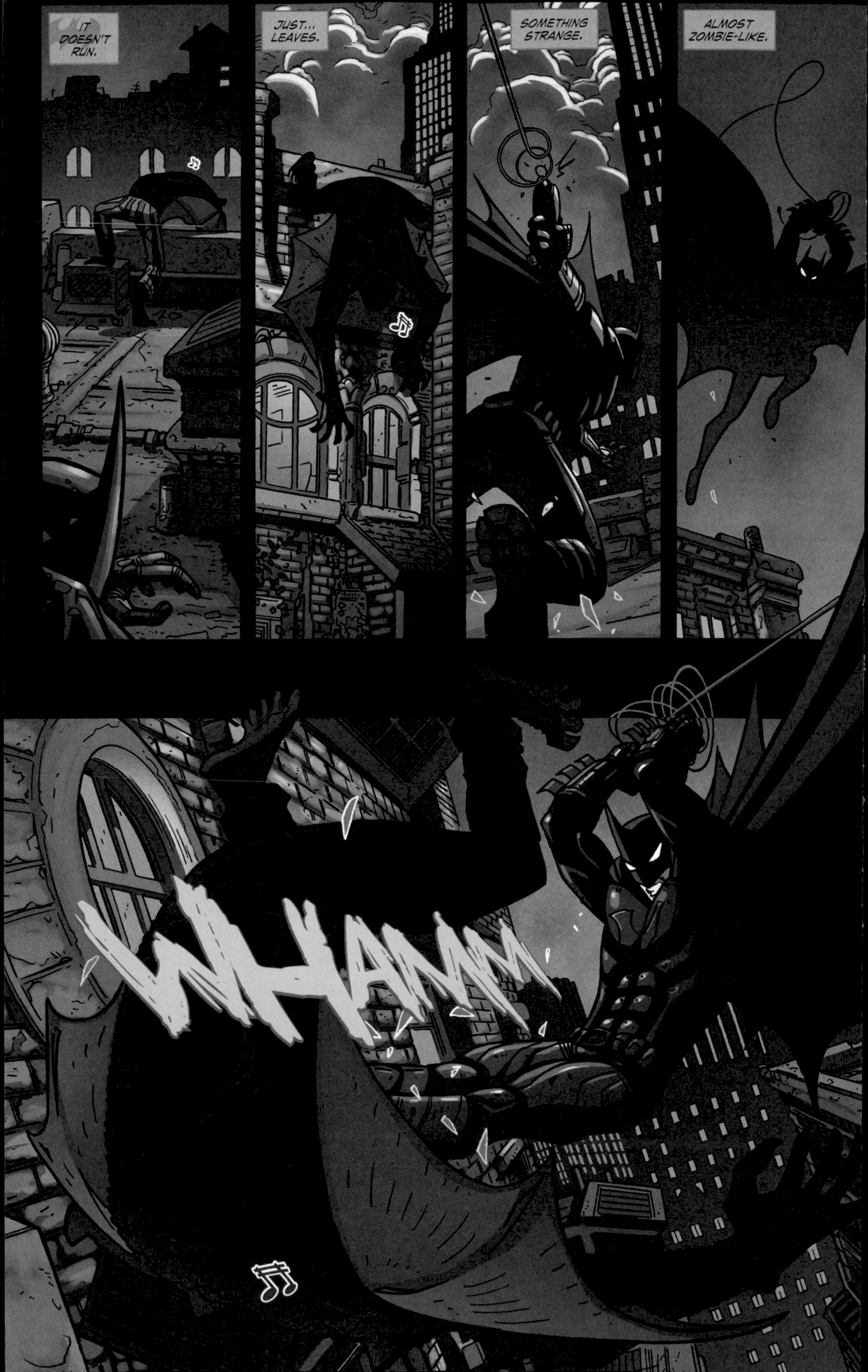
IT DOESN'T RUN.
JUST... LEAVES.
SOMETHING STRANGE.
ALMOST ZOMBIE-LIKE.
WHAMM

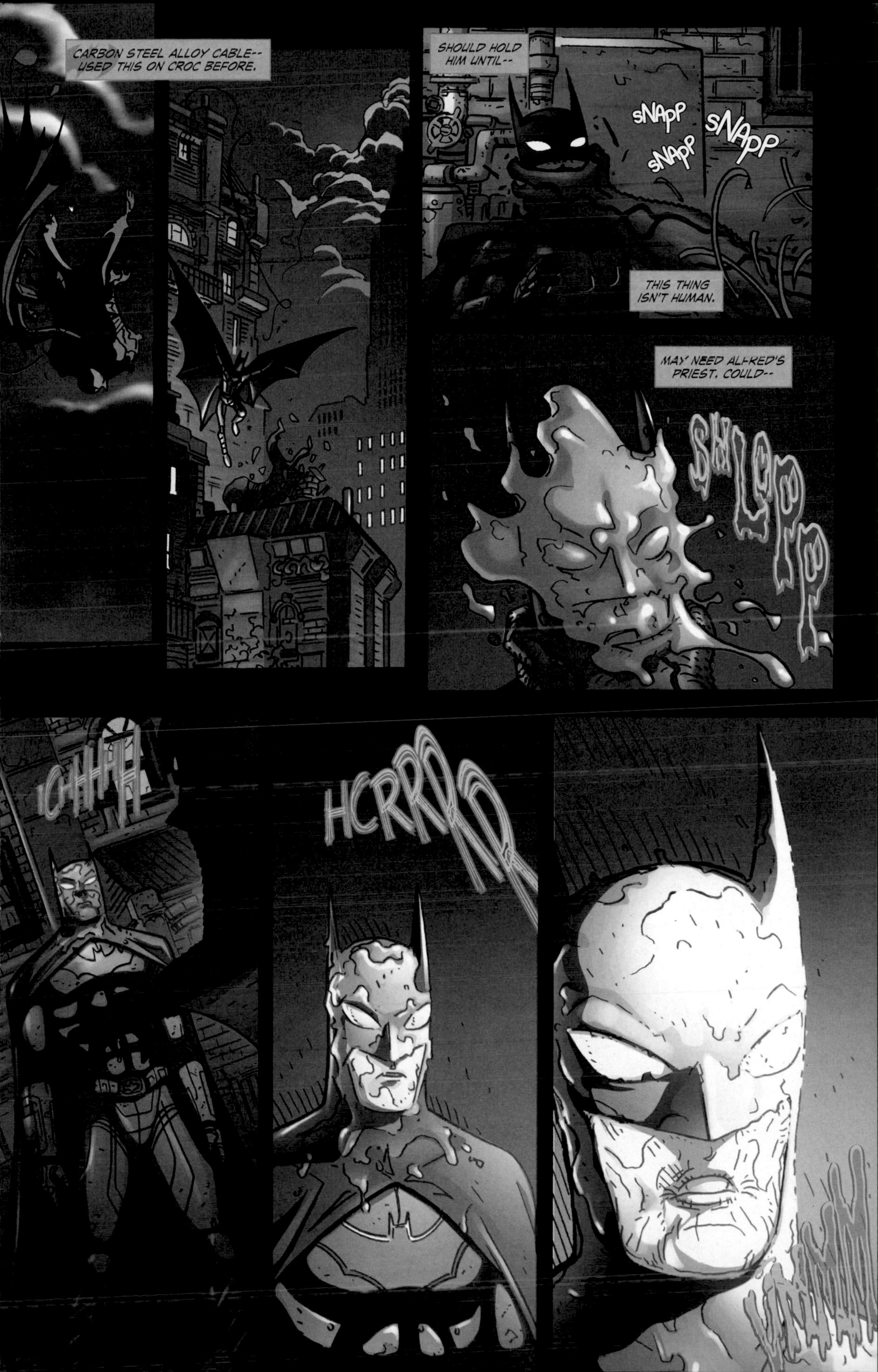

CARBON STEEL ALLOY CABLE--
USED THIS ON CROC BEFORE.
SHOULD HOLD
HIM UNTIL--
SNAPP
SNAPP
SNAPP
THIS THING
ISN'T HUMAN.
MAY NEED ALFRED'S
PRIEST. COULD--
SHLOPP
ICHHHH
HCRRRR

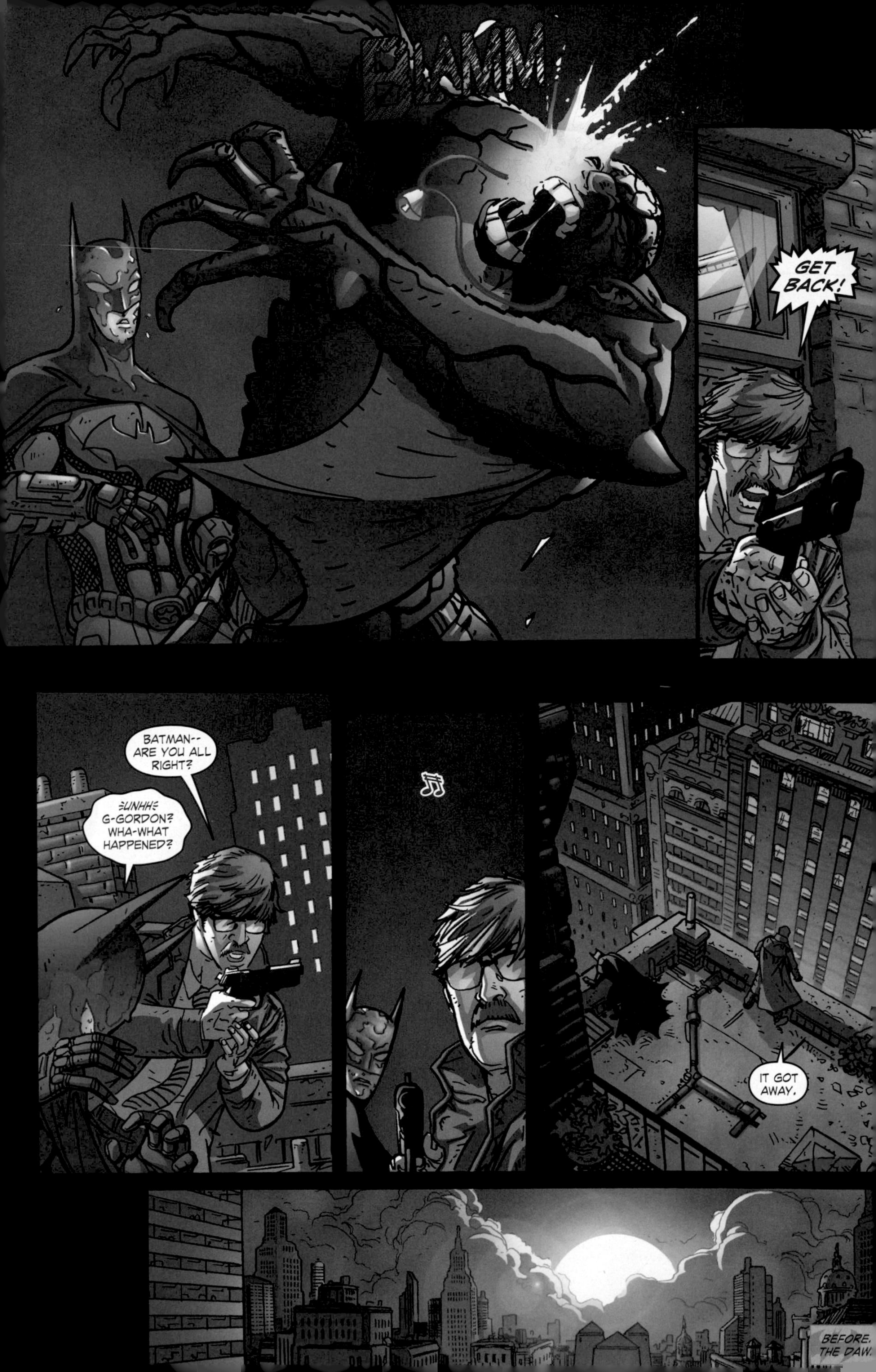
BLAMM!
GET BACK!
BATMAN-- ARE YOU ALL RIGHT?
UNHH G-GORDON? WHA-WHAT HAPPENED?
IT GOT AWAY.

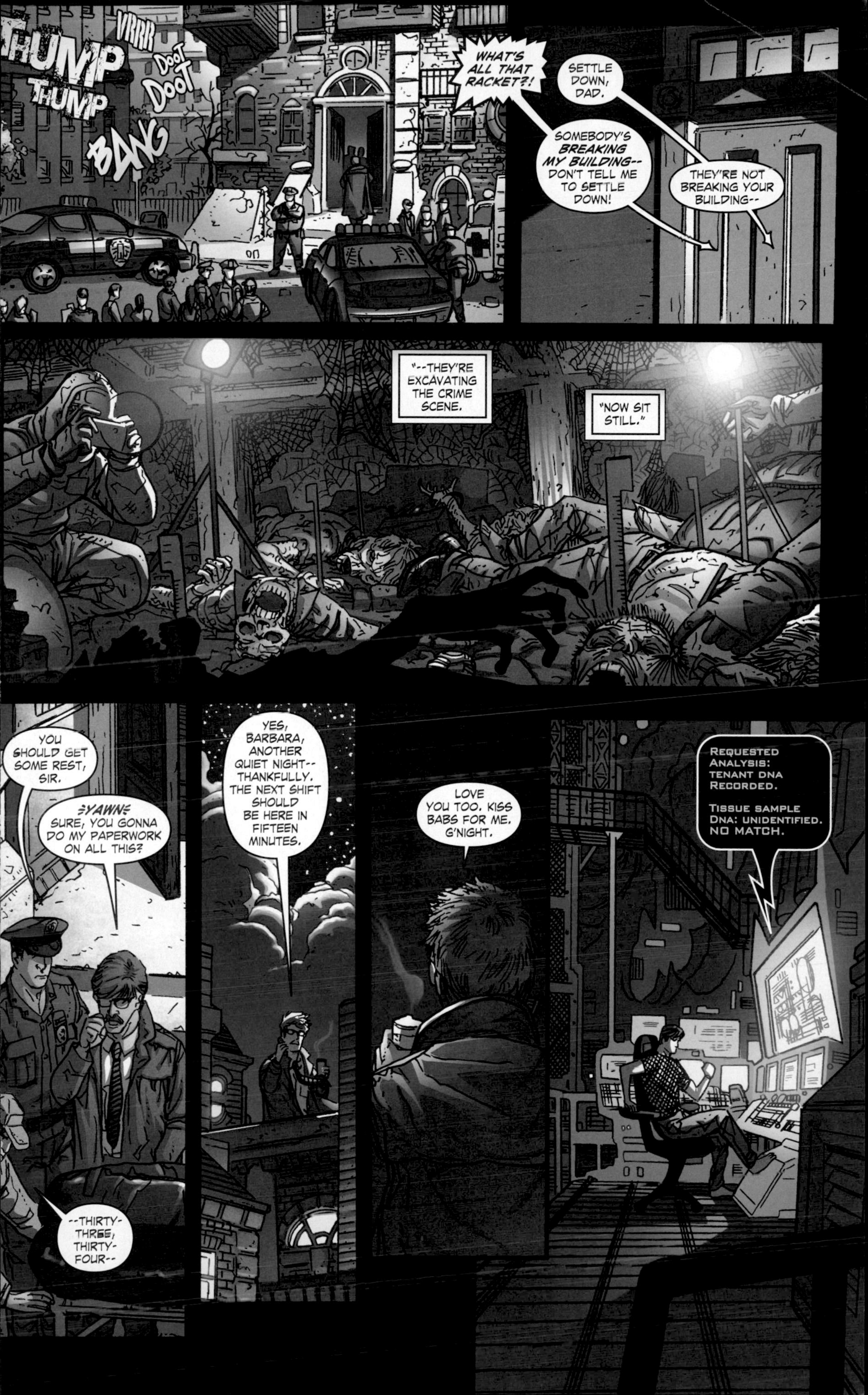
THUMP
VRRR
THUMP
DOOT DOOT
BANG
WHAT'S ALL THAT RACKET?!
SETTLE DOWN, DAD.
SOMEBODY'S BREAKING MY BUILDING-- DON'T TELL ME TO SETTLE DOWN!
THEY'RE NOT BREAKING YOUR BUILDING--
"--THEY'RE EXCAVATING THE CRIME SCENE.
"NOW SIT STILL."
YOU SHOULD GET SOME REST, SIR.
≶YAWN≶ SURE; YOU GONNA DO MY PAPERWORK ON ALL THIS?
--THIRTY-THREE, THIRTY-FOUR--
YES, BARBARA, ANOTHER QUIET NIGHT-- THANKFULLY. THE NEXT SHIFT SHOULD BE HERE IN FIFTEEN MINUTES.
LOVE YOU TOO. KISS BABS FOR ME. G'NIGHT.
REQUESTED ANALYSIS: TENANT DNA RECORDED.
TISSUE SAMPLE DNA: UNIDENTIFIED. NO MATCH.

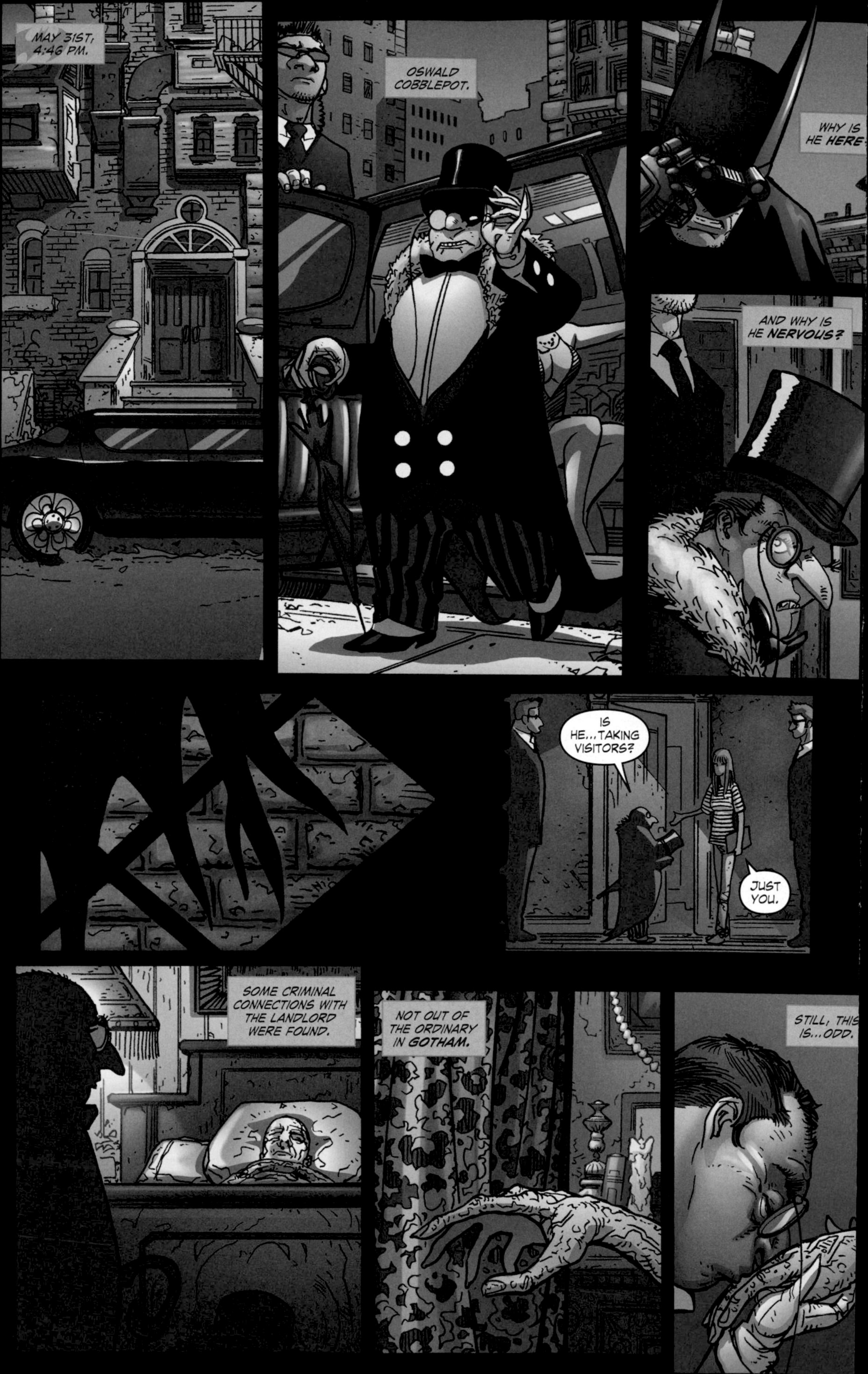
MAY 31ST, 4:46 PM.
OSWALD COBBLEPOT.
WHY IS HE HERE?
AND WHY IS HE NERVOUS?
IS HE...TAKING VISITORS?
JUST YOU.
SOME CRIMINAL CONNECTIONS WITH THE LANDLORD WERE FOUND.
NOT OUT OF THE ORDINARY IN GOTHAM.
STILL, THIS IS...ODD.

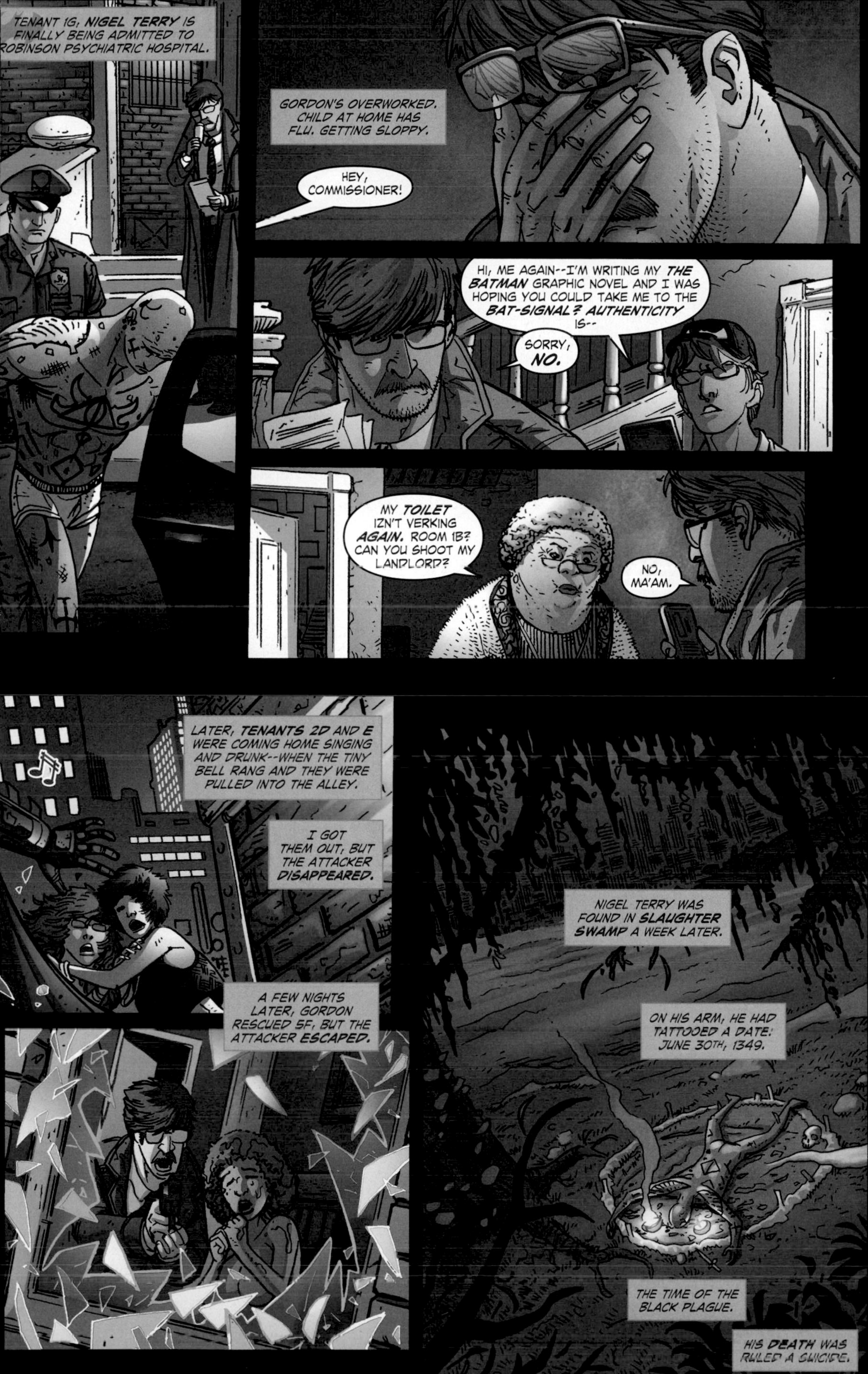
TENANT 1G, NIGEL TERRY IS FINALLY BEING ADMITTED TO ROBINSON PSYCHIATRIC HOSPITAL.
GORDON'S OVERWORKED. CHILD AT HOME HAS FLU. GETTING SLOPPY.
HEY, COMMISSIONER!
HI, ME AGAIN--I'M WRITING MY THE BATMAN GRAPHIC NOVEL AND I WAS HOPING YOU COULD TAKE ME TO THE BAT-SIGNAL? AUTHENTICITY IS--
SORRY, NO.
MY TOILET IZN'T VERKING AGAIN. ROOM 1B? CAN YOU SHOOT MY LANDLORD?
NO, MA'AM.
LATER, TENANTS 2D AND E WERE COMING HOME SINGING AND DRUNK--WHEN THE TINY BELL RANG AND THEY WERE PULLED INTO THE ALLEY.
I GOT THEM OUT, BUT THE ATTACKER DISAPPEARED.
A FEW NIGHTS LATER, GORDON RESCUED 5F, BUT THE ATTACKER ESCAPED.
NIGEL TERRY WAS FOUND IN SLAUGHTER SWAMP A WEEK LATER.
ON HIS ARM, HE HAD TATTOOED A DATE: JUNE 30TH, 1349.
THE TIME OF THE BLACK PLAGUE.
HIS DEATH WAS RULED A SUICIDE.

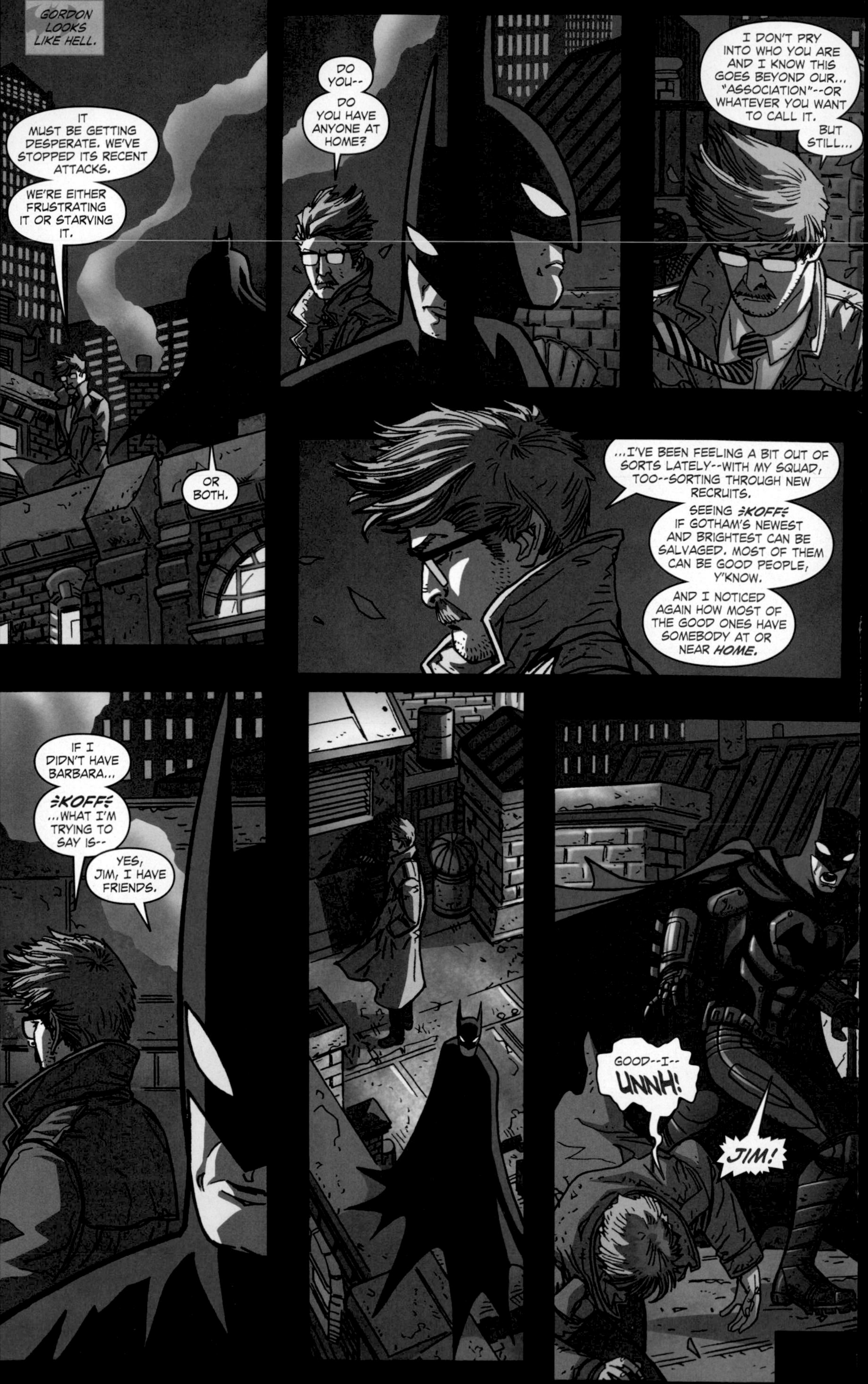
GORDON LOOKS LIKE HELL.
IT MUST BE GETTING DESPERATE. WE'VE STOPPED ITS RECENT ATTACKS.
WE'RE EITHER FRUSTRATING IT OR STARVING IT.
OR BOTH.
DO YOU--
DO YOU HAVE ANYONE AT HOME?
I DON'T PRY INTO WHO YOU ARE AND I KNOW THIS GOES BEYOND OUR... "ASSOCIATION"--OR WHATEVER YOU WANT TO CALL IT.
BUT STILL...
...I'VE BEEN FEELING A BIT OUT OF SORTS LATELY--WITH MY SQUAD, TOO--SORTING THROUGH NEW RECRUITS.
SEEING *KOFF* IF GOTHAM'S NEWEST AND BRIGHTEST CAN BE SALVAGED. MOST OF THEM CAN BE GOOD PEOPLE, Y'KNOW.
AND I NOTICED AGAIN HOW MOST OF THE GOOD ONES HAVE SOMEBODY AT OR NEAR HOME.
IF I DIDN'T HAVE BARBARA...
KOFF ...WHAT I'M TRYING TO SAY IS--
YES, JIM, I HAVE FRIENDS.
GOOD--I-- UNNH!
JIM!

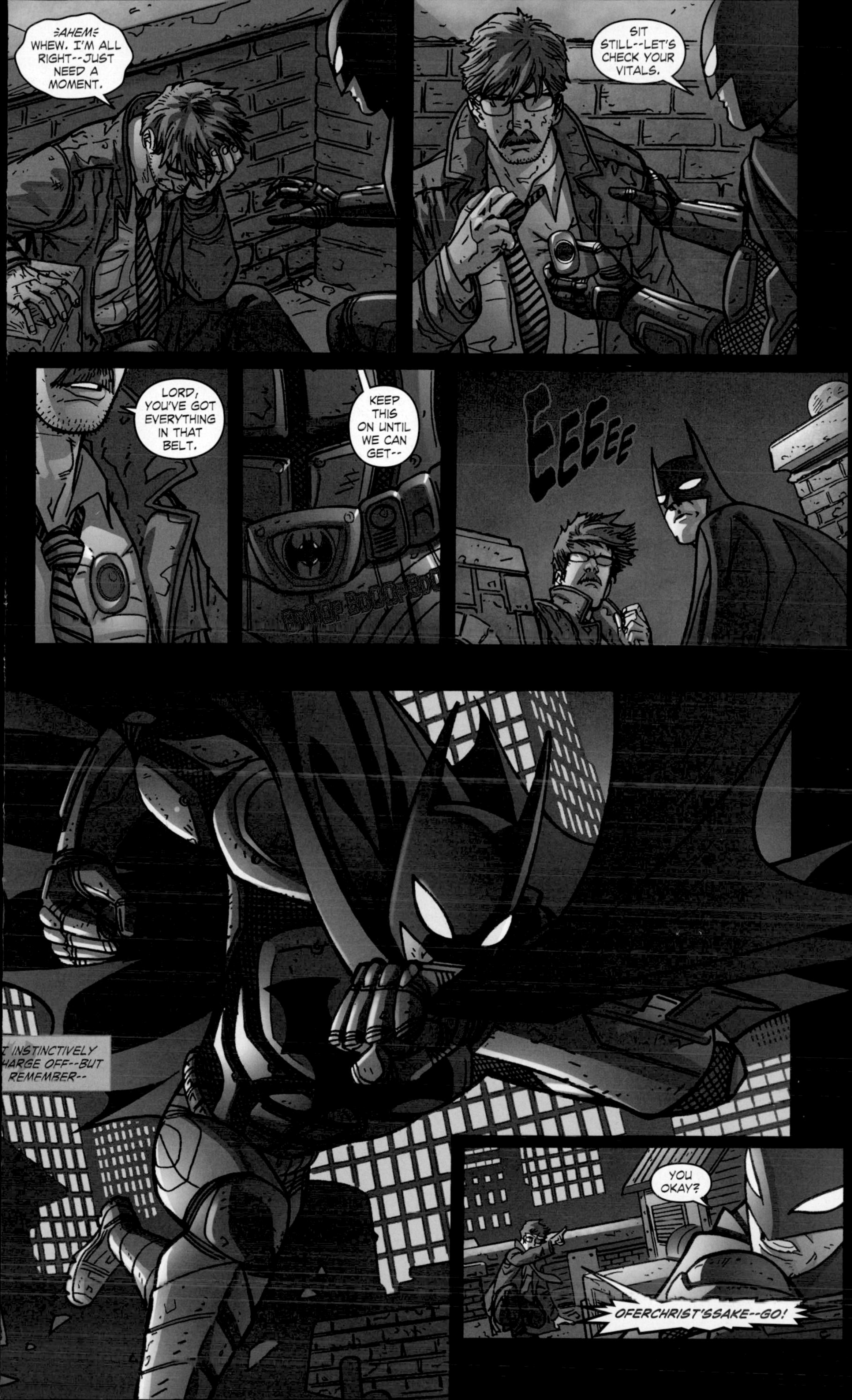
=AHEM= WHEW. I'M ALL RIGHT--JUST NEED A MOMENT.
SIT STILL--LET'S CHECK YOUR VITALS.
LORD, YOU'VE GOT EVERYTHING IN THAT BELT.
KEEP THIS ON UNTIL WE CAN GET--
EEEee
I INSTINCTIVELY HARGE OFF--BUT REMEMBER--
YOU OKAY?
OFERCHRIST'SSAKE--GO!

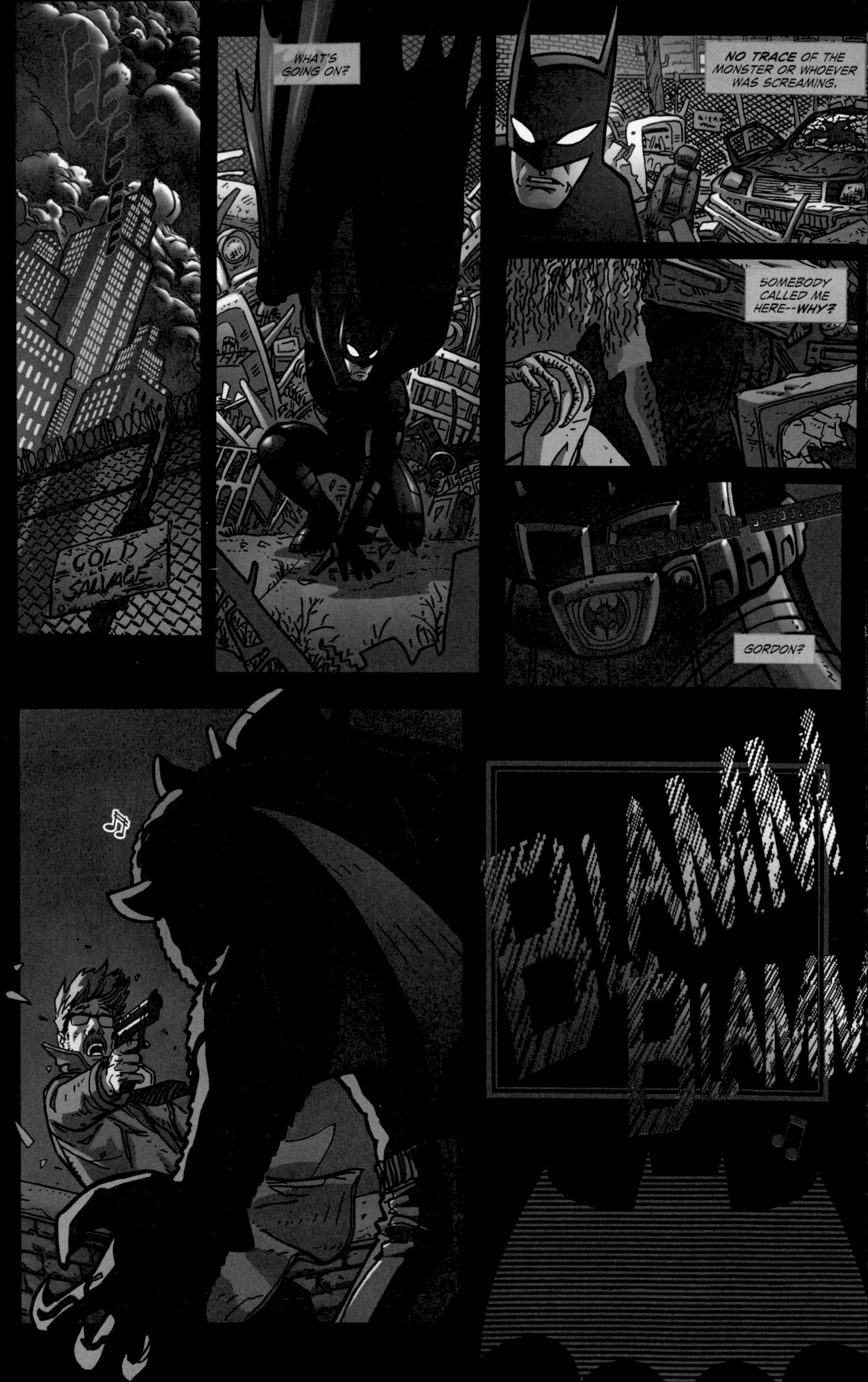
COLD SALVAGE
WHAT'S GOING ON?
NO TRACE OF THE MONSTER OR WHOEVER WAS SCREAMING.
SOMEBODY CALLED ME HERE--WHY?
GORDON?
BLAMM BLAMM

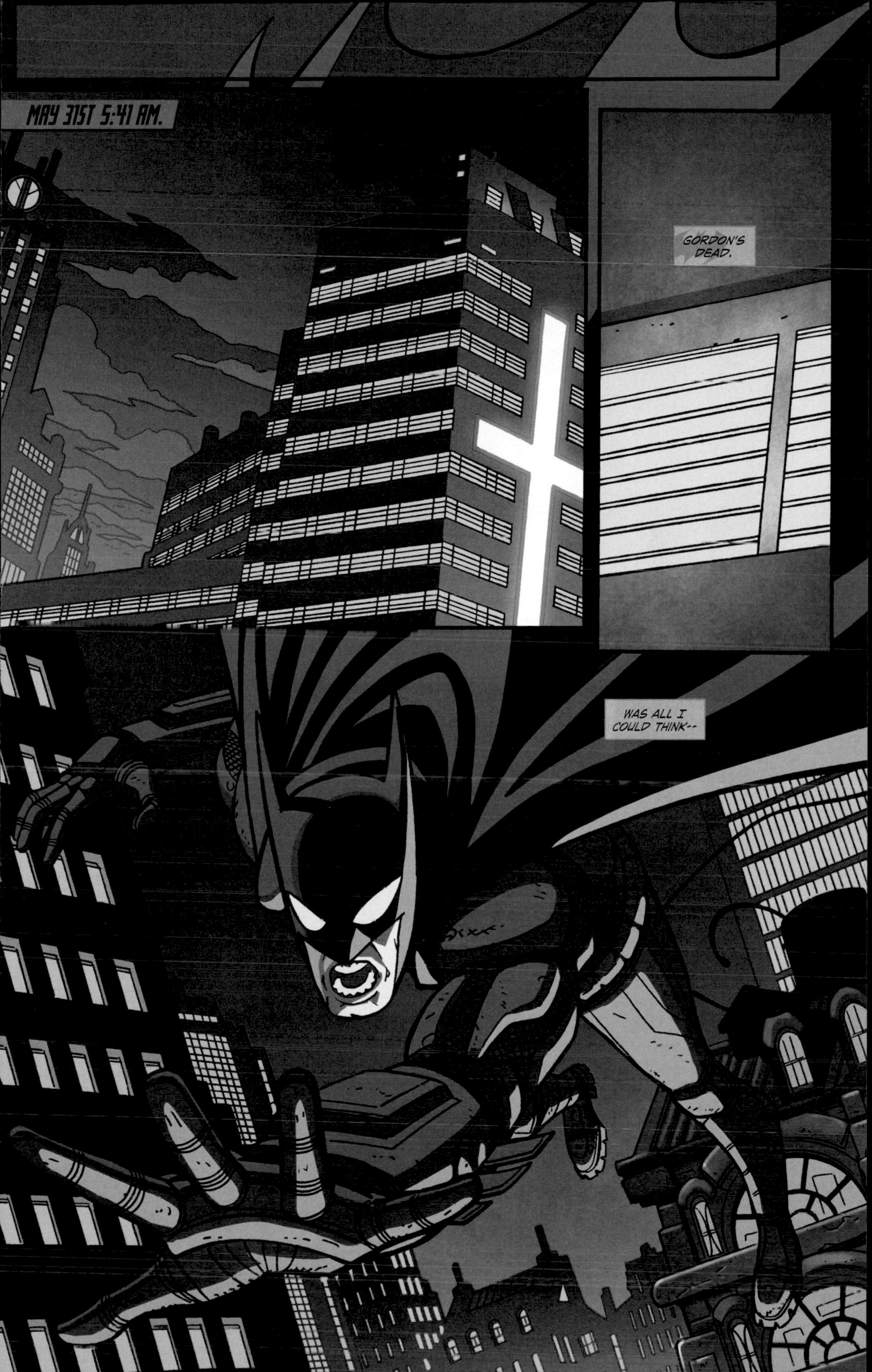
MAY 31ST 5:41 AM.
GORDON'S DEAD.
WAS ALL I COULD THINK--

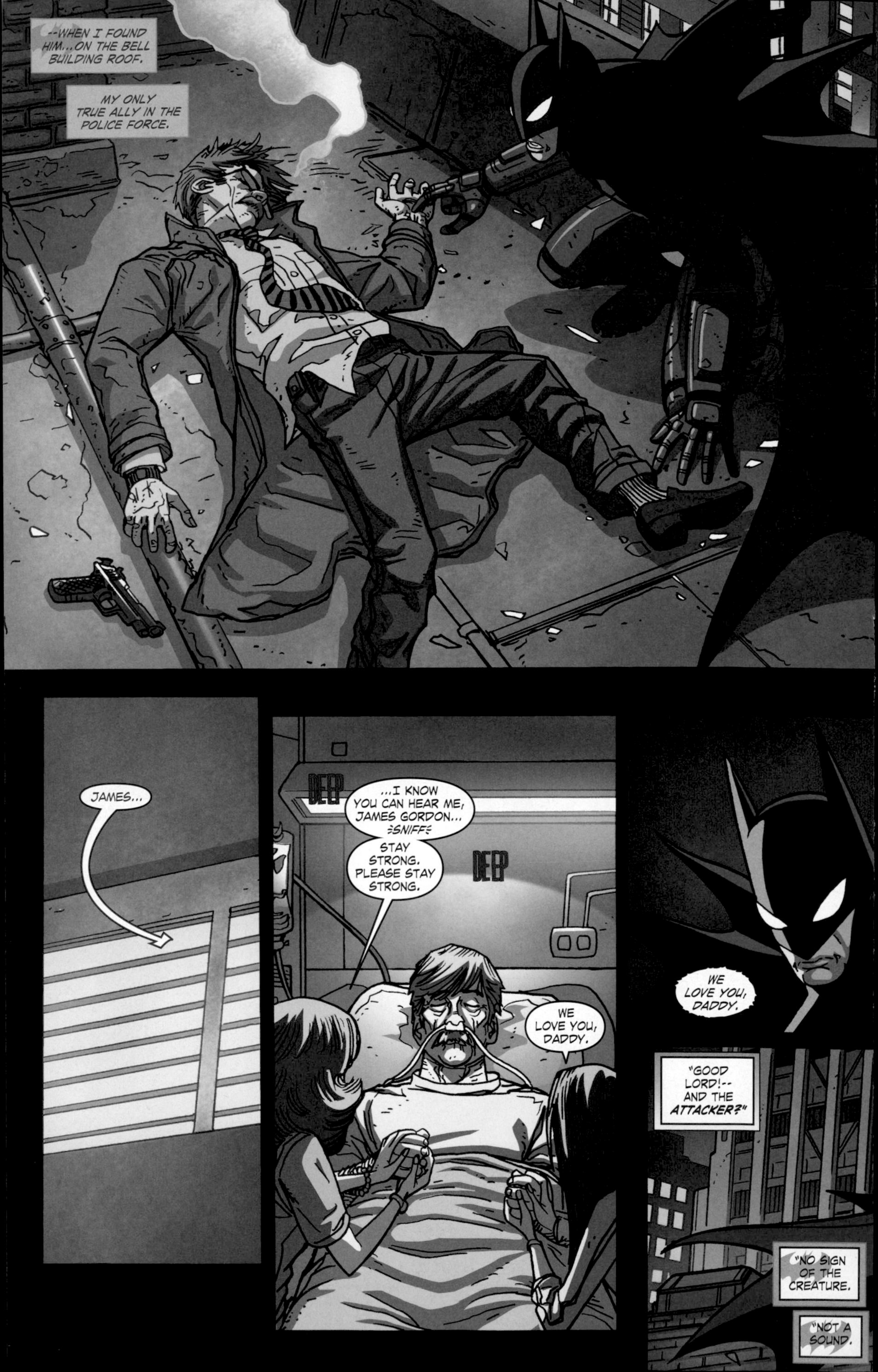
--WHEN I FOUND HIM...ON THE BELL BUILDING ROOF.
MY ONLY TRUE ALLY IN THE POLICE FORCE.
JAMES...
DEEP
...I KNOW YOU CAN HEAR ME, JAMES GORDON... SNIFF
STAY STRONG. PLEASE STAY STRONG.
DEEP
WE LOVE YOU, DADDY.
WE LOVE YOU, DADDY.
"GOOD LORD!-- AND THE ATTACKER?"
"NO SIGN OF THE CREATURE.
"NOT A SOUND.

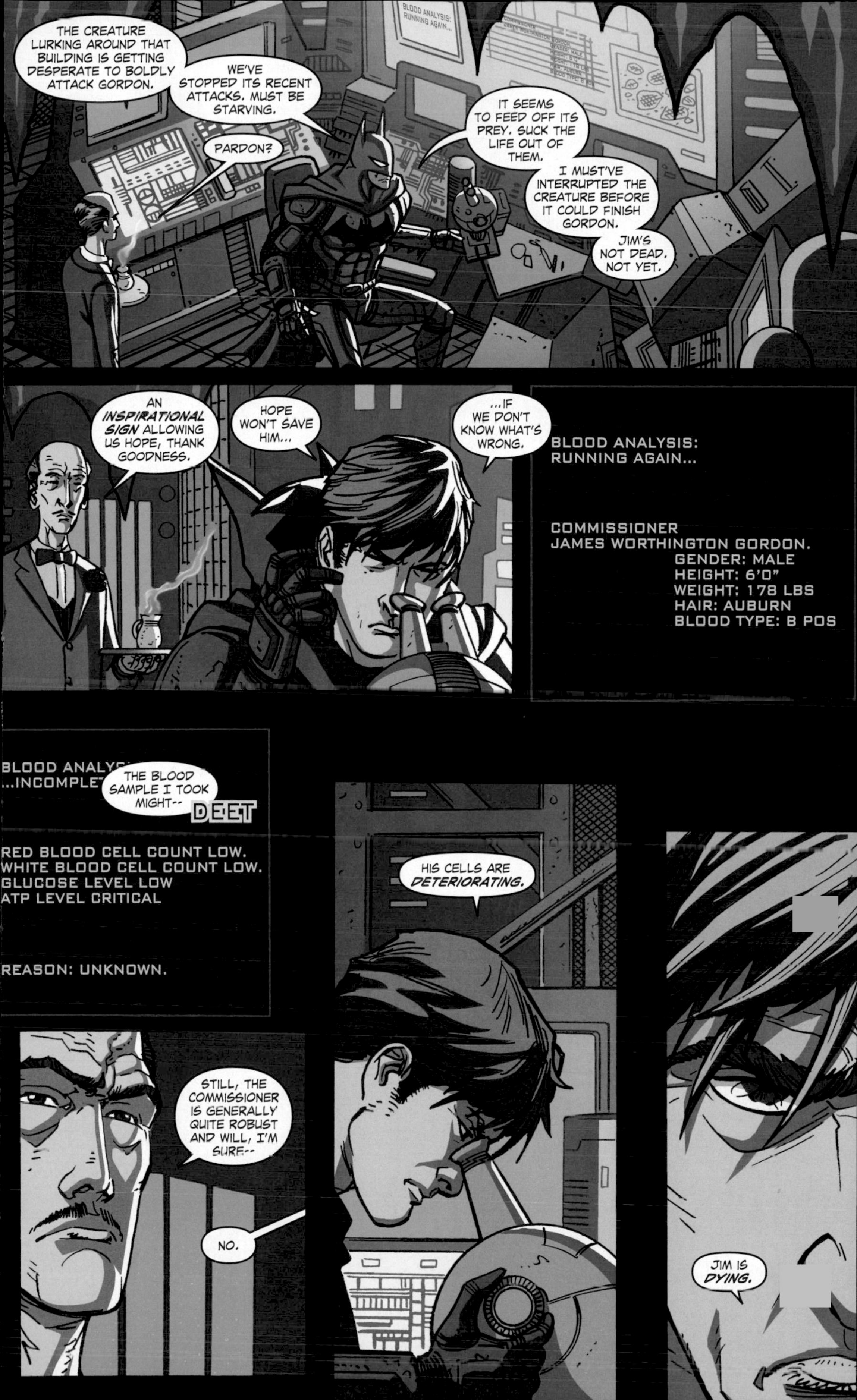

THE CREATURE LURKING AROUND THAT BUILDING IS GETTING DESPERATE TO BOLDLY ATTACK GORDON.
WE'VE STOPPED ITS RECENT ATTACKS. MUST BE STARVING.
PARDON?
IT SEEMS TO FEED OFF ITS PREY. SUCK THE LIFE OUT OF THEM.
I MUST'VE INTERRUPTED THE CREATURE BEFORE IT COULD FINISH GORDON.
JIM'S NOT DEAD. NOT YET.
AN *INSPIRATIONAL SIGN* ALLOWING US HOPE, THANK GOODNESS.
HOPE WON'T SAVE HIM...
...IF WE DON'T KNOW WHAT'S WRONG.
BLOOD ANALYSIS: RUNNING AGAIN...
COMMISSIONER JAMES WORTHINGTON GORDON.
GENDER: MALE
HEIGHT: 6'0"
WEIGHT: 178 LBS
HAIR: AUBURN
BLOOD TYPE: B POS
BLOOD ANALYS
...INCOMPLET
THE BLOOD SAMPLE I TOOK MIGHT--
DEET
RED BLOOD CELL COUNT LOW.
WHITE BLOOD CELL COUNT LOW.
GLUCOSE LEVEL LOW
ATP LEVEL CRITICAL
REASON: UNKNOWN.
HIS CELLS ARE *DETERIORATING.*
STILL, THE COMMISSIONER IS GENERALLY QUITE ROBUST AND WILL, I'M SURE--
NO.
JIM IS *DYING.*

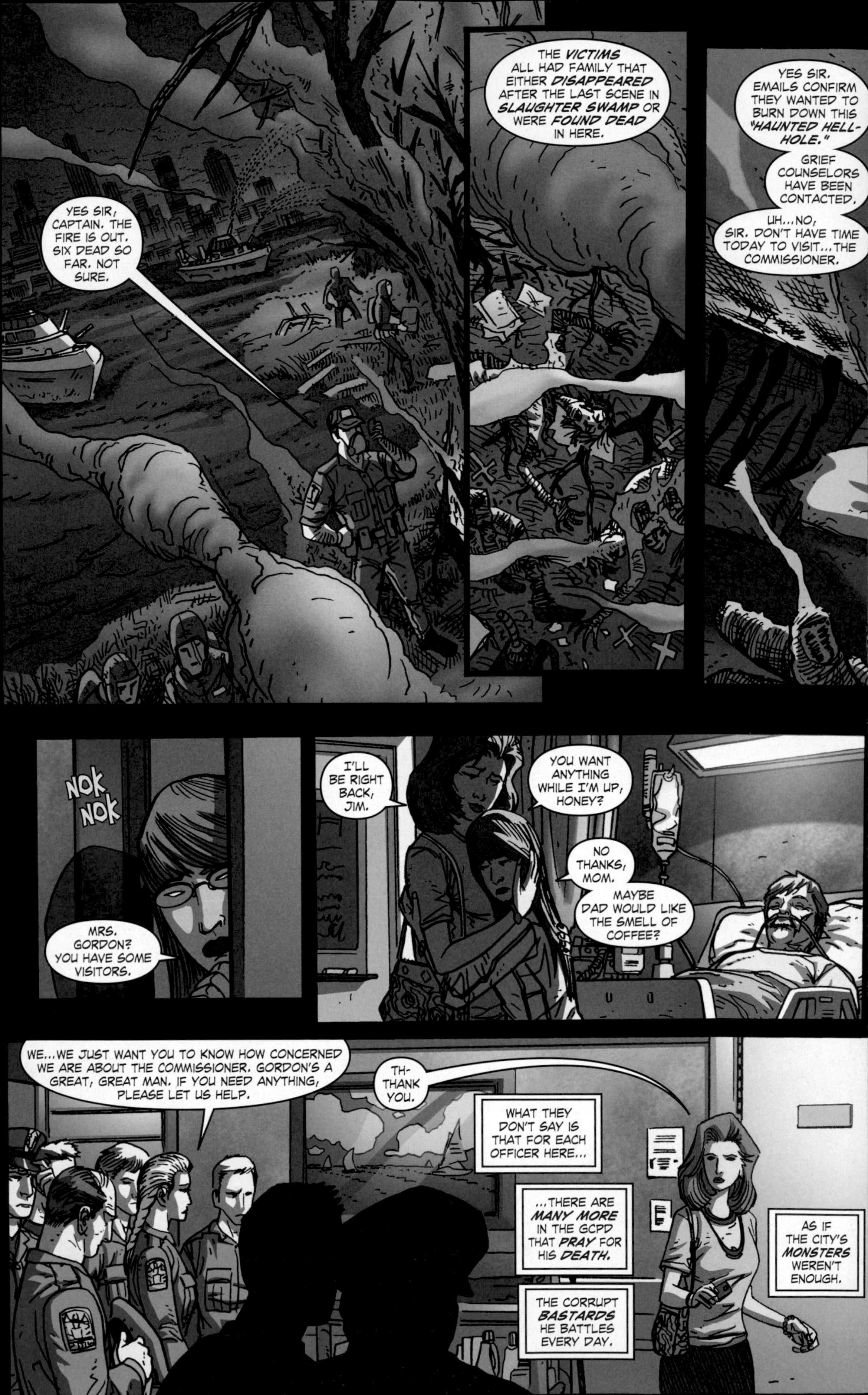
YES SIR, CAPTAIN. THE FIRE IS OUT. SIX DEAD SO FAR. NOT SURE.
THE VICTIMS ALL HAD FAMILY THAT EITHER DISAPPEARED AFTER THE LAST SCENE IN SLAUGHTER SWAMP OR WERE FOUND DEAD IN HERE.
YES SIR. EMAILS CONFIRM THEY WANTED TO BURN DOWN THIS "HAUNTED HELL-HOLE."
GRIEF COUNSELORS HAVE BEEN CONTACTED.
UH...NO, SIR. DON'T HAVE TIME TODAY TO VISIT...THE COMMISSIONER.
NOK NOK
MRS. GORDON? YOU HAVE SOME VISITORS.
I'LL BE RIGHT BACK, JIM.
YOU WANT ANYTHING WHILE I'M UP, HONEY?
NO THANKS, MOM.
MAYBE DAD WOULD LIKE THE SMELL OF COFFEE?
WE...WE JUST WANT YOU TO KNOW HOW CONCERNED WE ARE ABOUT THE COMMISSIONER. GORDON'S A GREAT, GREAT MAN. IF YOU NEED ANYTHING, PLEASE LET US HELP.
TH-THANK YOU.
WHAT THEY DON'T SAY IS THAT FOR EACH OFFICER HERE...
...THERE ARE MANY MORE IN THE GCPD THAT PRAY FOR HIS DEATH.
THE CORRUPT BASTARDS HE BATTLES EVERY DAY.
AS IF THE CITY'S MONSTERS WEREN'T ENOUGH.

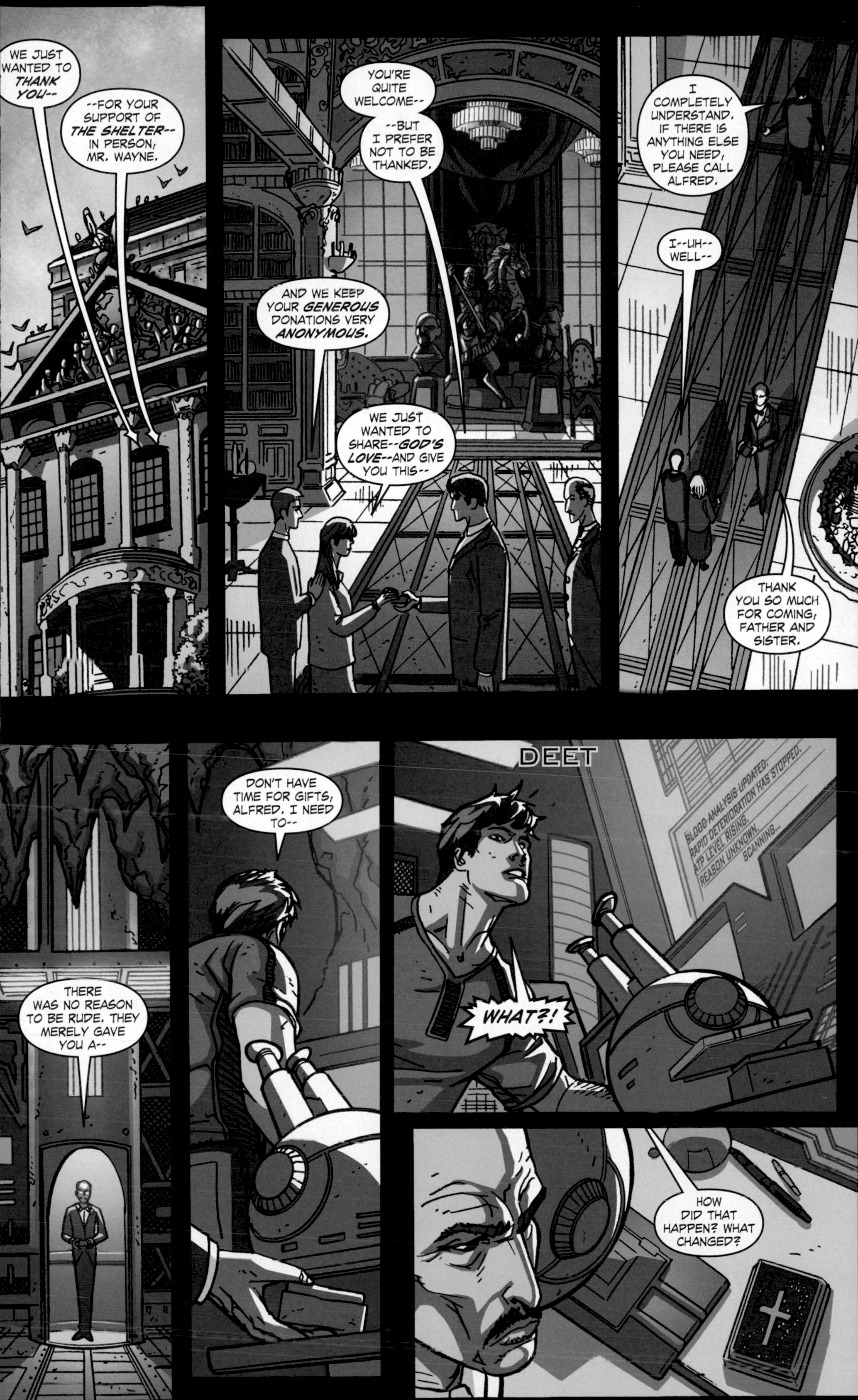

WE JUST WANTED TO THANK YOU--
--FOR YOUR SUPPORT OF THE SHELTER-- IN PERSON, MR. WAYNE.
YOU'RE QUITE WELCOME--
--BUT I PREFER NOT TO BE THANKED.
AND WE KEEP YOUR GENEROUS DONATIONS VERY ANONYMOUS.
WE JUST WANTED TO SHARE--GOD'S LOVE--AND GIVE YOU THIS--
I COMPLETELY UNDERSTAND. IF THERE IS ANYTHING ELSE YOU NEED, PLEASE CALL ALFRED.
I--UH-- WELL--
THANK YOU SO MUCH FOR COMING, FATHER AND SISTER.
THERE WAS NO REASON TO BE RUDE. THEY MERELY GAVE YOU A--
DON'T HAVE TIME FOR GIFTS, ALFRED. I NEED TO--
DEET
BLOOD ANALYSIS UPDATED.
RAPID DETERIORATION HAS STOPPED.
ATP LEVEL RISING.
REASON UNKNOWN.
SCANNING...
WHAT?!
HOW DID THAT HAPPEN? WHAT CHANGED?

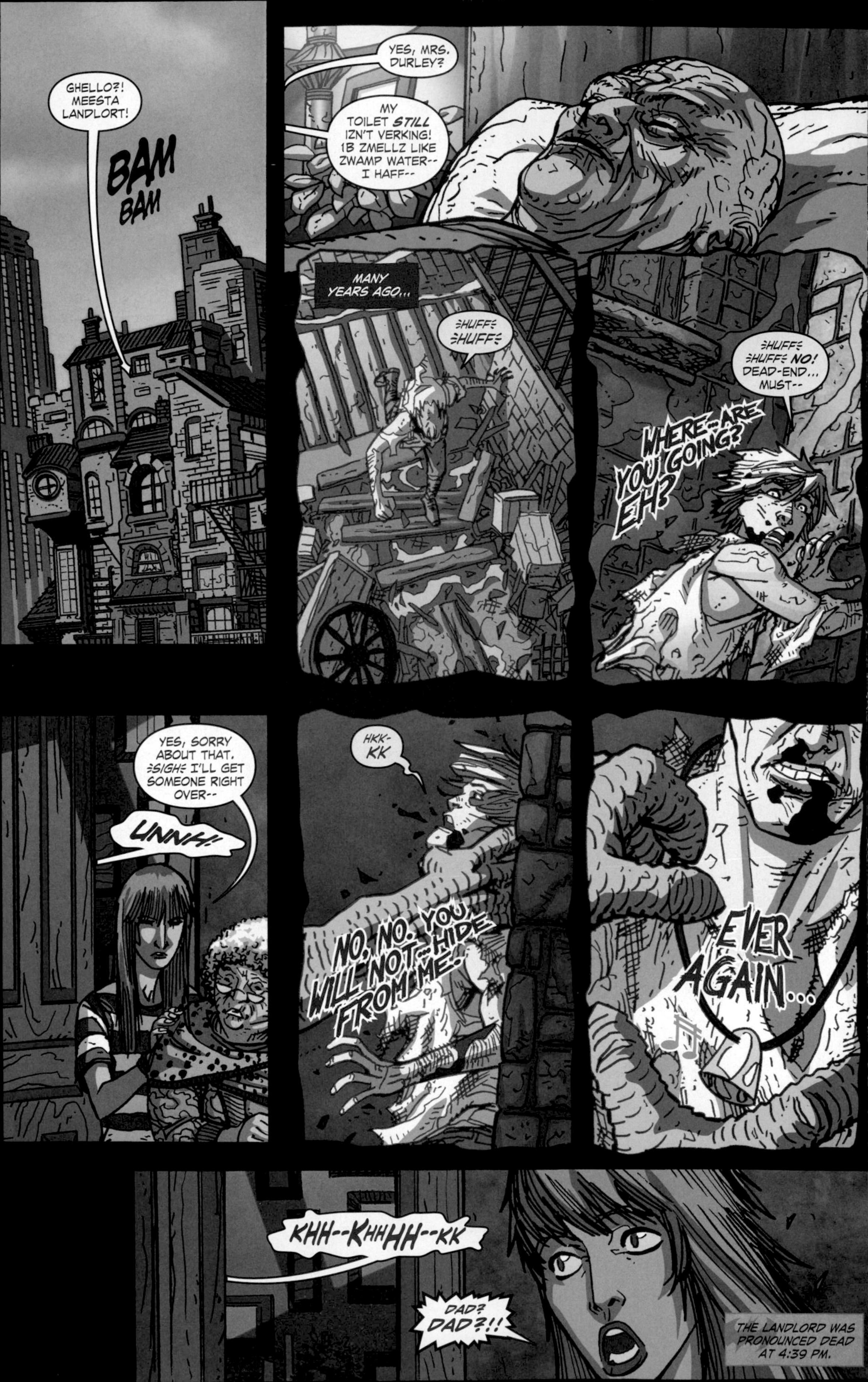
GHELLO?! MEESTA LANDLORT!
BAM
BAM
YES, MRS. DURLEY?
MY TOILET STILL IZN'T VERKING! IB ZMELLZ LIKE ZWAMP WATER-- I HAFF--
MANY YEARS AGO...
HUFF HUFF
HUFF HUFF NO! DEAD-END... MUST--
WHERE--ARE YOU GOING? EH?
YES, SORRY ABOUT THAT. SIGH I'LL GET SOMEONE RIGHT OVER--
UNNH!
HKK-KK
NO, NO. YOU WILL NOT--HIDE FROM ME.
EVER AGAIN...
KHH--KHHHH--KK
DAD? DAD?!!
THE LANDLORD WAS PRONOUNCED DEAD AT 4:39 PM.

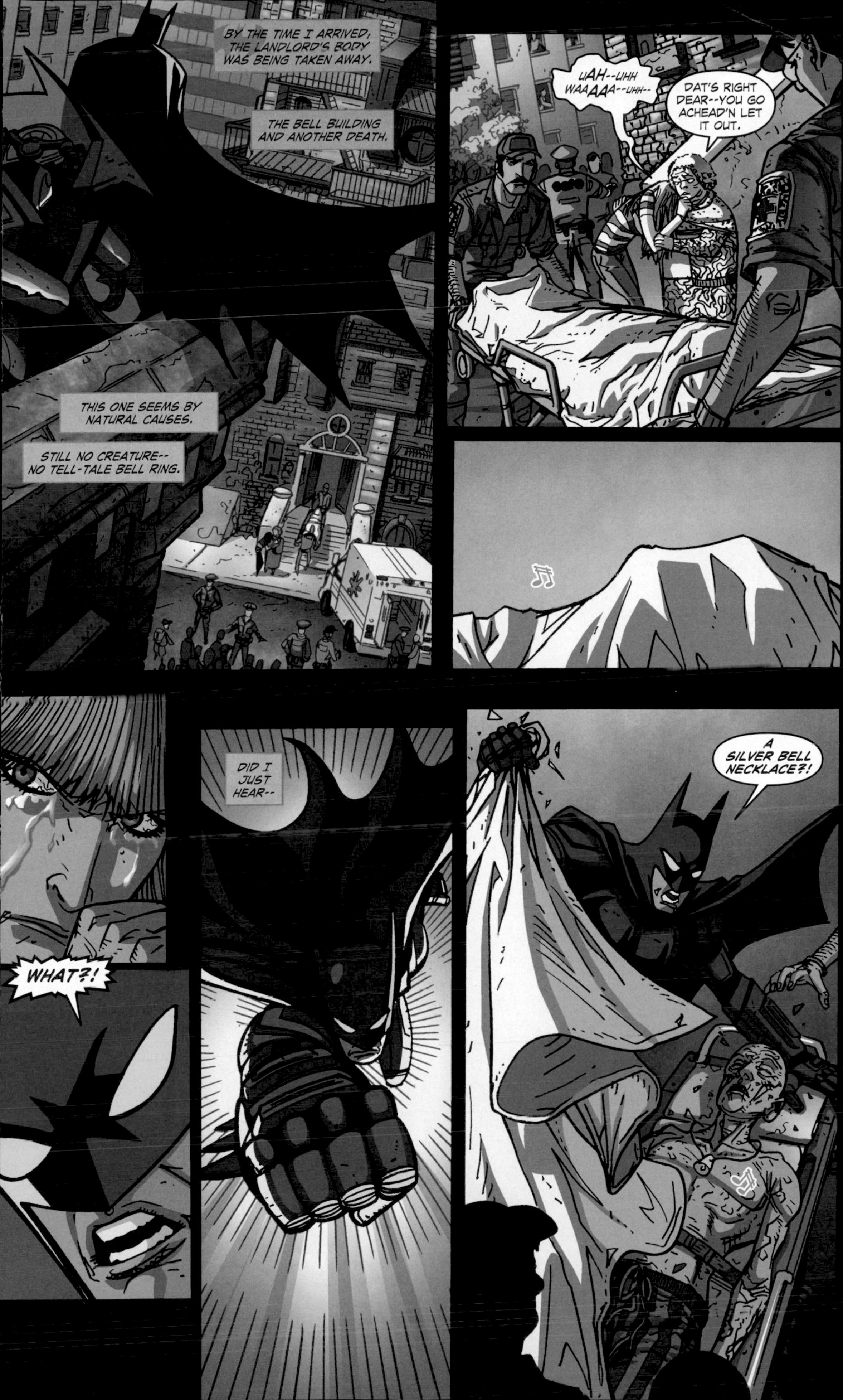
BY THE TIME I ARRIVED, THE LANDLORD'S BODY WAS BEING TAKEN AWAY.
THE BELL BUILDING AND ANOTHER DEATH.
THIS ONE SEEMS BY NATURAL CAUSES.
STILL NO CREATURE-- NO TELL-TALE BELL RING.
UAH--UHH WAAAAA--UHH--
DAT'S RIGHT DEAR--YOU GO ACHEAD'N LET IT OUT.
WHAT?!
DID I JUST HEAR--
A SILVER BELL NECKLACE?!

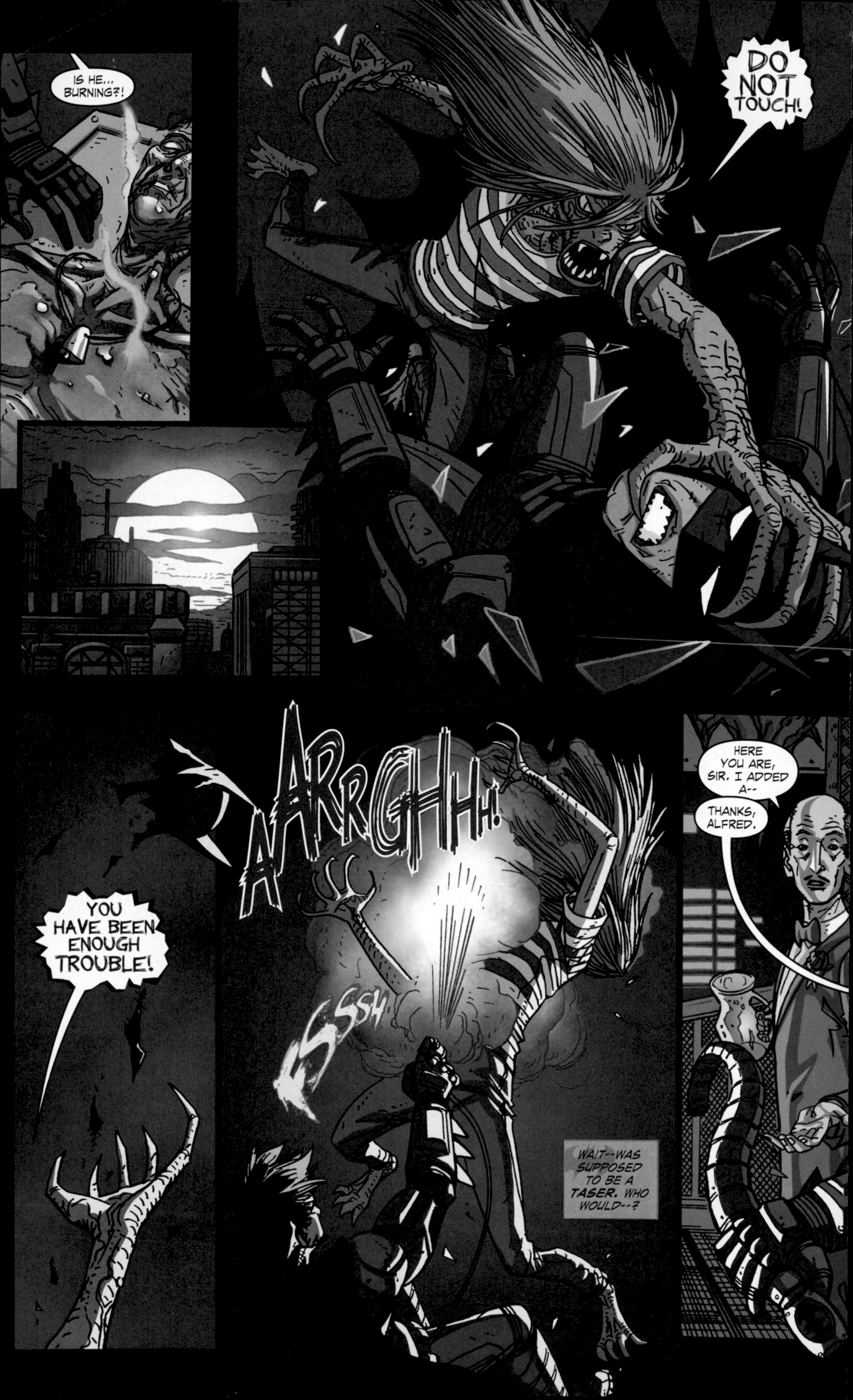
IS HE... BURNING?!
DO NOT TOUCH!
AARRGHH!
YOU HAVE BEEN ENOUGH TROUBLE!
SSSH
WAIT--WAS SUPPOSED TO BE A TASER. WHO WOULD--?
HERE YOU ARE, SIR. I ADDED A--
THANKS, ALFRED.

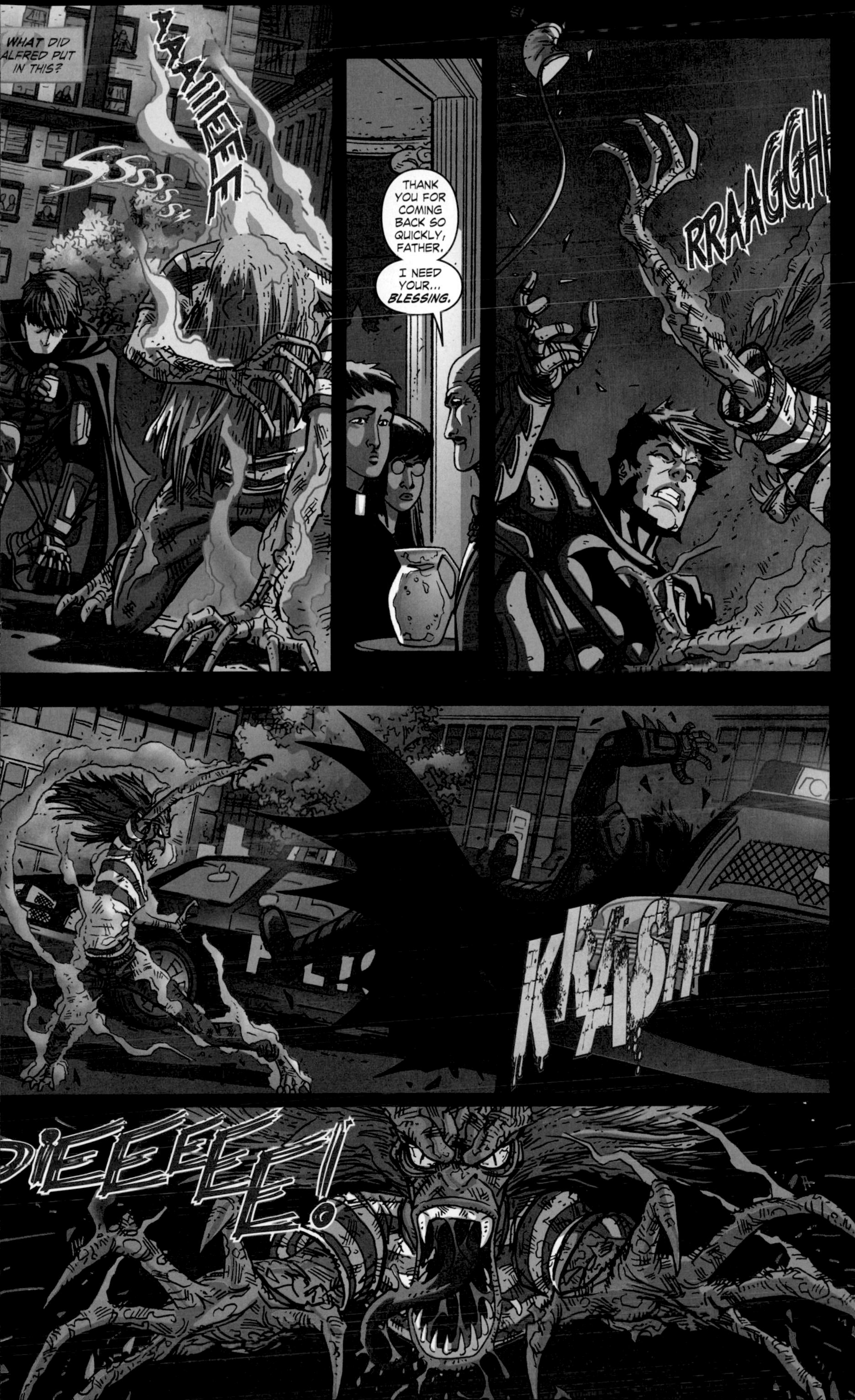
WHAT DID ALFRED PUT IN THIS?
RAAIIIEEEE
SSSSSSH
THANK YOU FOR COMING BACK SO QUICKLY, FATHER.
I NEED YOUR... BLESSING.
RRAAGGH
KRASH!
DIEEEEE!

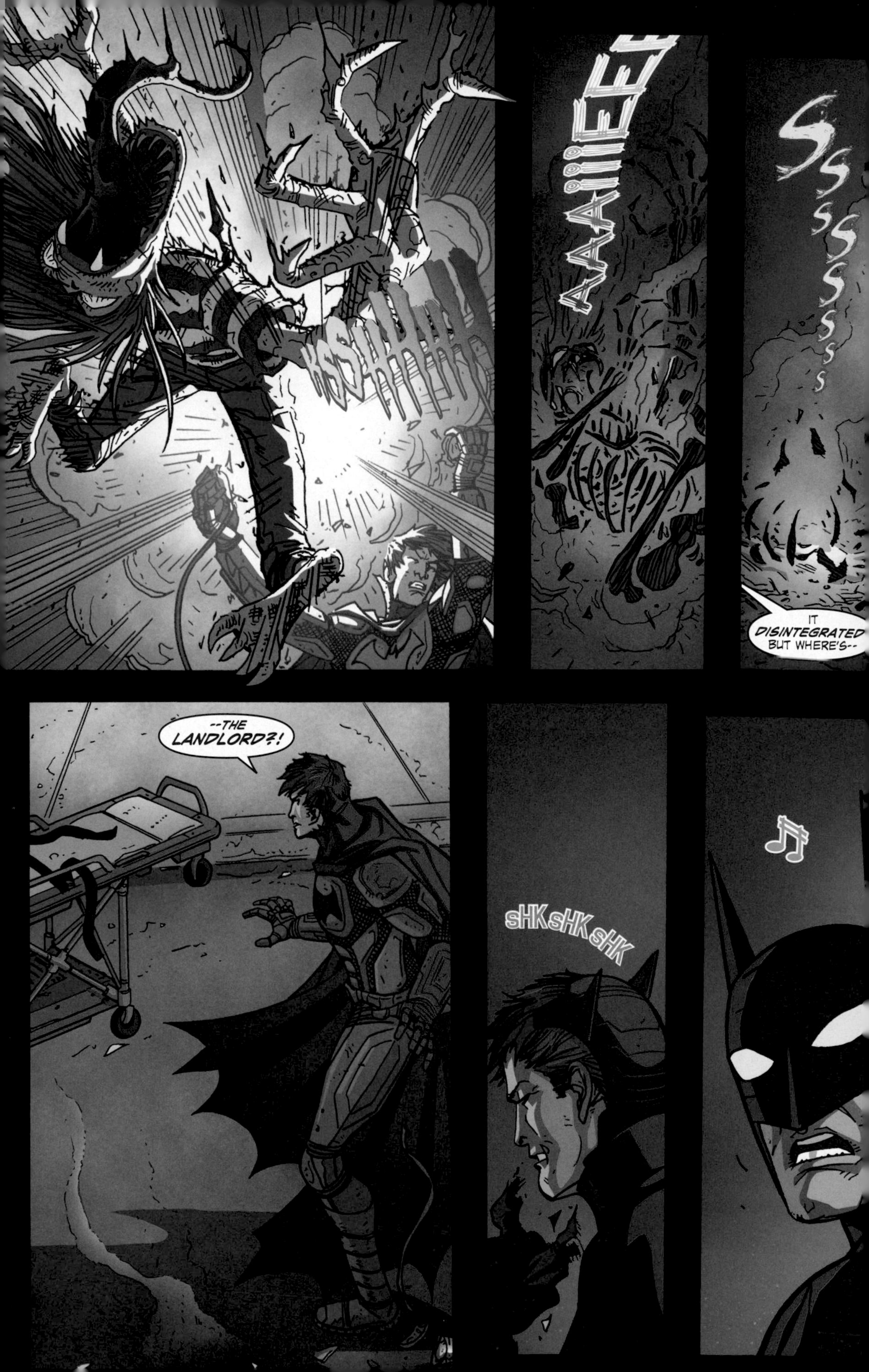
KSSHHHHH
AAAIIIEEE
SSSSSSSSS
IT DISINTEGRATED BUT WHERE'S--
--THE LANDLORD?!
sHK sHK sHK

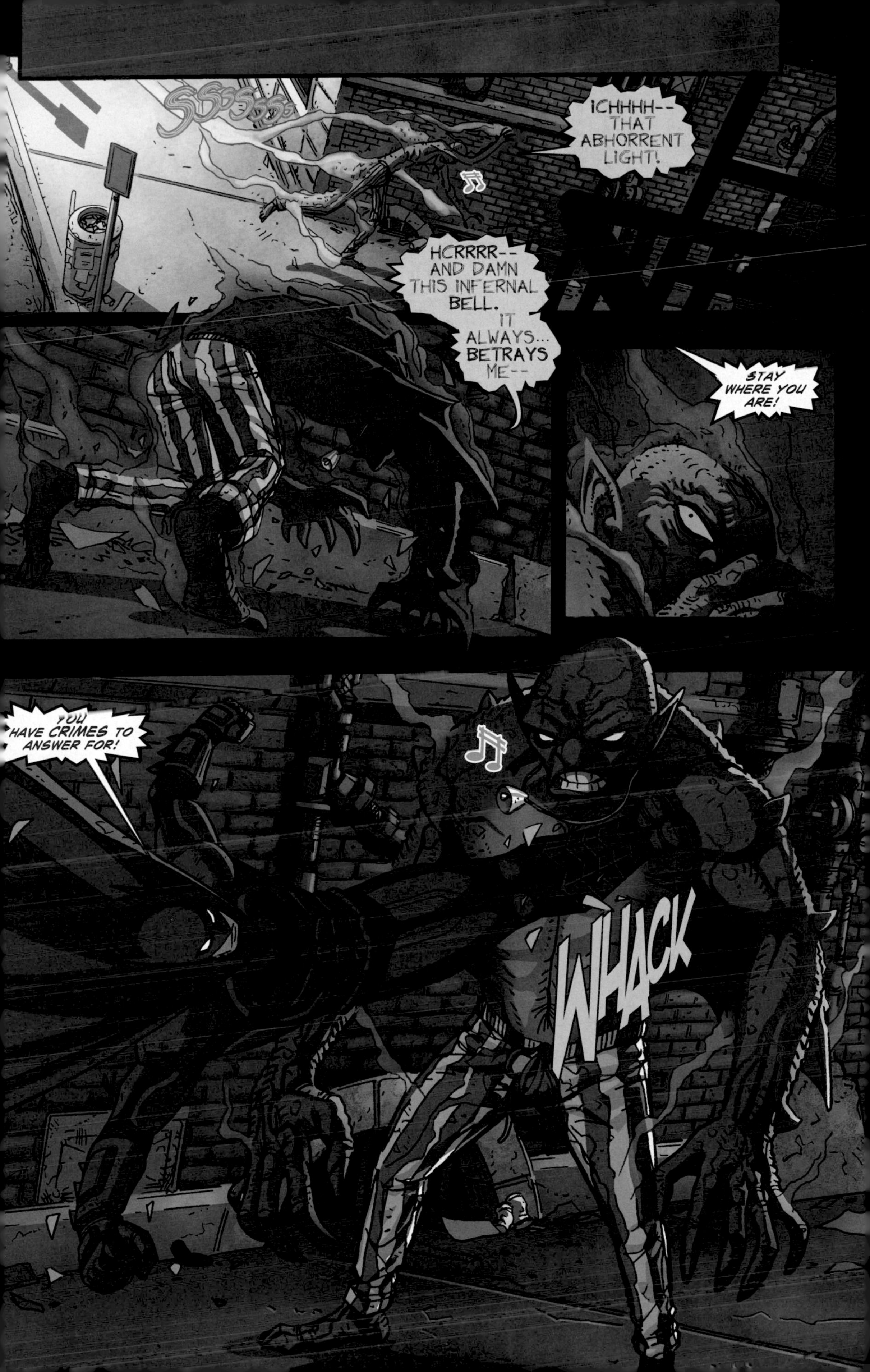
SSSSSSS
¡CHHHH-- THAT ABHORRENT LIGHT!
HCRRRR-- AND DAMN THIS INFERNAL BELL.
IT ALWAYS... BETRAYS ME--
STAY WHERE YOU ARE!
YOU HAVE CRIMES TO ANSWER FOR!
WHACK

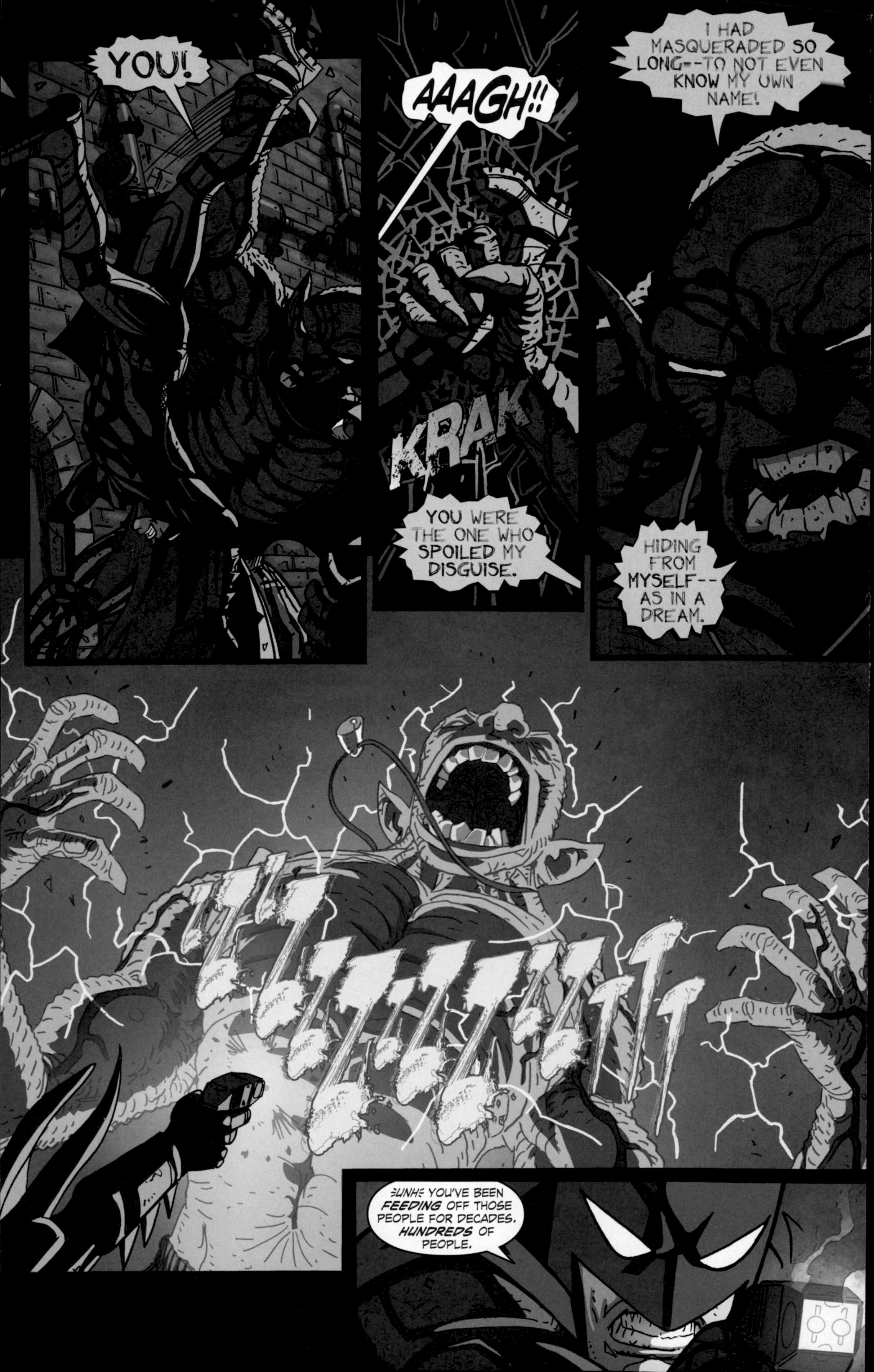
YOU!
AAAGH!!
KRAK
YOU WERE THE ONE WHO SPOILED MY DISGUISE.
I HAD MASQUERADED SO LONG--TO NOT EVEN KNOW MY OWN NAME!
HIDING FROM MYSELF--AS IN A DREAM.
ZZZZZZZZZZT
UNH YOU'VE BEEN FEEDING OFF THOSE PEOPLE FOR DECADES. HUNDREDS OF PEOPLE.

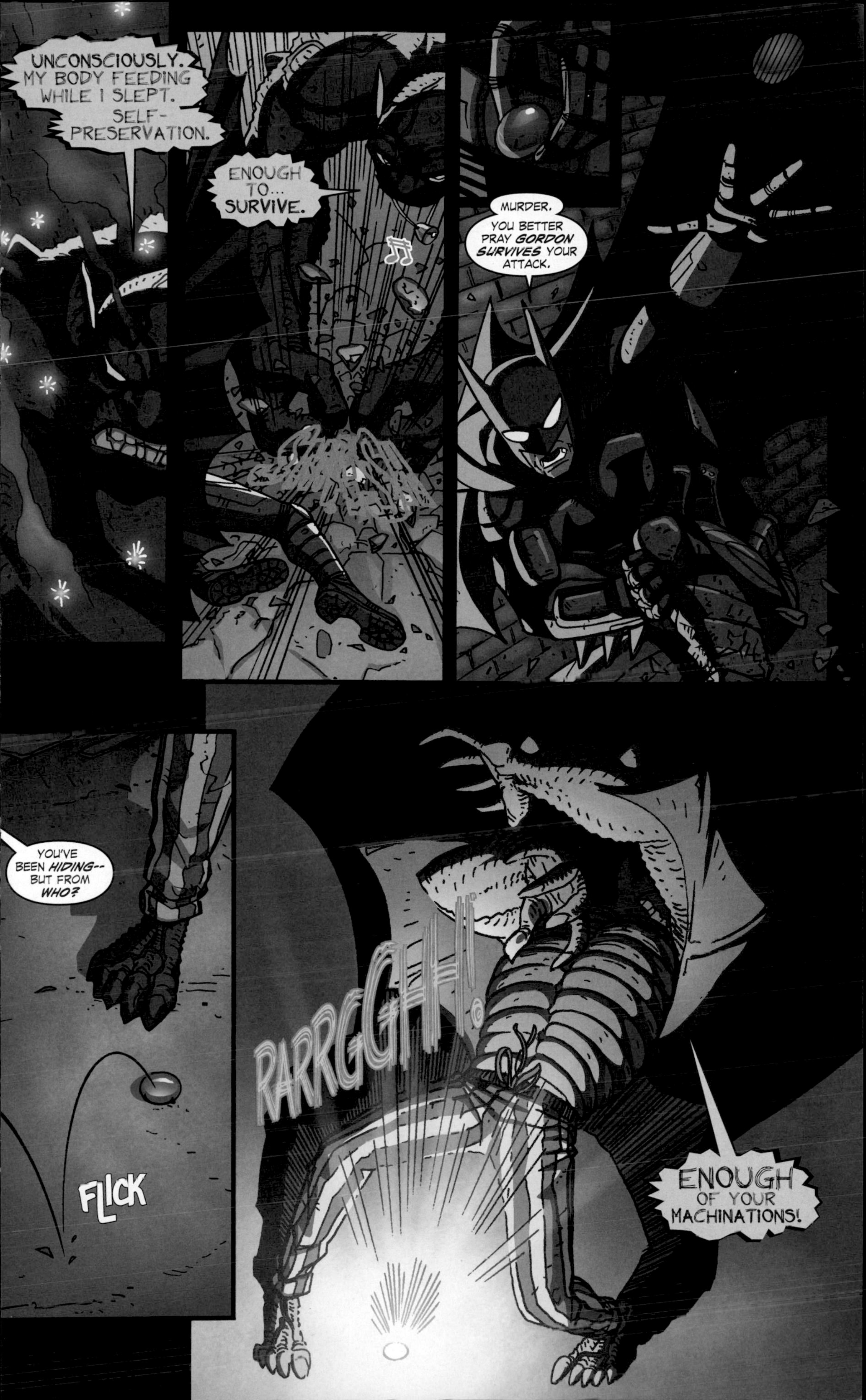

UNCONSCIOUSLY. MY BODY FEEDING WHILE I SLEPT. SELF-PRESERVATION.
ENOUGH TO... SURVIVE.
MURDER.
YOU BETTER PRAY GORDON SURVIVES YOUR ATTACK.
YOU'VE BEEN HIDING-- BUT FROM WHO?
FLICK
RARRGGH!!
ENOUGH OF YOUR MACHINATIONS!

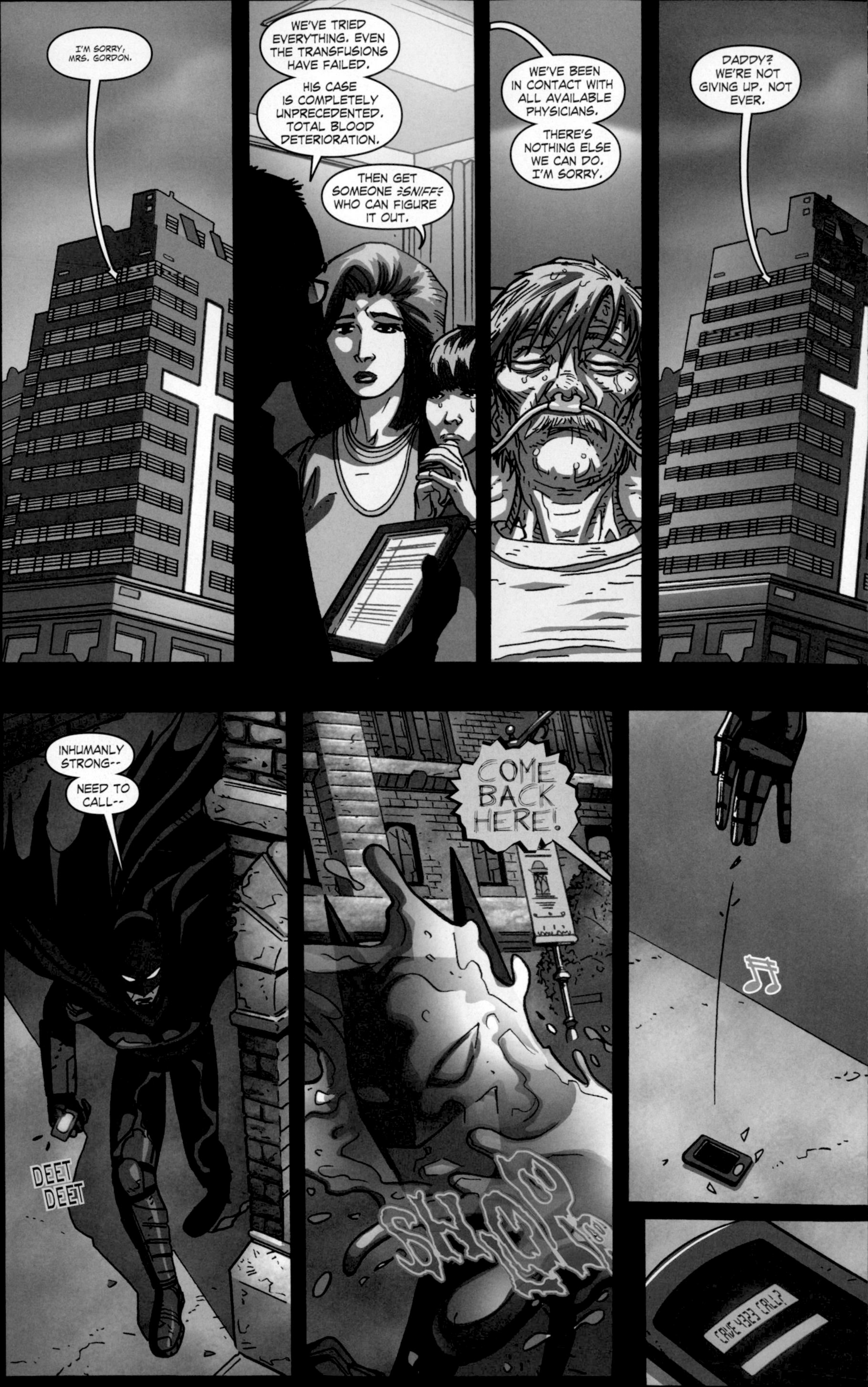
I'M SORRY, MRS. GORDON.
WE'VE TRIED EVERYTHING. EVEN THE TRANSFUSIONS HAVE FAILED.
HIS CASE IS COMPLETELY UNPRECEDENTED. TOTAL BLOOD DETERIORATION.
THEN GET SOMEONE *SNIFF* WHO CAN FIGURE IT OUT.
WE'VE BEEN IN CONTACT WITH ALL AVAILABLE PHYSICIANS.
THERE'S NOTHING ELSE WE CAN DO. I'M SORRY.
DADDY? WE'RE NOT GIVING UP. NOT EVER.
INHUMANLY STRONG--
NEED TO CALL--
DEET DEET
COME BACK HERE!
SHOP
CAVE 4323 CALL?

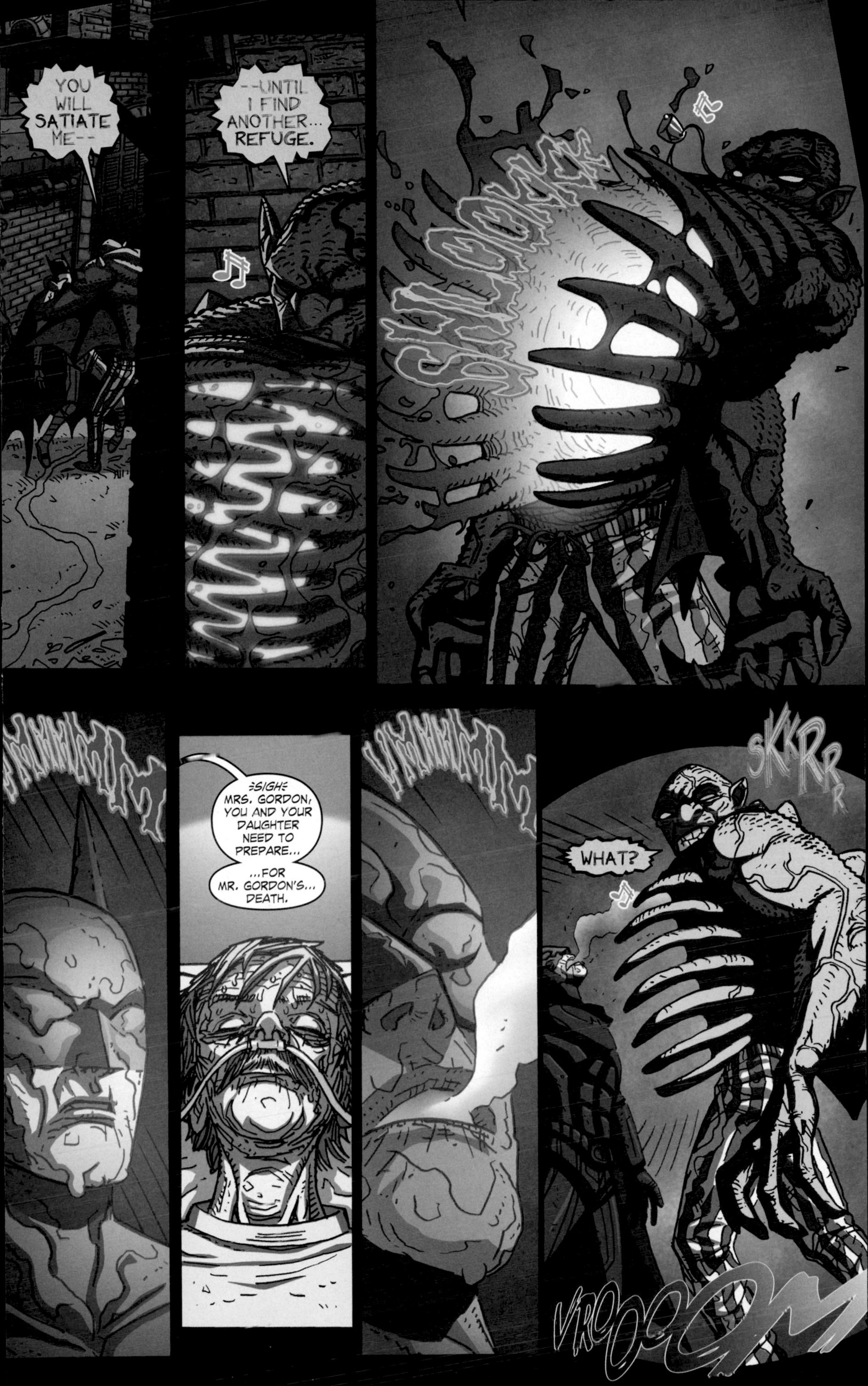
YOU WILL SATIATE ME--
--UNTIL I FIND ANOTHER... REFUGE.
SHLOOMCK
VMMMMMM
≡SIGH≡ MRS. GORDON, YOU AND YOUR DAUGHTER NEED TO PREPARE...
...FOR MR. GORDON'S... DEATH.
VMMMMMM
SKKRRR
WHAT?
VROOOOOM

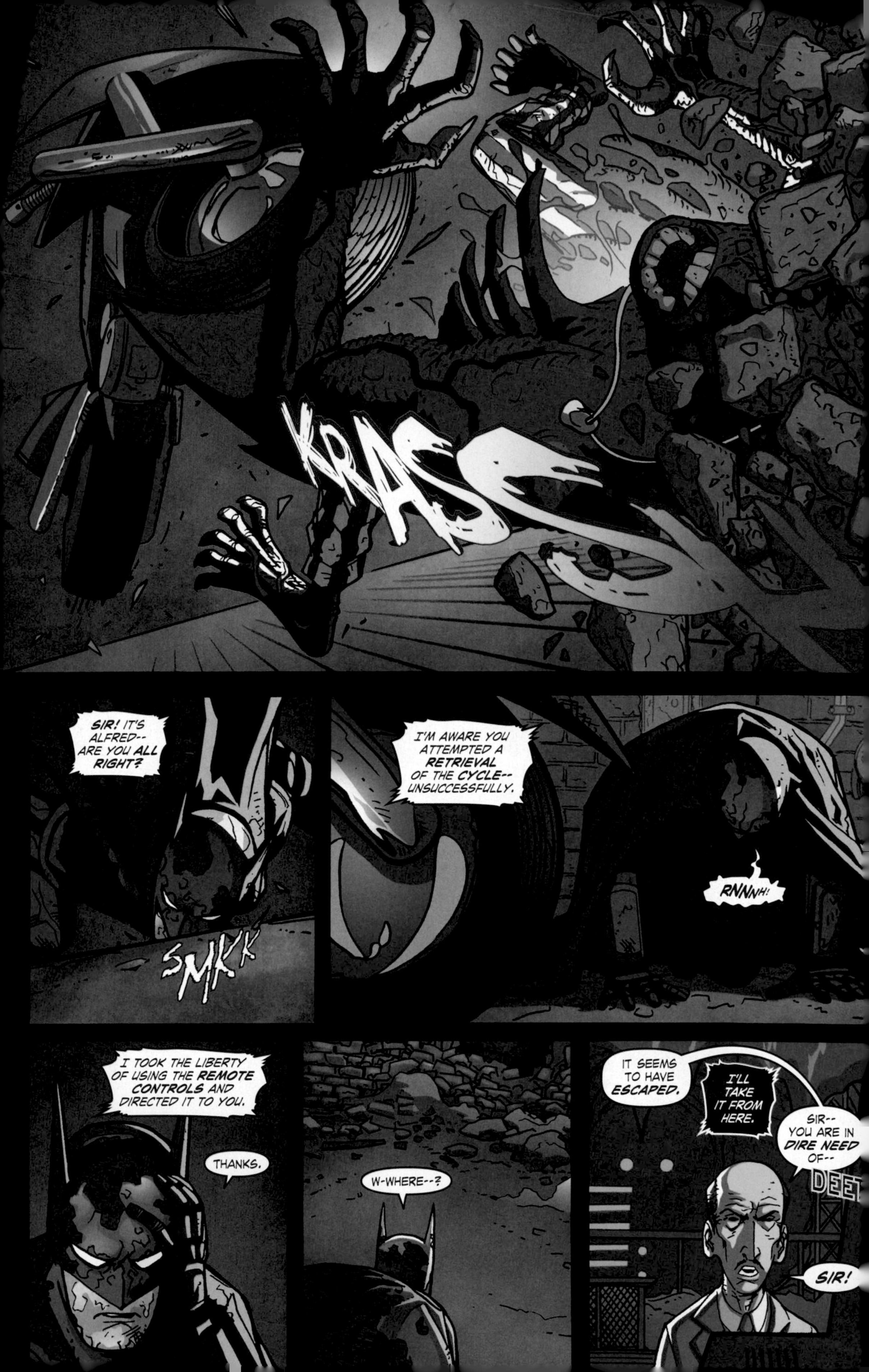
KRAS
SIR! IT'S ALFRED-- ARE YOU ALL RIGHT?
SMKK
I'M AWARE YOU ATTEMPTED A RETRIEVAL OF THE CYCLE-- UNSUCCESSFULLY.
RNNNH!
I TOOK THE LIBERTY OF USING THE REMOTE CONTROLS AND DIRECTED IT TO YOU.
THANKS.
W-WHERE--?
IT SEEMS TO HAVE ESCAPED.
I'LL TAKE IT FROM HERE.
SIR-- YOU ARE IN DIRE NEED OF--
SIR!

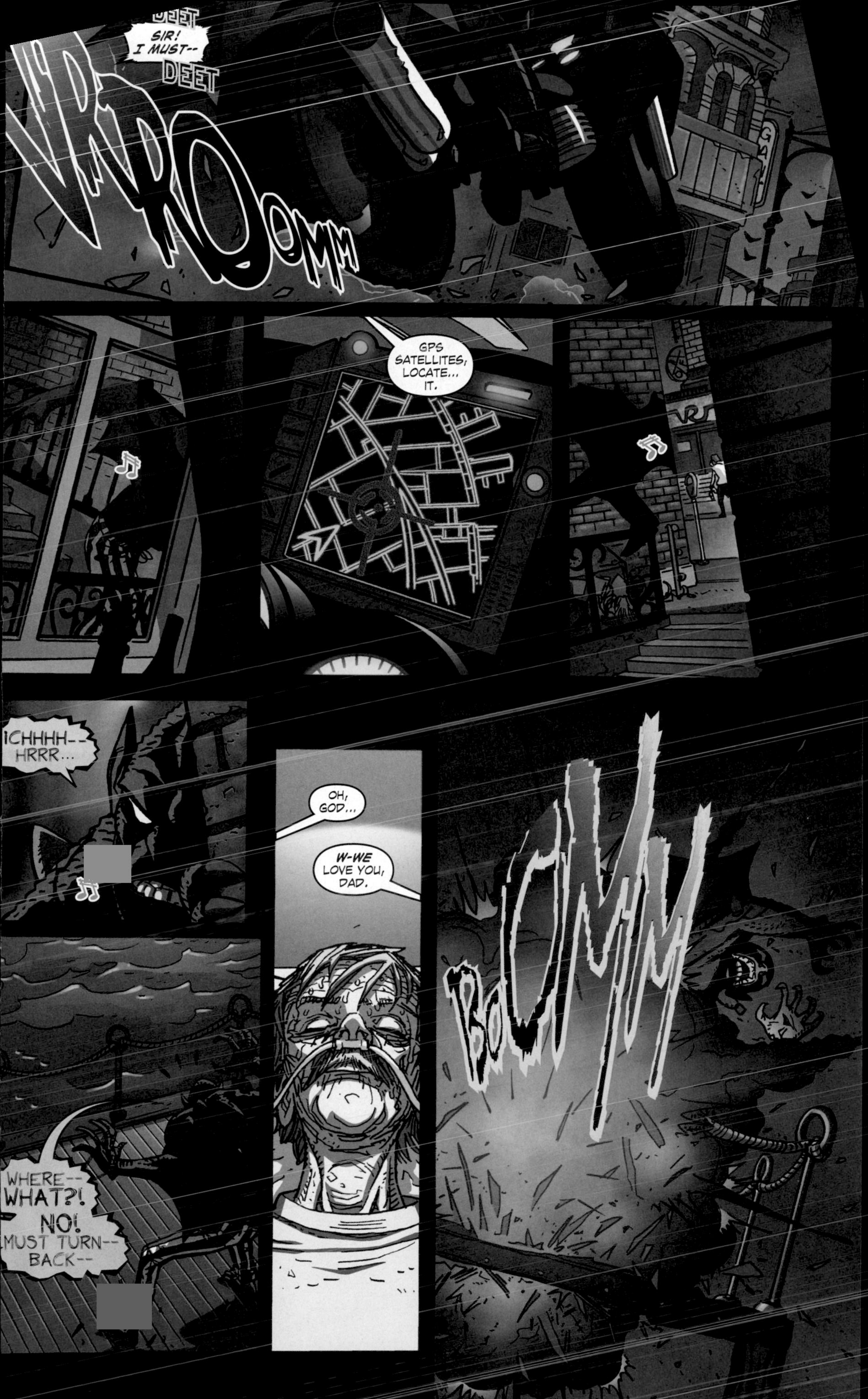
DEET
SIR! I MUST--
DEET
VRROOOMM
GPS SATELLITES, LOCATE... IT.
¡CHHHH--HRRR...
OH, GOD...
W-WE LOVE YOU, DAD.
WHERE--WHAT?! NO! MUST TURN--BACK--
BOOMM

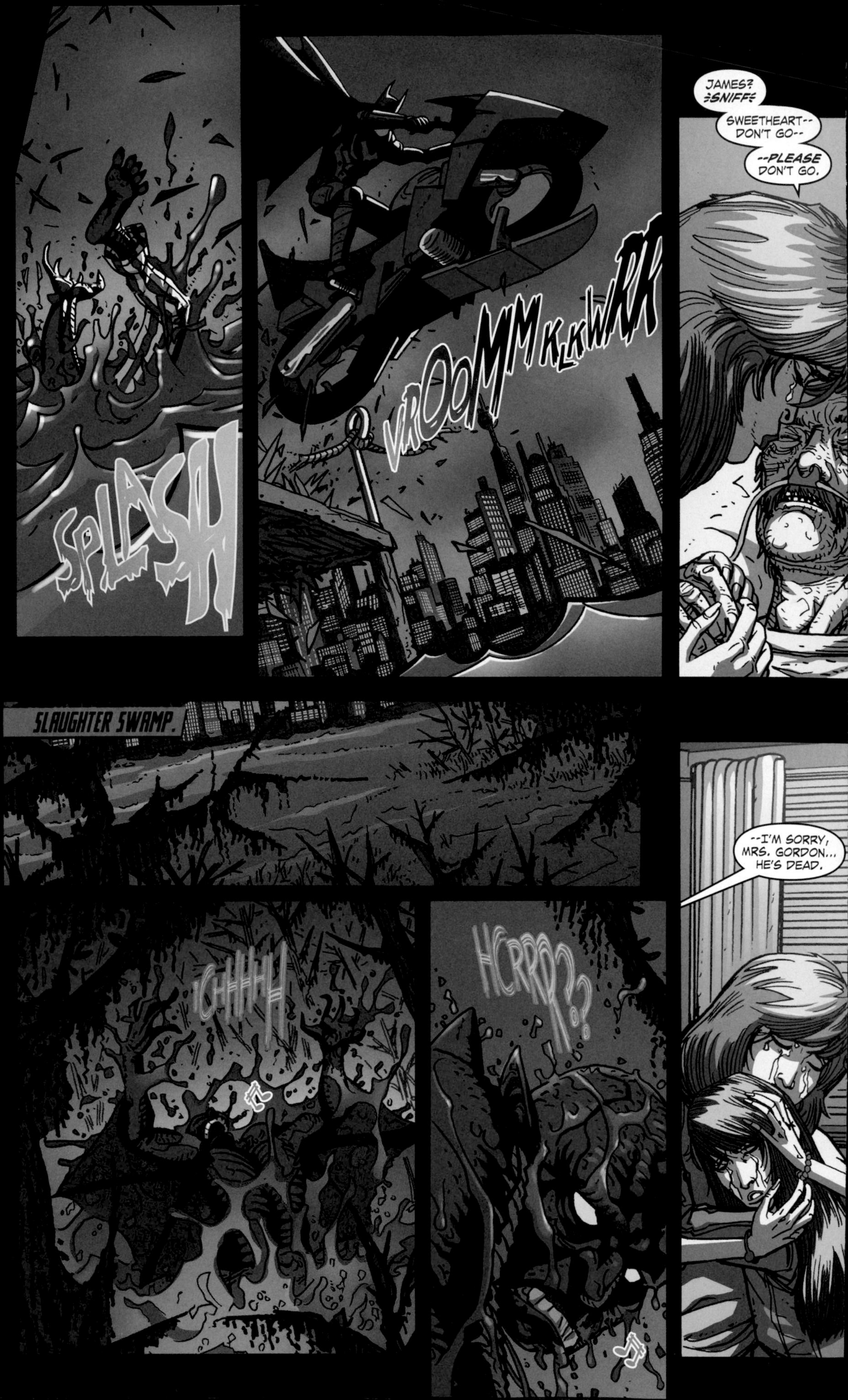
SPLASH
VROOMMM KLKWRR
JAMES? SNIFF
SWEETHEART-- DON'T GO--
--PLEASE DON'T GO.
SLAUGHTER SWAMP.
--I'M SORRY, MRS. GORDON... HE'S DEAD.
HCRRR??

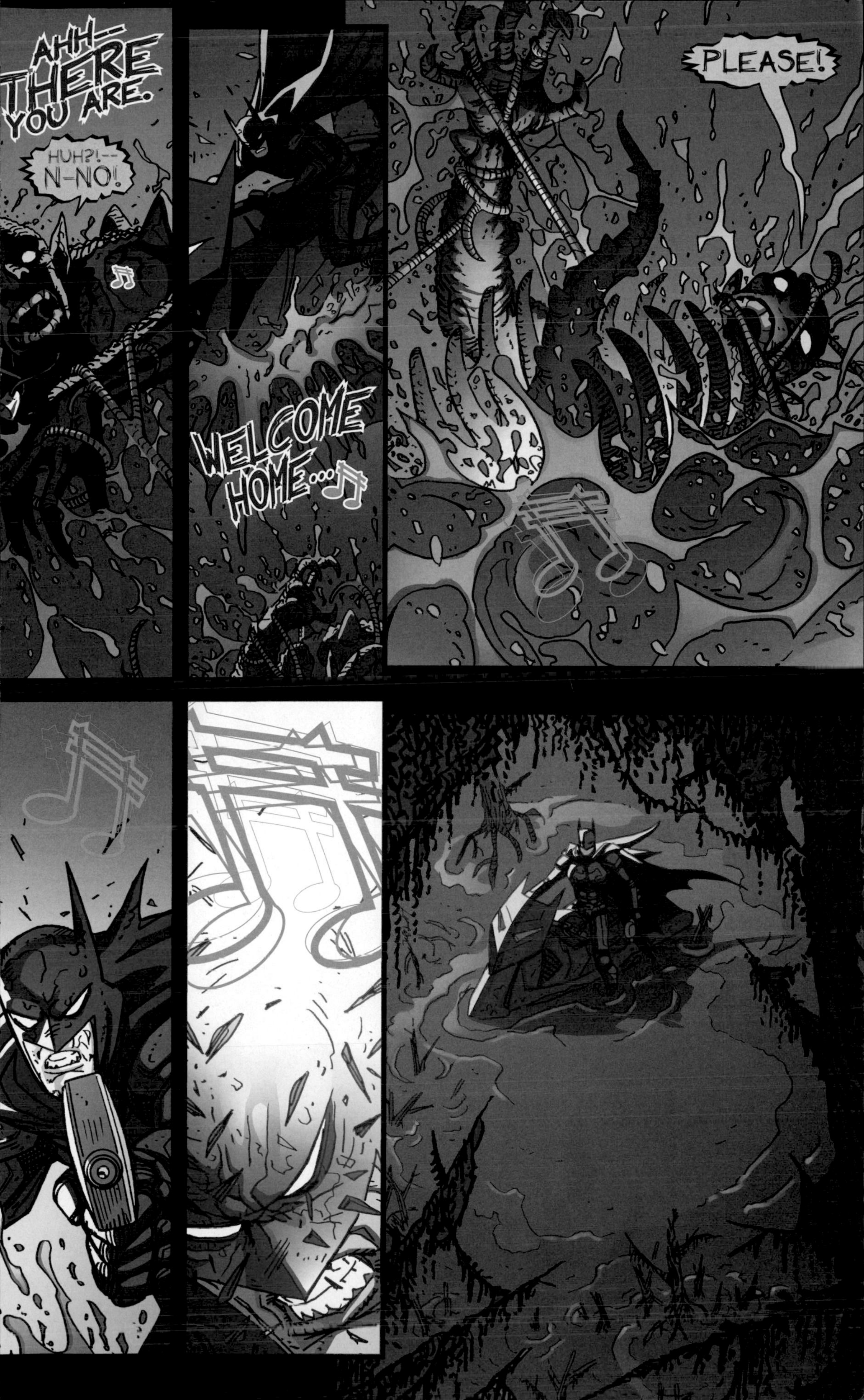
AHH— THERE YOU ARE.
HUH?!-- N-NO!
WELCOME HOME...
PLEASE!

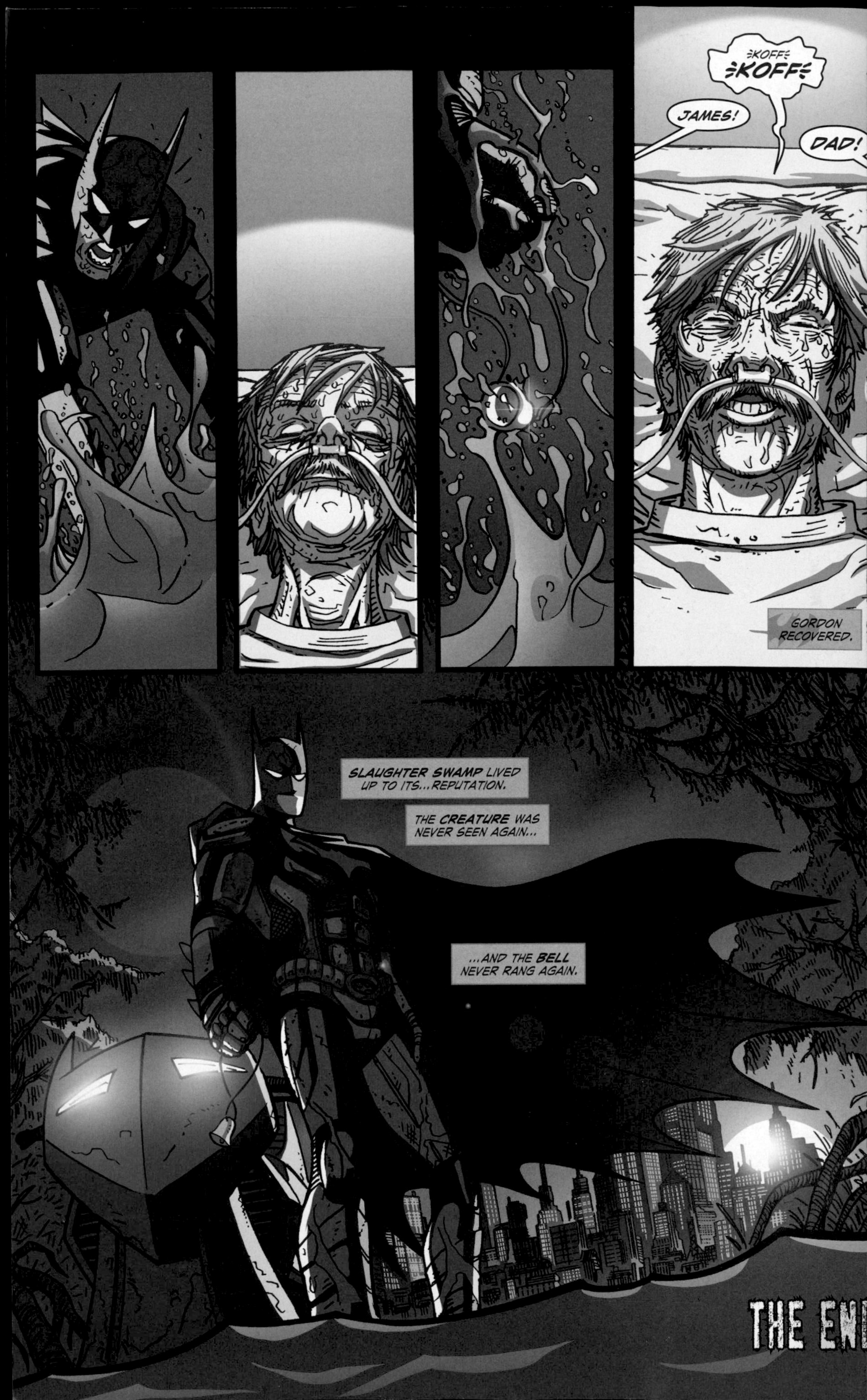

KOFF KOFF
JAMES!
DAD!
GORDON RECOVERED.
SLAUGHTER SWAMP LIVED UP TO ITS...REPUTATION.
THE CREATURE WAS NEVER SEEN AGAIN...
...AND THE BELL NEVER RANG AGAIN.

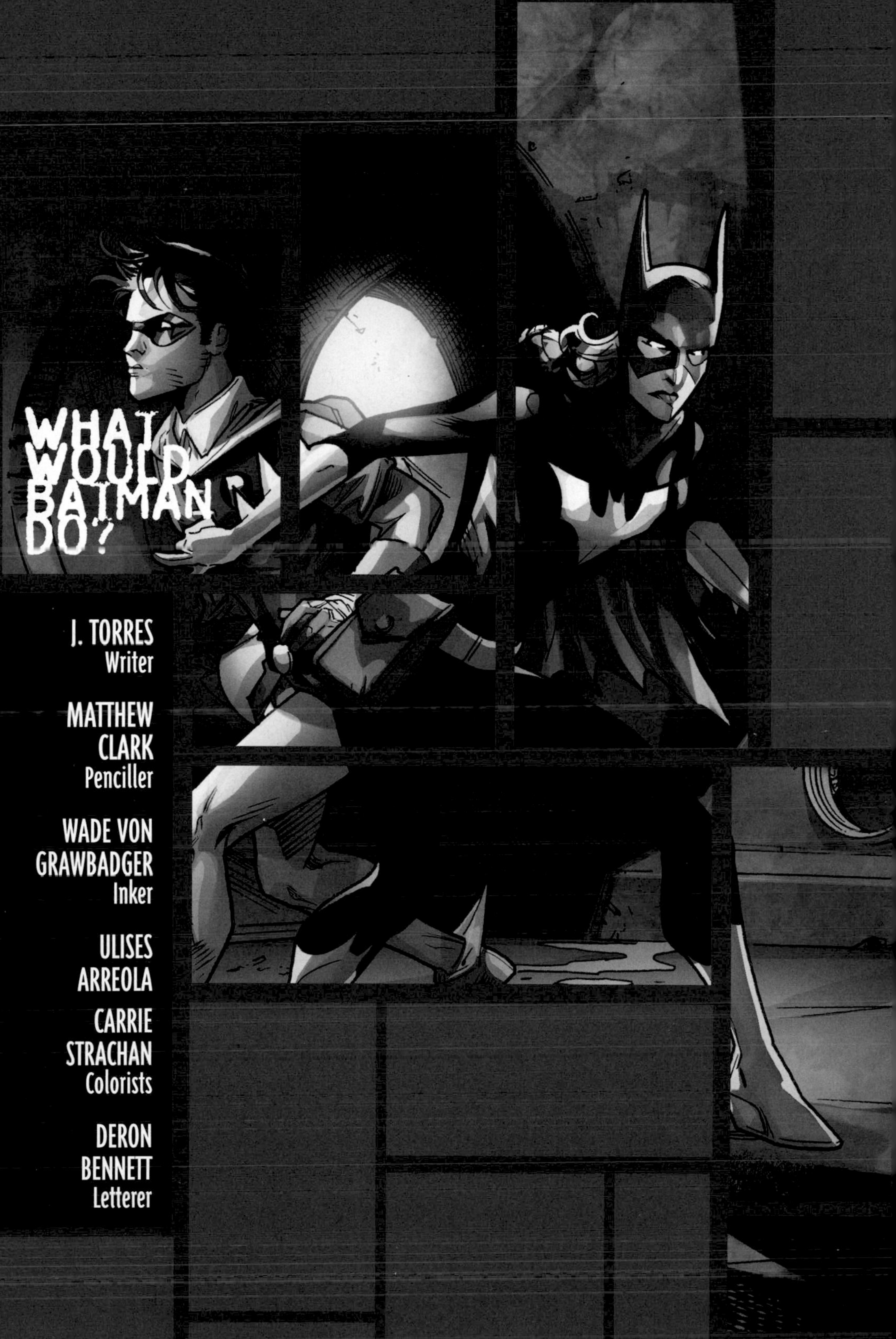
WHAT WOULD BATMAN DO?

WHAT WOULD BATMAN DO?

J. TORRES
Writer

MATTHEW CLARK
Penciller

WADE VON GRAWBADGER
Inker

ULISES ARREOLA
CARRIE STRACHAN
Colorists

DERON BENNETT
Letterer

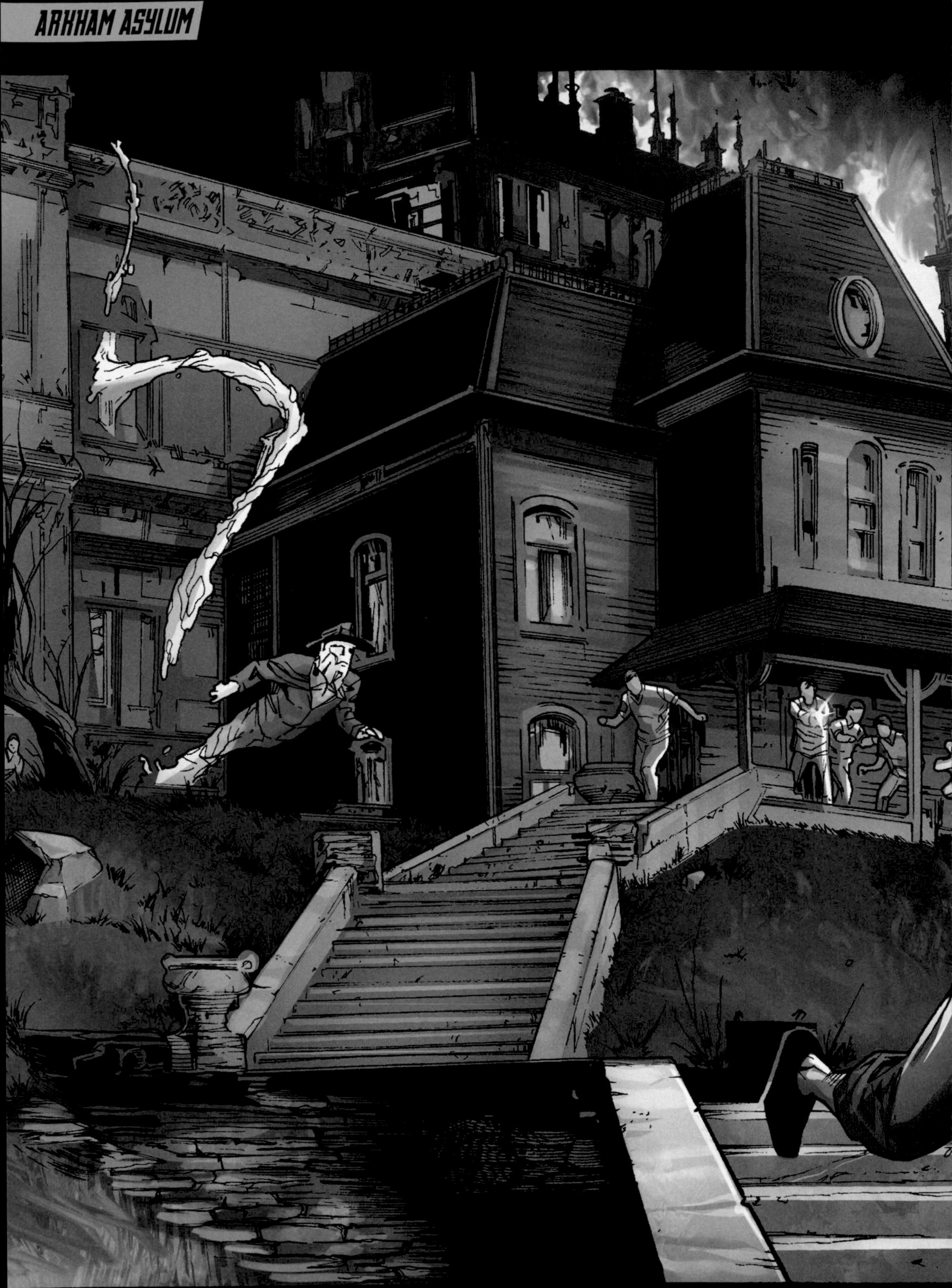
ARKHAM ASYLUM

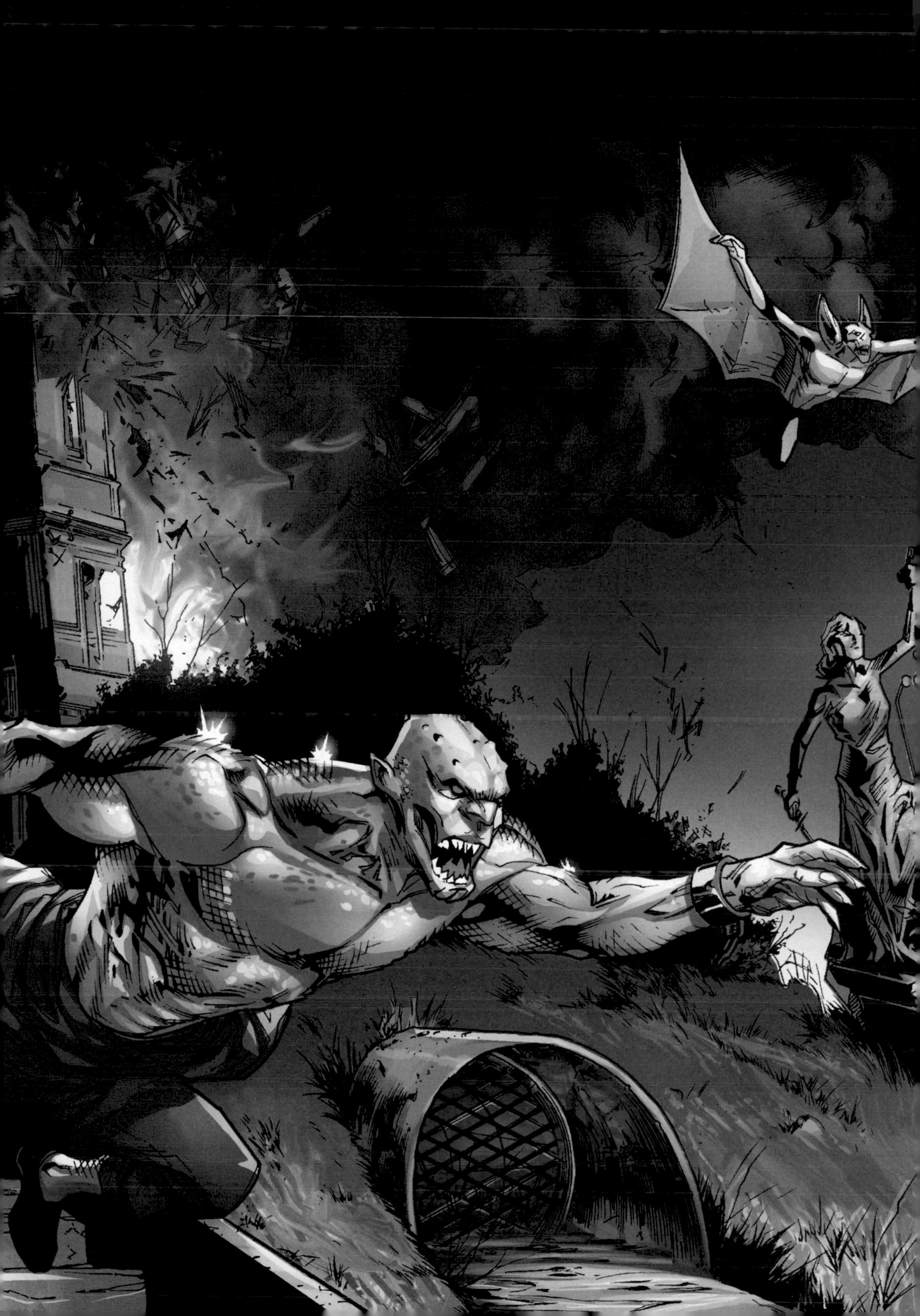

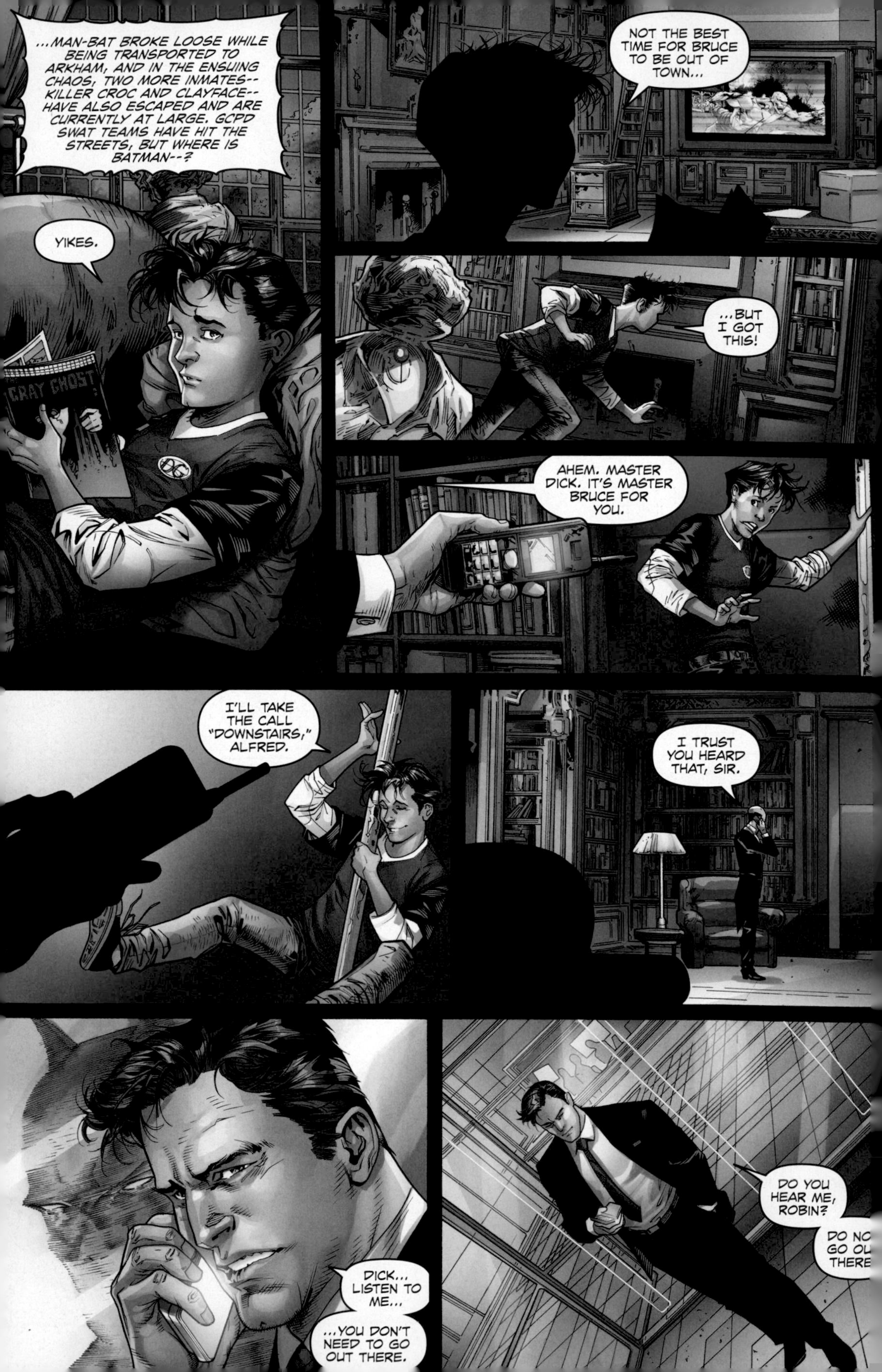
...MAN-BAT BROKE LOOSE WHILE BEING TRANSPORTED TO ARKHAM, AND IN THE ENSUING CHAOS, TWO MORE INMATES--KILLER CROC AND CLAYFACE--HAVE ALSO ESCAPED AND ARE CURRENTLY AT LARGE. GCPD SWAT TEAMS HAVE HIT THE STREETS, BUT WHERE IS BATMAN--?
YIKES.
THE GRAY GHOST
NOT THE BEST TIME FOR BRUCE TO BE OUT OF TOWN...
...BUT I GOT THIS!
AHEM. MASTER DICK. IT'S MASTER BRUCE FOR YOU.
I'LL TAKE THE CALL "DOWNSTAIRS," ALFRED.
I TRUST YOU HEARD THAT, SIR.
DICK... LISTEN TO ME...
...YOU DON'T NEED TO GO OUT THERE.
DO YOU HEAR ME, ROBIN?

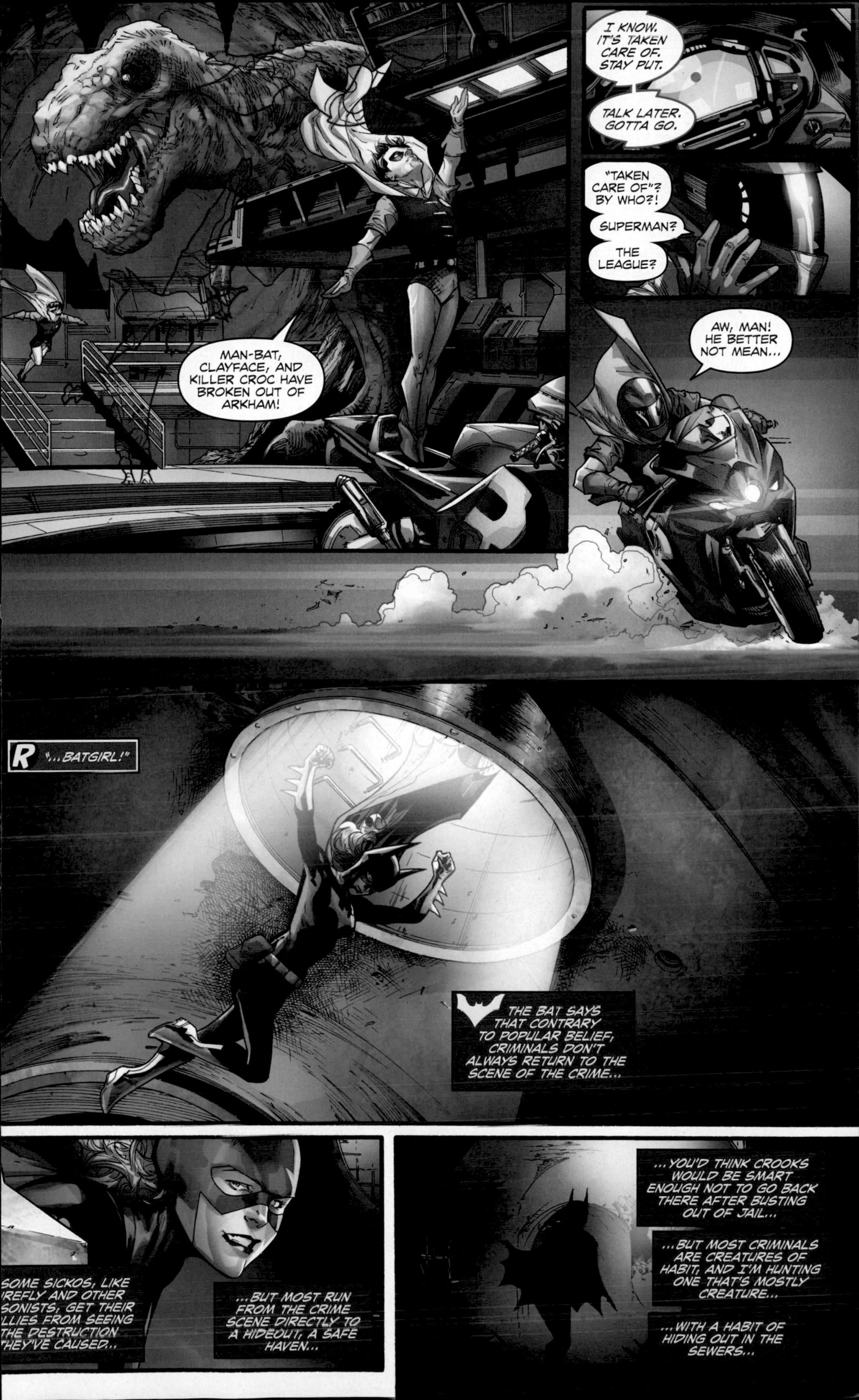
MAN-BAT, CLAYFACE, AND KILLER CROC HAVE BROKEN OUT OF ARKHAM!
I KNOW. IT'S TAKEN CARE OF. STAY PUT.
TALK LATER. GOTTA GO.
"TAKEN CARE OF"? BY WHO?!
SUPERMAN?
THE LEAGUE?
AW, MAN! HE BETTER NOT MEAN...
"...BATGIRL!"
THE BAT SAYS THAT CONTRARY TO POPULAR BELIEF, CRIMINALS DON'T ALWAYS RETURN TO THE SCENE OF THE CRIME...
SOME SICKOS, LIKE IREFLY AND OTHER SONISTS, GET THEIR LLIES FROM SEEING THE DESTRUCTION THEY'VE CAUSED...
...BUT MOST RUN FROM THE CRIME SCENE DIRECTLY TO A HIDEOUT, A SAFE HAVEN...
...YOU'D THINK CROOKS WOULD BE SMART ENOUGH NOT TO GO BACK THERE AFTER BUSTING OUT OF JAIL...
...BUT MOST CRIMINALS ARE CREATURES OF HABIT, AND I'M HUNTING ONE THAT'S MOSTLY CREATURE...
...WITH A HABIT OF HIDING OUT IN THE SEWERS...

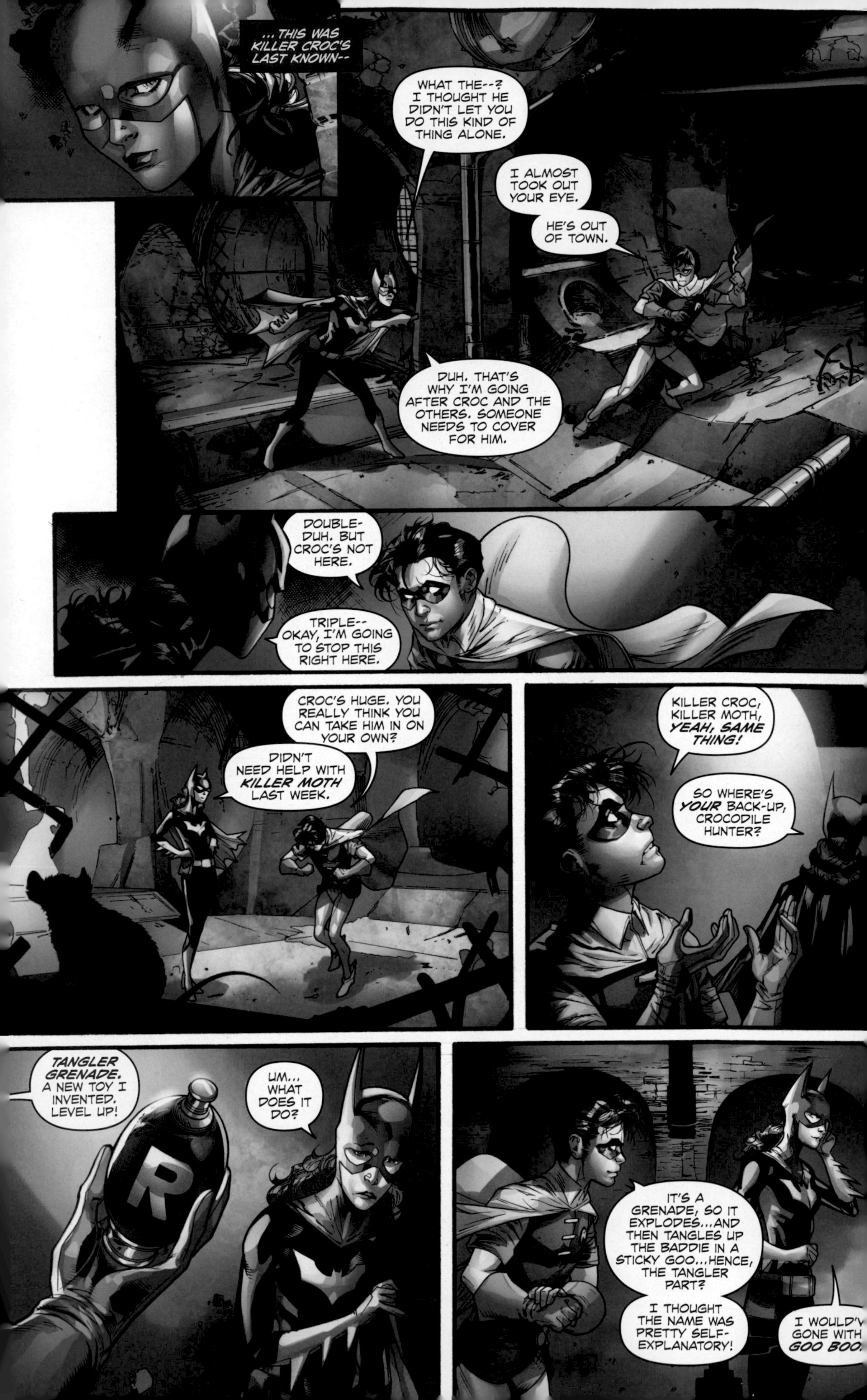

...THIS WAS KILLER CROC'S LAST KNOWN--
WHAT THE--? I THOUGHT HE DIDN'T LET YOU DO THIS KIND OF THING ALONE.
I ALMOST TOOK OUT YOUR EYE.
HE'S OUT OF TOWN.
DUH. THAT'S WHY I'M GOING AFTER CROC AND THE OTHERS. SOMEONE NEEDS TO COVER FOR HIM.
DOUBLE-DUH. BUT CROC'S NOT HERE.
TRIPLE--OKAY, I'M GOING TO STOP THIS RIGHT HERE.
CROC'S HUGE. YOU REALLY THINK YOU CAN TAKE HIM IN ON YOUR OWN?
DIDN'T NEED HELP WITH KILLER MOTH LAST WEEK.
KILLER CROC, KILLER MOTH, YEAH, SAME THING!
SO WHERE'S YOUR BACK-UP, CROCODILE HUNTER?
TANGLER GRENADE. A NEW TOY I INVENTED. LEVEL UP!
UM... WHAT DOES IT DO?
IT'S A GRENADE, SO IT EXPLODES...AND THEN TANGLES UP THE BADDIE IN A STICKY GOO...HENCE, THE TANGLER PART?
I THOUGHT THE NAME WAS PRETTY SELF-EXPLANATORY!
I WOULD'V GONE WITH GOO BOO

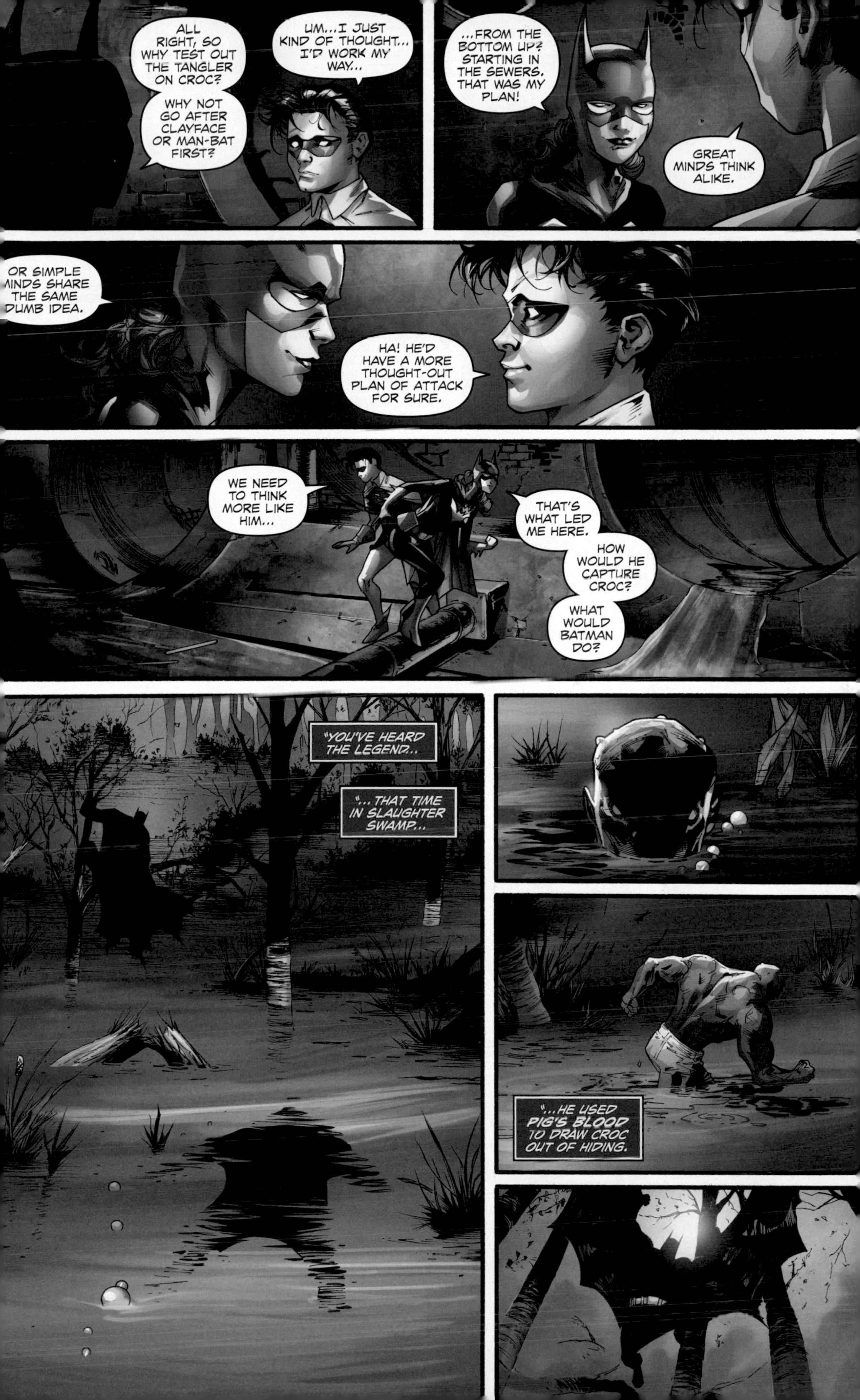
ALL RIGHT, SO WHY TEST OUT THE TANGLER ON CROC?
WHY NOT GO AFTER CLAYFACE OR MAN-BAT FIRST?
UM...I JUST KIND OF THOUGHT... I'D WORK MY WAY...
...FROM THE BOTTOM UP? STARTING IN THE SEWERS. THAT WAS MY PLAN!
GREAT MINDS THINK ALIKE.
OR SIMPLE MINDS SHARE THE SAME DUMB IDEA.
HA! HE'D HAVE A MORE THOUGHT-OUT PLAN OF ATTACK FOR SURE.
WE NEED TO THINK MORE LIKE HIM...
THAT'S WHAT LED ME HERE.
HOW WOULD HE CAPTURE CROC?
WHAT WOULD BATMAN DO?
"YOU'VE HEARD THE LEGEND...
"...THAT TIME IN SLAUGHTER SWAMP...
"...HE USED PIG'S BLOOD TO DRAW CROC OUT OF HIDING.

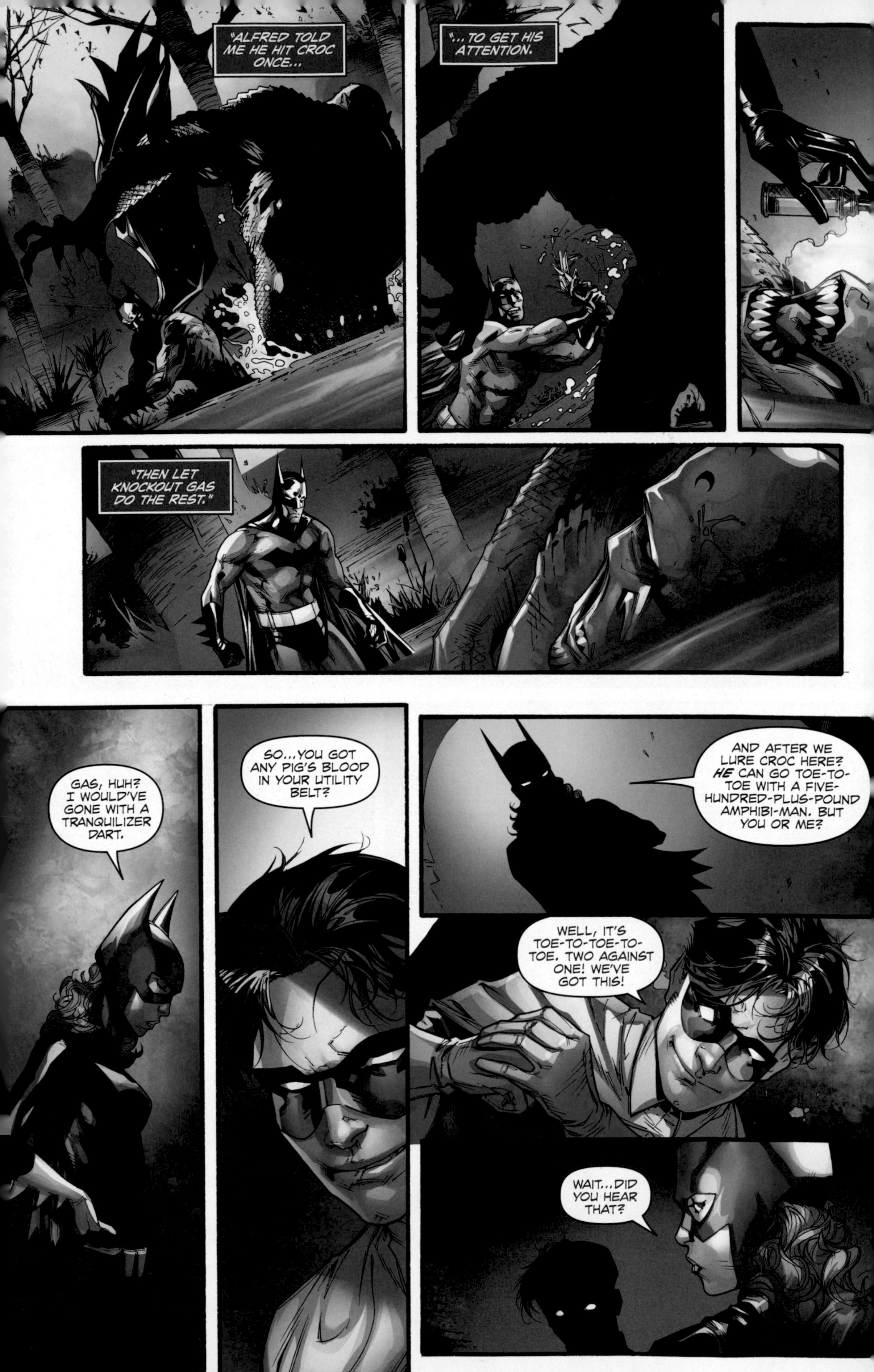
"ALFRED TOLD ME HE HIT CROC ONCE...
"...TO GET HIS ATTENTION.
"THEN LET KNOCKOUT GAS DO THE REST."
GAS, HUH? I WOULD'VE GONE WITH A TRANQUILIZER DART.
SO...YOU GOT ANY PIG'S BLOOD IN YOUR UTILITY BELT?
AND AFTER WE LURE CROC HERE? HE CAN GO TOE-TO-TOE WITH A FIVE-HUNDRED-PLUS-POUND AMPHIBI-MAN. BUT YOU OR ME?
WELL, IT'S TOE-TO-TOE-TO-TOE. TWO AGAINST ONE! WE'VE GOT THIS!
WAIT...DID YOU HEAR THAT?

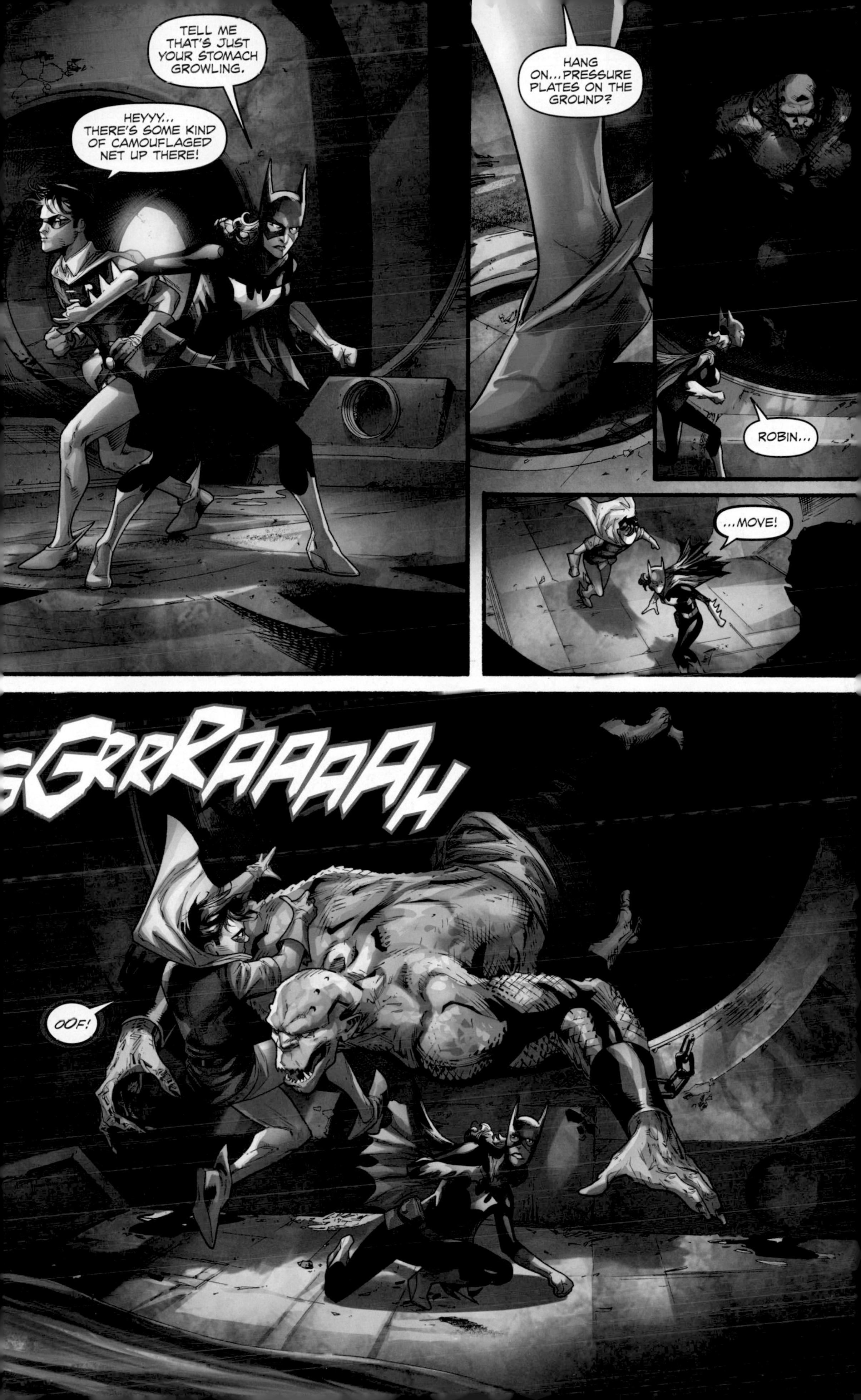

TELL ME THAT'S JUST YOUR STOMACH GROWLING.
HEYYY... THERE'S SOME KIND OF CAMOUFLAGED NET UP THERE!
HANG ON...PRESSURE PLATES ON THE GROUND?
ROBIN...
...MOVE!
GRRRAAAAAH
OOF!

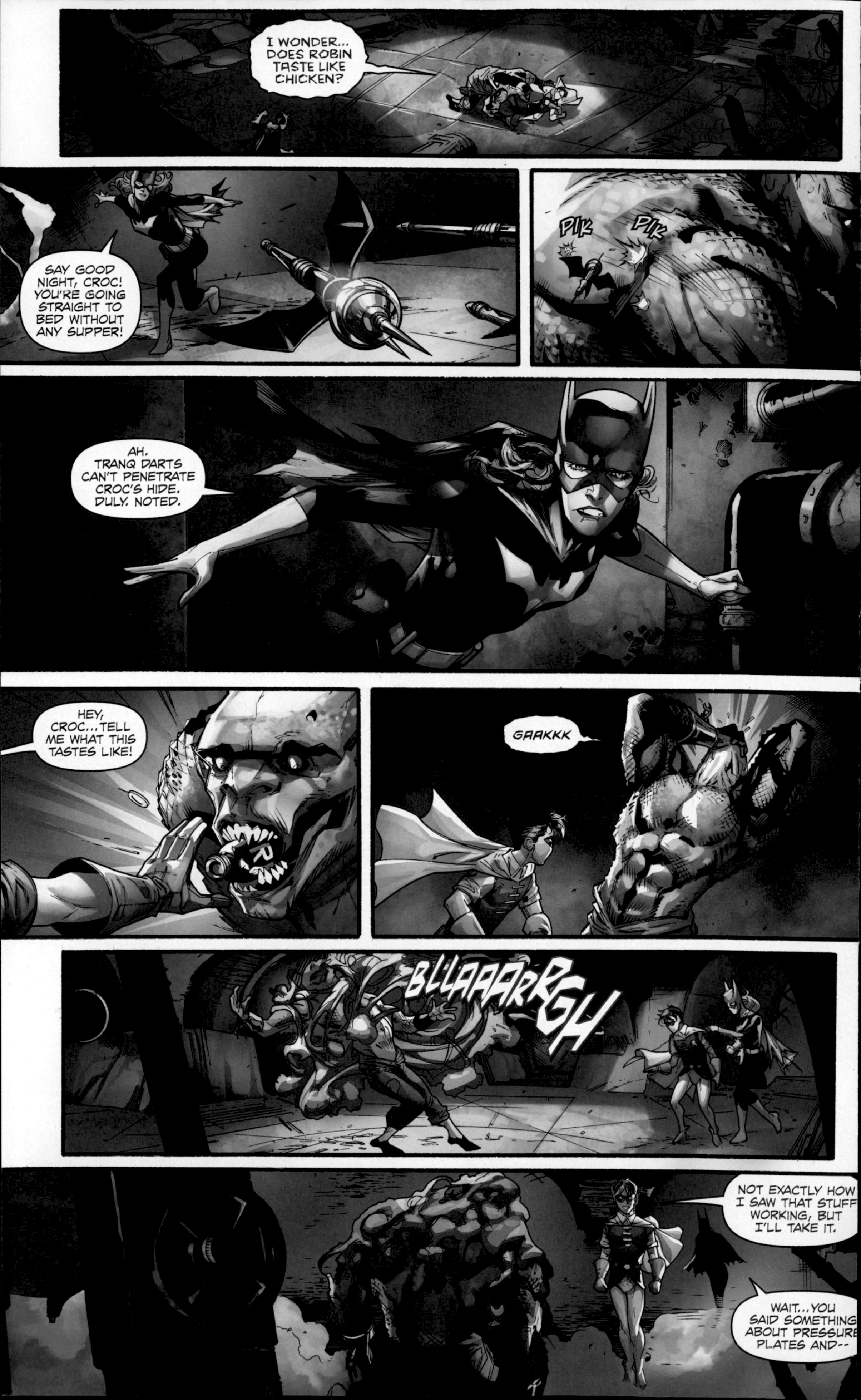
I WONDER... DOES ROBIN TASTE LIKE CHICKEN?
SAY GOOD NIGHT, CROC! YOU'RE GOING STRAIGHT TO BED WITHOUT ANY SUPPER!
PIK
PIK
AH. TRANQ DARTS CAN'T PENETRATE CROC'S HIDE. DULY. NOTED.
HEY, CROC...TELL ME WHAT THIS TASTES LIKE!
GAAKKK
BLLAAARRGH
NOT EXACTLY HOW I SAW THAT STUFF WORKING, BUT I'LL TAKE IT.
WAIT...YOU SAID SOMETHING ABOUT PRESSURE PLATES AND--

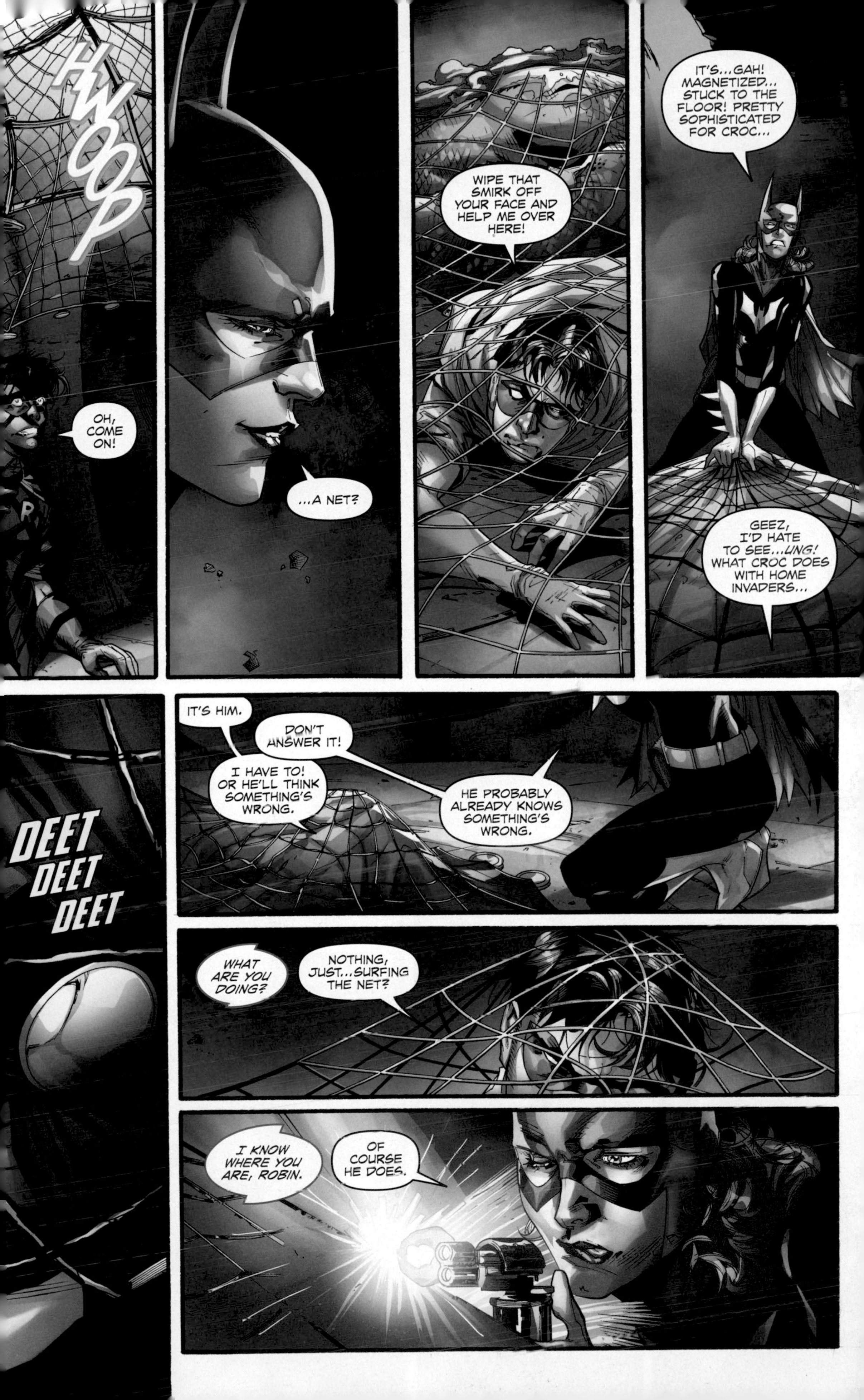
HWOOP
OH, COME ON!
...A NET?
WIPE THAT SMIRK OFF YOUR FACE AND HELP ME OVER HERE!
IT'S...GAH! MAGNETIZED... STUCK TO THE FLOOR! PRETTY SOPHISTICATED FOR CROC...
GEEZ, I'D HATE TO SEE...UNG! WHAT CROC DOES WITH HOME INVADERS...
DEET DEET DEET
IT'S HIM.
DON'T ANSWER IT!
I HAVE TO! OR HE'LL THINK SOMETHING'S WRONG.
HE PROBABLY ALREADY KNOWS SOMETHING'S WRONG.
WHAT ARE YOU DOING?
NOTHING, JUST...SURFING THE NET?
I KNOW WHERE YOU ARE, ROBIN.
OF COURSE HE DOES.

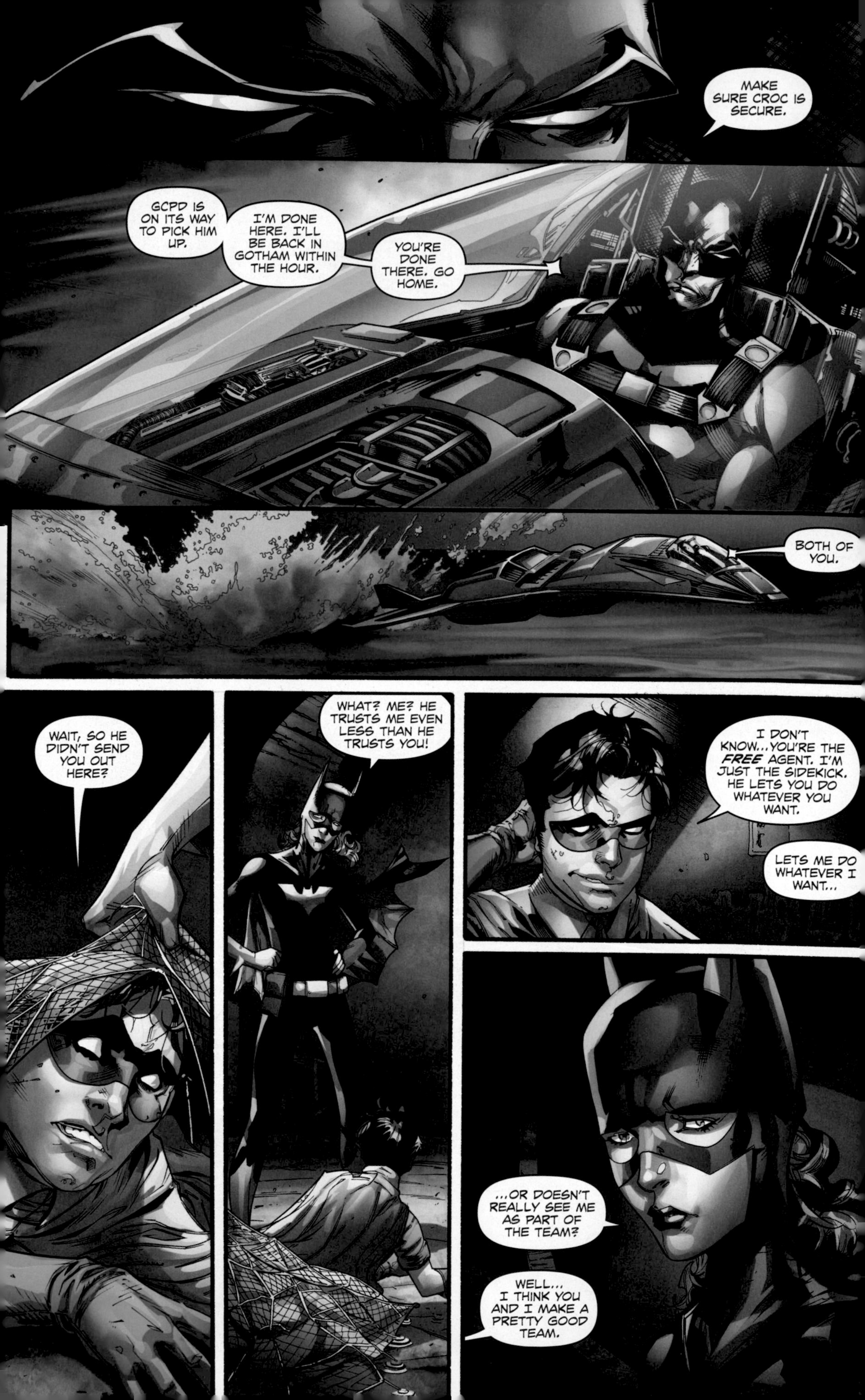

MAKE SURE CROC IS SECURE.
GCPD IS ON ITS WAY TO PICK HIM UP.
I'M DONE HERE. I'LL BE BACK IN GOTHAM WITHIN THE HOUR.
YOU'RE DONE THERE. GO HOME.
BOTH OF YOU.
WAIT, SO HE DIDN'T SEND YOU OUT HERE?
WHAT? ME? HE TRUSTS ME EVEN LESS THAN HE TRUSTS YOU!
I DON'T KNOW...YOU'RE THE FREE AGENT. I'M JUST THE SIDEKICK. HE LETS YOU DO WHATEVER YOU WANT.
LETS ME DO WHATEVER I WANT...
...OR DOESN'T REALLY SEE ME AS PART OF THE TEAM?
WELL... I THINK YOU AND I MAKE A PRETTY GOOD TEAM.

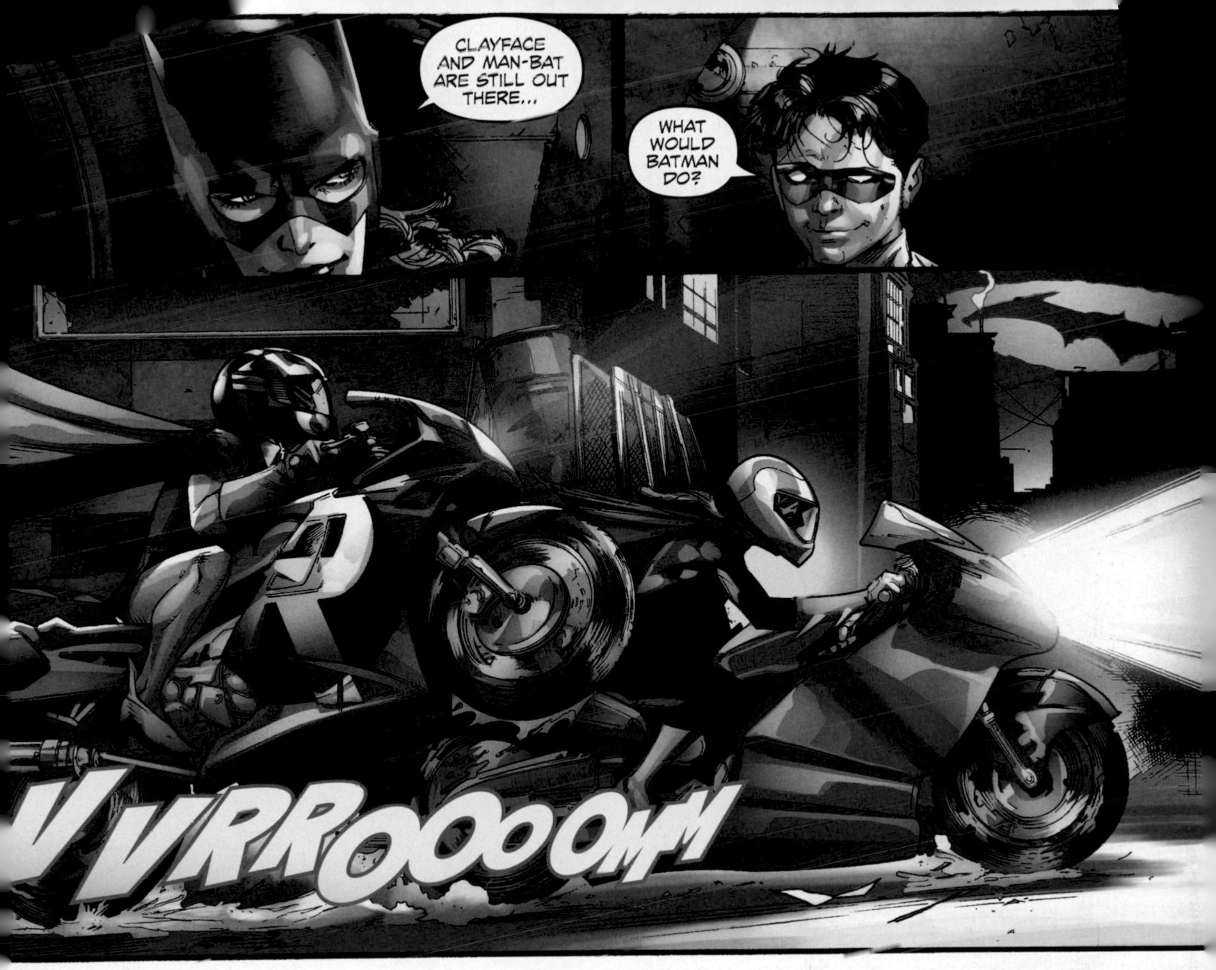
CLAYFACE AND MAN-BAT ARE STILL OUT THERE...
WHAT WOULD BATMAN DO?
VVRROOOOOMM

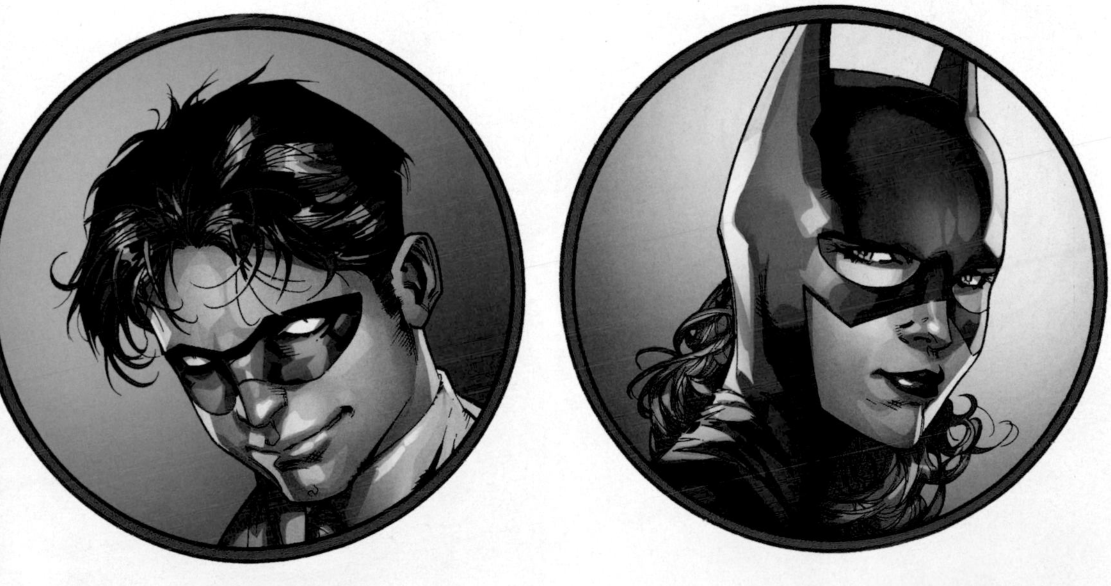

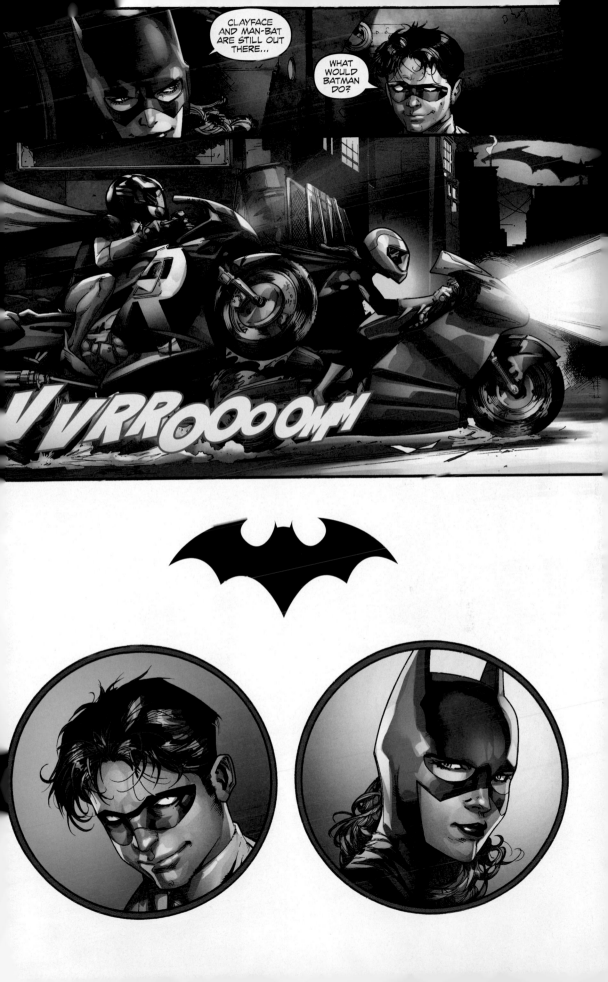

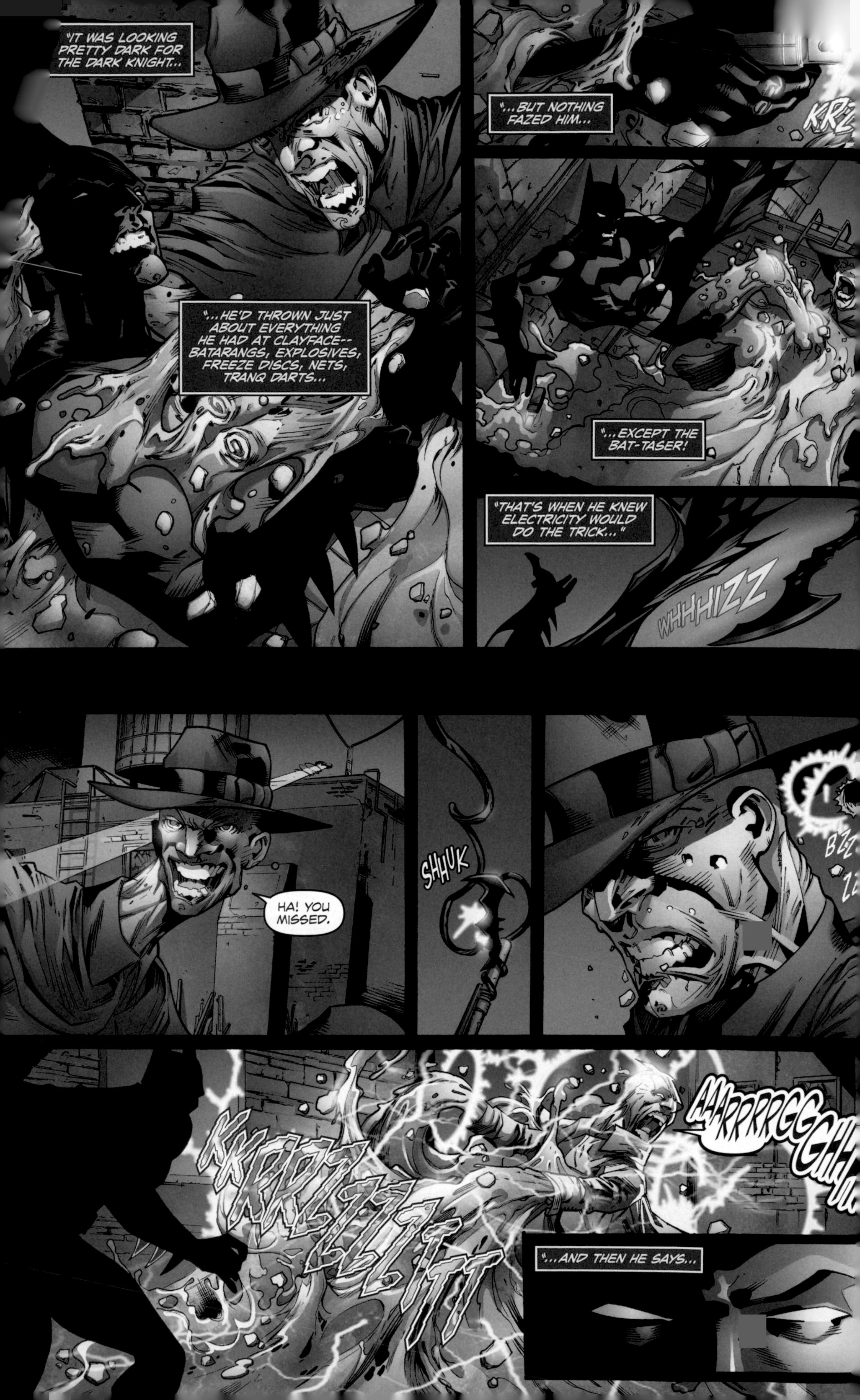
"IT WAS LOOKING PRETTY DARK FOR THE DARK KNIGHT...
"...HE'D THROWN JUST ABOUT EVERYTHING HE HAD AT CLAYFACE--BATARANGS, EXPLOSIVES, FREEZE DISCS, NETS, TRANQ DARTS...
"...BUT NOTHING FAZED HIM...
KRZ
"...EXCEPT THE BAT-TASER!
"THAT'S WHEN HE KNEW ELECTRICITY WOULD DO THE TRICK..."
WHHHIZZ
HA! YOU MISSED.
SHHUK
BZZ
KRZZZZZZZTTT
AAARRRRGGGHH
"...AND THEN HE SAYS...

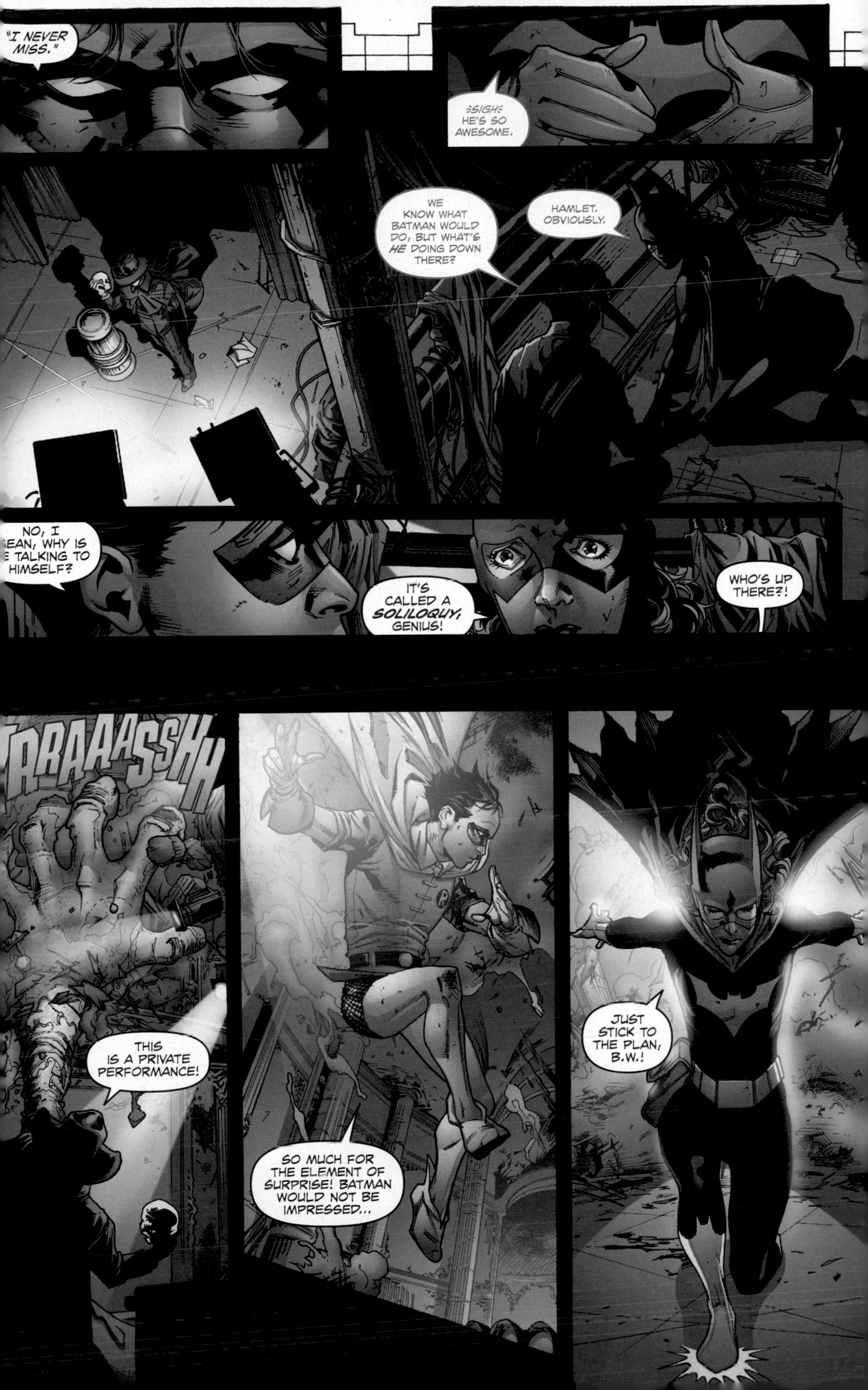
"I NEVER MISS."
=SIGH= HE'S SO AWESOME.
WE KNOW WHAT BATMAN WOULD DO, BUT WHAT'S HE DOING DOWN THERE?
HAMLET. OBVIOUSLY.
NO, I EAN, WHY IS E TALKING TO HIMSELF?
IT'S CALLED A SOLILOQUY, GENIUS!
WHO'S UP THERE?!
RRAAASSHH
THIS IS A PRIVATE PERFORMANCE!
SO MUCH FOR THE ELEMENT OF SURPRISE! BATMAN WOULD NOT BE IMPRESSED...
JUST STICK TO THE PLAN, B.W.!

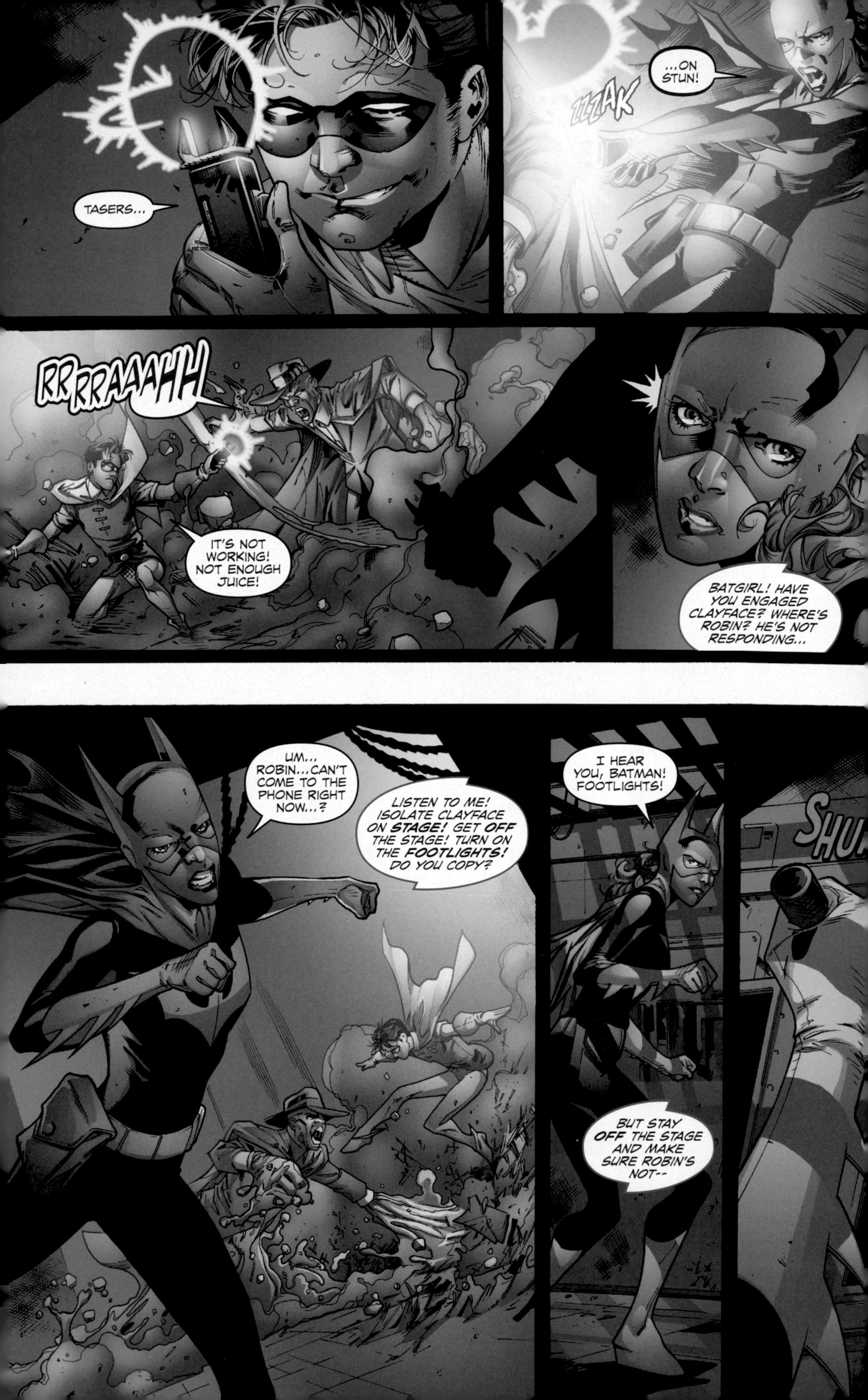
TASERS...
...ON STUN!
ZZZAK
RRRRAAAHH
IT'S NOT WORKING! NOT ENOUGH JUICE!
BATGIRL! HAVE YOU ENGAGED CLAYFACE? WHERE'S ROBIN? HE'S NOT RESPONDING...
UM... ROBIN...CAN'T COME TO THE PHONE RIGHT NOW...?
LISTEN TO ME! ISOLATE CLAYFACE ON STAGE! GET OFF THE STAGE! TURN ON THE FOOTLIGHTS! DO YOU COPY?
I HEAR YOU, BATMAN! FOOTLIGHTS!
BUT STAY OFF THE STAGE AND MAKE SURE ROBIN'S NOT--

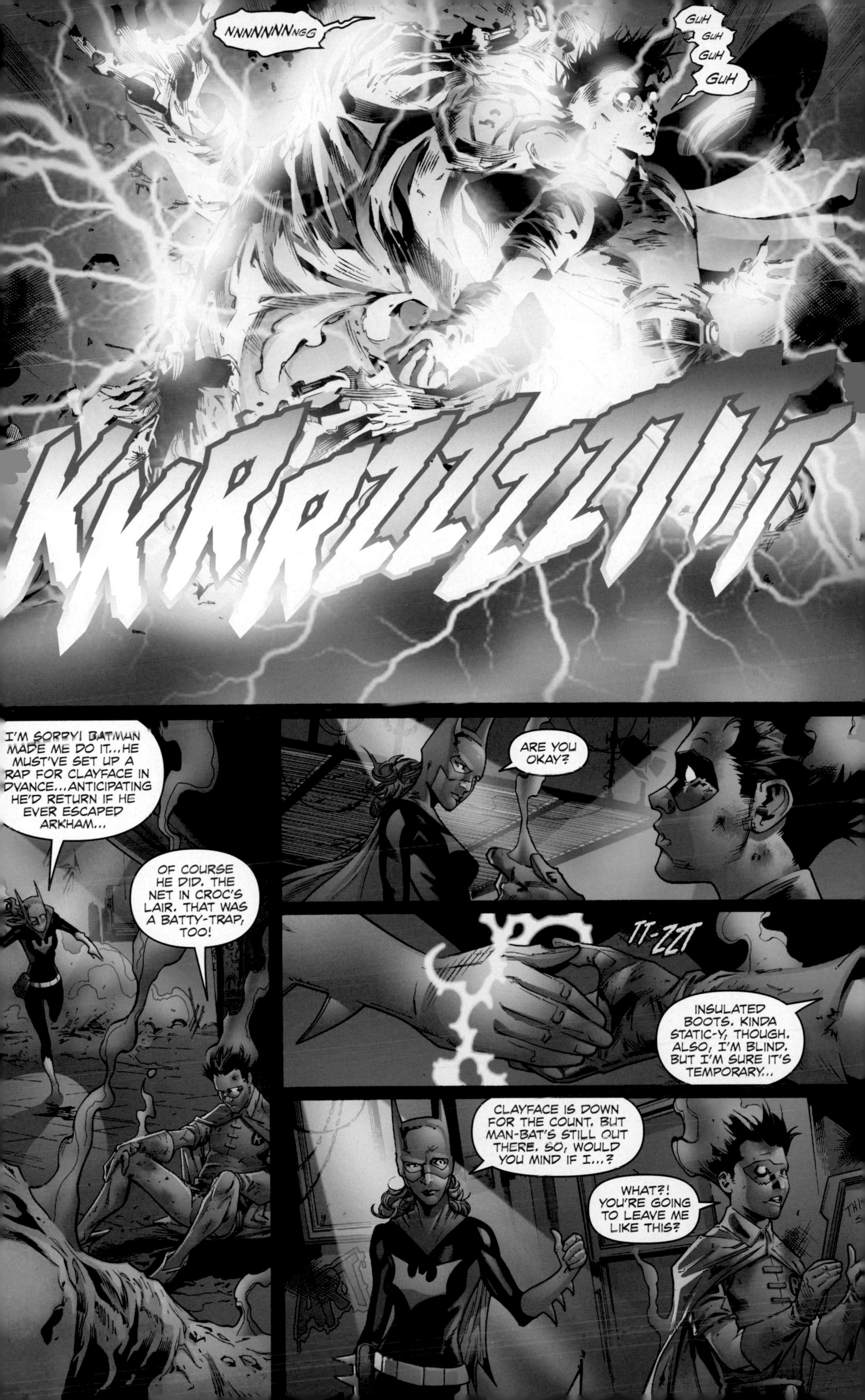
NNNNNNNNngg
GuH
GuH
GuH
GuH
KKRZZZZTTT
I'M SORRY! BATMAN MADE ME DO IT...HE MUST'VE SET UP A RAP FOR CLAYFACE IN DVANCE...ANTICIPATING HE'D RETURN IF HE EVER ESCAPED ARKHAM...
ARE YOU OKAY?
OF COURSE HE DID. THE NET IN CROC'S LAIR. THAT WAS A BATTY-TRAP, TOO!
TT-ZZT
INSULATED BOOTS. KINDA STATIC-Y, THOUGH. ALSO, I'M BLIND. BUT I'M SURE IT'S TEMPORARY...
CLAYFACE IS DOWN FOR THE COUNT. BUT MAN-BAT'S STILL OUT THERE. SO, WOULD YOU MIND IF I...?
WHAT?! YOU'RE GOING TO LEAVE ME LIKE THIS?

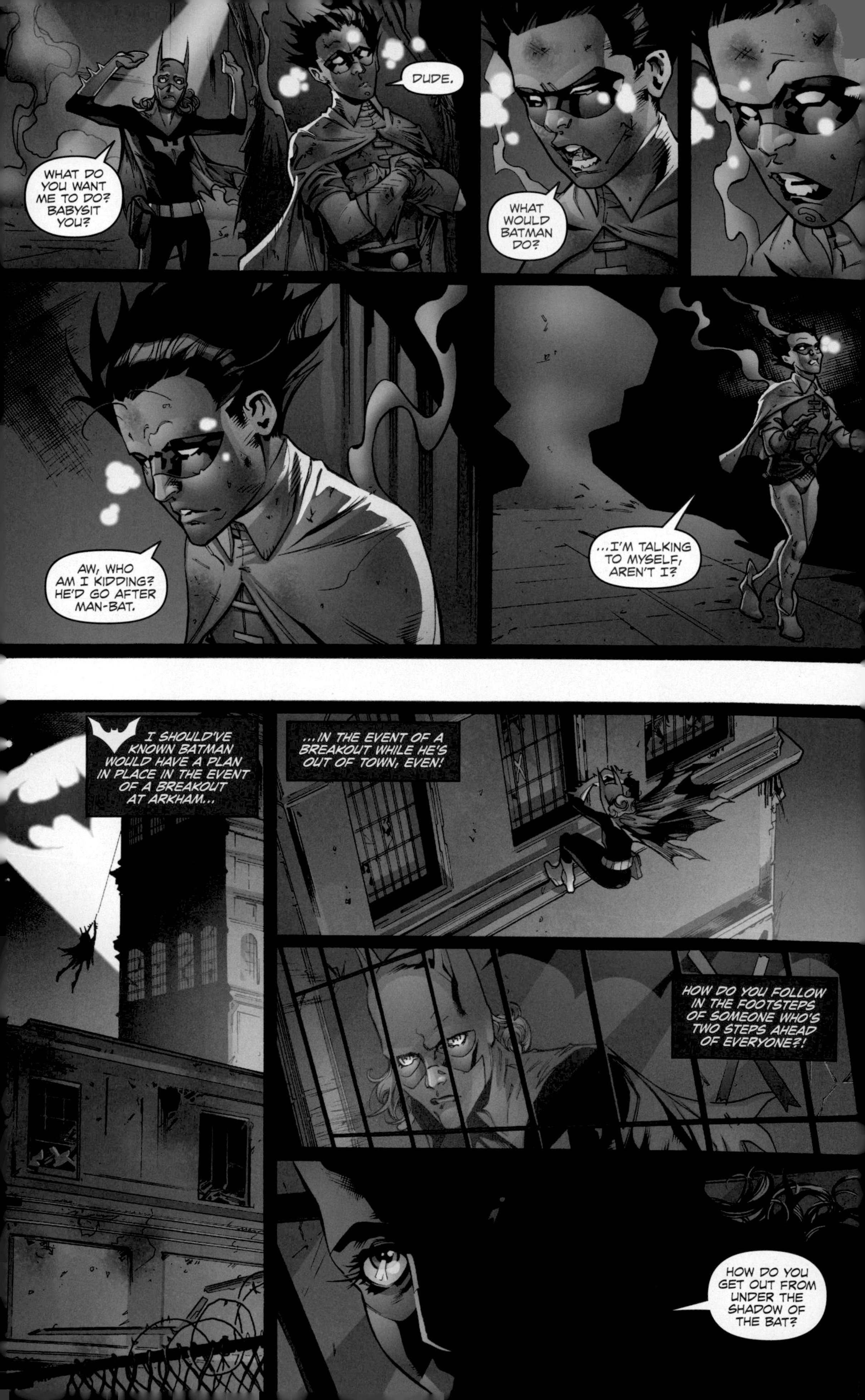
WHAT DO YOU WANT ME TO DO? BABYSIT YOU?
DUDE.
WHAT WOULD BATMAN DO?
AW, WHO AM I KIDDING? HE'D GO AFTER MAN-BAT.
...I'M TALKING TO MYSELF, AREN'T I?
I SHOULD'VE KNOWN BATMAN WOULD HAVE A PLAN IN PLACE IN THE EVENT OF A BREAKOUT AT ARKHAM...
...IN THE EVENT OF A BREAKOUT WHILE HE'S OUT OF TOWN, EVEN!
HOW DO YOU FOLLOW IN THE FOOTSTEPS OF SOMEONE WHO'S TWO STEPS AHEAD OF EVERYONE?!
HOW DO YOU GET OUT FROM UNDER THE SHADOW OF THE BAT?

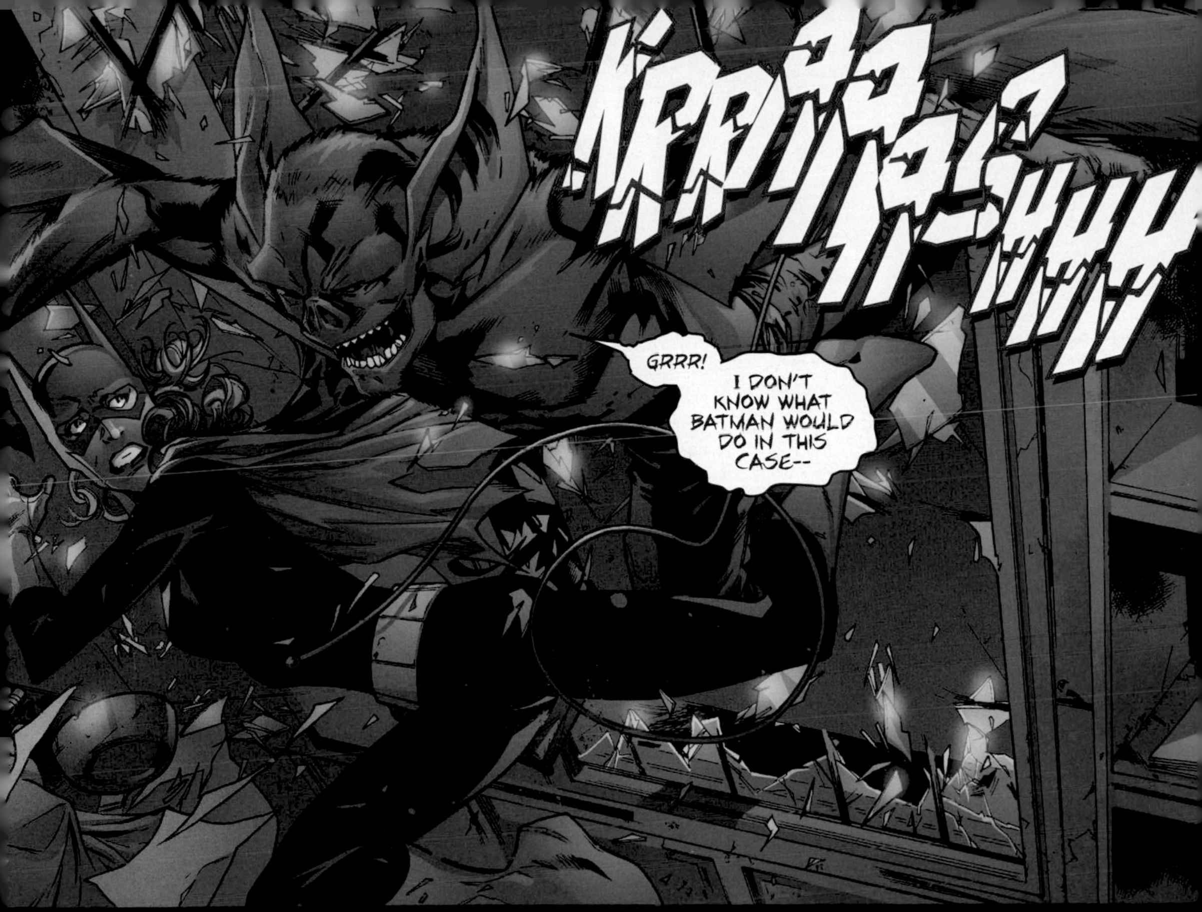
GRRR!
I DON'T KNOW WHAT BATMAN WOULD DO IN THIS CASE--

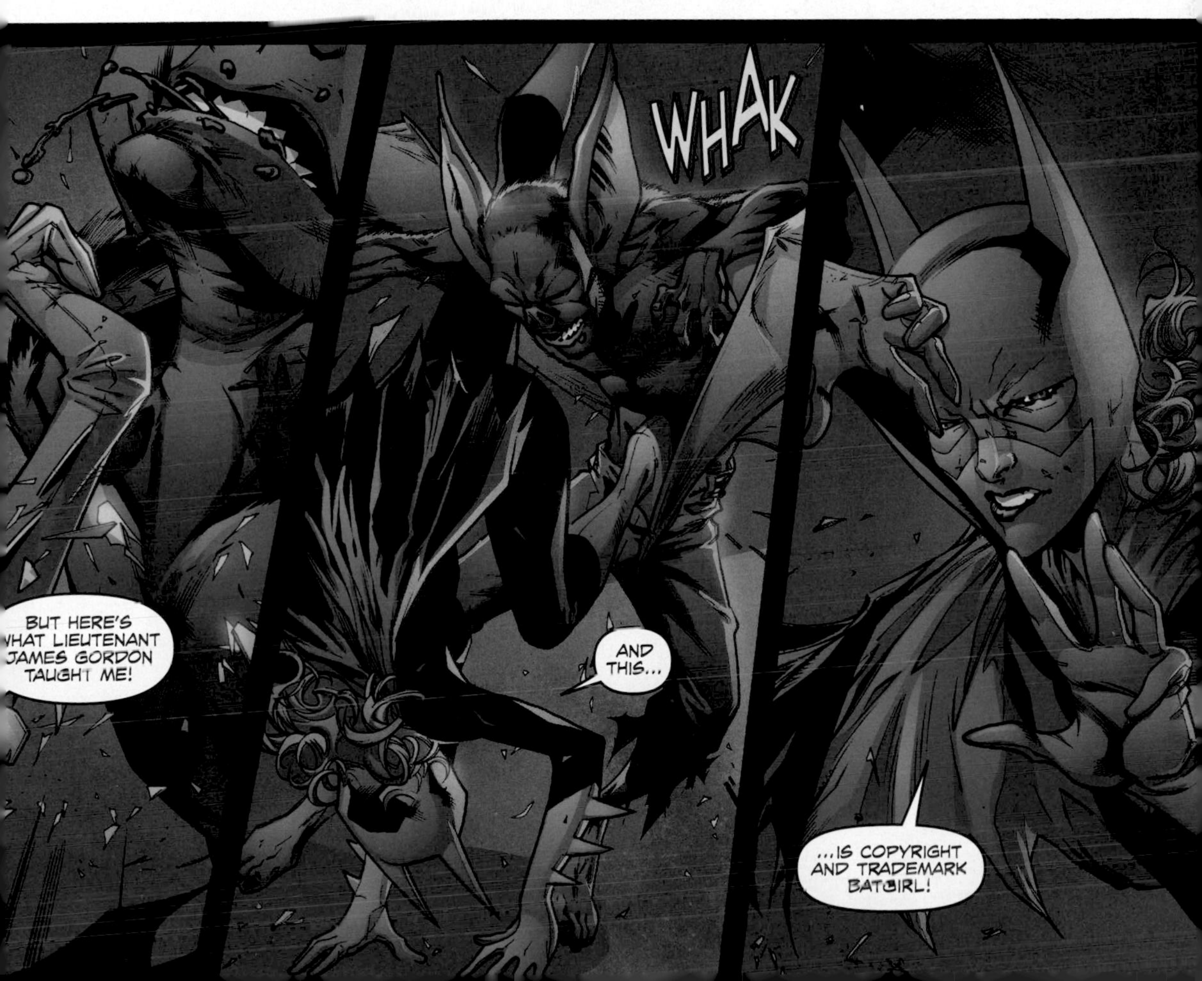
WHAK
BUT HERE'S WHAT LIEUTENANT JAMES GORDON TAUGHT ME!
AND THIS...
...IS COPYRIGHT AND TRADEMARK BATGIRL!

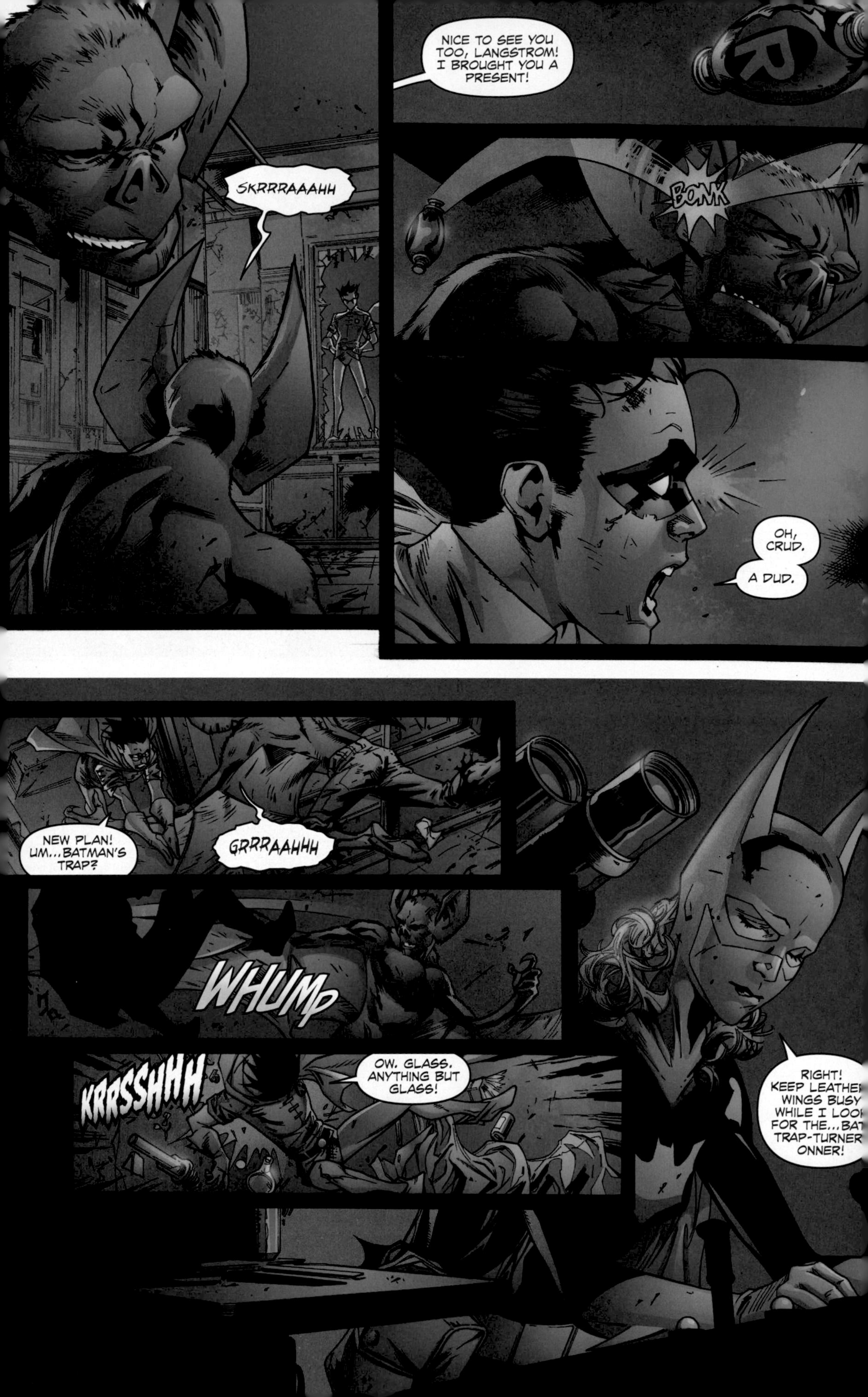
SKRRRAAAHH
NICE TO SEE YOU TOO, LANGSTROM! I BROUGHT YOU A PRESENT!
BONK
OH, CRUD.
A DUD.
NEW PLAN! UM...BATMAN'S TRAP?
GRRRAAHHH
WHUMP
KRRSSHHH
OW. GLASS. ANYTHING BUT GLASS!
RIGHT! KEEP LEATHER WINGS BUSY WHILE I LOOK FOR THE...BAT TRAP-TURNER ONNER!

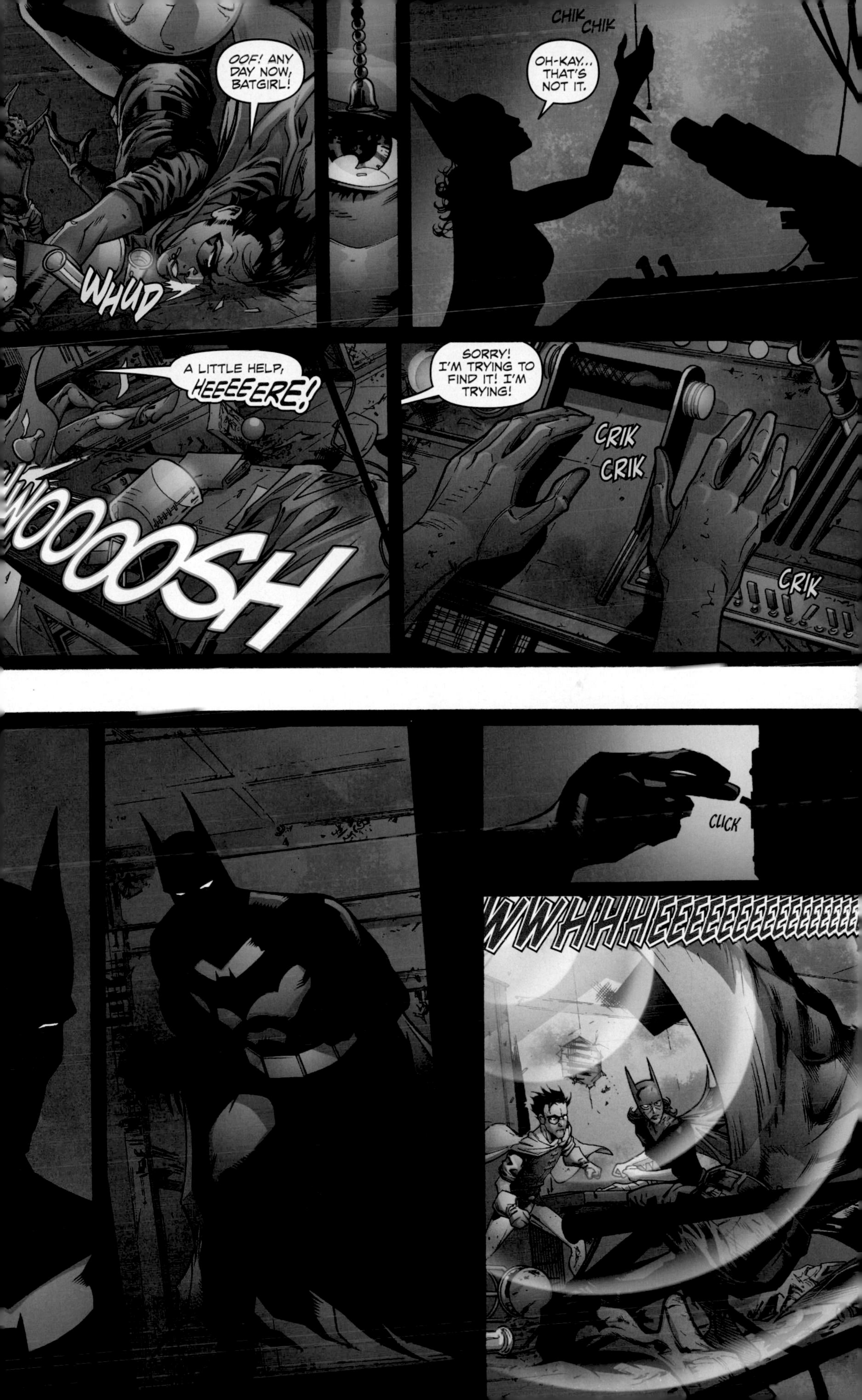
OOF! ANY DAY NOW, BATGIRL!
WHUD
CHIK CHIK
OH-KAY... THAT'S NOT IT.
A LITTLE HELP, HEEEEERE!
WOOOOSH
SORRY! I'M TRYING TO FIND IT! I'M TRYING!
CRIK
CRIK
CRIK
CLICK
WWHHHEEEEEEEEEEEEEE

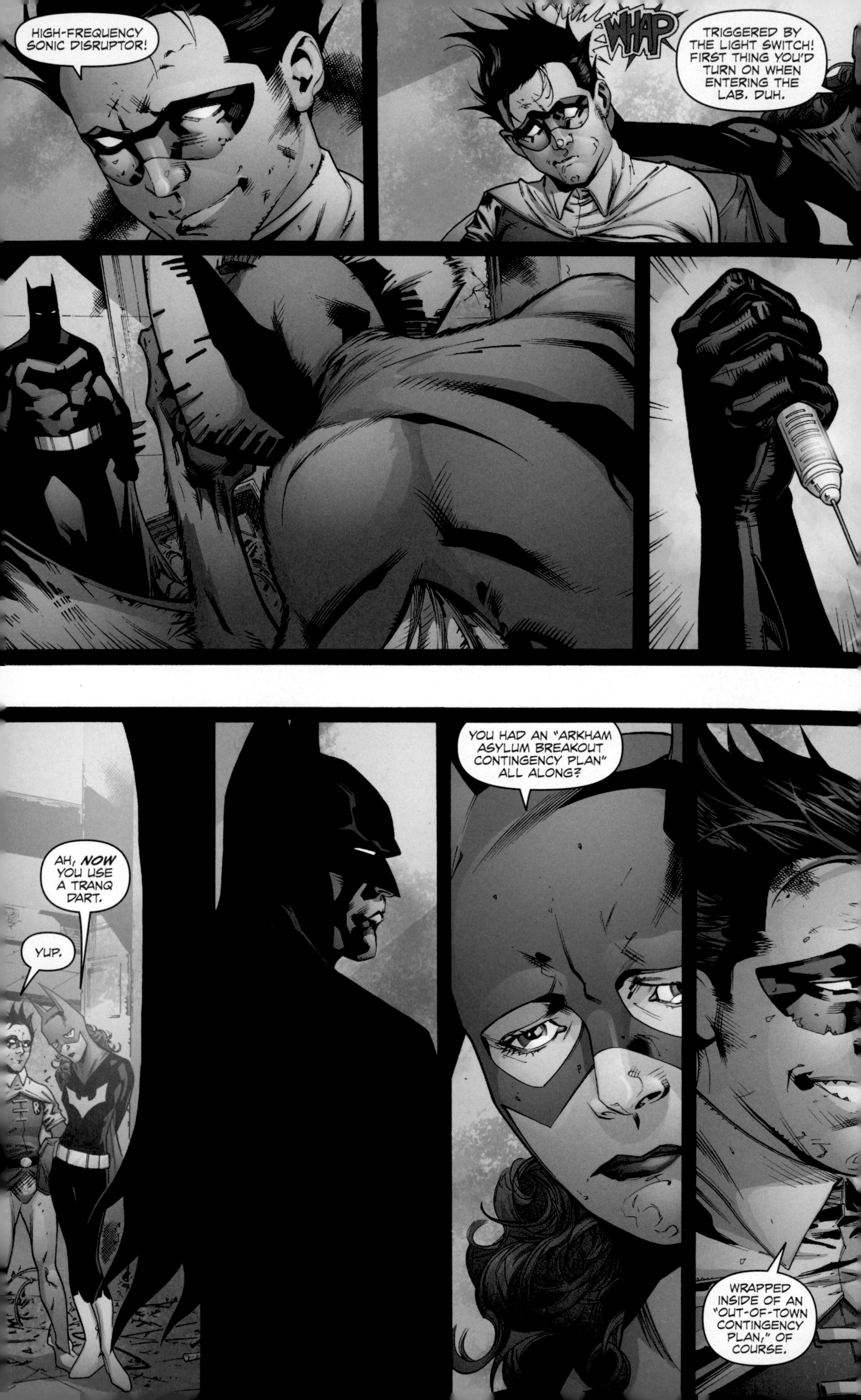
HIGH-FREQUENCY SONIC DISRUPTOR!
WHAP
TRIGGERED BY THE LIGHT SWITCH! FIRST THING YOU'D TURN ON WHEN ENTERING THE LAB. DUH.
AH, NOW YOU USE A TRANQ DART.
YUP.
YOU HAD AN "ARKHAM ASYLUM BREAKOUT CONTINGENCY PLAN" ALL ALONG?
WRAPPED INSIDE OF AN "OUT-OF-TOWN CONTINGENCY PLAN," OF COURSE.

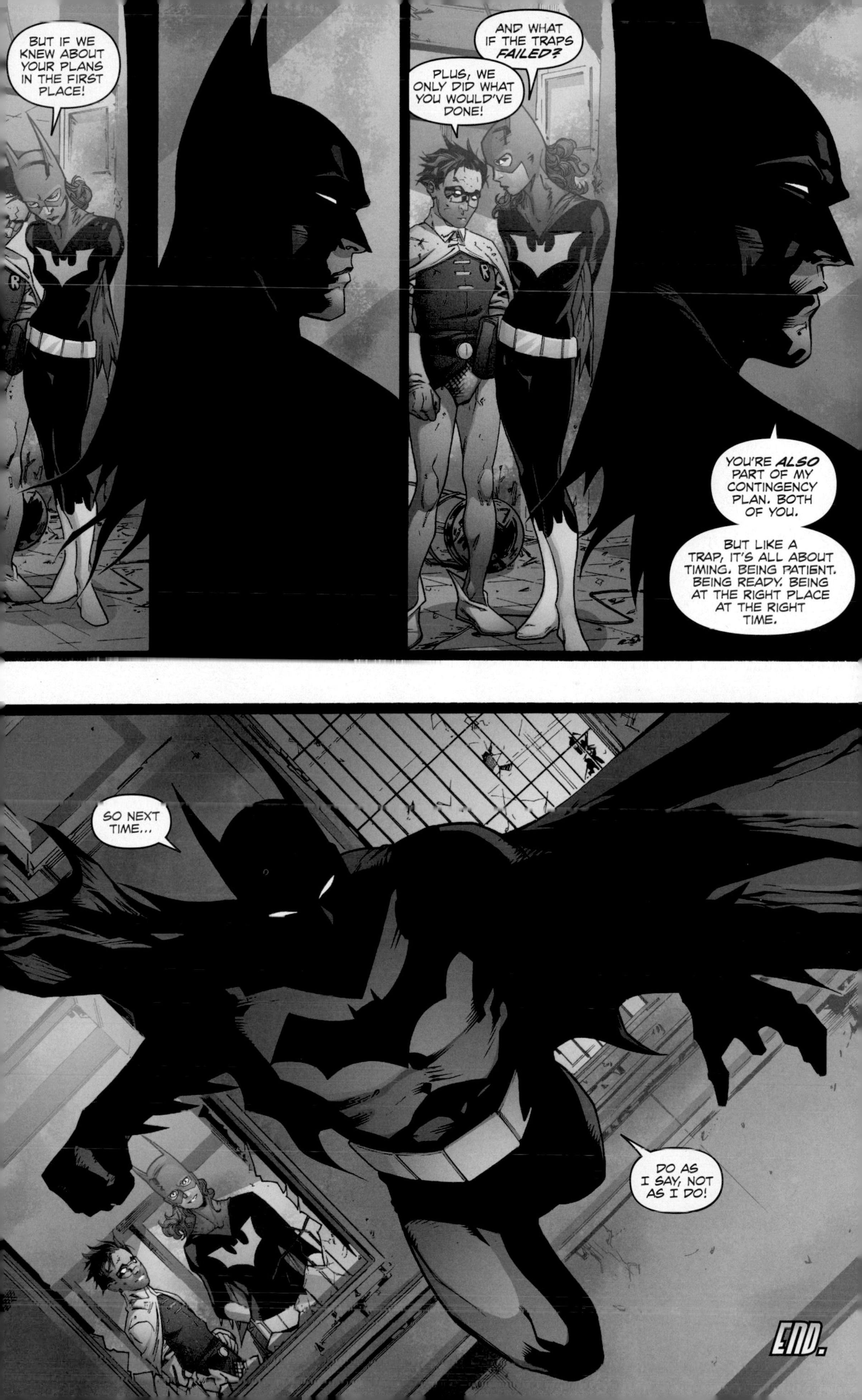
BUT IF WE KNEW ABOUT YOUR PLANS IN THE FIRST PLACE!
AND WHAT IF THE TRAPS FAILED?
PLUS, WE ONLY DID WHAT YOU WOULD'VE DONE!
YOU'RE ALSO PART OF MY CONTINGENCY PLAN. BOTH OF YOU.
BUT LIKE A TRAP, IT'S ALL ABOUT TIMING. BEING PATIENT. BEING READY. BEING AT THE RIGHT PLACE AT THE RIGHT TIME.
SO NEXT TIME...
DO AS I SAY, NOT AS I DO!
END.

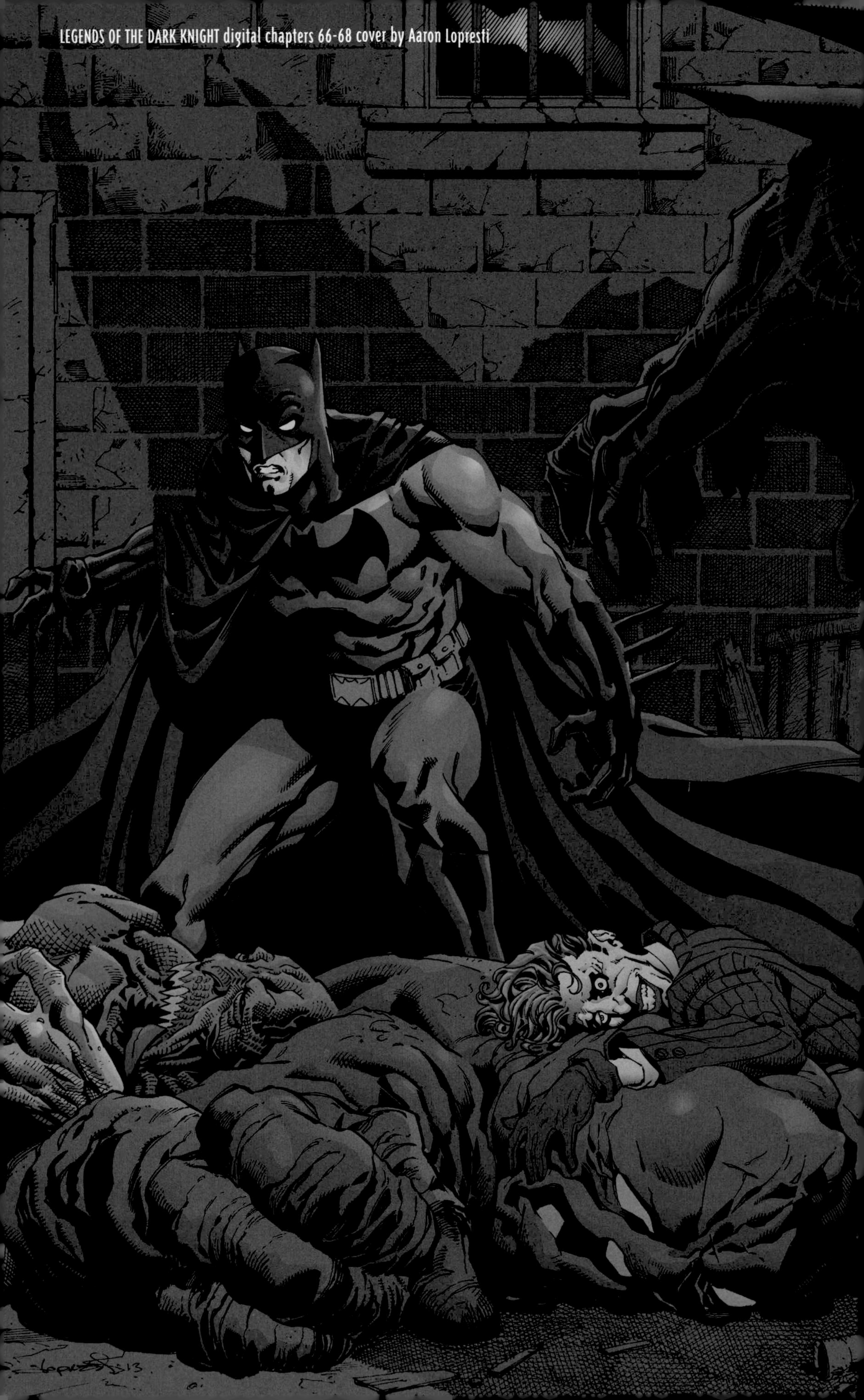
LEGENDS OF THE DARK KNIGHT digital chapters 66-68 cover by Aaron Lopresti

LEGENDS OF THE DARK KNIGHT digital chapters 70-73 cover by Scott Kolins

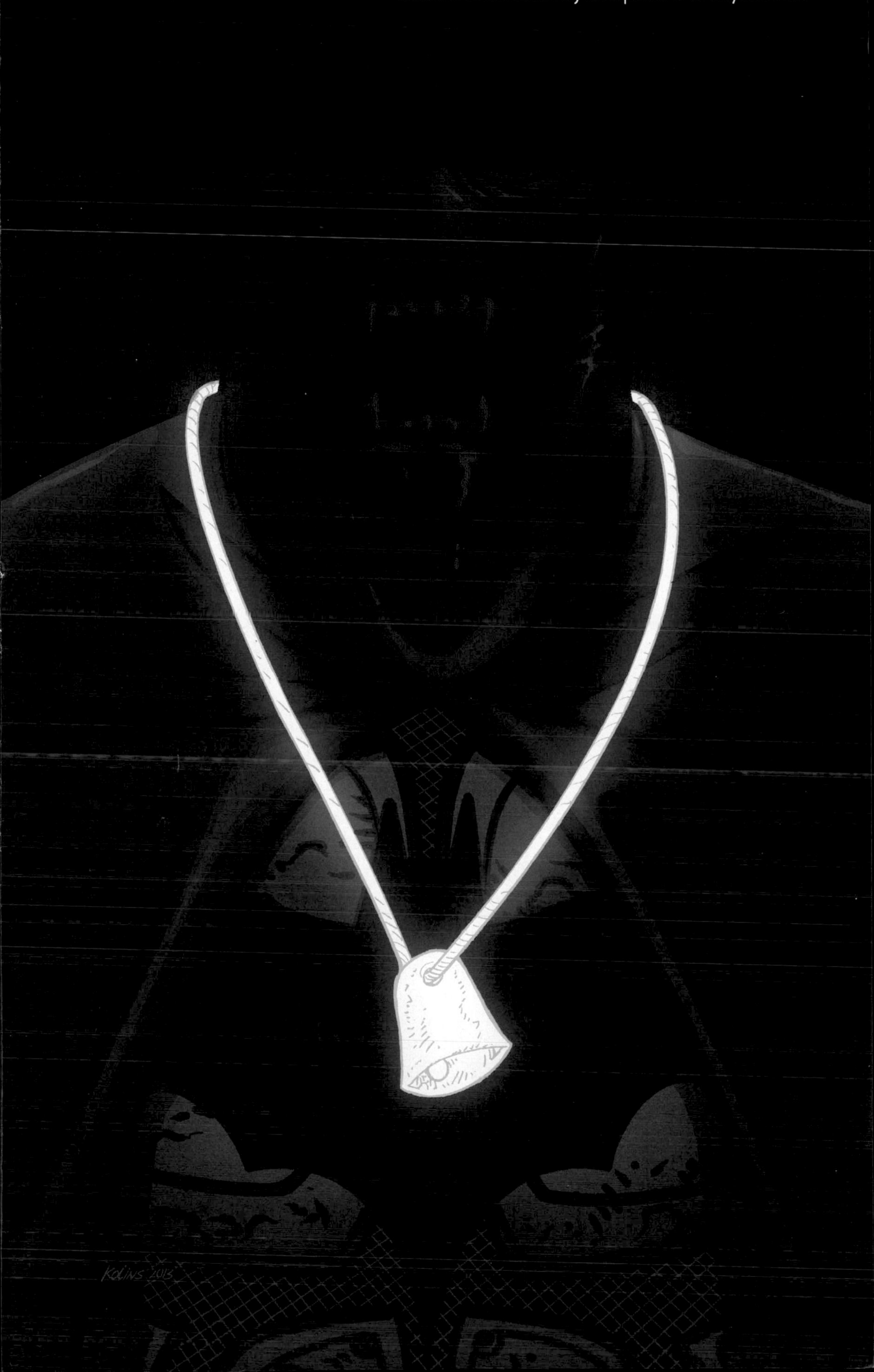
KOLINS 2013

LEGENDS OF THE DARK KNIGHT digital chapters 74-76 cover by Francesco Francavilla

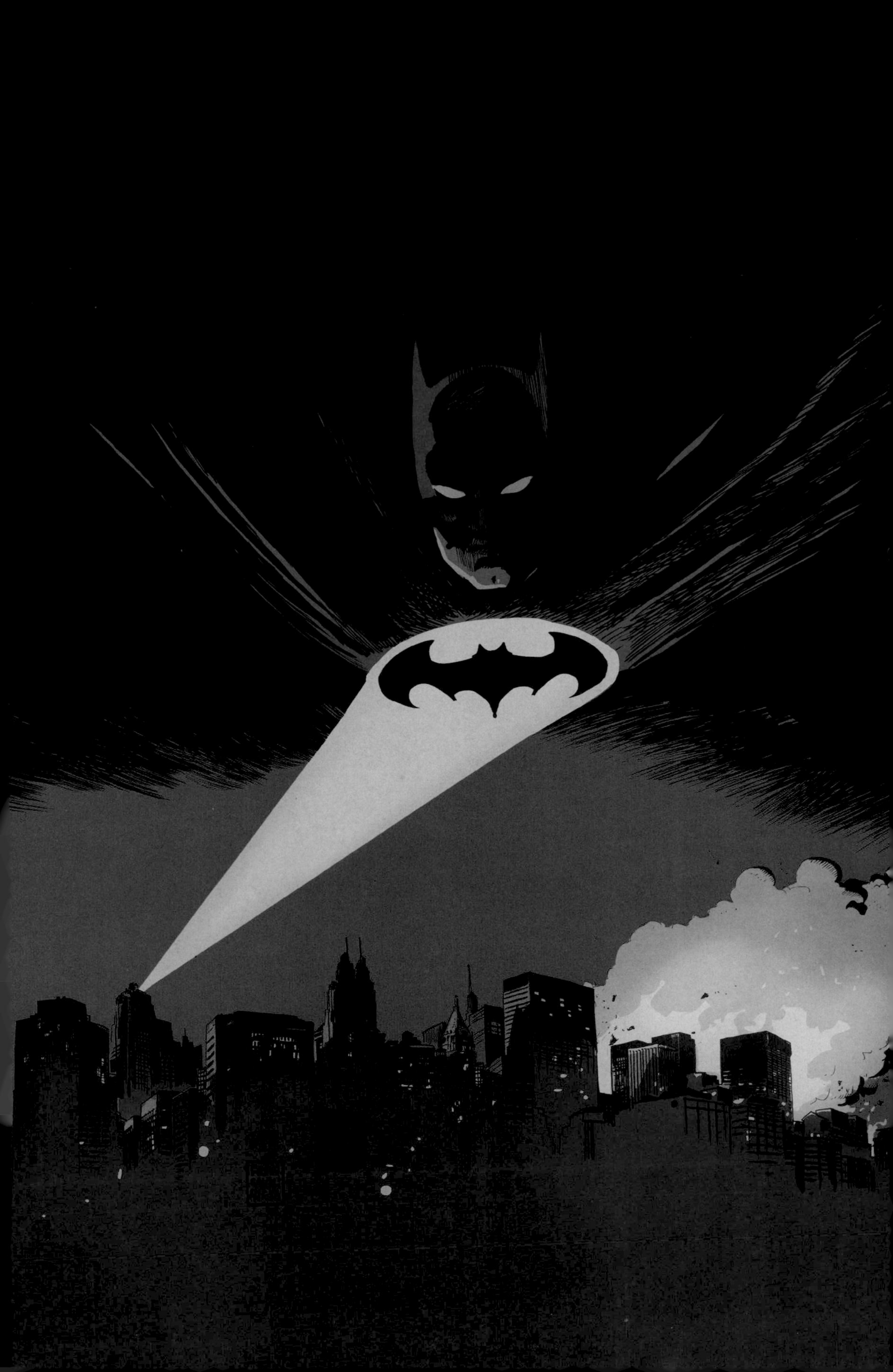

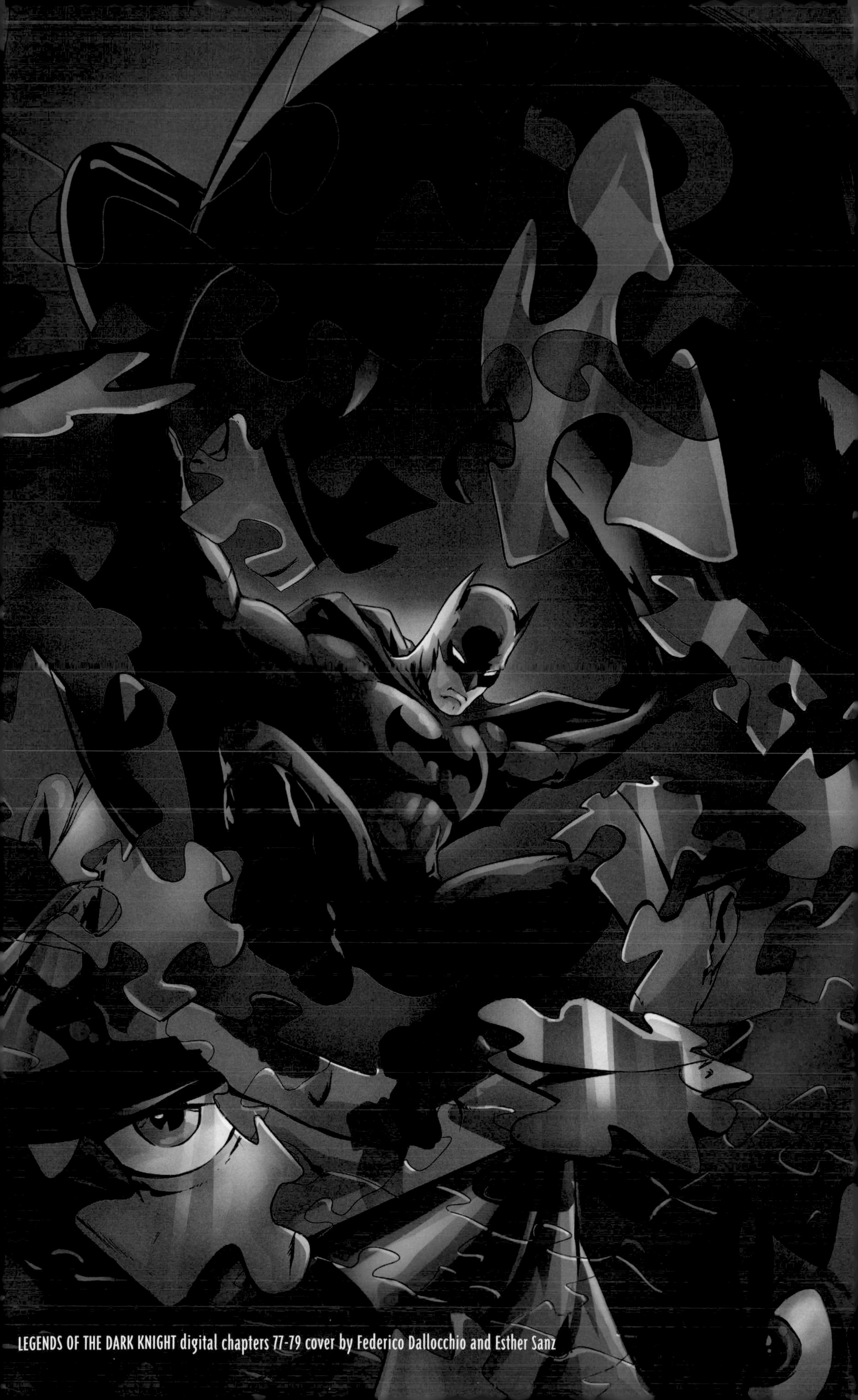

LEGENDS OF THE DARK KNIGHT digital chapters 77-79 cover by Federico Dallocchio and Esther Sanz

LEGENDS OF THE DARK KNIGHT digital chapters 80-82 cover by Cully Hamner

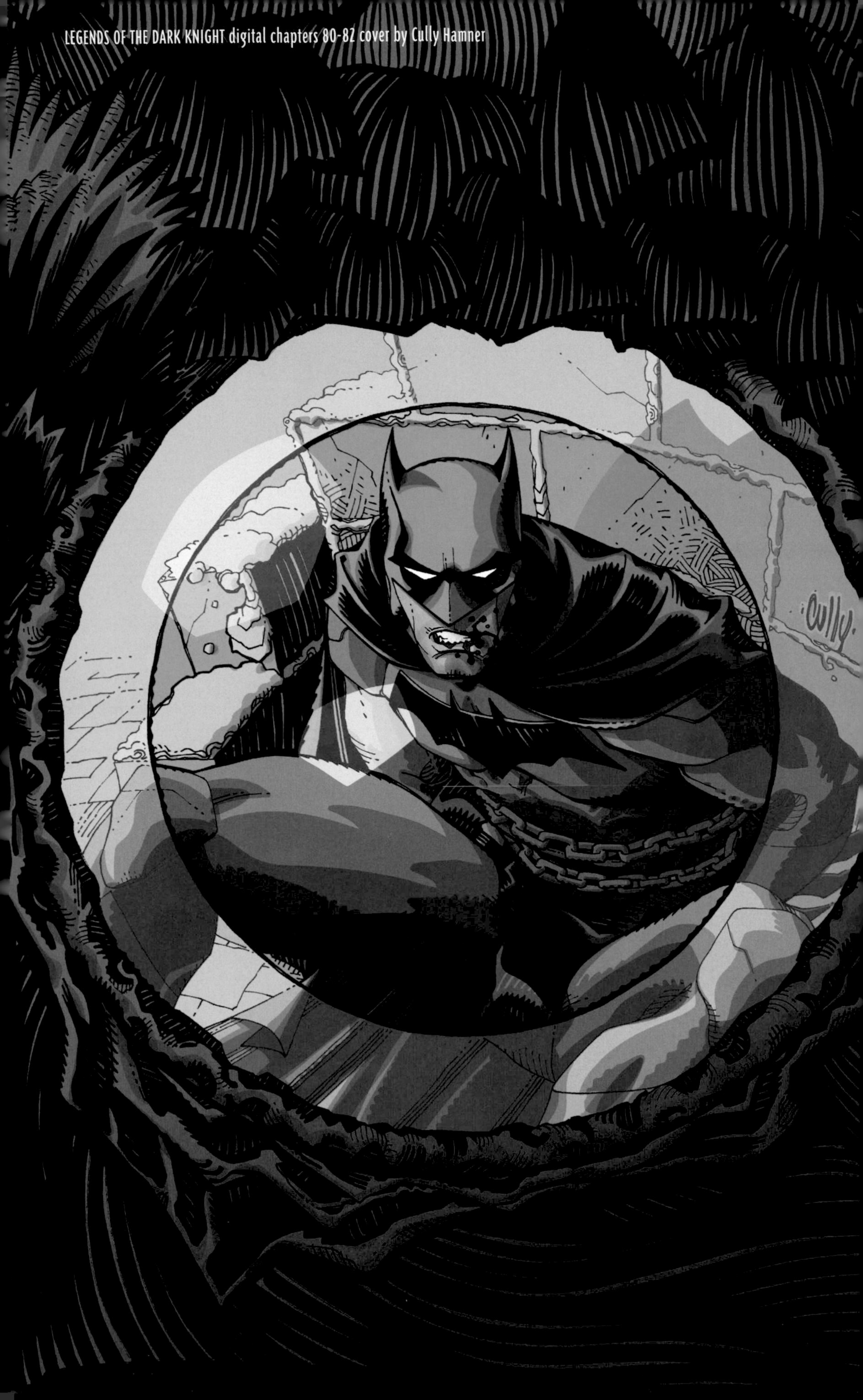

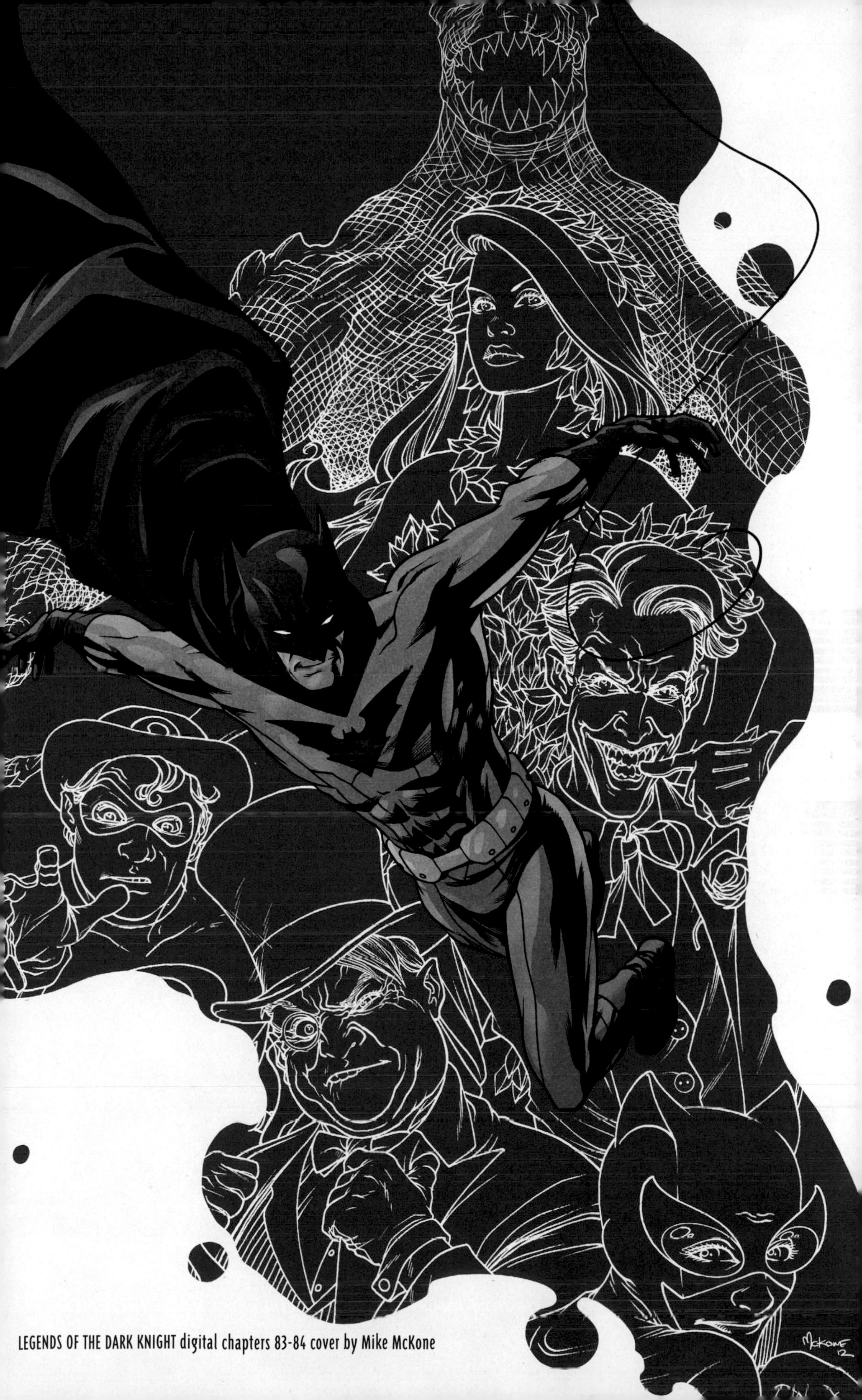
McKONE '12

LEGENDS OF THE DARK KNIGHT digital chapters 83-84 cover by Mike McKone

"Finch's detailed, moody style works well Gotham City and its Dark Knight"—NEWSARAMA

"Finch's quality of art lives up to the hype with his detailed panels and sharp lines—all designed to explode off of the page."—TAMPA BAY EXAMINER

START AT THE BEGINNING

BATMAN: THE DARK KNIGHT
VOLUME 1: KNIGHT TERRORS

BATMAN: THE DARK KNIGHT VOL. 2: CYCLE OF VIOLENCE

BATMAN: THE DARK KNIGHT VOL. 3: MAD

PENGUIN: PAIN & PREJUDICE

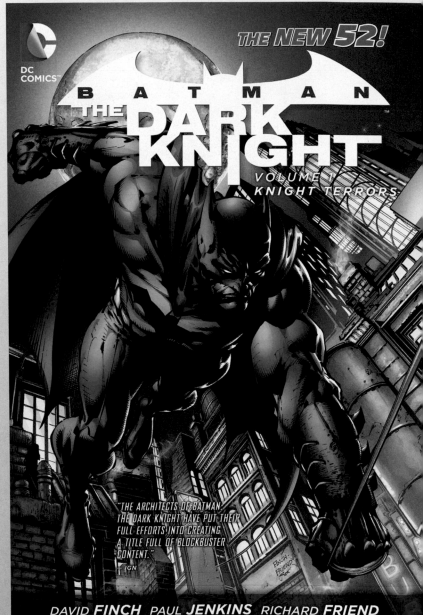

START AT THE BEGINNING!

BATMAN VOLUME 1: THE COURT OF OWLS

BATMAN VOL. 2: THE CITY OF OWLS

with SCOTT SNYDER and GREG CAPULLO

BATMAN VOL. 3: DEATH OF THE FAMILY

with SCOTT SNYDER and GREG CAPULLO

BATMAN: NIGHT OF THE OWLS

with SCOTT SNYDER and GREG CAPULLO

SCOTT **SNYDER** GREG **CAPULLO** JONATHAN **GLAPION**